Win A Few

Win A Few

The Autobiography of
THE SOLDIER OF ORANGE

Foreword by Len Deighton

ERIK HAZELHOFF

Titles by the same author:

RENDEZVOUS IN SAN FRANCISCO
HET SMEULENDE VUUR (The Finnish-Russian War)
SOLDAAT VAN ORANJE-40-45
DE VERRE TAMBOUR (The Distant Drummer)
SOLDIER OF ORANGE
IN PURSUIT OF LIFE

Portions of these books have been included in this updated edition

Note: Photographs are from the author's archives, except where credited. Persons with questions regarding copyright ownership kindly contact Debbie@jetlaunch.net

Edited by Karin Hazelhoff Roelfzema

Book designed by Debbie O'Byrne at www.jetlaunch.net

ISBN-13: 978-1-938886-71-3

ISBN-10: 1938886712

Printed in the United States of America

REVIEWS FOR *WIN A FEW*

"Your writing is not only captivating but from your soul…I will now carry your stories with me forever"

—Rear Admiral D. McCain,
Deputy Chief of Staff, Pacific Fleet

"What a life! What a book! It is unbelievable that so many adventures can be encompassed in only one man's life. Erik's book is breathtaking and moving, and I read it all in one sitting. Hats off to him!!"

—Paul Verhoeven, Director: 'RoboCop,' 'Basic Instinct'

"It was even possible for a man to remember flying on an RAF raid over Berlin with nostalgia, for all the appalling Bomber Command casualty rates (q.v.) which indicate how dangerous the job was."

—Angus Calder, Author: 'Wars'

"This exciting and beautifully written autobiography…… reveals him to be one of the genuine heroes of the 20th century."

—Mary Whipple: Favorite Reading

"This book is a lot of fun and so finely written that the pages just whip by."

—Honolulu Star Bulletin

"A writer of no mean merit…couldn't put it down."

—Eastern Daily Press UK

"There are "intellectual" biographies and autobiographies, works that purport to demonstrate cultural pedigree, and then there are vital autobiographies . The latter type signifying more than a mere succession of events — instead, the pulse of a conscious vitality that recognizes itself as passing through life "…The work is tale that, in juxtaposing life's most vexing and sublime aspects, also succeeds in demonstrating its unity."

—Pedro Blas Gonzalez, Reviewers Bookwatch

CONTENTS

Foreword by *Len Deighton*...1

Chapter 1 *The Shark and the Crocodile*...........................2

Chapter 2 *Of Pigeonholes and Gauchos*...........................17

Chapter 3 *Rendezvous in San Francisco*...........................30

Chapter 4 *War "They Have Come!"*................................47

Chapter 5 *The Lure of Freedom*.....................................59

Chapter 6 *Under German Occupation*..............................76

Chapter 7 *Escape to England*...97

Chapter 8 *Contact Holland*..110

Chapter 9 *Secret Landings and Exile Intrigues*................128

Chapter 10 *The Wild Blue Yonder*.................................145

Chapter 11 *Pilot, 139 Squadron, RAF*...........................159

Chapter 12 *Target Berlin*..174

Chapter 13 *The Outbreak of Peace*................................190

Chapter 14 *Living with Royalty*.....................................206

Chapter 15 *America Here I Come*..................................218

Chapter 16 *Hollywood*..237

Chapter 17 *To Arms For Ambon!*..................................250

Chapter 18 *Standoff in the Philippines*............264

Chapter 19 *Running the Indonesian Blockade*.................278

Chapter 20 *Early Adventures in Television*...................298

Chapter 21 *Director, Radio Free Europe*.....................311

Chapter 22 *Ups and Downs of a Businessman*.................324

Chapter 23 *Soldier of Orange*...........................342

Chapter 24 *Echoes of Java*............................355

Chapter 25 *Hawaii No Ka Oi*...........................377

Chapter 26 *Grande Finale*.............................395

Biography...411

FOREWORD

by Len Deighton

This is an infuriating book. How can one man have lived a hundred lives? A hundred lives! And not dull - get up in the morning and brew coffee - lives, like mine. These are amazing lives: comic, heroic, epic, tragic and sometimes futile. Here is his story and, by happy coincidence, Erik Hazelhoff was born with a fierce and fluent talent for writing.

Nothing stops him, whether it's a ticking bureaucrat or a ticking time-bomb, Erik the amateur pilot flying countless missions over wartime Germany or the short-sighted applicant surviving countless physical examinations in order to join the RAF's most elite Pathfinder Force. Equally gripping is his postwar encounter with an American employment agency, and his adventures in the jungles of Hollywood.

But he always emerges apparently unscathed: like a plastic duck plunging over Niagara Falls he always surfaces and darts away to new waters.

For if there's something endearing about him, it's the cheerful way in which he faces every fresh trial. And his optimism is well founded. When someone asks him for a light it is likely to be a billionaire, when he shelters from bombs under a table he may meet a member of the royal family there. Penniless in Manhattan: hold on, here comes a school friend. There's no point in resenting his vast good luck, it's just the way he is.

Erik's life story, which covers the twentieth century both in time span and much of its turbulent content, provides many truthful insights. They contradict the glossy and simplistic history of these times that books and television present. They also bring him in contact with some of the world's most fascinating personalities, from Holland's Queen Wilhelmina to

America's Charles Lindbergh, the CIA's Allen Dulles to Hollywood's Rutger Hauer, from Freddy Heineken to Lawrence Olivier.

But his writing talent feeds most voraciously upon his love for flying and aircraft. He glosses over his courage which took him back to occupied Holland as a secret agent again and again, but for me it's his many adventures in the air that are most vivid and memorable. His descriptions of flying a De Havilland Mosquito over snowy Northern Europe or a tiny Republic Seabee over tropical jungle, are graphic and poetic. And it's always 'we'. For even when flying solo, Erik includes his plane.

But I won't go on and on. Here's Erik's life story. Or, to be precise, one hundred of them.

—L.D.

                 *   *   *

Since the above was written, Erik has again provided for us a momentous and innovative surprise. His life has always provided an inspiration for me and many others like me. As a distant member of Erik's family—the uncle of my wife Ysabele, I admired his unwavering integrity and determination.

I have no doubt that the talented people who created 'Soldier of Orange' the daring and incomparable musical faced many difficulties and hurdles just as Erik did. And like him they persisted and succeeded in producing for us an entertainment of a style so grand and original that it has already become a milestone in theatrical production. And furthermore it is what Show-Biz people call a boffo hit. I knew Erik well enough to know that he is in God's Heaven and smiling down at us.

Len Deighton is a British military historian, poet, graphic artist and a globally acclaimed writer of novels and non-fiction. His best known books have been made into films and one 13-part TV series; The Ipcress File, Funeral in Berlin, and Game, Set & Match.

CHAPTER 1

The Shark and the Crocodile

It always bothered my father that Holland remained neutral in the war. What war? Europe remembers only one, aside from some racial and religious infighting traditionally popular in the Balkans. Americans, in their heady rush of newfound power, have provided themselves with a wider choice: Korea? Viet Nam? Grenada? Panama? Desert Storm, Yugoslavia, Iraq? Still, World War II was the big one, it happened to all of us, the good guys won, the end of an epoch, beginning of the yankee-doodle era... Wow! Was there ever such a show before? - Yes, there was, twenty-five years earlier, known as The Great War, and it saddened my father that we stayed out of it.

He was in his twenties and recently married when the First World War broke out. As the guns of August 1914 thundered over Belgium into France, the Dutch stolidly accepted their preposterous good fortune that the German general staff, as an afterthought, decided to skirt the Netherlands' southern border and leave the tiny country to the north untouched. Its queen, Wilhelmina, only thirty-four but already sixteen years on the throne, proclaimed strict neutrality and urged her subjects "to count your blessings and be great in everything in which a small nation can be great". The two, to my father, were incompatible.

At first this seems remarkable, because militarism is as alien to my family as it is to our people. It implies a taste for discipline, and anyone who ever spent a day in Amsterdam can attest that in Dutch society this concept is open to broad interpretation. The rule of law is constantly being challenged by the dictates of common sense, and the inevitable clashes are resolved by peaceful and ingenious compromise. For instance,

Wedding Day of my Parents - 1911

"No Trespassing" signs are generally respected, as long as they don't stand where we have to go, and "Beware of the Dog" is interpreted as a warning to bring along a sturdy stick with which, if necessary, to whack the bastard over the head. Even the dreadful Eighty Years War, by which the United Netherlands wrested their independence from Spain in the 17th. century, constituted a victory of rowdy improvisation over the forces of law and order. A suitable slogan for Dutchmen the world over, then and now, would be: "Liberty yes! Discipline no!"

My father's militant attitude, although exceptional, was still part of a recognized national syndrome: Patriotism grows in direct ratio to the distance between a Hollander and his country. In the light of this axiom, his chauvinism was at least understandable: he lived in the Colonies with his bride, in far-off Java. But he was a true product of Amsterdam where my grandfather, a tall, thin barrister with a wooden leg, maintained high visibility in local Society, based not so much on his legal acumen as on the fact that he owned the first automobile in the Netherlands - a local product called "Spijker", all polished brass and huge lanterns and a curved honker with a rubber squeeze-ball. He insisted on driving it himself, but found it socially improper for his chauffeur to sit in the passenger seat beside him and ordered the poor man to stand on the running board all the way. Together they rattled and puffed from his stately townhouse in the Vondelpark to his office on the Herengracht, along curved canals and over steep little bridges, Grandpa rising from the open gondola ramrod straight in his black suit like a chimney with the chauffeur hanging on for dear life, pursued by noisy urchins and the bawdy greetings of passing boatmen, honking his horn with the squeeze-ball but never too busy to doff his hat to the ladies.

Next he scandalized my grandmother, a haughty dark beauty such as are still found scattered around the Netherlands, particularly in the south, as startling mementos of lonely Spanish soldiers - officers, mind you! - who occupied our country four centuries ago. He stunned her by running for public office, and then winning to boot! Such things simply were not done in our circles, where publicity was tantamount to disgrace. For the family - her brother was American writer Hendrik Willem van Loon's father - this political success became an acute social embarrassment, but Grandpa couldn't care less and continued to honk his way to council meetings. He actually succeeded in getting a law passed, his only one, a national ordinance against billboards to which even today Holland owes its uncluttered vistas of endless skies. "If you believe in something," he proclaimed after this triumph, shaking his finger at his three sons like Moses on the mountain, "then you must fight for it. Always."

My father, who as a boy looked deceptively like Little Lord Fauntleroy but had a mind of his own, took him at his word. He believed all right, but having no stomach for the rigors of the Dutch Reformed Church he turned his back on all religion as "unreasonable" and became an Anglophile, with Rudyard Kipling as his prophet and the White Man's Burden as his credo. He strove - and succeeded - to learn flawless English, practiced the Stiff Upper Lip and once or twice came perilously close to Dressing For Dinner. The years went by and at the age of eighteen his brothers went to university, one to Leiden, the other to Delft, but my father packed a bag, kissed his parents goodbye and took a boat ten thousand miles around the world to the Netherlands East Indies. He believed in Empire.

He also believed in money. The Dutch colonies, a mighty string of islands large and small straddling the equator from India to Australia, contributed vast sums to the economy of the Netherlands Kingdom, where their torrent of raw materials supported a second industrial revolution. Careers in the tropics, before DDT, antibiotics and above all air-conditioning, tended to be short, telescoped to fit a limited sojourn in the murderously hot and humid climate. My father didn't complain - years in the Indies counted double for pension purposes and salaries were augmented by *tantièmes*, a system of bonuses as percentage of profits peculiar to the produce business. At the outbreak of the war, a confident young colonial and just married, he was about to become Administrator and Chief Planter of eight coffee and rubber plantations in the highlands of Java, now part of Indonesia but then often referred to - with a proud colonial flourish - as "the pearl in the emerald girdle of the Dutch empire." He seemed well on his way to wealth.

Holland wasn't doing badly, either. The torrent of riches from the colonies fed the insatiable demands of the belligerents, for which the little uncommitted country became the marketplace. It also settled smoothly into the traditional roles of neutral havens in wartime as financial centers and bases for espionage, to which it even contributed the glamour spy of World War One, a Frisian girl called Greta Zelle who became famous as Mata Hari before paying for it with her life.

None of this escaped my father, who spent long nights bent over a primitive radio listening to news from Singapore. He fretted about unprincipled Dutch war-profiteers and paid informers, while his many British friends returned home to England to join their units or volunteer for famous regiments dressed in plumed helmets or tartan kilts. Together with his young wife he saw them off aboard the Rotterdam Lloyd ships tied up at Tandjong Perak, the harbor of Surabaya. When the steam whistle roared two blasts - "All ashore!" - and the band on the quay struck up Aloha 'Oe, my mother invariably burst into tears while her husband said his final goodbyes and apologized one more time for the neutrality of the little country of which he was so desperately proud.

From my own standpoint, nothing much happened the next few years: my father got rich and my mother pregnant, and they had a daughter. Then, on April 3rd 1917, as far as I was concerned the balloon went up. In Washington that day, much to everyone's indignation, senator Robert la Follette, progressive Republican from Wisconsin, held up the vote on his country's declaration of war. The Senate vowed to stay in session until the measure was passed, and acted accordingly: the United States of America entered World War I on the side of the Allies, thereby determining the outcome of "the war to end all wars". My mother in faraway Surabaya, pregnant again, picked this day to give birth to a son. If, as the Romans would have us believe, "nomen est omen",then her maiden name, Vreede - Dutch for Peace - gave a wrong signal about me to the world.

* * *

If you go past the Black Cave without a pebble in your mouth, you drop down dead. Stone dead. Is it true? Is it not true? The trail winds through the darkest part of the forest, barely visible. White chalices of *ketjubung*, lilies gazing earthwards, glow in the green dusk, the air is heavy with their strange fragrance. Poisonous, hold your breath!

It is dead silent, no leaf trembles, not a bird sings. No ray of sunshine penetrates the foliage; the light is flat, without shadows. Behind the next curve lies the Cave. My heart throbs in my throat but I keep going, around the bend... and there it is, a dark slash in the rocks.

Don't quit now, above all don't quit. The forest grows denser still, the light weaker and more gray. From the Cave wafts a threat, foul and deadly, as if something black is breathing in my direction. A shiver runs through my bones, my knees buckle.

Keep going... keep going... a few more steps and it will be over. I look straight ahead, not right, not left, above all not at the Cave.. What about the pebble, could it be true? My father laughed and scoffed and called it nonsense, but the old man in the village, old skin-and-bones with the red lips, swore that it was true. "Just try it, if you don't believe me."

I slip the pebble into my mouth and taste its power. Now go on, don't look back, whatever you do... Don't look back, just keep going... I'm past, I've done it! It is getting lighter. I've done it, I'm still alive. I am six years old.

We're in the mountains, my parents, my sister and I, taking a break from the heat in the coastal plain. The Koch lands, as some of my father's plantations are called, lie scattered over the volcanoes of East Java but their administrative headquarters are down in Surabaya, where we live. We're staying with the resident manager at Sumber Agung, one of the highest coffee and rubber lands of the group, on the slopes of Gunung Lawu. The plantation is like a park, miles and miles of crisp coffee bushes, man high, shaded by regimented lines of rubber trees. When my father inspects the gardens with the manager, on horseback, I ride along with them on a black pony called Untung. The small, brown men and women in the fields are cheerful and courteous; when they happen to be standing on higher ground when we ride by, they crouch down and apologize. They laugh a lot, too, I can hear them behind us when we have passed.

Occasionally we come to the boundary and look over a stretch of solid forest into a valley where rice paddies are sculpted from the mountainside, emerald green around a village that seems to have been dropped haphazardly from the trees - palm frond roofs on bamboo and matting. From all sides paths lead to it, along which bevies of young people, naked from the waist up, swing their way down the mountain. The men carry baskets bobbing up and down from poles across their shoulders; the girls balance towering stacks of fruit or produce on their heads above straight backs and young breasts. Those who are single, irrespective of gender, wear a red *hibiscus* flower behind one ear. They chatter and sing, and when they meet on the paths laughter rises from the valley. In the far distance, way down in the plain, heat shimmers hazily over endless sugar cane.

This is the village where the old man lives. His young grandson Ahmed, my faithful companion around here, takes me to see him from time to time; not at his house, which would be unthinkable for a Dutch boy, but to the place where he spends most of his days, squatting in the embrace of a banyan tree, chewing *sirih*, a kind of betel nut, spitting juice which stains his lips like blood. He always wears the same old sarong and artfully folded batik headgear, nothing else, skin and bones showing ribs as delicate as a bird's. We sit on some stones and talk to him, in Malay for my benefit, as I don't speak the local Javanese. Between grunts and spits he tells us strange tales, which Ahmed swears are true.

We ride on and come to the lake. "You went fishing here yesterday, they tell me," the manager remarks, turning around on his horse. "Catch anything?"

I did, but what can I say? I can't tell them the truth, they'll laugh at me. It all comes back clearly:

Ahmed and I have borrowed his grandfather's boat and are fishing in the lake. The water is clear, a light glassy brown.

"Do you see him?" Ahmed asks.

I shake my head. I look as deep as I can, sunrays shiver through the water like dancing spider webs. I see nothing. I keep looking and looking and then I see him, way down deep, a Dutch gentleman floating on his back. He is wearing a white suit and a sun helmet, why not? He drowned himself here, purposely, many years ago. How does Ahmed know? "Everybody knows," he says.

There he floats, barely visible in the sun-shadows. Shshsh... little bubbles rise from his nose, a good sign because in reality those bubbles are air escaping from the mouth of a *kotès* that has taken my bait. The float on my line slowly sinks below the water-surface, about a foot. There it stands for a minute or so, motionless, then shoots down. I jerk the tip of my bamboo rod upwards, the line tightens and shivers and suddenly a fat,beautiful,shiny fish hangs wriggling in the sun. I thank the Dutch gentleman. Surely, somehow he had something to do with it.

"I caught a *kotès*," I tell the manager.

The plantation house of Sumber Agung where we are staying is huge, with a wide verandah overlooking the front lawn surrounded by flowerbeds, mostly *cannas*, red and orange. Here the manager receives the foremen every morning at dawn to discuss the work of the day, and anybody else from the village that has something on his chest and wishes to see him. My father joins him. He sits in a chair with a cup of coffee as the visitors come up the stairs, slightly crouched and stooping so as not to compete with his preeminent position. They stay on the floor, squatting, but the mood is relaxed, gracious and businesslike, with a generous sprinkling of easy laughter. They speak Malay, a foreman sometimes translating to whichever of the 300 Indonesian languages and dialects is in local use. Women are welcome and often preponderant, dressed in their fineries, especially now because my father is a striking man.

In the evening the manager and his guests gather on the verandah to separate day from night, enjoy the short tropical sunset and prepare our minds for dinner. The men drink *stengas*, whisky and soda, which the houseboy brings them unasked, noiseless as a ghost. The setting sun's garish colors paint a fitting backdrop for the wild peacocks that fly past against a yellow sky, some pausing in the giant eucalyptus trees across the lawn, screeching piercingly. My father tells of his day, we listen respectfully; my mother rarely takes her eyes off him. During the early phases of the moon we watch it rise, until the number two boy lights the lamps to announce that dinner is served.

One night we observe a total eclipse of the moon. A dark bite slowly eats the surface. Evil spirits are trying to swallow him, the *tong-tongs* in the neighboring hamlets throb through the night to chase them away.

I am well prepared. My sister told me all about it, shadow of the Earth and all that. I may be only six but I am not stupid! I listen to the men in the village taking turns beating on the hollowed-out tree trunk, the muffled sound alarms the darkness and reaches up to the moon, but the shadow keeps on growing, swallowing him. Now he is almost totally gone, on all sides *tong-tongs* join in the frenzy, the night is alive with sound. The tension is unbearable - will he ever come back?...

"Off to bed," my father commands at the first crack of light on the moon's other side. We did it! We did it! He's coming back! "Tomorrow very early we return to Surabaya."

My sister and I sleep in the guest quarters, which are connected to the main house by an outside walkway, paved and covered, about a hundred feet long. "Be sure you go together," he adds. "And don't dally."

He need not worry. Some time ago, right here on this walkway, a boy sauntering off to bed was fatally mauled by a *tutul*, a Javanese panther. How do we know? Everybody knows.

* * *

At the age of six I thoroughly approved of Life. From the beginning everything had gone entirely to my satisfaction. As far back as I could remember, which at that time must have been the cradle, I had been well treated. My parents obviously loved me, and the feeling was mutual. My sister, Ellen, due to our vast age difference of two years, largely left me alone. The women servants, *babu* Pah and *babu* Pih, looked after me, but being happy I required a minimum of discipline and was reasonably free to do as I pleased. Growing up, I discovered to my surprise that my friends and playmates were not hard to beat at games and sports. All in all, I felt in tune with the universe, a functioning part, ready to accept whatever I did not understand. Which included the occasional spirit, for whom I always had the greatest respect.

In Surabaya we lived on Kajoon, overlooking the river Brantas. When after the monsoon rains the broad, brown stream roiled furiously our yard boy, the *kebon*, would wink at me and say, "They're at it again."

Of course I knew what he meant: the shark (*sura*), who swam up from the sea, and the crocodile (*buaja*), who drifted down from the mountain, had resumed their epic battle for supremacy over the river. Sura - buaja... Surabaya.

In front of the house, dominating the entire garden, stood a gigantic banyan tree. As soon as I could climb, which was shortly after I could walk, I made it my headquarters. After breakfast I frequently disappeared in it to spend all day in its upper reaches, sixty feet or more off the ground, invisible to my worried parents who towards dinnertime would lure me down with promises of food. "You don't seem to fall out much," the kebon remarked one evening. "That tree is your friend."

The house itself, shaded by the banyan, was a classic Dutch-colonial building, large and white with pillars each side of the marble steps. It was designed to resist the heat with walls a brick-length thick and tile floors, deep verandahs fore and aft and a twenty-foot high ceiling. Swinging half-doors, like in a Western bar, connected ample, open rooms that caught the slightest movement of the tepid air.

It was a happy home, which my mother filled with bustle and cheer. She came from an old colonial family and was born in Java, as was her mother before her. Contrary to the British, the Dutch did not frown on mixed marriages - at least, officially - and as Hollanders had lived in the Indies for more than three hundred years, far from home, many families had through the centuries absorbed a drop or two of Indonesian blood here and there. Members of such clans were, in the vernacular of the time, "suspect", as were many of our friends. In polite circles the problem was simply never mentioned, as a matter of manners, because unofficially it took a person down a couple of rungs on the social ladder. *"Ces sont des choses qu'on ne discute pas,"* my mother would say, always in French for some mysterious reason, which presumably had to do with the delicacy of the subject. She herself had Delft-blue eyes, auburn hair and the advantage of an impeccable European education, but, to put it mildly, her viewpoints and attitudes clearly pointed to a long family involvement with Indonesian culture.

So she took Ellen and me to see Balinese dancers whose art and concentration turned them into monkeys; and to the yearly cattle races on Madura where the jockeys stood upright, like Roman gladiators, on a harnessed brace of flower-decked bulls; and to the Borobudur temple, whose more than 500 Buddhas told the story of their religion in stone; and to the horrors of the volcanic Idjen plateau, where the earth breathed sulfur and a bottomless lake rested on a bed of poisonous fumes; and to *gamelan* concerts whose hypnotic music put you in a trance; and to *wajang* shadow plays in which legendary heroes battled hideous spirits and four-armed monsters; and to American movies at the *Pasar Malam* projected on a transparent cotton screen for white viewers on one side and brown ones at the back, the former rooting for the cowboys and the latter for the Indians in a never-ending dialog of cheers and catcalls. - Such was my preschool education, and it was my mother who provided it.

Except for the cowboy movies my father had little interest in all this. As a solid Dutchman he based himself on reality, despised spirits and denied the existence of all other unsubstantiated entities. Besides, he had no time. He was busy building Empire and, concomitantly, his own fortune. Weekends he played golf on a course where snakes hid out in the holes, hissing ferociously, sometimes shooting away into the *alang alang* grass with the ball in their mouth.

This was as close as he ever came to adventure. Always an exceptionally handsome man in a straight-nosed, clean-shaven, British way, his good looks were matched by sterling qualities, such as kindness, fairness, honesty, loyalty and diligence. It made him into a perfect gentleman, courteous and reliable, and consequently not very exciting. He disliked taking risks, those indispensable stepping stones to glory in any field of human endeavor, and consequently never in his life exceeded conventional business success. For him, it sufficed.

In spite of his position in the commercial world he was financially unsophisticated. Not that it mattered. Much money was being made in coffee and rubber, of which the tantième system diverted an exorbitant amount into the planters' pockets. As one of them my father was highly in favor of this and invested it all in Dutch blue chips such as Royal Dutch Shell, Philips Electrical and Unilever. He never sold a single share, until he prepared his affairs for leaving the Indies and then his timing was perfect: three months before the crash of 1929 he converted all his stocks into bonds, and earned the family's undying gratitude.

For Empire building his timing was less fortunate. Since the turn of the century the Ethical Movement, which put the interest of the colonized above that of the colonizers, had been gaining ground in the Netherlands. My father detested it. On Java the Indonesian intellectual Ahmed Sukarno was about to proclaim his *Partai Nasionalis Indonesia*, which carried "Merdeka" (Freedom) in its banner. My father's comment was, "Lock him up." Only in the Simpang Club, where he played bridge once a week, could he still count on a sympathetic audience for his increasingly archaic viewpoints.

He was an empire builder because he was a conservative, not because he was a racist. On the conventional political scale he would probably register slightly to the right of Genghis Khan, yet he was also a true son of Amsterdam, the cradle of tolerance, racial and every other kind. He loved the Javanese, but as a man of his time he took the 'white man's burden' seriously and treated them as wards. Such were the enormous responsibilities which colonialism created, as they created huge profits. Both, according to my father, were equally legitimate and should continue. Change was the enemy, not race. - I loved him, of course, but in those early years we rarely got close.

* * *

In the middle of all this, free, unsuspecting, not a care in the world, I suddenly had to go to school. It began disastrously. The first morning opened with a race between classmates, to be repeated every day for a month, to finish first in arranging the letters of our primer *Ot en Sien* - the Dutch equivalent of Dick and Jane - on the word-boards in front of us. Of course I expected to win, hands down, but to my consternation a Chinese girl, Elvira Tan, beat me; her name remains forever graven in my memory. This was entirely unacceptable to me and every morning for a month I hurled myself into the fray, bloody but unbowed, gritting my teeth in the quest for victory. The rest of the class stayed so far behind, they might as well have stood on the sidelines. But no matter how light-ning fast I manipulated the tiny chips, there were always two or three left when Elvira's silvery little voice announced her triumph. I was perplexed, I didn't know whether I should love her or murder her. Even so, I learned my lesson: I was not going to win every battle in my life.

Every weekday morning thereafter at six o'clock, instead of escap-ing into the banyan tree, I sat opposite my father for breakfast, marveling at his white, starched, long-sleeved suit with the stiff collar, two inches high, tightly buttoned up at his throat as a precaution against sweaty emanations on this long, hot, humid, pre-deodorant day. I wore shoes, among other nonsensical clothing. At half past six sharp Monhadji drove up in the Minerva to chauffeur us downtown, to school and office. We sat silently in the back seat, I with my books next to my father, the Administrator and Chief Planter, with his little aluminum lunch pail - he worked from seven in the morning to six in the evening without leaving his office. Getting rich wasn't easy; neither was getting smart.

Learning proved no problem, I knew quickly enough how to handle decimals and that the Netherlands East Indies, when stretched across the USA, would reach from San Francisco 800 miles into the Atlantic Ocean. My troubles lay deeper. Every day we were taught some facts and figures that did not fit the mystical concepts that had buttressed my world so far. The basics of Dutch education, one of the toughest in existence, were being grafted onto the exotic infrastructure which of necessity would have to support them for the rest of my life. With it came the first rudi-ments of Western civilization, which unraveled reality as I understood it without as yet providing an alternative. In short, I was lost.

I looked to my parents for help. My father was of no use at all. Not surprisingly he stood behind every hard-nosed fact that the school rammed down my fragile universe. In his eyes, I was finally on the right track.

My mother, to my disappointment, didn't do much better. I presume she considered that, whatever her personal feelings, the school taught me what I had to know to become a proper Hollander. But she had a joker up her sleeve. "Why don't you go see Opa?" she suggested.

If my grandfather in Amsterdam had attained a certain notoriety, my mother's father was downright famous. Opa Vreede qualified as a legendary sports hero. He had gone to Leiden, Holland's oldest and most

prestigious university, to study Law, but got involved in the more serious task of stroking the senior fours of Njord, the Student Rowing
Association. As sculling, after the example of Cambridge and Oxford,
had become the prime competitive sport at Europe's universities, with
senior fours as the traditional main event, he quickly became known.
The fact that in five years he never lost a race - in the Njord boat "Sans
Nom" made him a legend. Still today his oars hang in the Association's
clubhouse in Leiden.

Meanwhile he studied Law, obtained a doctor's degree and joined
the legal establishment in the Indies, where he married into my mother's
family. His wife died young, but his career soared, until at its height he
suddenly resigned as Vice-President of the Council of Justice and bought
a commercial limestone quarry with a spooky mansion at the edge of the
jungle, somewhere near Semarang. The romance of this move totally
escaped my father, of course, and yet when quite predictably the quarry
went bankrupt shortly thereafter, he dutifully invited his father-in-law to
move in with us. From then on Opa Vreede lived in the first room of the
left outbuilding of our house on Kajoon.

He was a big man who looked like a retired sea captain, with white
hair and a mustache above a trim Vandyke beard. Every morning at
breakfast we saw him walk by in a flowery kimono on his way to the
other wing for his daily bath - half a dozen buckets full from the cistern,
after a quick check for scorpions and centipedes - and a mood of expectation gripped the household. As soon as the door closed behind him
he launched into a full-throated version of *La Donna è mobile*, always the
same, and the servants would cover their mouths to hide grins from ear
to ear. The bath lasted the length of the aria, no more no less, after which
the day could proceed as ordained.

I took my mother's advice and was invited to visit Opa in the small
hours of the afternoon. On the table in the center of his room lay a heap
of rowing medals in anticipation of my favorite stories. But I wanted his
opinion and told him my problems. He was singularly unimpressed.

"Give it time," he said mildly. "More problems have been solved by
time than by people." Then, as the house lay silent around us, stunned
by the midday heat, the stroke of the "Sans Nom" with his grandson on
his lap and the medals glowing in the shuttered glare, told me tales of
his student days and convinced me once again that at the other end of
the world, in Holland, in Leiden, some of the best years of my life were
waiting to be lived. On both points he proved right.

As the years went by, school kept grinding away at me. I saw much less of my mother, and Ellen had discovered Rudolph Valentino and Clara Bow and moved into regions where I didn't care to follow. But the more I got educated, the better I got along with my father. We actually discussed matters and were well on our way to becoming friends. Finally, ten days before graduation, he even invited me to lunch at the Simpang Club.

We ordered the Special, a bowl of fried rice with spices and on a separate plate a fried egg, sunny side up. My father's side dish was hideously undercooked and glassy, quivering whenever someone walked past. He shoved it aside and ignored it. He appeared preoccupied and under stress. After we had finished the rice almost in silence, he said, "You and your sister are going home to Holland next month."

I had been expecting it, of course. We had avoided the subject as much as possible, miserable as it made us, but it had to come up sometime. Ellen was attending high school in Bandung, but she was a girl and I knew well enough that I, as every one of my male friends, had to go to high school in the Netherlands in order to become a true Hollander." Do I have to?" I tried, in spite of this.

"Don't ask silly questions," my father answered wearily. "We got word from The Hague and everything is set. The Hein family can accommodate Ellen, and you'll live with professor Geerts. They're good homes. Mother and I shall follow in a year or so, as soon as I made my business arrangements."

My father leaving the Indies? This seemed unthinkable. Coffee and rubber were his life, I could not imagine him without it. But he loved us and wanted to keep the family together. His son, now that the time had come, had to go home to the old country, inevitably. It was a price every colonial family had to pay. So we all had to go back to Holland. How would he take it? And how would my mother, to leave the country of hr birth? How would Ellen, and for that matter, how would I?

There was little more to say. My father called for the bill and asked for the complaints book, a sizable tome for members' gripes; his side dish, now cold, still stood quivering on the table. He paid and then took the book from the waiter. He opened it, casually slid the egg off the plate between two clean pages and slammed it shut.

We stepped down the marble stairs into the hot Surabaya afternoon.

* * *

Once again the little band plays Aloha Oe on the quay in Tandjong Perak. This time it's for us. Ellen and I are standing on the deck of the Rotterdam Lloyd ss. *Sibajak*, hand in hand. Our parents have left the ship, we are on our own. My sister trembles beside me.

"Just look at it this way," my father had suggested, trying to keep our spirits up. "You are leaving your motherland to go to your fatherland. The two are one, as it should be, now and forever. So you're really not going anywhere."

Like hell we're not, we are going ten thousand miles away from the Indies, my sister and I. We've been to Holland on home leave, enough to know that the two are as different as night and day. And look what we're leaving behind; there they stand on the quay next to my parents, in their best sarongs and blouses, our friends, almost family... head boy Ali, second boy Njo, babu Pah, babu Pih, Monhadji, the kebon, kokkie, small and still. Occasionally the women flutter little white handkerchiefs, specially washed and ironed for the occasion. We wave back silently, in tears. My mother does not move.

Three blasts on the steam-whistle, deafening. The hawsers are dropped off the dock. The Sibajak starts slipping away and as the black wedge of water between ship and quay side widens relentlessly, people shout back and forth, "*tabeh!... tabeh!... farewell!... farewell!*".... through the last sliding notes of Aloha Oe... But already we are in different worlds.

August 1930, I am thirteen years old and on my way to become a proper Hollander. I am ready, but will it be easy? In the Netherlands everything is like it is, a bike is a bike and a cheese is a cheese. But is that really all? Where I come from the shark and the crocodile do battle, a banyan tree is my friend, evil spirits swallow the moon, and tell me, has anyone yet gone past the Black Cave without a pebble in his mouth?

CHAPTER 2

Of Pigeonholes and Gauchos

A windmill, a pair of wooden shoes, a bunch of tulips... don't let it fool you, behind these bucolic symbols hides one of the most contentious countries in the world. After 1917, when its Constitution was revised, it outdid itself by transforming its structure into a socio-political society based on "pillars", and as the system gradually consolidated itself throughout the land, people spoke of "pillarization". It changed the life of the nation and everyone in it.

During my high school years in Holland, pillarization - which survived into the Sixties - was at its peak. Five pillars supported the dome of public life: a Dutch-Reformed, a Liberal Protestant, a Catholic, a Socialist and a Humanist. Everyone in the country automatically fell within the scope of one of these, depending on his religious and philosophical concepts. This involved not only politics, but also schools and universities, the labor movement, newspapers and radio, hospitals and sports clubs, and gradually spread across the private sector until the pillars dominated the existence of every individual, from the choice of kindergarten to that of undertaker.

Daily routine also became ruled by pillarization - where you lived and how, what you did for fun, whom you chose to be your doctor, your dentist and even your grocer: a good Catholic would turn to shops and craftsmen of his own faith, and they themselves employed only Catholics. Many Dutchmen therefore lived in their specific little world, shut off from their fellow countrymen, cultivating their own habits and traditions in, as it has been called, hostile coexistence in peace. As always in our history, they respected each other's viewpoints and treated one another other civilly, but there was little left of trust and fellowship.

That was not all. Cutting across this five-way vertical split of the nation, ran a horizontal grid of class distinctions of which the Aztecs would have been proud. The two combined created a rigidly compartmentalized society, in which every person was assigned his pigeonhole with remarkable consistency.

When sometime after my parents' homecoming I joined the oldest soccer club of Holland, HVV, hated in the league as a bulwark of privilege and tradition, every game we played represented ninety minutes of unadulterated class warfare. We knew where we stood and made no bones about it. Once, during a game in Gouda, I had to take a corner-kick which on the home team's cramped facility brought me dangerously close to the hostile supporters. One of them succeeded in hooking the handle of his umbrella around my ankle, just as I was about to take off. To loud cheers of the public I fell flat on my face.

"Dirty proletarian!" I hissed at him as I got ready for a second try.

"Rich blood sucker!" he jeered back, and having thus accurately placed each other in our respective pigeonholes, we parted not without a mutual bond of satisfaction.

Escape from one's social compartment was impossible, your fellow Dutchmen wouldn't let you, not up, not down, not left, not right. Your name and family, your mother's background, what your father did for a living, your home address, your school or job, your choice of words, and especially that scourge of social equality- your accent, it all slid smoothly into our human computers for purposes of identification. As a rule people kept their distance, as a safety zone in which to legitimize each other and if necessary drive you back, for whoever burst out from his assigned position in society was a threat to the existing order.

At first I couldn't care less, of course. I felt entirely at ease in the pigeonhole into which I had apparently landed, somewhere fairly elevated, and it made no difference to me whether my milk came from a catholic or a protestant cow, nor if the bastard who had just hooked me with his umbrella was a socialist or a humanist. As far as I was concerned, Holland turned out to be a teenager's paradise.

Most importantly, our family was together again; after a year of preparations and goodbyes my parents had left the Indies with heavy hearts. We lived in The Hague, although my father's new position as president of a distillery forced him to drive 20 miles to Schiedam every day, a considerable distance in the Netherlands. He took the job for the money, but was socially unhappy to be producing genever (Dutch gin) and cordials instead of coffee and rubber, clearly a rung down the ladder. At the age of 42, with the first signs of a middle-age belly, there was little left of the proud empire builder on his stallion in the coffee fields of Sumber Agung, and he knew it. We were reunited, and he had paid a high price for it. But live in Schiedam, a harbor and factory town? Never! The Hague at least had class as the seat of government and home of the Queen. On this point we all agreed.

This especially pleased my mother. The Hague—short for 's Gravenhage, the 'Count's country home'—was the preferred final destination of former colonials, so she regained many old friends. The Netherlands' third city, it lies just behind the dunes along the North Sea coast, about halfway between Amsterdam and Rotterdam, two towns which don't agree on much except that The Hague is la-di-da and stuck up. The Indies' presence was so pervasive that a typically Dutch evening on the town invariably involved a superb Indonesian rijsttafel for dinner We gradually lost our tropical pallor and melted into our European surroundings.

What my sister, Ellen, thought of it all was impossible to ascertain, as she had discovered romance and was up to her ears in boys. She had grown into a tall, attractive blonde with huge eyes of an unusually light blue color, which blazed with intelligence. I liked her well enough, but she had always been and would forever remain a complete mystery to me. Sometimes you could hardly blame me for this.

Once, on a ski-vacation in Switzerland, she announced her engagement to a Polish count, a shadowy figure whom none of us ever met. It was a socially intriguing notion, but when after our return to Holland my parents raised some practical points concerning the marriage, she eloped to Poland. She got as far as the railroad station in downtown The Hague, where she changed her mind. She took a taxi home, where I happened to open the front-door to her.

"How's your count?" I inquired tactlessly.

"What count?" she answered, with her sweetest smile. It was the last anyone ever heard of him. I was relieved when she ultimately went off to college, where she graduated summa cum laude in Law and faded temporarily out of my life.

Personally I liked The Hague for three reasons. First, it had an excellent school, which was after all the purpose of my coming all the way from Surabaya. Its 6 day, 42 hour week and mountains of homework left me barely enough time for the other two: the proximity of Scheveningen, our massive beach resort, and even closer, down the road from our house, HVV and my regular buddies.

Here I floated along blissfully close to the surface of life, safe and sound in my luxurious pigeonhole. The soccer-fields were never greener, the beaches of Scheveningen never more golden, the sails never whiter on the countless lakes of the Low Countries, and, soon, the girls never more alluring and unfathomable. School, although time consuming, presented no problems; in absence of my Nemesis, Elvira Tan, I had a firm grip on first place in my grade. Whenever winter would freeze the canals, classes were suspended to free us for skating - on wooden, not silver skates - from village to village, stopping at tiny stalls on the ice for hot chocolate or genever from stone crocks.

Otherwise our world moved on bicycle, for no one under thirty owned a car. Everybody pedaled, to everywhere, for anything. Our country even boasted a regiment of soldiers on bicycles, fully equipped with rifles and backpacks and their entire military band on wheels. We heard rumors of teenagers in America actually owning their own car, but didn't quite believe it. As we went courting on our bikes - no mean achievement - the thought of having a vehicle at one's disposal for that purpose was just too stupendous to contemplate. Who needed it? Who could want anything more than Holland offered us?

The years went by, happy-go-lucky, and then one day, without warning, I thought of the man in the bamboo village, old skin-and-bones with the red lips, and of Ahmed, his little brown grandson with the serious eyes and flashing smile. Of Gunung Lawu and the lake, of the river Brantas, the banyan tree and the kebon winking at me. I thought of the Indies out there and of the whole world out everywhere, outside my cozy little pigeonhole with life moving by. I panicked, because I could see my entire future laid out before me, inescapably: I would graduate from high-school, step into Opa Vreede's shoes at Leiden University, get a degree and settle into one of the traditional careers of our family: the law, big business or, if all else failed, the Royal Navy. Surely there was more to it all?

Outwardly nothing changed: I gave it my best at school, played bad but enthusiastic soccer and chased the girls. But under it all grew an unsettling urge to break out of my constraints and investigate life as others lived it, and in the process perhaps discover new realities. My pigeonhole began to feel like a prison cell, locking me away from a vast, inviting world of unknown places, people and experiences. It was time I flew the coop, but how? - My first effort shipwrecked on predictable cliffs.

As I fancied my voice - unwisely - I took a crash course in playing the guitar. As soon as the combination of the two satisfied my modest ambitions, I put on some ratty clothes and made for the Wagenstraat, a particularly uninviting part of downtown The Hague, far from my usual hunting grounds. For breaking out, surely this was the spot. Putting my bike against a wall I took up a protected position in a shop entrance, unpacked my guitar and placed the empty case at an inviting angle. Then I opened my mouth to entertain the shoppers... Nothing came out.

For the first time in my life I was about to beg for something, but I just could not do it. A few passersby looked at me curiously, so I pretended to be admiring the merchandise in a shop window, which unfortunately displayed fancy ladies' underwear.

I gritted my teeth and tried again - was it really such a disgrace to make a buck? No, but throwing yourself on the naked charity of your fellowman requires a level of humility difficult to achieve, at least for me. On this I had not counted, and only by the greatest effort did I finally manage to strum a few chords and raise my voice. Even to me it sounded like a rooster with a cold.

Things got better as I went along, to the extent that I began to observe my potential benefactors. All I saw was bleak suspicion. Was it the cold, perhaps, that prevented them from digging into their pockets for a spot of change? Even my prize rendition of "Old Man River" drew nothing but skittish glances, and yet, suddenly there lay a shiny quarter in my box! It represented the first money I ever earned, and had it been pure gold it could not have excited me more. I had burst out of my pigeonhole! I was being accepted by another world! It seemed worth all the effort and embarrassment, until I noticed that some son-of-a-bitch denizen of this new world had made off with my bicycle.

It was a long walk home. When I came to a row of imposing homes along the Koninginngracht I couldn't resist one more try. It had gotten dark, and on an upper floor behind a brightly lit window, uncurtained as is the custom in Holland, a party was in progress. This seemed a natural for an easy haul, so I unboxed my guitar, crossed over and rang the bell. The moment the door opened automatically at the bottom of steep, endless stairs, I launched into a sailor's chantey out of Gilbert and Sullivan. To my horror I recognized the face staring down at me from the top of the steps: it belonged to my ex-girlfriend whom I had taken great pains to avoid for the last six weeks. "Erik!" she chirped. "What a wonderful surprise! How did you know it was my birthday?"

I was right back in my pigeonhole.

* * *

My next effort, a year or so later, produced a stunning revelation: if I wrote something, people would sometimes pay to read it. I was ecstatic. Now surely, being recognized as a writer, even getting paid for it, would free me from my rigid position in society... Not so in Holland. In the prewar Netherlands of my circles writing was not considered a serious occupation. Authors and journalists, which of course existed, tended to dispute this, but they themselves were not taken seriously. Writing as a hobby - fine, but as soon as it got published and made money it became a social embarrassment.

What was serious in Holland was Trade, the lifeblood of the country and its history, and the biggest Dutchmen were the big businessmen. They didn't write books and stories, nor did other respected citizens such as lawyers, doctors or diplomats. Before World War II there may have been disagreement about the rest of the Dutch social totem pole, but not about the lowly standing of contemporary creative expression, be it in paint, stone, harmony, or words, with film stars at the very bottom. An occasional giant might break the bonds, but rarely before dying first, and then often after a penurious life. The run-of-the-mill artists, actors and writers were invariably poor, a condition which does not foster social prominence in the Netherlands, and the twilight zone of journalism barely escaped a similar fate. At age sixteen I got an article published, five columns in the respected Algemeen Handelsblad, but to protect my social reputation I hid my exuberance and signed it with only my initials.

The subject of all this excitement was a trip on a fishing trawler out of the Dutch Reformed stronghold of Katwijk. Once again I was restless for an unknown facet of life, and felt pretty confident that the KW 20 could provide it. I was not disappointed. After talking my way aboard as deck hand, I almost immediately regretted it. The straw bag I had brought, which was to fit into my bunk, showed signs of fleas which the bosun fixed by pouring a pint of motor oil over it, on which I had to sleep for at least two weeks. "You brought them," he explained. "We never have fleas on board. They can't stand the smell of fish."

As it turned out, we didn't spend much time sleeping anyway. The KW 20, a classic wooden diesel-powered North Sea vessel, was trawling for bottom fish such as sole. halibut and flounder. This meant that every three hours, day and night, all hands were called on deck to pull in the net, clattering about on wooden shoes trying to keep our balance in six inches of sea-sludge and slithering creatures. Mostly the wind howled, whipping rain and hail into our faces, and at night waves broke over our heads in inky darkness. After setting the net again and sorting the catch into ice baskets by the light of storm lanterns, there was often less than twenty minutes left before the next haul.

Aboard KW20

The fleas also had my sympathy. Aside from the all-pervading smell of fresh fish, creatures got stuck on deck in every nook and cranny, and started to rot whenever the sun came out. This stench would follow us down into our social center, the forecastle, a nine by nine by six feet triangle in the nose of the ship, to be joined there by more subtle aromas such as cooking fat, wet clothes, diesel exhaust, cheap tobacco and unwashed men. Why wash, if every three hours we were showered by the dregs of the sea? So we didn't, nor did we ever changed our clothes.

Even so, it was cozy below deck. At meal time we sat on benches around the bare, wooden table, six burly men and me, filling the little room to bursting. As the ship bucked and shuddered we listened to the waves breaking against the other side of the wall, while the skipper read to us from the Bible. Then came the food, every day the same, bread and margarine in the morning, potatoes with pork fat at noon, rice-soup and fish for dinner. The bread started out fresh, then soon petrified and turned brown with cockroach traces. For this abundance the fishermen thanked God before and after every meal and sang psalms of gratitude, interminably, led by the skipper who improvised the melody. The men sang lustily, including the cook who was tone-deaf, and when their voices rolled around that tiny dry hole on the vast sea, he spirit of the Lord was clearly present. When we finished we threw the rest of our food on the floor and hoisted ourselves into the bunks behind us for a few minutes sleep before the watch's next "Haul, men! Haul!"

After this adventure my pigeonhole suddenly didn't look so bad after all and for two years the world outside seemed to consist only of places like Cannes, St. Moritz, Mallorca and Paris. In fact, I suffered a complete relapse into the main concern of teenagers, which is to have a good time. Girls overwhelmed my life, with soccer a close second, and behind those fascinating alternatives even school took a beating.

Meanwhile the first ripples of a new drift touched the Netherlands, a whiff of change. Of course we could hear Adolph Hitler ranting beyond our eastern border day after day, but who would pay attention to a jerk like that? This was more subtle. Movies, up till now predominantly American in Holland, were being slowly pushed aside by German films, and where before it had been Gary Cooper, Claudette Colbert and Clark Gable, now we rushed to see Willy Fritsch, Marlene Dietrich and Heinz Rühmann. The Mills Brothers and Boswell Sisters still hung on, but the big singing star was Zarah Leander. In a sport I fancied, auto racing, Mercedes Benz reigned supreme with drivers like Von Brauchitz, Stuck and Rosemeyer, save for one Italian, Nuvolari, on Ferrari. British and French tourists dwindled while Scheveningen, Zandvoort and other Dutch beach resorts bulged with Germans. Nothing bad about it, just new.

In the summer of 1936, a few weeks after graduating from high school, I startled my parents with the news that instead of entering Leiden university in the Fall I was off to South America. This time my father wished to know more. Lighting one in his endless chain of cigarettes, he confronted me. "Why do you want to go to South America?"

The answer, though crystal clear to me, I considered too complicated for any parent to understand. My moment of truth had arrived: Did my future lie in Holland, as a lawyer or businessman, or in the world beyond, the great unknown, perhaps as a writer? To my father this was bound to seem a fairly straight forward choice, but I firmly believed - and still do - that you can eat your cake and have it, too. Not always, of course, but often enough to present a real alternative, always worth trying. South America would be a test, decisive yet not irrevocable, a solution with a backdoor just in case, perhaps the ultimate escape yet not eliminating the possibility of a hasty retreat to Leiden next year. Despairing of my parents' understanding of such matters I mumbled something about gauchos and learning Spanish, and shrugged my shoulders.

My father looked at me silently for a long moment. Then, to my great surprise and embarrassment, he placed his hand on my head as if I were a little boy and said: "You must do what you must do. Everyone said I was crazy when I went to the Indies. I seem to remember a classmate of mine, way back from Amsterdam, now lives in Argentina somewhere. Raises cattle on the Pampas, or something. Pretty nice fellow, I recall. Maybe he could use you."

* * *

Rincon de Aguaceros lay thirty miles from the town of Mercedes, in the province of Corrientes in northeast Argentina. It was a relatively small ranch, or estancia, some 3000 acres nestled in the bend of the river Aguaceros, and supported around 2000 head of cattle and 4000-odd sheep. The road out of the sleepy little ocher-colored town ended abruptly and we ran into open country. The 1931 Ford pickup twisted and bucked, but fortunately it had been dry and we ground along at a noisy 25 mph followed by a swirling cloud of dust. In the far distance the estancia complex with surrounding trees stood like a rectangular smudge on the horizon in an otherwise completely bare, slightly undulating landscape: the Pampas.

Don Mauricio Pieper - Maurits Pieper from Amsterdam - el patron of the estancia, had welcomed me with an easy smile as I stepped off the train in which I had rumbled 30 hours from Buenos Aires to Mercedes. He was a lanky, 49-year old Hollander with a brush of iron-grey hair. His open, weathered face creased into a network of laugh lines around startlingly blue Dutch eyes. Without much talk we climbed aboard the truck and drove to the distant smudge. Gradually it grew into a low, U-shaped house with red walls and a tin roof surrounded by some outbuildings and eucalyptus trees, a shabby version of Sumber Agung. Just clear of the trees, straight out of The Grapes of Wrath, an iron windmill silhouetted against the evening sky.

After washing up we immediately installed ourselves on the front verandah, where two chairs had been put in readiness side by side. A half-breed Indian girl, smiling shyly, brought us maté, Argentina's national tea drink, in a hollow gourd with a silver straw, vile tasting stuff but very invigorating. Every two minutes she returned, sliding like a ghost in and out of the darkening house, to pour fresh hot water on the tea.

"Do not thank her," Pieper cautioned me. "It's the signal that you've had enough." After the next pouring, I thanked her.

A Coleman lamp was lit in the room behind us, splashing its dead white glare on the bare walls. "Our only light," Pieper grinned amiably. "We carry it along with us. But there are some candles in your room. - Guillerma!" he yelled.

The girl, a dusky teenager with amber eyes, seemed to materialize from the dark. "Out," he said, with a wave behind him. She faded away and the lamp went out. He followed her fondly with his gaze. "Nice kid," he commented. "I named her after Queen Wilhelmina. - You're not hungry, are you? We have an early moon tonight, let's watch it rise. Do you mind?"

It was stupendous. As the moon lifted from the horizon like a red balloon, it unleashed pandemonium on the Pampas. The main players were frogs, led in their exuberant composition by a silvery fine "auu! auu!" from dozens of little frog-throats in vague locations, plaintive and distinct as babies' voices. These were accompanied by dry, rhumba-like clicks of even smaller creatures, and from time to time cut through by the rapid, earsplitting plop-plop-plop-plop of the larger marsh species. All this performed against the steady backdrop of low, soft drum beats of the giant toads, which grow as large as rabbits. The concert, accentuated now and then by the cry of a chaja night bird, created an ultimate void, profoundly lonely, the silence of the Pampas.

We listened and looked, without speaking, while Guillerma floated in and out soundlessly with the hot water kettle. The ground remained dark under the rising moon, except for three or four pools of weak, unearthly glow - superstitiously feared by the peones, the local cowboys - where cattle carcasses belatedly expelled the sun's ultraviolet rays. In one direction flickering lines of orange fire, set that morning, consumed the grass to make room for new growth. Close by in the trees myriads of fire flies flashed their silent seduction. Behind the house a voice began to sing an intricate Indian melody, accompanied by soft clapping of hands, and laughter. "Our peones," Don Mauricio explained with a smile.

Guillerma poured again, and at last Pieper thanked her. "Let's eat," he said, whacking me on the shoulder. We went inside and sat on both sides of the Coleman lamp. The meal consisted of asado (roast) of tender lamb spareribs, and strawberries with thick cream for dessert. The beer was Heineken's. My host spoke little, but seemed to be pleased with my presence. One thing appeared certain: I was going to like it here.

However, after 27 days on a ship out of Rotterdam the mere distance from home had already decided the main issue. I had made up my mind: I would get my fill of Argentina, which might take a few months, and then return to the Netherlands. My father had known exactly what he was doing. In spite of many foreign vacations and spells of restlessness, I had never before been separated from my country. Before burning any bridges he wanted me to test my roots and experience the strength of my bonds to our fatherland. He never doubted the outcome - I was homesick from the very first day. Holland, pigeonholes and all, was clearly where I belonged. I would go home, enter Leiden University in the autumn, study Law and grow up a Dutchman, maybe even a big businessman. And I would write a little on the side, as a hobby, as befits a gentleman.

With this finally settled there was nothing more to worry about; I could enjoy Rincon de Aguaceros to the fullest, and did. I learned to ride and rope, brand and cut, worm and de-horn, shear and castrate, skin and stretch, cook asado and drink wine from a buckskin. We hunted fowl in the marshes by day and crocodiles in the river by night, chased the fast nandu (ostrich) and the wily dorado (river trout). I learned Guarani songs from the peones - Dionysio, Pancho, Luis, Chico and Herrera - and most of all, became friends with Don Mauricio Pieper.

He was a cowboy with the soul of a saint. "My philosophy," he explained to me in the course of our endless maté sessions, "is to trust every creature on Earth, including humans." He would shrug his shoulders, blue eyes beaming from the creases. "You get screwed sometimes, but less often than you'd think. And on balance, you will gain a lot more in life than you'll lose." This advice alone has since proven well worth my bizarre journey to distant Argentina.

He clearly practiced what he preached. One look at his staff when I first arrived, and I started worrying about my gold watch. Guillerma and her old mother in the kitchen seemed all right, but I had my doubts about his five peones with their unkempt, bushy mops of hair, wild mustaches, patched clothes, bizarre hats, foot long knives in their belts and spurs the size of silver dollars which forced them to walk on their toes, jingling with every step. I checked my room for a drawer to lock away my money, but could not find one. When I asked Pieper to keep it in a safe place for me, he smiled.

"Every place here is safe," he said. "There are no locks on this estancia. My men are Indians, Guarani. They're honest, they don't steal. They might stick a knife in you if you don't treat them right, but otherwise you have nothing to worry about."

That bit about the knife worried me, honest or not, so I asked him about right and wrong treatment in Guarani circles.

"The keyword is Dignity," Don Mauricio explained. It was around noon, and once again we were sitting side by side on the front porch sipping maté, evidently Pieper's favorite pastime. Guillerma with her hot water kettle slid in and out of the kitchen, where the usual never-ending torrent of tango's flowed from the radio. This time she made twenty-three trips before I thanked her. "They're very strong on dignity. So never scold one in front of the others or you risk your life."

Armed with this wisdom I spent six wonderful months in their company, admiring their skill and courage, enjoying their humor, exuberance and kindness, and carried away by the amazing melodious perfection of their songs. And, of course, always most respectful of their dignity.

Week after week I kept delaying my departure, and then came the locusts. I was actually packing my bag to leave when Guillerma burst into the room as if she'd seen a ghost. "The langostas are coming!" She had set the scene:

It's early morning. In the northern sky hovers a massive cloud, a rainstorm perhaps, hugging half the horizon. But its color is strange, russet with dark patches, and around the edges here and there a delicate pink wisp. It slowly drifts in our direction, dragging a black shadow over the countryside below. Already the forerunners are beginning to come down on us, quiet as snowflakes with a soft rustling of wings, large, red locusts three inches long. The cloud grows, changes shape, starts churning and shimmering, and takes us into its shadow. The peones are burning wet wood, waving bright blankets and banging pans, but inexorably it keeps drifting in on the soft breeze, a solid sheet of voracious creatures several hundreds of feet thick.

Now the sky darkens, a dull roar like a distant waterfall fills the air above us, the hollow sound of billions of wings which flicker blindingly around, painting the world red. In torrents they descend upon us and cover everything in a writhing layer, which rises wing tip to wing tip around us with every step. Swinging a simple stick around kills hundreds. Branches break noisily under their weight while they devour every leaf in sight, the air smells sour from their droppings which rustle through the trees like rain. And above, hour after hour after hour, the reddish river streams on, until finally the flow thins and the orgy rolls onwards. The locusts take off from the ground in sudden rushes of wings, scattered at first, then in one giant roaring wave - and all are gone. The rust colored cloud, glimmering here and there, slowly drifts away, a clear blue sky beams down on the devastated earth below.

It seemed too good to pass up. I stayed an extra day and wrote an article about the onslaught, which Holland's biggest newspaper, the Telegraaf, printed on the front-page of its weekend edition. I signed it with my initials; for a non-writer, I was doing OK. Then I returned to Buenos Aires, hopped on a boat to Rotterdam and registered to enter Leiden University in the Fall of 1937.

And Don Mauricio Pieper? Fate gave him what he deserved. Shortly after my departure he moved from Rincon de Aguaceros to a modern estancia nearer Buenos Aires. He married Guillerma and had four sons. When World War II broke out and boosted Argentine beef prices, he became a millionaire. And he lived happily ever after.

CHAPTER 3

Rendezvous in San Francisco

Inside they were waiting for me, the bastards. I took a deep breath and leaned against the door. When it gave, the noise hit me like a blow. I staggered back – too late; a bony hand grabbed me by the throat. With shouts of triumph they dragged me down a dark hallway that smelled of beer and sweat. At an entrance to the right I dug in my heels, as a matter of principle, which cost me a sleeve and all the buttons of my shirt. A powerful brute picked me up from behind and shoved me into the air, and for a moment I had a splendid view of the scene at my feet, before crashing into it like a sack of potatoes.

Before me lay a vast, rectangular, high ceilinged room with graceful windows. Red plush curtains screened out the afternoon, chandeliers sparkled. Between a bar at one end and a huge fireplace at the other, pandemonium reigned; a heaving, yelling, sweating sea of humanity in which here and there heads shaven as bald as my own bobbed about forlornly like little white buoys in a storm. I caught a glimpse of a mournful apparition crouched in the bar sink, stark naked, flapping his arms like a demented duck, then I tumbled into the debris of overturned tables and chairs and broken glass. It was the first day of initiation, 1937, at Leiden, Holland's oldest, world famous university, and I landed on the floor of Minerva, hallowed home of the Leiden Student Corps.

Except in areas of marginal importance such as classes, curriculum, exams and the rest of the educational poppycock, the Corps considered itself the heart of Leiden's academic life. It boasted no more than a few hundred active members, all distinctly male, but as the heart of Leiden it clearly had to be the hub of Holland, and seeing that the Netherlands constituted the core of Europe and Europe of the world... well, anyway, the Corps was important.

Furthermore, it passionately believed that, if not in the eyes of God at least in those of every sane Dutchman, all men were created unequal. Know your place, and shut up. In this universal system, Divine Providence had reserved a very special niche for the Corps member, the Leidener. Provided, of course, that he belonged; if not, he was destined to fade from the scene sooner or later. This did not depend on brains, talent, or even money. On the contrary, every success in the field of human endeavor except rowing and sex was suspect, particularly the passing of exams on schedule, which required tact and humility.

Belonging was a matter of style: not what you did, but how you did it, even when you did nothing. Yours truly, in the dirt and beer and glass, with torn shirt and shaven head and generations of Leideners among his ancestors, belonged. I cautiously surveyed the scene of action. Fetuses - our generic name for the next three weeks - were sitting around on the floor, our habitat, looking miserable while everybody else was having a good time. Students drank beer and genever, and through the ruckus and laughter sounded wet slaps on bald heads. To my left a fetus in extremis was acting out a fried egg on the reading table, tears streaming down his face. To my right another was being dragged across the floor by his collar, through the dirt and debris. He winked at me cheerfully as he slid by. Elsewhere others stood forlornly in the chaos, like lost lambs, until a new group of tormentors pounced on them and dragged them away. Through it all four servers, smart in their black and silver uniforms, carried large trays of drinks, moving about as if it were the most normal thing in the world. Which it was, if you went to Leiden.

At first I was lucky. As I tried to sneak away, some dignified Leidener intercepted me. "Your name, fetus!"

I gave him my name and he made the connection with my grandfather, the legendary rowing-hero. As a result we discussed him for at least ten minutes, in every respect a normal, pleasant, social conversation, apart from the fact that I was lying flat on my back with my interlocutor's right foot firmly planted on my chest. Without a word of goodbye he suddenly moved on, leaving me vulnerable and unprotected. In a relatively quiet corner I spotted a table occupied by exalted seniors, its ample cloth promising a superb hideout. On hands and knees I scooted through the bedlam, but was caught at the very last moment. A tough hour followed, in which gallons of beer streamed down my spine, with

me steadfastly defending my entire male lineage against accusations varying from general debauchery to treason at the battle of Waterloo. Finally,
in a moment of confusion, I managed to escape and slip under the tablecloth. Sitting in the filth, gray-flanneled legs all around me, I became
aware of another bald presence in the gloom. "Krediet," it whispered,
politely. "Chris Krediet."

"Of Doctor Krediet? From Scheveningen?" Always establish with
whom you're dealing.

"My father." Careful not to disturb our hosts above, we shook
hands, a civilized gesture from a world which seemed eons behind us.
Then we settled down comfortably for a chat, like a subculture of hair-
less troglodytes.

We almost made it till dinnertime. Sitting opposite each other, legs
crossed, we were discussing the French race, specially its female gender.
Chris, waving a finger in the air the way Dutchmen converse, held the
floor. "You've got to understand...."

At this moment the entire table above our heads keeled over. A
fearful crash, glasses shattering, chairs toppled, Seniors jumping about
yelling and swearing at some petrified fetus who had caused the disaster,
and there we were, in the bright light, miraculously revealed at the core
of the commotion. I got out of there fast and kept going, but when I
looked back from a safe distance Chris was still sitting serenely in the
ruins, cross-legged, straight and bald, motionless, like some strange ar-
cheological discovery. Then the dinner bell rang.

We had barely sat down, eighty-four bald heads side by side at long,
narrow tables, when a beery voice lit into the Io Vivat!, the official Corps
song. A bloodcurdling command brought us to our feet, and as we chimed
in, the doors at the end of the hall parted and in strode the Collegium,
the ruling body of the Leiden Student Corps: five dignified young men
resplendent in morning coats and blue ribbons with silver insignia, like
Greek gods down from Olympus for an evening's slumming in Hades.

The President, Student next to God, led the way to the head table
set apart from the mob, casually treading on a fetus whose back had been
designated stepping stone to the dais. He was quite short, yet he easily
eclipsed his taller companions. After sitting down he gave us a sign that
we could proceed, a haughty little nod, and I sensed his charisma flow
through the room. His dark good looks, wide-set brown eyes and thin
mustache gave him an air of ruthlessness. His name was Ernst de Jonge,
and I firmly resolved to stay out of his way.

Fate would have it otherwise. Some acolyte called out my name and ordered me to entertain the Collegium with a song in Malay, the language of my youth. I chose the melancholy love song *Terang Bulan* (Full Moon). Apparently my rendition was not universally admired, for someone at the head table threw a soup tureen which exploded on my head.

Later that evening, after a trip to the hospital, alone in my room with eight stitches in my head and dizzy from loss of blood, I opened the door in response to a gentle knock. The perpetrator of the evil deed had come to apologize. He was friendly and concerned, and seemed an altogether different person from the potentate of a few hours ago. It was Ernst de Jonge.

We sat down and talked through the night, sustained by a bottle of Armagnac, the President and the fetus. Could anything be more glorious? Opa Vreede, with his heap of glittering medals in far away Surabaya, had been right. Leiden was the center of the world.

* * *

The main purpose of initiation rites is to show freshmen their place in the student community and mold them together into a cohesive body for the rest of their lives. On Chris and me it didn't work. We were somewhat older and vastly more experienced than the others, and had come to Leiden for a college degree, proper contacts and a good time, in that order.

Baldheaded or not, the individual shone through. Most evenings we spent from midnight till dawn in Minerva as tradition dictated, but otherwise we cherished our privacy. A few others felt likewise and became our friends. Together we stumbled into the future.

By Christmas our hair had grown back. Now we occasionally ventured into the university and some of us actually went so far as to buy a textbook. But soon the nights were getting shorter and we walked home from Minerva by daylight. Early tulips broke the ground, and that meant the rowing season. Magnificent brutes with blue-and-white scarves down to their knees began gracing Leiden's streets, harbingers of the Varsity. A hundred miles to the east tiresome old Hitler kept ranting on the radio, and by the way, Austria disappeared from the map, absorbed "home" into the Third Reich. Well, what can you expect? Once a Kraut, always a Kraut.

Suddenly it was summer, 1938. The academy closed its doors, sanctioning our state of idleness. This was girl time: sailing on the Kaag and Brasemer lakes, sunning on the beach at Scheveningen, dancing through the nights and plunging into every other activity that, with a reasonable dose of luck, could lead to sexual triumph. Contentedly I flowed along, absorbed in the absurd details of student life, without the slightest inkling of the ambush which the United States of America had in store for me.

To most of us in Leiden, a better name for America would have been the Dark Continent. We knew nothing about it. We had all gone to superior high schools and passed the toughest examination of our entire lives, and - to speak for myself – had studied history, geography, biology, physics, chemistry, algebra, geometry, and six languages, including 17 hours a week of Latin and Greek; but I never received one single hour of instruction about the USA, its history, its sociology, its political structure, its literature, its anything. The country was never discussed, radio and newspapers rarely referred to it, we were simply not aware of it.

Prime among the reasons was lack of interest. America had little to offer us. Liberty? We enjoyed our own, thank you. Money? We were doing fine, better in many respects than the USA. Technology, innovation? Dutch scientists stood in the forefront of progress. Cars? We preferred the Jaguar, Mercedes and Ferrari. Movies? They had been shoved aside by German productions.

The reverse was equally true, in spades. Americans by and large had no real use for Europe, let alone Holland. Their economy was continental, not international, and if they never sold a Buick in Amsterdam few people cared. They had their own dreams and problems, which left no room for foreign involvement. They might mistake Antwerp for the capital of the Netherlands and Wilhelmina for queen of Denmark - I, a freshman at Holland's best academy, would have been hard put to place Chicago in Illinois and Roosevelt in the White House. Why? Because there was no radio, television or any other affordable means of transatlantic communication, and it took a journey of ten days by boat to get there. The absence of planes and electronics kept us separated.

Nevertheless, we were under its spell. It was Cowboys and Indians from childhood on, but we made the connection via Germany. Around the turn of the century Karl May, the son of a weaver in Saxony, wrote books - some say in jail - about the white hunter Old Shatterhand and his Indian friend, Winnetou, and is responsible for the fact that an entire generation of Dutchmen knows that Apaches were the good guys and

Comanches the bad. He never left Germany, but for us in Leiden the American West existed as he described it, Death Valley, Llano Estacado, Rocky Mountains, Red River and all.

During high school it was music, blues, jazz, swing and big band magic. We wound up our portable phonographs with the cute dog on it and filled every spare minute with America's greats, from old Leadbelly and Satchmo to Benny Goodman and the Dorsey Brothers. In one sense at least it pulled us closer. We knew Basin Street from its blues and Rampart Street from the parade, took the A-train to Duke Ellington's Harlem and shuffled off to Buffalo, hi-de-ho'ed with Cab Calloway and choo-choo'd to Chattanooga. Without it, life would have been unthinkable. But beyond this, the US-of-A might just as well have been Outer Mongolia.

Then, on July fifth in the summer of 1938, I met my first American girl, ever. Chris and I, after spending the whole glorious day on the beach in Scheveningen, decided on a final bottle of Moselle in the Kurhaus Bar, home to Gregor Serbán and Holland's best Romanian gypsy orchestra. Of course we ran into Aad Robertson, fraternity brother and one of our good friends, looking like film star Robert Taylor and clearly on the prowl. We sat at the bar, ordered wine and surveyed the field. It was early, ten o'clock, but by eleven the elegant little place had filled up, with Serbán in full cry. Then some girls came in, students no doubt, well chaperoned, who whispered to each other in English. There were no seats, so we offered ours which they gracefully accepted. We hovered close by. "You from London?" Aad opened up in his best Oxford accent.

They were American. They were not shy, didn't giggle, and talked easily, as if conversation among strangers was the most normal thing in the world. Wine was new to them, but they seemed to like it so we ordered more. I concentrated on a blonde with shoulder-long hair curled inward, most unusual and very shiny. She was more pretty than beautiful, attractive, clean looking with fine, blue eyes. And she talked up a storm.

She told me about her town, about her school, her brother, a drive-in restaurant and an outdoor cinema, a picnic in the mountains, about her new bathing suit, as if we had been pals forever. Whether it was this intimacy, or her eyes, or the wine, or embarrassment about my ignorance - I had a sudden desire to know more about America.

"Well, why don't you come and visit me?" she countered. "Next month is my birthday, August fifteenth, you're invited."

"Where do you live exactly?"

"Sausalito. Across the bridge from San Francisco."

Serbán, Serbán, how you played that night! Did you know what you were doing? Your violin turned mice into men and men into gods, and then it was too late: I heard myself accept.

"Really? All the way to San Francisco? - You must be filthy rich," she chirped in awe.

That was the last impression I wanted to make in that pricey little joint. Furthermore, it wasn't true, for my father had put me on a student's allowance which left no room for extravagance. But on a wall in my room hung a passage by Jack London which had caught my eye: "It's the lightning flash that guides a man. He must lay his course in the blue dazzle, then follow it in the dark. And when he reaches the end, it always lightens again." As life has taught me, it does.

"Oh no. In fact, I'm flat broke. I'll make you a bet. I'll get to Sausalito by August fifteenth, on ten dollars or less." That gave me a month and ten days. Surely, America couldn't be all that big? Or was it? Five weeks, ten dollars, could it be done?

"You're on!" she cried enthusiastically, and called on all her friends to witness the bet.

"Can Aad and I be witnesses, too?" Chris asked innocently, but with a most wicked grin. I knew I was trapped. I looked around me in a daze. Amazing how one's immediate future can change from one moment to another! I was off to the Dark Continent.

"Midsummer night's madness," Aad concluded.

✱ ✱ ✱

A foreigner's experience of the USA runs in a fairly predictable cycle. The initial impression is one of bedlam, which through diminishing stages of mere confusion rapidly evolves into a false sense of simplicity. After about six months the visitor is convinced that he has the country all figured out. Then a development occurs which does not quite fit into his concept, then another, then more, creating moments of doubt, which steadily increase in number and intensity throughout the years.

In about a decade, if he sticks around, he reaches his moment of enlightenment, which teaches him that he does not understand one damned thing about America. After this crisis, slowly and painfully, real understanding may come to him, or it may not, depending on his intelligence and sensitivity.

Unfortunately, the apex of confidence comes after six months, so that is when he writes his book. The result is commensurate. I wrote mine after one. It was, for lack of a more forgiving expression, Leiden'ish. And a roaring bestseller.

I didn't mean to write a book, but mistakenly thought a press card might help me get a ship to New York as a first step in winning my bet. On the strength of my ancient Dutch Reformed fishing story and Mauricio Pieper's locusts, the Rotterdamsch Nieuwsblad decided to take a chance with me. In return I committed myself to writing a minimum of ten articles of around 3000 words each, all on spec, as we had no means of communication during my trip. When I protested that such an avalanche of words might prove to be boring, the editor answered archly, "Our readers like to be bored occasionally." Frankly, it was not what I had in mind.

As it turned out, they ultimately printed 25 articles, almost 100,000 words, still under pseudonym to protect my reputation, and when these were almost inevitably turned into a book I took the plunge and put my name on the cover. The press card was never used; after worming my way into his office, the president of Holland-America Line proved to be a Leidener himself, class of 1915. He took me out to lunch and in a sentimental moment, between the Bordeaux and the Armagnac, hired me as apprentice officer on the ss. Spaarndam for a round-trip to New York.

The book became a bestseller - by Dutch standards, of course - not mainly by virtue of its literary qualities, but because it gave young people in Holland a lighthearted peek into a world which offered much they craved. Accuracy often suffered. My first night in New York I slept in Central Park and marveled at the abundant company I had. Already I planned my next article around Americans as outdoor people, who in summer evidently preferred sleeping in the park to their beds at home, when one of them explained that he didn't have a home nor a bed to sleep in. It was 1938, the tail end of the Great Depression, a detail which had escaped my notice.

On the other hand, I showed them a country of vast distances and endless space, of kind and helpful people, of sometimes astounding trust. On a farm near Wauconda, Illinois, where I worked for two days - 12 hours, $ 1.50 per day – before getting fired for insufficient milking experience, the owner lent me his car the very first afternoon to mail one of my articles in town. The next night he left me in charge of the farm and everything in it, including two children, while he and his wife visited her parents. Europeans and Americans see fault with each other, but I'd much rather be a European stranded in America than the reverse.

Once somebody turned the tables on me. Just outside Salina, Kansas, on a hot, grueling day in the Dust Bowl, a large convertible pulling a caravan stopped to pick me up. A middle-aged couple filled the car and directed me to the trailer behind. It was a simple affair, a comfortable couch, coffee-maker on the table, two or three chairs. On the couch sat a pretty girl, maybe fifteen years of age. There were no front windows.

As the car pulled into route 40, the caravan swaying behind, my young hostess invitingly patted the couch beside her. I hesitated; under-age girls are dangerous stuff, especially in America. Even so, I saw no reason to reject her innocent gesture, it all seemed perfectly safe. After all, her parents were within easy calling distance and trouble was the last thing I had in mind.

The girl seemed to have other plans, quite convincingly, and I couldn't figure her out. I'm a good resister but I have my limits. Finally, slightly out of breath, I said, "I guess any moment now you're going to yell for your daddy, right?"

1938: 'The Umbrella Boy'

"They wouldn't hear me. There is no way I can reach them," she said, and then added darkly, "As long as we are moving, there's just nothing I can do to stop you."

Well, from one thing comes another, and an isolated caravan on a lonely highway presents a remarkably seductive environment, especially when it's moving. She may have been fifteen, but she certainly knew how to make love. Afterwards she brewed me some coffee and when I had finished my cup she coolly picked up an intercom hidden behind some books and said, "Dad? Could you stop, please? This fellow wants to get off."

Dust bowl, hot or not, off I got. So much for American innocence. More importantly, my countrymen read about a land without pigeon-holes, where everyone could aim his life in any direction, up, down, left, right, and nobody cared about his name, religion or social background, his accent or what his father did for a living. In human relations Americans are prepared to skate on thinner ice than their European counterparts.

They also tasted adventure. Before World War II hitchhiking did not exist in Europe, and riding freight trains was - and is - totally unheard of. I proved to them that in the USA the former could get you from New York to Denver, and the latter from Denver to San Francisco, altogether in three weeks time, free of charge, without spending even ten dollars. No wonder the book was a bestseller. Young Dutchmen left in droves and some aren't back yet.

On arrival in New York I took a pair of shoe bags out of my suit-case and filled them with toilet articles and writing gear. The luggage I checked in a hotel. I was wearing a gray suit, dark blue open-collar shirt and good shoes, and put the little bags around my neck. To compliment this travel outfit I bought a black umbrella for 98 cents and rigged it to stay up above my head with minimal support. It served to protect me from rain and sun and landed me in some newspapers along the way; I could not have made a better investment. Finally, not wanting to be taken for a mere tourist, I changed my name to Jerry Gail, under the misappre-hension that in America this would be taken as more authentic than my own. Then I aimed for the setting sun.

Immediately I ran into an old problem. My obvious means of trans-portation, hitchhiking, is nothing less than begging for a ride, requiring the same humility as raising my voice in the Wagenstraat for money. Car after car whizzed by, while I tried to screw up the courage to raise my thumb. Gritting my teeth I finally succeeded. A car stopped, a break-through which elated me no less than that first quarter in my guitar-box.

Not until Chicago did a real crisis occur. Even hitchhiking requires technique. In the absence of road signs I learned to depend on route numbers, displayed on little shields along the way and printed on maps, which were given out free of charge at gas stations. Experience taught me never to ask directions from an individual, to stay on highways and distrust short cuts, and to avoid police officers at all cost. This knowl-edge, combined with short-term odd jobs along the way such as wood chopping and dish washing, and an occasional free handout, kept me sol-vent, fed and moving at a reasonable clip. Until I bogged down in Illinois, just outside Chicago.

I had broken my own rules and, looking for a shortcut, ventured onto country roads. In no time I was lost, with dusk approaching. When I walked into a town called Aurora, it began to pour. Every strange suburb is a depressing mixture of city and country: streets with houses but no traffic, trees and shadows but no nature. Darkness fell, gusts of wind shook my umbrella, the rain hung like smoke around the dripping streetlights. All at once San Francisco seemed a mirage. Not a living soul was in sight, no cover to be found, I felt abandoned, forsaken... Then a miracle happened. An angel in the guise of an out-of-work piano-tuner drove up, took me aboard his car and promptly informed me that he'd gotten tired of his wife, his job and pianos in general and was on his way to start a new life in San Francisco, California. Would I like to come along?

Temptation - in this moment of crisis I had suddenly all but reached my goal and won my bet. No uncertainties of a trek through a strange continent, no dangers, hardships or anxiety about an unknown future, they would all dissolve in the safe comfort of a big Buick. But so would all expectations.

"Well?" asked the angel, when I failed to answer. "How far would you like to come?"

"To the next stoplight, please," I said. I knew it all along: It's still the journey, not the goal.

After this experience I stuck to route 6 as far as Omaha, dipped south to Kansas City, then took Route 40 all the way to Denver. The Kansas City Times of July 29 and the Denver Post of August 3 wrote me up as "Umbrella Boy", with pictures, and for several days I floated along on the wings of publicity, until on the cold and blustery afternoon of August 5th I crossed the Great Divide at Berthout Pass, 11,306 feet high in the Rocky Mountains. On the other side they hadn't heard of me, and not of hitchhiking either.

* * *

Night covered the Colorado River valley like a cloak From time to time summer lightning flickered in the east, revealing towering clouds above the Great Divide in shades of gray. A single bolt occasionally flashed across the lowering sky, pouring blue light into the gap between massive mountains, which in the sudden glare appeared about to topple down on the few dozen small, square houses of Granby. Thunder crashed and rumbled and rolled around until it found its way out, westward. The mountains growled and grumbled until gradually silence returned.

Midnight. The railway yard of the Western Pacific lay deserted. A few heavy drops of rain wetted the rails until they gleamed, red and green, in the lights of a signal post. In front of the sad little station a lamp, screeching monotonously in the wind, cast a white, swaying circle into which suddenly a man stepped out of the night. He made straight for the unlit waiting room and let the door slam shut behind him. "Hello boys!" he greeted us. "Having a good time?"

His eyes were used to the dark or he would have missed us. The youngster on the floor next to me reacted with a sudden snore, peeked at the newcomer who stood shaking the rain from his beard, and mumbled, "Hiya grandpa." In a corner somebody coughed.

Then silence, except for the heavy breathing of the boy, fast asleep again. Now we were five in the bare little room, each with his small bag or bundle, and coal dust in his ears: hobos.

It wasn't my first experience in the world of freight trains. The previous week, at the Port of Entry between Kansas and Missouri, I had met a man called John. We had hitched a ride together, but the cattle truck dropped us off in the middle of the night at some deserted spot twenty five miles outside Topeka.

We were lucky to find a gas station, always a haven of hospitality, and with nothing better to do we stood shaving side by side in the fastidiously clean wash room. Suddenly John gave a shout, which almost cost me an earlobe. "Shh! Listen!"

Not knowing what to listen for, I didn't hear anything.

Suddenly, there it was, faint and faraway: the three-toned roar of an American steam locomotive's whistle. It had no special meaning for me, yet, and still I felt its power and fascination, the mysterious attraction of its sonorous call through the night.

"Come on!" John yelled, grabbing his bundle. I dumped my shaving gear in the shoe bags, snatched my jacket and umbrella and ran out into the darkness: we were going to hop a freight and become hobos! John, half his face covered in shaving cream, pounded along by my side. Quick, across the road... through the ditch... in the distance lights were glowing, we could hear the rumble of iron wheels... come on! across the field... the rails!

Two, four, six, eight, a switch-point, good, it'll have to slow down. There's the light beam, duck! behind a bush... Slowly, groaning, brakes screeching, the engine approached, blew a cloud of humid steam over us, inched by us thundering and hissing. A sudden blast of scalding steam and we were in the dark, facing the rumbling row of black freight cars. We had entered the world of the hobo.

"You ever ride the freights?" John called out. "Never mind, I've ridden plenty. Just do as I tell you. - Hop on that car. Quick, it's gaining speed." I did as he told me, while he ran alongside. "Grab that ladder and climb up to the roof. Get that damned umbrella out of the way and hold my stuff... hurry, for Christ's sake!" I took his bundle and with both hands free he pulled himself aboard between two cars. "OK, I've got her. Climb up, sit on the ridge. I'm right behind you."

We sat side by side on the roof of a train, which moved faster and faster through the night. What a blast! In jerks the locomotive worked itself up to top speed.. heads down! a bridge..signal posts flashed by, the wheels rumbled and rattled, sparks spat from the smokestack, the wind blustered and every so often the whistle roared... Leiden seemed a long way off.

We stuck it out as far as Manhattan, Kansas. By that time the cinders had made my eyes burn, the shaving foam on John's face looked like patches of blackberry jam, the glamour was definitely wearing thin. "If you have to ride atop," John explained belatedly, as we sneaked out of the railway yard, "always pick the middle of the train. Too far ahead, you get more cinders. Too far back, the bumps get rougher."

That night we talked for many hours, and John told me all he knew about hobos and bulls, reefers and boxcars, mud holes and jungles. We slept on a warm asphalt road with our heads on the sidewalk, until early traffic forced us to pull up our legs.

Then, knowing that to make time a hitchhiker must be alone, we tossed a coin at the junction of routes 24 and 40, and separated. Route 40 brought me to Denver.

After two luxurious days as "Umbrella Boy" in the Mile High City I had set out in fine spirits for Salt Lake City and points west, but the tide had turned. I spent eight hours on the road without catching a ride. At a place called Eddie Ott's somebody warned me: no rides between here and California, rough country and too few people. But I didn't believe him and walked my way up into the Rockies and across Berthoud Pass, 11,000 feet high on a cold and blustery afternoon in my thin clothes, waving my useless umbrella at the few passing motorists. A train whistle, far away, made up my mind as I approached Granby. I knew enough to ride the freights alone. Two hours later I had crossed the yard, stepped out of the night into the swaying white circle and taken my place amongst my fellow hobos in the waiting-room.

* * *

"Any freight ever touch this goddam hole?" grumbled someone.

"Patience, lad," the old man counseled. "Five more hours till daybreak. You'd be frozen dead if you were atop now."

He was right, of course, we were still above eight thousand feet and without any protective clothing. Better take it easy.

Just then the now familiar three-toned blast of a steam whistle roared somewhere in the night. Instantly we were on our feet. Outside footsteps approached, a light flicked on and in the doorway stood a railway man, Western Pacific on his work shirt.

"Relax, boys," he said, "this is the Streamliner, it barrels right through here." He pulled a watch on a metal chain from his breast pocket. "Three and a half hours from now a freight comes through, the 2412. No stop, but she'll slow down at the block signal. Might have a boxcar or two."

We sat down again. "You don't have to worry about railway men in mud holes," John had told me. "In fact," he added with a wicked grin, "we hobos get better service than the passengers." Not unreasonable, considering that there were a lot more of us than them, some two million against a handful. Better to work with us than against. That left only the bulls, thugs hired to keep us off the freights, loved by nobody, with their billy clubs, their big mouths and punk attitude. Even the townspeople are on our side, according to John. We keep to ourselves, work for our bread, cook and socialize in our jungles on the fringes of railway yards, and use the freights only for transportation. And what about the country?

Don't sell us short. How would they get by without their mobile workforce? A new lode of copper goes into production in Idaho, they need labor. The hobos hear about it, in a few days freights from Oregon to Minnesota bring in hundreds of men to mine the ore. The peach crop in California? Well, the hobo army pulls west again, saving the harvest. It doesn't cost anybody a cent, and who else would sit for days and nights in heat and cold, eyes burning with cinders, coal dust all over, risking their lives on roofs, in tunnels, on railway yards, in reefers, with bulls ready and willing to crack open their skulls at first opportunity?

Listening to John I soon fervently agreed: Where would America in the Great Depression be without us, hobos? Suddenly it was time. A whistle blasted unexpectedly near and the next moment the 2412 struggled into the yard. Already we were outside, running through the dark to the block signal. Up close the engine seemed huge, its eye gleamed, and as it bore down on me I shivered with excitement. Then came the magic moment. The wall of light and power, engine thunder and whistle roar, screeching brakes and hissing steam inched past, bright and hot, and instantly I found myself in another world, cool, dark and intimate, silent except for the rhythmic clacking of the wheels and the groaning of couplings. Hobos ran alongside the train. Boxcars? No boxcars. Hoppers? Gondolas? Flatcars? Nothing, only reefers. The freight started to pull away. Running fast, I spotted a grab iron and yanked myself aboard, almost losing my umbrella. I scampered up the reefer; thank God, it was empty.

America's rails carry a lot more comfortable freights, all the way from boxcars to jimmys, but reefers were the most numerous and had their points. Short for refrigerators, you could recognize them by four small trapdoors in the roof, two on each end, which were left open when the reefer was not in use. Underneath each set of doors lay a narrow, deep little cellar the width of the car. These were cozy and protected, but connected to the main refrigeration area by a coarse screen in the floor. Hobos sat in these spaces, two by two, like wasp larvae in the back of giant caterpillars. The danger was sleep. Prior to loading and freezing, the small doors were shut and locked virtually soundproof, with the result that inexperienced or careless hobos, caught inside, would come out with the beef sides, and just as stiff.

When I aimed my pocket light into the first space I saw a big, black man who looked like good company. His shoulders just about filled the width of the little cellar. The moment he spotted my umbrella he motioned me down and made room for me.

His name was Shorty and we had a good time together, talking and taking turns sleeping while the other kept guard. As the sun came up I was tempted to go on the roof, but Shorty had a phobia and assured me that the freight was crawling with bulls. He implored me not to endanger us both, so I stayed down.

Suddenly there was a shock, screeching of brakes, a loud crash and we were thrown against the forward wall. The train stood still and in the silence shrill whistles blew and voices sounded. In spite of Shorty's protests I clambered up the ladder and very carefully peeked outside. I saw railway men running along the track, talking excitedly, holding a conference, and then way up front a car that had run off the rails. The freight itself seemed deserted, not a single rider in sight. Around us, the mountain scenery was spectacular.

When I reported to Shorty he insisted that it was all a ruse by some misguided bull to catch us, which gained credibility when someone outside walked along the cars, banging the sides and calling out: "Come on out, boys, give us a hand! Come on out! No questions asked!"

I climbed up to investigate, and looking around saw a head carefully poking out of the reefer roof further back, and another one up front, and more. Gradually the entire train began to ooze hobos, cautious at first but then, when all seemed on the level, exuberantly waving and shouting at each other, making for the derailed car. A quick estimate put the number of men riding the 'deserted' freight at an even hundred. Every one went to work in a festive mood. Within an hour the damage was repaired, the whistle blew twice ("high!..ball!..") and the 2412, its roof ridge solidly lined with hobos like sparrows, resumed its run through the American west.

Shorty and I sat side by side, enjoying our unexpected legal status and admiring the early morning view. The rays of the sun crowned the mountain tops, slid down huge walls of slate, chased the shadows from the valley and ended up playing with the trout, which jumped like sparks from the green Colorado River below. The endless train wiggled like a jointed toy snake around the steep slopes, on a single track carved from rock, and whenever the tiny engine became visible its impatient puffs reached us in waves. It plunged into mysterious black holes, and reappeared triumphantly long before we followed it into the tunnel. Finally it gave a long, sonorous blast on its steam whistle.

The stationmaster of Grand Junction heard the signal. He pulled his Ingersoll from a vest pocket, studied it carefully and said to the telegraph operator: "The 2412 bound for Salt Lake City. One hour behind schedule."

* * *

My experience on the 2412 hooked me on freights, as only hobos will understand. I stuck with them all the way to Sacramento, California, then bought a ticket for a bus to San Francisco with money from the Salt Lake Tribune, who had revived the Umbrella Boy and paid him generously for it. On August 10th I won my bet, five days within the allotted time.

When I called my girl in Sausalito, she had a tough time remembering me. It was mutual, there had been plenty of American girls since the Kurhaus Bar. She gallantly invited me to spend the weekend with her - and, as I rightly assumed, her family - but as it was only Wednesday I expressed regrets.

Besides, there was work to do. In a telegram to General Delivery the Rotterdamsch Nieuwsblad had accepted my first five articles and requested twenty more. Writing these along the way had been one of my major problems, and I looked forward to producing the rest in comfort behind a proper desk. It would be tough enough to do, in Leiden in the summertime.

Also, after the vastness of America and the great distances covered, I really wanted to go home. But not before seeing Hollywood. As the Los Angeles Times was kind enough to interview—and pay me, I received a splendid reception from Metro-Goldwyn-Mayer. They took me to the studios where films were being shot and introduced me to every star present, so that in one afternoon I met Louise Rainer and Ferdinand Gravet, Wallace Beery, Mickey Rooney, Jeanette MacDonald and Nelson Eddy, Loretta Young and Dennis O'Keefe, and in the cafeteria I ran into one or two others on my own. All were unbelievably gracious.

The next day I set out for Holland; it seemed a long way off. Having tired of freight trains for a while, I hitchhiked through the desert - no trace yet of Las Vegas! - to the Port of Entry between Nevada, Arizona and Utah. To my great surprise I succeeded in hitching a ride on an interstate truck, generally regarded as impossible by the open road community. The driver seemed vague about his route, but it was to include towns like Pocatello, Butte and Bismarck, which sounded somewhat northerly to me, but so what?

We drove for days, and finally I'd had enough. With fifty dollars left from the Los Angeles Times, I got on a Greyhound bus as a paying passenger. The adventure was over, next stop New York City. On August 22, after crossing on the ferry to Hoboken, I boarded the ss Statendam for Holland as apprentice officer. The Dutch genever tasted of home.

In Leiden nothing had changed. I met Chris Krediet and Aad Robertson in the Kurhaus Bar in Scheveningen to report on my adventures, but they were only mildly interested. However, Serbán was hot and the wine was cool, so we raised our glasses in a toast to Sir Neville Chamberlain and his brilliant success in Munich at the expense of Czechoslovakia. Why not? The entire Western world was jubilant about "peace in our time". Except our friends the Czechs, who wept in the streets of Prague. Prague? Where the hell's Prague?

CHAPTER 4

War -"They Have Come!"

N ewspapers, radio and television bring war into our living rooms - the problem is, we do not care. Over coffee, beer or coke it loses its impact. Unless the gun that shoots at us is genuine, we do not frighten; unless the man it kills is our brother, we do not weep. Under cover of indifference World War II crept up on us.

Shortly after my return from America, something odd happened in Minerva. A sophomore named Jean Mesritz climbed on the reading table, traditionally the pedestal for distinguished guest speakers, and called for attention. It was unusual enough to quiet down the room. "Is everybody comfortable?" he asked.

What the hell? A few students sniggered, the rest looked up curiously.

"I mean–is there enough beer to go around? Is everybody happy?" He was not altogether sober.

"Why don't you tell us what's on your mind?" a senior suggested. "Or else, shut up and come down."

"I should like to ask you," Mesritz continued politely, "as we are sitting here drinking beer, how many of you realize what's going on just a hundred or so kilometers east of here?"

We assumed we knew what he was talking about. This was 1938. Hirohito fought in Manchuria, Mussolini in Ethiopia, Franco in Spain, but the greatest fascist of them all, Adolph Hitler, was rapidly rising to world power just the other side of our border.

"I mean, it's fine for us to drink beer, nothing wrong with it. But how many of you realize that right now, right next door, Jews are getting beaten up, their shops smashed, and God knows what else? Or haven't you heard?"

The stories had reached us. Fresh from his triumph in Munich, where Czechoslovakia had been dismembered and Sudetenland fell into his lap without a shot, Hitler had unleashed his Nazis into the streets to harass and terrorize the Jews in Germany. You could listen to his insane harangues on the radio, night after night, but we always turned him off.

"You know about it, but it doesn't bother you, right? Let's have another beer and to hell with Hitler and his Jews, right?"

We were getting uncomfortable. The news did disturb us, when we happened to think of it, but no more than the eternal famine in India, or the musical chairs of governments in France. It did bother us, but not enough.

"Order! Order!" somebody called out. A few beery voices joined in. "Order!"

Of course, there was no doubt about Mesritz being totally out of line. To address the assembled students, permission is required from the Minerva Committee. If everyone could just get up and speak, chaotic conditions would ensue. Besides, worst of all, it was against tradition.

The room became rowdy. However, in proper Leiden style it all turned into harmless farce as a group of juniors rushed the reading table, shouting German nonsense and flashing wild Hitler salutes, and good-naturedly captured the speaker, who put up little resistance before giving up gracefully. They hoisted him onto their shoulders and, half in protest half in triumph, Jean Mesritz was carried around the room. He ended up in an easy chair by the fireplace, with a large glass of beer before him.

"What was that all about?" I asked Chris on our way home. Although close to six in the morning, it was still pitch dark. In the narrow little streets our footsteps resounded on the cobblestones.

"Jean Mesritz? Himself Jewish, I guess. Or at least a little."

This astounded me. Jean was a handsome, well-built fellow without the slightest resemblance to the often fat-bellied, hook-nosed caricatures in the Nazi press being hawked on street corners by hoodlums in black uniforms. We went to high school together and had been friends for years. On the subject of girls, who fell for his intelligent, light eyes and matte complexion, he had always been my mentor. For a while we had jointly taken boxing lessons, where he quickly cured me of any ambition I may have had in that direction. Jean Mesritz Jewish? It had simply never come up. Why should it? What difference did it make? - Autumn... winter... we began to take up our studies, to the extent of inquiring after the names of our professors and the schedules of our classes. In this we were interrupted by Christmas vacation, when traditionally half of Holland invades the Alps to spend two weeks tumbling from snowy mountains into snow-white beds, preferably in enchanting company. Barely returned home we learned that German armies had marched into Czechoslovakia. Now we knew where Prague was.

Somewhere in the Balkans or something, and no Dutchman in his right mind took the Balkans seriously.

In the Spring of 1939 the civil war in Spain ground to an end, at a cost of 700,000 men and women killed in battle, 30,000 executed and assassinated and 15,000 lost in air raids. In the USA President Roosevelt asked for three additional appropriations to upgrade air and naval forces, and for repeal of the arms embargo on, amongst others, Britain. In August, Albert Einstein informed him that an atomic bomb was feasible. We, on the other hand, spent most of the summer on the beach in Scheveningen.

On Sunday morning September 3rd we were playing tennis for a change, Chris, Aad Robertson and I, and my new roommate, Paul Erdman. Early autumn lay heavy over the lush countryside, the sun beat down from a cloudless sky. A radio in the clubhouse played light music from the BBC in London, and Sir Edward Elgar's "Land of Hope and Glory" wafted through the open windows.

"What's the score?" Paul called across the net after a while. I had no idea. While we were thinking about it, the music suddenly stopped. An English voice spoke, somber and emphatic. World War II had broken out.

For a moment we paused. We stood like statues, just for a moment. The sweet smell of hay came from across the meadows, bees buzzed in the silence. Paul's immaculate flannels stood out creamy white against the red court. Somewhere a train whistled, a far, small sound in the sultry air. From the window streamed the chords of a military band, the British national anthem, "... God... save... the... King..."

"Well, what's the score?" Paul asked again, when the music died down. I still didn't know.

"Why don't we start all over?" I called back, hitting a ball in his direction.

After the game I got on my bike and pedaled to the highest top of the nearby dunes. To the west stretched the North Sea, steel-blue, silver scaled, rimmed by a ribbon of surf. The beach shimmered in the sun, all the way from Scheveningen in the South, past Katwijk, to the knotty point of Noordwijk in the North. Behind the dunes lay Holland, a strip of pastel colors dwarfed by sky; green polders, here and there a glint of water, distant steeples and the arms of windmills penciled on the haze, orange roof tiles of a sleepy town. In the Netherlands all was well.

Then, at three a.m. that night I heard on the radio that the ss Athenia, a passenger ship, had been torpedoed, "many persons including women and children are feared lost at sea..." And a presence, barely a memory, vague and awesome, softly seeped into my quiet room. Outside in the dark something black had breathed in my direction.

* * *

Rendez-vous in San Francisco came out three weeks later. It took six months to finish the articles and work them into a cohesive story, and even though the Dutch government immediately proclaimed our neutrality, I thought the outbreak of war meant the end of the book's chances. On the contrary, people flocked to buy it as a balm for the suddenly increased tensions. The publisher linked its publicity and sales with those of three other novels: Daphne du Maurier's Rebecca, Howard Fast's O Absalom and A.J.Cronin's The Citadel, an extravagant compliment which also helped. I went on a lecture tour, including Leiden, where I expected the hall to be packed with my fellow students. It was packed all right, but not a single Leidener was present, except Chris and Paul. By writing and lecturing I had exceeded the bounds of my pigeonhole, now my peers were putting me back in my place.

But by producing a book and putting my name on it I had escaped forever, and I didn't give a good goddam anymore. My real friends, Chris Krediet, Aad Robertson, Paul Erdman and Jean Mesritz, came around and stuck with me, the rest tried to claw me down for a while but in due time resigned themselves to the inevitable. I had flown the coop, they could take it or stuff it.

Chris Krediet, Erik Hazelhoff, and Aad Robertson

Perhaps it was the urge to prove myself on this new course that made me accept the next assignment. In November the USSR bombed and invaded Finland, and this time the Dutch cared. It constituted a simple, straightforward land grab by a Great Power on its blameless, small neighbor, a war we understood.

After a history of often bloody involvement with Russia, the Finns had declared their independence - not for the first time - in December, 1917. Their famous general, Carl baron Mannerheim, defeated the Red Armies and fortified the Karelian peninsula, gateway to St. Petersburg (Leningrad), a city whose foundations had been built by Finnish slave labor in the early 18th century with fearful loss of life. Now Stalin wanted Karelia, as well as some other border corrections, specially up north. But to nobody's surprise the Finns, a tough lot if there ever was one, fought like tigers. On the strength of Rendezvous in San Francisco my publisher offered me a similar deal for Finland: a series of articles and a book. The deal may have been the same, the job wasn't, as I found out when I reached the war zone. Death has presence. Not only in the pathetic reality of his defeated victim, but also subjectively as a dark prince who prowls around, determining by his own arbitrary logic who shall be next. A country at war is his element, he has a job to do and a right to be there. He asserts his power, he exults. When the Swedish airliner landed by flares on a blacked-out airstrip near Turku, Finland, his sinister aura was there to greet me. It never left me through six miserable, dark and hideously cold weeks.

It was a tragedy. The war lasted three-and-a-half months, in which time the Finns lost 30% of the 200,000 men they managed to put in the field. They were overwhelmed by a force of 1.2 million Russians, but not before inflicting triple the number of casualties on the Soviet troops, illiterate farm boys who were invariably mystified by finding themselves out in the arctic snow in the middle of winter. The terms of the peace, signed on March 13, 1940, were surprisingly moderate, although Finland did lose the Karelian Isthmus and the Rybachiy Peninsula off Murmansk. In the end nobody, let alone I, knew what it was all about.

I felt totally out of place. What was I doing here? On the day after my arrival I set out for the front near Rovaniemi.

Suddenly the train stopped in the middle of endless snow fields broken by patches of fir and birch, like Siberia in a movie. The locomotive blew its whistle and everybody seemed to know what it meant. Doors smacked open, passengers hurled themselves out of the cars and started to barge frantically through hip-deep snow towards a bunch of trees. I heard engines, and standing in the door, the last man out, I looked up. Above me a triangle of silver planes gleamed against the blue sky, fifteen in rigid formation, high and almost motionless, and while I stood looking, right before my eyes, dozens of little blocks tumbled down from them, now and then flashing in the sun, and rapidly fell away towards me in curving strings.

When finally I realized that they were bombs, I found that I couldn't move... the blinding, white snow everywhere, the shrill scream of the whistle with its steam jetting straight up in the air, the glittering silver dots against the flawless blue, the steady drone of airplane engines, the strings of bombs, everything sharp and brittle and rigid like a dream so vivid it refused to burst. How did I get here? What for? This wasn't my fight, to hell with Finns and Russians! I wanted to live, not die in this cold, alien place. Damnation on my publisher, on my own ambition and stupidity, my heroics, and if I ever came out of this alive I swore I would never, never leave my safe, secure little Holland again.

Apparently the bombs weren't meant for us, they fell miles away in the forest. I forgot my frantic oaths, and anyway, within three months the opportunities for death and heroics would be as good, if not better, in the Netherlands than almost anywhere else in the world.

Incidentally, the book got written. Not surprisingly it turned out fiercely anti-Russian, and as the beginning of World War II found Hitler allied with Stalin for the purpose of gobbling up Poland, the German occupation authorities in Holland seized all copies and forbade further printings. When in June, 1941, Hitler invaded the USSR, the situation reversed itself and the book was vigorously promoted for Nazi propaganda objectives, smearing my good name as a loyal Dutchman. To top it all - in 1949, four years after the end of World War II, some mysterious postwar German authority sent me a precisely documented royalty check to cover all sales, pro and con, accurate to the last Pfennig.

* * *

As Thomas Jefferson and his Commission of Five were drafting the American Declaration of Independence, they paid considerable attention to a document from Holland's history. In 1581 the lowlands renounced their allegiance to King Philip II of Spain, and the leader of the revolt, Prince William (the Silent) of Orange, spelled out his motivations in language which admirably fitted the scene in Philadelphia, two hundred years later. Both occasions led to war, but it took the Dutch eighty years to achieve their independence.

A signal victory in this grueling war was the battle for Leiden, which after four months of brutal isolation remained under siege by Spanish legions. Inside the town the situation became so desperate that part of the citizenry, tired of eating rats, chewing shoe leather and burying their relatives, tried to force burgomaster Van der Werf into surrendering. He handed them his sword, with the words, "Cut up my body and still your hunger with my flesh. But as long as my heart beats, I shall with God's help resist the despised Spaniards." Or words to that effect.

Outside the walls, William the Silent and his men had breached all surrounding dikes. A fleet from Zeeland stood poised to relieve the city, but was prevented from sailing by a stubborn easterly wind which kept the sea from flooding the land. A week went by and hope faded, then finally the wind swung around to the west and water began to gush into the fertile countryside which averaged ten to twelve feet below sea-level. At last the Dutch fleet with its flat-bottomed boats weighed anchor and set sail for Leiden, fighting the Spaniards in a series of naval engagements amidst the tops of orchards and the roofs of farms. After two days, only one main enemy stronghold stood between the Zeelanders and the starving burghers of Leiden who, peering from their city wall, could see both the Dutch fleet and the Spanish fort, less than seven hundred paces away.

In the night of October 2nd, 1574, the west wind howled over the drowned land and all sides dreaded the coming dawn. At midnight the storm reached its peak and with a sudden rumble part of the city's wall collapsed: after four months of heroic resistance, with salvation in sight, all seemed lost. But the Spaniards, unnerved by the water rising all about them in the pitch-black night, had mistaken the tumult for the sound of impending battle and abandoned their position. A thirteen-year old boy, setting eel traps for his family during the night, had witnessed the stealthy retreat. No one would believe him, so he rowed to the deserted fort. When at first light the Zeelanders attacked they were greeted only by a boy standing on the highest rampart, waving both arms above his head. Leiden was saved!

In recognition of their contribution to the cause of freedom, William of Orange offered the city of Leiden this choice: a ten year suspension of all taxes, or a university. The burghers chose the university. It was constructed within one year in the same location where it rises today, a solid, dignified building along a canal called the Rapenburg, once the city moat.

Directly opposite, across a humpbacked little bridge, stands number 56 Rapenburg, student house since 1579. On the first floor, overlooking the canal, the bridge and the university, Paul Erdman and I shared rooms. To everyone's surprise, our cohabitation worked out well. Chris would have been my first choice, considering our common background and many other similarities, but he was too much of a loner and preferred solitude in some obscure lodging under the eaves, where he submerged himself in Voltaire, Kant and Nietzsche. We immensely enjoyed each other's company, yet he somewhere guarded a hunk of privacy which kept him isolated, clearly by choice.

Paul and I on the other hand both appreciated our splendid ambiance and comfortable quarters, which remained the basis of our relationship. He was born and raised in Holland, the only son of a prosperous legal expert in The Hague. For a Dutchman he was neither tall nor short, about six feet, just like me, and with his blue eyes and fair skin we could have been taken for brothers, except that he exuded a curious air of refinement. You couldn't imagine him with dirty fingernails, and we teased him about his blond curls which he vainly tried to control with heavy doses of pomade. His expensive clothes were always superbly correct, but just as you started to doubt his moral fiber, you ran into a will of steel: Paul Erdman knew exactly what he wanted and was not to be denied.

Mostly, our styles were different. He often irritated me by small acts of perfection, such as picking every last little bone out of the smallest sardine, or peeling tomatoes. Being excessively tidy he made my inspired informality seem grubby by comparison. Yet, it was hard not to like him, with his eminently decent face and kind eyes, which conveyed more steadiness than sparkle. You felt you could rely on him, because he would never surprise you, which, of course, also made him a bit of a bore. On top of this he was a serious student, bless him, not from intellectual curiosity but because most of all he wanted to become a jurist, like his father and his grandfather. At almost any price.

We got along, but we never got close. We had our separate bedrooms, a living room and bathroom, and shared the best student location in Leiden, on the corner of the Rapenburg and an alley called the Kloksteeg, where the Pilgrim Fathers lived for sixteen years prior to their departure for Plymouth Rock. We were content.

Apart from Finland, nothing much happened in the winter of '39-'40. Hitler and Stalin divided Poland, but our little speck of land, surrounded by violence on an epic scale, conducted its business as usual, as if war were a foreign product unsuited to the Dutch marketplace. The Kaiser bypassed our country in World War I, so why not the Führer in World War II? Some reserves had been called up, which brought a sprinkling of uniforms to Minerva, but it merely added spice to our lives. Of my close friends only Jean Mesritz fell into that category. Resplendent in black and gold and the French-type kepi of an officer in the Royal Hussars, he reported sharply improved results with the ladies. It almost compensated for the loss of his walking-cane, the Leidener's most precious status symbol.

Jean Mestritz

My own position in this respect was curious. In 1937 I had been called up for military service in the light infantry, but was discharged after four days as unfit on account of "shortcomings". I was so delighted, that I ran happily out of the gate without ever inquiring after the nature of these shortcomings. Admittedly my eyesight was poor, minus two, but not bad enough to warrant military exclusion. I did, however, engage the army psychologist in a deep conversation about the right of refusal to kill another human being on command, unless one is in agreement with the justification of that order. The doctor protested that this would amount to a right for every soldier to refuse participating in a war, unless he agreed with the purpose of that war. "That is exactly what I have in mind," I confirmed, which did not seem to please him. Two weeks later my discharge became final.

One early morning in the spring of 1940 our landlady, who ran a tobacco shop on the ground floor of 56 Rapenburg, banged on my bedroom door. "Sir! Quick, come and look! That crazy Mr. Robertson!"

The room that Paul and I shared, on the corner above the shop, had a tiny balcony, six feet by two, facing the little bridge. I dashed to the glass doors and out, in my pajamas. A platoon of soldiers came marching down the Rapenburg, then swung left across the canal straight towards me, and there, at the very end, towering above the rest of the recruits in an ordinary private's uniform several sizes too small, stepped my friend and fraternity brother Aad Robertson. He waved at me joyously behind the sergeant's back. Then they were right below me.

"What the hell!" I shouted. "What are you doing in that monkey suit? Come upstairs! When can you come?"

"This afternoon," he called back, blithely ignoring the sergeant. "Fix me some lunch!" And off he went, twice turning around to wave.

Apparently Aad Robertson had volunteered for the army. I was dumbfounded. Of course, from Aad you could expect anything. He embodied the quintessential Student, with a capital S, in many respects a perfect counterbalance to Paul Erdman. Exuberant and outgoing, his high-spirited playfulness made him totally unpredictable, always up to something and full of outrageous ideas which he loved to put into action. He was absurdly handsome, yet warm and friendly and as popular with us as, unfortunately, with our girlfriends. Although his mother was German he liked the Anglo-Saxon sound of his family name and sometimes put on unmistakably British airs. He looked downright preposterous in that private's uniform. I could hardly wait for an explanation.

At around noon we gathered around the sherry bottle, Paul, Chris and I, and Jean Mesritz whom I had invited for lunch to be present at the dénouement. He had tactfully exchanged his lieutenant's uniform for the gray slacks and brown sports jacket of the Leidener. As always, I was delighted to see him. Quietly intelligent, he had a tendency to retreat into his own world, from which he was usually roused with respect because of his size. He made himself comfortable and smiled at me.

We waited. I poured another round of sherry. Paul, still in his dressing gown, sat peacefully peeling a tomato, watched with undisguised distaste by Chris, who usually joined us for lunch. Jean picked up my Laws of the Netherlands from the floor and became immersed in it. The only one still missing was Aad, but he was on his way, striding down the Rapenburg which curved silent and dignified on both sides of the canal. From the window I could see him coming, tall, slim, very British in his off-duty tweeds. Now he strolled past the university, looking up at the somber hulk before turning left. One more little bridge and we heard him clumping up the stairs. "Christ!" he said, pausing dramatically in the doorway. "To think that I may have to go to war with this bunch of nitwits."

For an instant the present trembled. Aad's barbed jest, under the circumstances, had unleashed an alien genie, War, which warped the grid of my perception. I looked around the room and saw four strangers, out of proportion in a chaotic world, about to explode to their destinies: Aad Robertson, Aryan superman; Jean Mesritz, doomed Jew; Paul Erdman, bloodless intellectual; Chris Krediet, involuted enigma. As for myself, I could smell the sweet scent of ketjubung, the poisonous lily, in the jungle dusk.

The genie slipped back into his bottle, obligingly, and the moment passed. I tapped on the floor with my cane - a series of taps to attract the landlady's attention, followed by one tap for each cup of coffee. Aad flopped down on the couch with his feet between the tomato sandwiches, until Paul lit a match and threatened to burn his pants. Jean seemed lost in civil law. The landlady brought a tray and put it on the table; the coffee in the cups showed how badly the room sagged. As she bent over, Aad pinched her bottom. She whacked his hand and left, coyly slamming the door.

After establishing that Robertson's joining the army, when he could have gotten a student deferment like Chris and Paul, could only be described as a preposterous stunt, we opened another bottle and continued arguing in our usual desultory manner, which ultimately reduced every subject to a joke. The sounds outside reflected the passing of the day: students on their way to class, their steps echoing sharply in the narrow Kloksteeg, then flattening out on the Rapenburg and up the humpbacked bridge. Now and then we recognized someone by a single word, a laugh. Canes rapped the cobblestones, followed by quiet periods when our more dedicated colleagues had disappeared in the building across the canal, whose medieval presence had looked down on our fathers and forefathers. In no time at all the day was done. We said good night and parted, having solved all the problems of the world.

I stepped out on the little balcony, perched almost above the bridge. An early spring, hot as summer, had ambushed Europe. Under its cloudless skies Norway had just been invaded, Denmark wiped off the map. But Leiden slumbered in the velvet night. The air smelled of canals and distant fields of hyacinths.

Somewhere a barge puff-puff-puffed down the Old Rhine through the heart of town. Behind me the Pieters Church, chiming midnight, dropped the notes into the alleys at its feet, gently, for the houses were old and leaned to each other for support. The voices of my friends faded away along the Rapenburg, until I could only hear the tapping of their canes across the water. - At 4:00 a.m. that morning, May 10, 1940, Queen Wilhelmina of The Netherlands awoke her daughter, Princess Juliana, with the words: "They have come!"

CHAPTER 5

The Lure of Freedom

L ife is a continuum of value judgments. Every waking moment we are confronted with alternatives, our mental computers make the choices, the totality of these decisions determines how we live. In peacetime, when we have to fit into society, we are supposed to judge by rational standards. In wartime, when insane thoughts and deeds are expected of us, we can only fall back on our emotions. The magic which allows us to switch from the one to the other, is called patriotism.

Without patriotism war is unthinkable, which is why nations build up vast reserves of it, even in peacetime. Natural love of country is artificially boosted by flags, anthems and more or less constant indoctrination. These tactics are ominously successful. Americans sincerely believe and constantly proclaim that the USA is "the greatest country in the world". By and large Englishmen, fresh from recent world domination, look down on their former colonies. The French, although a miserable failure in World War II, are convinced to the last man and woman of their superiority over both, and anybody else for that matter. Germans, while presently somewhat chastised, have historically shown strong tendencies towards the Herrenvolk concept. Japan's entire culture proclaims its uniqueness above all others, while the Chinese have regarded the lot of us as "barbarians" for the last twenty centuries. Any individual included in the above paragraph is invited to a moment of introspection in which to confirm or reject its assumption.

Less generally known is the fact that smaller nations, like the Portuguese, Finns, Poles, Argentines, Iranians and Greeks also feel superior to everyone else, at least morally, and are if possible even more abundantly endowed with nationalism.

Near the top in this respect stood the Dutch in 1940, opinionated, rich and smug after a century of peace and prosperity. I myself was a prime example, and when war called upon all good men to abandon reason in favor of patriotism, no one complied more readily and without reservations. Usually such enthusiasm is rewarded by a quick exit from the stage of Life, but with uncanny protection from whatever powers may be, I emerged from World War II sufficiently intact to tell the tale.

Wars unfold in scenes of stupendous drama, but are mostly remembered by defining moments of a personal nature, insignificant details in the flow of history. Although equally authentic, they merely weave a human trail through the vast scenery of the times. For a Hollander like me it all started with the invasion of the Netherlands in the early hours of May 10, 1940.

I must have had an inkling. About a year previously I started to feel uncomfortable about our house in The Hague, which stood close to the Waalsdorp military barracks. Nothing definite, but I began to dislike its aura. It also had become too large for my parents by themselves, now that my sister, Ellen, had gotten married to a Leidener and moved to Eindhoven. By skillful use of this argument and dogged perseverance, which surprised even me, I finally persuaded my father to move to Park de Kieviet in Wassenaar, a neighboring suburb of trees, flowers, ponds and ducklings behind the Meyendel dunes.

On New Year's Eve shortly afterwards, I went further.

At midnight I walked around our new house with a glass of champagne in my hand, in the ice cold pitch dark, drinking toasts to the future at its four corners and communicating with it in my best childhood tradition. When a few months later the Germans attacked Holland without declaration of war and in the first minutes of the invasion dropped four bombs on The Hague, three on the Waalsdorp barracks and the fourth in our old back garden, blasting deadly glass through all of our former rooms, I felt a profound sense of gratitude focused somehow on faraway and long ago, old skin-and-bones and his grandson Ahmed, my first connections with a spiritual world. They hadn't let me down. How did they know? "Everybody knows."

The night of the invasion never reached darkness, reflecting the glow of perfect spring days on either side of it.

After listening to my friends' footsteps fading away along the Rapenburg, I decided to take a ride on my motor bike. It took me to my parents' home in Wassenaar, where I stayed to get some sleep. It was not to be. At 4.00 o'clock, sunrise, antiaircraft guns behind the duck pond opened up and from my bedroom window I saw a Junkers transport lumbering over the edge of town, dropping parachutes like larvae from its tail. Suddenly life was chaos, and as there wasn't much I could do about it I went downstairs to brew a large pot of coffee.

My mother appeared in her night clothes, pretty shaken, and embraced me as if I had already one foot in the grave, which did nothing for my morale. Just as I was about to push her away, I grasped her emotional condition. Here stood Corrie Vreede, born on Java half a world away, a sweet and above all cheerful girl. At the age of eighteen she ran into my father, and from then on only one thing really mattered to her: husband and children. That became her mission in life. And then, at the peak of her happiness, some infamous bastard rises to power in Germany and sends thousands of soldiers across the border to murder her son, and those of all the other Dutch mothers, and destroy all for which she has ever lived. - Instead of disentangling myself I hugged her back and kissed her, perhaps not such a good idea because she promptly burst into tears.

When my father came down we settled around the radio, which warned that German paratroopers were dropping on Wassenaar and in the dunes around us. My first wartime decision seemed imminent. At any moment I expected to see a helmeted head poke through the kitchen window, and then? Would we offer him a cup of coffee, or was I expected to hurl myself at the enemy with one of our fearsome new steak knives? The crisis resolved itself because no one turned up, but it put me on notice to expect baffling problems.

I did not have to wait long. Later that morning Chris picked me up on his BMW motorbike to volunteer for the army in The Hague. Returning to Leiden he dropped me at the turnoff for Park de Kieviet, and I continued on foot. On the way home I was joined by a milkman on his rounds, glad to have company. After a few hundred yards we were stopped by a Dutch lieutenant. "You can't go any further," he said. "Park de Kieviet is in enemy hands."

Park de Kieviet in Nazi hands? It sounded so bizarre, I almost burst out laughing. How about my parents?

"Aw, come on, captain," the milkman protested. "I'm only a milkman. I've got to make my rounds. I want no part of all this." The lieutenant shrugged his shoulders.

We kept on going, the milkman and I. After all, he had to get rid of his milk and I had to get home. Just outside our driveway six German paratroopers stepped out of my mother's rhododendrons. After the first shock I got another surprise: they were just boys, younger than Chris or me. They bought four bottles of milk, keeping one hand on their automatic carbines.

They paid the exact amount in Dutch cash, then handed the milkman a tip. "Thank you, sir," said the milkman. "Auf Wiedersehen," they mumbled, as they faded into the bushes.

"Auf Wiedersehen," I stammered back.

War wasn't at all the way I had imagined it.

* * *

On the fourth day after the invasion I thought we had won. In some sharp fighting all around Wassenaar the parachutists had been defeated by Dutch army units, and everything seemed close to normal. We knew little about the rest of the country, but the tone of radio and newspapers contributed to our hopeful mood.

Riding home from Leiden on my bike after a few beers at Minerva, impatiently awaiting my call-up for the army, I saw a curious cloud on my left. It towered to great height in the otherwise flawless sky, churning russet at its base, then upwards in rose-colored convolutions to a snow-white crest well above thirty-thousand feet - a giant strawberry sundae. It was fearsome. I slowed down for a closer look and to estimate its location: south, about twenty miles. Rotterdam, no doubt about it.

I raced home to Wassenaar and burst into the kitchen. My father held up his hand, they were listening to the radio.

It was all over. From the beginning Rotterdam, at the confluence of Europe's biggest rivers, had emerged as the key to the military situation. Its bridges had fallen undamaged to the treacherous predawn assault of May 10, but Dutch marines put up fierce and effective resistance at the northern end, preventing the Wehrmacht from breaking into the heart of Holland. Time was of the essence to the German High Command in the Netherlands, already behind schedule in relation to General Von Rundstedt's giant offensive against France and the British Expeditionary Force to the south. Rather than slug it out it was decided to bomb the heart out of Rotterdam instead.

At 1:25 p.m. on May 14, the first Heinkels appeared on the eastern horizon. Subsequently one hundred heavy bombers of the Luftwaffe, unopposed since the small Netherlands Air Force had fought itself to extinction in the first two days of war, eradicated the entire center of Rotterdam - 625 heavily populated acres - in twenty minutes of leisurely area bombing, killing and wounding thousands. Utrecht then Amsterdam would be next, the Germans promised, unless all resistance ceased immediately.

Blackmail on an epic scale underlay the capitulation of Holland's armed forces that same afternoon.

Sitting around the kitchen table, we were joined by my uncle Humphrey from Paris, who was staying with my parents for tulip time. He fancied himself as an expert on World War I.

"You'd better destroy your wines," he advised. "In France in 1914, the Boche got drunk and shot or raped every one in sight." His brother glared at him, outraged, as if this suggestion had finally brought home the reality of defeat. Then he got up and walked out. My mother stared out of the window, silent, dry-eyed.

I finished my fourth cup of coffee and followed my father out of the room. In the hall he put his arm around my shoulder. As always, he was ready and eager to do his patriotic duty, but the first World War had passed him by and now he was fifty, too old to fight, too young not to resent it. Kipling's manly mystique forbade public display of emotion, so we walked down the corridor, his face averted to hide the tears. Then he turned into the cellar and began to pour our wines down the drain.

After a moment's consternation, not unreasonable for a Leidener, I pitched in beside him, opening cases, pulling corks, tipping bottles, watching the sparkling fluid gurgle away down the sink. I understood my old man. As head of our family he desperately wanted to protect us from the nameless dangers that were upon us, but there was nothing he could do. In his fury and frustration he had latched on to my uncle's dubious suggestion.

At least it created an illusion, which was better than nothing. We went at it with a vengeance. Occasionally, when a particularly noble vintage confronted us in its dusty cradle, my father would pull the cork with reverence, smell it appreciatively and take a swig or two for old times' sake. Then he handed it to me for my opinion. We'd cluck and shake our heads and pour the rest of the bottle, if any, down the sink. When we got to the champagnes, for which our home had a certain reputation even in Wassenaar, we felt it our duty to toast the fortunes of the British, the French, the Americans, anybody whose efforts might hasten Hitler's demise, which on second thought included the Dutch, the Poles, the Danes and the Norwegians. After that we drank to individual heroes who had promoted the cause of liberty in general - William of Orange, George Washington, José Marti, Andreas Hofer, Garibaldi, Mahatma Gandhi, Pancho Villa - and as we ran out of names we had also run out of champagne. When uncle Humphrey, intrigued by sounds of unseemly merriment, had the temerity to appear at the door, we captured him, dragged him outside and locked him up in our bomb shelter.

I wandered out into the garden. A breeze stirred the warm scents of evening, in the lilac bush near the gate sang a nightingale. I sat down on a little knoll with my back against a tree and tried to concentrate on the flow of events.

Capitulation.

Surrender.

I began to cry. I sobbed for a while, feeling myself in tune with the singing bird, the smell of flowers, the trees, the Dutch earth on which I sat, the limpid night around me, and old skin-and-bones. Then I threw up all over the primulae.

* * *

Of one thing Chris and I were sure: the capitulation marked the beginning, not the end of our war. Being goal oriented by nature, we began at the conclusion. Before the month was over, we had carefully designed an eight course victory dinner. Not long afterwards the German authorities closed Minerva, which had boasted one of the best wine cellars in the Netherlands. On a dark, wet night we broke in through the roof, stumbled down the pitch black stairs, across all the spooky, familiar rooms and kicked our way into the caves. Menu in hand, we chose the accompanying wines for the future great occasion from a dizzying array of legendary vintages, not a bottle under two hundred dollars, a generous supply for a party of five. Better us than a bunch of Nazi officers pigging it at Minerva's expense, especially after my father's recent sacrifice. We hid our booty in two baskets and sneaked them out the back door to Chris' attic. Now all we needed was victory.

Under all the Leiden bravado, it was a resounding vote of confidence. To us, the question was not whether we were going to win the war, but how. Chris talked vaguely about army dispatch riders on Norton 500's, but I aimed higher. Notwithstanding my military discharge, "shortcomings" and dubious eyesight, I saw myself as a pilot in the Royal Air

Force, pure and simple. The vision was sustained by my conviction, which determined my attitude of those days, that if others had succeeded in learning to fly, or any other skill for that matter, then I was capable of the same, given time and opportunity. Obviously we had to get to England first, somehow.

There were obstacles. Squeezed between Germany and the sea, Holland lay farthest from the neutral steppingstones to Great Britain: Sweden, Switzerland and the Iberian peninsula. The rest of Europe was occupied by German troops. The direct route to England was blocked by more than a hundred miles of the most deadly body of water in the world, the North Sea. Dozens of ships perish every year in its unpredictable gales, which come roaring down the funnel from the Atlantic and Arctic Oceans, and on occasion all but sink the Netherlands itself. As a front-line in the war the Dutch coast, a straight, bare beach along a belt of dunes, bristled with German forces which made it well-nigh impenetrable from either side.

German Watch on the Dunes

Finally, trying to escape and getting caught produced a one-way ticket to the "Orange Hotel", Scheveningen's notorious SS-jail conveniently located on the edge of the Waalsdorp dunes, its favorite execution grounds. In the early years of the Occupation, before the establishment of overland escape networks, more than a hundred Hollanders in all manner of boats, dinghies and canoes set out on the direct route to England. Some the Germans caught, and of those who reached the open sea the overwhelming majority was never heard from again.

Considering the odds, it's no surprise that attempting to escape never became popular. Even if successful, it did not appear inviting. Night after night the BBC reported the terrible slaughter of British people by the Luftwaffe, and urged the nation to prepare for invasion. Winston Churchill sounded even less reassuring: "We shall fight on the beaches.... we shall fight in the streets..." Obviously, even if you made it there in one piece, all England had to offer was loneliness, danger and disaster.

In Holland, on the other hand, the fighting was over, the specter of death had passed. If you stuck to the rules and bowed to the victor, you could live in safety with your family and friends. Later, when terror and counter terror convulsed the Netherlands, Britain looked like a haven. But in the first two years of our war, 1940 to 1942, the opposite was true. To cross over to England you had to sacrifice all you loved, including probably your life, for this one privilege: to fight the Nazis as a free man or woman. Only a handful considered the privilege worth the sacrifice. For Chris and me there was never any doubt.

Meanwhile life in the Netherlands seemed to be sliding back into the past. All cars and motorcycles had disappeared, including taxis, impounded by the Wehrmacht. For private transportation we fell back on pedal bikes, which kept everyone in their home towns and villages. Even there, movement was restricted by a nationwide curfew from midnight to four a.m., which led to increased home life with frequent "sleep-overs", intentional or otherwise. But most of all it was the blackout, fiercely enforced, which hung like blindness over the land and kept people indoors after sunset, moving gregarious Dutch social life from café's and restaurants to gatherings around fireplaces in very private living rooms. All this was conducive to planning secret projects, but not to executing them.

In Leiden much of the scheming went on in Jean Mesritz' room at the foot of the Pieter's Church, where three centuries before some of the Pilgrim Fathers had worshiped. There, under the low ceiling and centuries-old beams, we studied all possible roads to freedom. South, through

Belgium, France, and across the Pyrenees into Spain? East and north, via Germany and Denmark into Sweden? All the way north to Finland's arctic open harbor, Petsamo? Up the Rhine through the enemy's heartland to Switzerland? The Nazis were everywhere, and each time we pulled out the atlas our eyes fell on that tantalizing stretch, so short on the map, a mere hundred-odd miles due west, the direct route. Across the impossible North Sea...

* * *

I like to go it alone. Right or wrong, I trust my judgment and prefer to be in a position to execute it instantly, without time-consuming consultation. Company is fine, but in moments of risk I want to be solitary. When the time came to skip, I told nobody and acted on my own.

Having never escaped from anywhere before, I went back to basics. My goal was England. Between Holland and England lay the North Sea. A sea is crossed by boat. Where was the nearest boat? In Scheveningen, both a beach resort and commercial fishing center.

I put on an old sweater and after a week in the harbor talking to fishermen, herring peddlers, German soldiers, police officers and local drunks, I knew among other things that commercial fishing would continue but all ships had to be back before dark every day and were restricted to a three-mile zone along the coast, patrolled by a converted tugboat manned by Wehrmacht personnel and armed with machine guns and antiaircraft cannon. At night it lay moored among the fishing boats, as headquarters for its soldiers who guarded the quays.

On the basis of this intelligence my plan was conceived. It should be possible to hide aboard a trawler in the harbor one night, equipped with an outboard engine, gasoline, a compass and a pistol. The next day, close to sundown, I would suddenly appear on deck, draw my gun and force the captain to put us out in the lifeboat. It sounded a little like Old Shatterhand, but so what?

Then all I had to do was make it to England. Of course, a dose of luck here and there would help, but why dwell on the weak spots - the longer you dwelled, the weaker the spots. I went down to the quayside to pick a ship.

A surprise awaited me: the trawlers carried no lifeboats. Now I remembered hearing about a recent ordinance banning all small craft from the coastal zone. Only German thoroughness would include the safety equipment of fishermen! Disgusted I turned to go home and think up a new scheme, when at the last moment I noticed a ship in the back row, the SCH.107. There, on her aft deck, lay the only lifeboat in the harbor, which greatly simplified my choice.

"They hit a breakwater last week," the herring man in the auction hall told me, eager to oblige. Holland's fishing towns had no taste for the Herrenvolk. "Fixed up sort of temporary. That's why she can carry a dinghy."

"Who's the skipper?"

"Fellow by name of Van der Zwan."

"Is he...uh...well, you know...okay?"

"Like so!" He gave the thumbs-up sign, sticking his smelly herring-thumb right under my nose.

If Van der Zwan was "like so!", perhaps he would give me a hand from the inside. With a gun stuck in his ribs, right in front of the crew, there was not much the Germans could pin on him. A gamble, but if it worked I would practically be in London.

The skipper's home turned out to be one of the little green houses at the foot of the dike, behind the South Boulevard.

At nine-thirty that night I knocked on his door in the pitch dark, unannounced, yet he let me in without questions. It was cozy inside and in no time we were sitting around the tea kettle, with his wife pouring. We discussed the weather, but as she showed no sign of retiring I put my cards on the table, in detail, with no frills except for a false name and a vague insinuation that Her Majesty the Queen would be tickled pink to see me arrive in England. I also offered double the value for the lifeboat, cash in advance.

"Well, well," the skipper said, shaking his head, and suddenly a large crock of genever was standing on the table. His wife produced two glasses, which he filled to the brim. "Tja, if you point one of those dangerous things at me... nothing I can do, what?" He opened his eyes wide, looking innocent, like a crusty old baby. "Bring some friends. Point all your guns at me, so I look good." He lifted his glass. "To the Queen!"

He wouldn't hear of getting paid for the boat, but his wife thought double its value would be just fine. I promised the money by noon the next morning, in order to tie things down. We drank some more genever, and that was that.

"Don't wait too long," Van der Zwan urged, as we stood outside the door, saying good night. I could hear the North Sea whisper on the other

side of the dike. "One of these days we're going to get German guards
on board. You can bet your life."

"Germans on board! When?"

"Pretty soon. Who knows? Next month? Next week? You never
know with these Krauts."

"Better do it tomorrow, then," I decided on the spot, panicking at the
idea that this unique opportunity might slip through my fingers. Suddenly
it was all set. I was to leave Holland, my home, my parents, everything,
the very next evening, August 13, 1940. - To organize an escape in twenty-four hours, without a car, under enemy occupation where possession
of every necessary element such as an engine, gasoline, a compass and
emphatically guns is unlawful and punishable by anything up to death, if
you can find them at all, I felt the need for help. Blackout or not, I got
on my bike and pedaled the fifteen miles to Leiden, where I huffed and
puffed up the Rapenburg, into the Kloksteeg to the house under the
Pieter's Church, ringing the bell just before curfew. The door was opened
by Erik Michielsen, a senior, in striped pajamas. Jean, he told me, had left
for The Hague.

I made up my mind in two seconds. Erik, a keen and determined
Leidener, undoubtedly one of Mesritz' plotters, would have to do instead
of Jean.

"You may come to England with me," I announced grandly, trying
to galvanize him.

"Awfully kind of you," he mumbled, rubbing his eyes, "but I'm already going. It's late, sleep well. See you on Piccadilly." I stuck my foot in
the door just as he tried to close it, and stepped inside.

His answer didn't surprise me; with the summer weather holding
steady the escape community buzzed with plans, although so far only
one had succeeded: three Leideners had recently crossed to England, a
hundred miles of open ocean, in a 12 ft. dinghy called "Bebek" - Malay
for "Duck" - proving to all of us that yes, it could be done! Michielsen
drew the blackout curtains and over a Heineken I pulled it out of him.
With Jean and two members of Njord, Opa Vreede's Rowing Club, he
had nailed two canoes together with cross-links and in this contraption
they planned to conquer the North Sea.

"Old boy," I snorted. "You can't paddle to England. You'll look ridiculous in the middle of that goddam sea in a canoe. Besides, you'll
drown."

In fact, I would be proven wrong - at least five men in three canoes made it across the North Sea from Holland to England in World War II. However, it didn't take me long to persuade Michielsen that my plan was better. All he really objected to was the smell of raw fish. After re-assurances on this point we joined forces without further ado, divided our activities for the coming day and, after a few hours sleep, went into action at first light.

* * *

Around ten o'clock that night Erik and I met in a shed at the southern end of the harbor, dressed as fishermen. Under some nets we found an outboard engine and four 5-gallon cans of gasoline, compliments of a certain Kobus, a friend of mine with black market connections whose patriotism far exceeded his social conscience - my youthful sallies into different strata of society finally paid off. Erik had brought a compass and Jean's service revolver, which against all orders had not been turned in. Finally, for provisions, my mother had parted with two round Edam cheeses from the family food hoard. The money for Van der Zwan, all from royalties of "Rendezvous in San Francisco", had been delivered at his home by, of all people, Paul Erdman.

In the clear, moonlit night the water in the harbor shone like black glass. It was easy to locate the SCH.107, too easy, she lay practically alongside the patrol boat. Two sentries with carbines paced back and forth, their steps echoing on the empty quay. Two more German soldiers stood on deck, smoking and talking. A few fishermen busied themselves around their ships with nets and other gear. We felt totally out of place.

Kobus had evidently wanted to ensure a fast crossing, the engine weighed a ton. It had been beautifully polished, and gleamed and sparkled in the moonlight. It was so heavy, we could only lift and carry it together. Our way to the SCH.107 led directly past the patrol boat.

I didn't like the situation one bit; it lacked a back door, an emergency exit. If anyone stopped us we were finished, plain and simple. What excuse could explain an oversized outboard motor in the harbor close to midnight, especially when garnished with twenty gallons of black-market gasoline, two Edam cheeses, a compass and a Dutch service revolver? They would probably shoot us for it.

We bundled the monster in our raincoats and staggered towards the trawler, as nonchalantly as two Leideners with an outboard engine can stagger through a fishing harbor under enemy occupation at night. The quayside seemed more deserted, the moon brighter than ever. We had waited until the sentries were out of the way, but the soldiers on deck stopped talking and stared at us as we approached. Keep going, I said to myself, don't look, just keep going. We shuffled by them in complete silence. It took a lifetime, and at any moment I expected to hear the fatal "Halt!"

Miraculously, it stayed quiet, nothing happened. One heave aboard, and it was done.

After two more trips with less spectacular cargo all our equipment lay safely stored on the SCH.107, under the nets below as Van der Zwan had instructed. Now came the long wait for our dawn of freedom. Feeling pretty good now, we sat on a hatch and lit cigarettes. Time passed slowly. A deep, vibrating drone began to fill the sky. I looked up. The mast cut black against the moon. Around it the night throbbed with German planes, wave after wave thundering westwards to bomb England, where in a few days we hoped to be... Did we really? I thought about my parents.

Parting had been tough. On my father I could count, as always. He stuck out his hand, in full control, but I could feel him tremble with the effort. He said just one word, in English:

"God speed!"

It was my mother who surprised me. "I don't think I'll ever see you again," she said, tearful but calm. "We want you to know that we are at peace with it. Better you die a free man than rot away in some Nazi prison." I could not know that when in the middle of the night a sudden gust of wind wrenched their bedroom window, it was my father who shot upright and cried, "O my God, Corrie, they'll drown like rats, those boys!" And he sobbed in my mother's arms.

The plan of the SCH.107 was realistic and sound. It had simplicity, speed of execution, and inside assistance reducing the risk. It aimed at England via the shortest route, the North Sea, in the safest conveyance, a lifeboat. It should have succeeded. It taught me a lesson I already knew: Luck is the great variable in Life.

We went below for a snooze on the nets. Shortly before dawn we heard footsteps on the deck above us. It was skipper Van der Zwan. "Gentlemen," he whispered down at us, his voice shaking with nerves. "Kindly come out of there. Here is your money back.

We're getting German soldiers on board, with rifles, tomorrow morning and every day after that. I have just been told. They can be here any moment. Please go, quickly. I want no trouble. My sincere regrets to her Majesty the Queen, but please go away."

When everything had been lugged back to the shed, Erik left for Leiden. I got on my bike and set out for Wassenaar, alone. It was a long and gloomy trip. At the edge of Park de Kieviet I sat up and sniffed - from here you could always smell the flowers in the gardens. Our house was dark, my parents were asleep. Feeling my way to the kitchen, I grabbed a beer and a piece of cheese, and tip-toed to my room. I checked the blackout curtain, switched on the light, closed the door tightly, turned the radio on to the BBC, poured the beer and put my feet on the table.

God, it was great to be home!

* * *

All next day I stayed in bed, but the following morning I dropped in on Jean under the Pieters Church, where I found all four members of the canoe plan in heated discussion. "Look who's here," Erik said snidely, as I stuck my head around the door. "The herring man. Nothing today, thank you."

This time it took a little longer, but when I offered to buy a sturdy boat with the Van der Zwan money, so that we could all go together, they dropped their plan for mine. In a wave of enthusiasm we decided to leave that very evening. With so many hands available, preparations ran smoothly. Jean took the cash to Warmond, a nearby marina, to buy a boat; Erik pedaled to Scheveningen on a carrier tricycle to collect the engine, gasoline and cheeses, and I called Kobus to provide us with suitable transport for bringing everything to a spot near Noordwijk, where one of the group had reconnoitered a footpath that led to the sea. The fact that the dunes which we would have to cross were strewn with manned pillboxes and rumored to be mined, we accepted as drawbacks of an otherwise solid plan.

In the short darkness between sunset and the beginning of curfew at midnight, our secret expedition thundered along sleepy country lanes and blasted to a stop at the foot of the Noordwijk dunes in a monstrous 22-wheel vehicle, proof of Kobus' determination to serve his country with nothing but the best, and the biggest. Jean seemed to have been touched by a similar spirit; the boat was as strong as a battleship and almost as heavy, so we had to mobilize six trusted Leideners from the Pieter's Church area as extra carriers. Boat and gear were unloaded, and when Kobus' behemoth finally pulled out empty and its roar died away in the night, silence fell over us like a cloak. Suddenly we felt exposed and vulnerable. In the dunes skull-and-crossbone signs grinned at our hushed little group from all sides, to inform us that we had entered a "shoot on sight" area.

It took us two hours of slave labor to get safely to the final ridge. Before us stretched the North Sea, black and baleful under a sliver of moon. We let the boat slip from our aching shoulders and collapsed in the sand; a German patrol would have heard us puff and pant a mile away. "Dear God," someone muttered, "It's like initiation all over again."

The last stretch had us scurrying across the beach in one haul. At close quarters the sea looked unexpectedly rough. In shallow water we loaded our gear and got aboard, Erik in the bow, the two rowers at the oars amidships, and Jean on the rear seat. There was a rush to push us off. I waded in, holding the stern to keep the boat head-on into the surf. When I lost ground, I hoisted myself aboard and sat down next to Jean. From the little band on the beach rose a muted cheer, barely audible above the roar of the sea; then they quickly dispersed. The bow shot up in the first wave, crashed into the trough, and all at once we were soaked through. There was little more than fifteen inches of freeboard and the water inside came up to our ankles, but we were on our way to England and freedom, a hundred-odd miles due west. It was August 15, 1940.

We intended to attach the engine as soon as the surf lay behind us, but after an hour of rowing the sea was getting no more tractable. Jean and I, equally seasick, took turns throwing up. Another hour and the moon shone through shreds of cloud on nothing but water - we were in open sea. We decided to hook on the motor, now or never.

While the engine was being handed to me from amidships, the rowers, who had been keeping the bow into the waves, were temporarily out of action. For a second the boat floundered, and at this precise moment a big roller hit us sideways; with the heavy machine in my arms I almost fell overboard. Our balance was radically upset and the sea poured in over the starboard gunwale.

We flung ourselves in the opposite direction and managed to right the boat, but the water sloshed after us and pushed the otherboard below the waves. In seconds it reached up to our knees. As a last resort I threw the engine, Kobus' pride, into the sea, but it was too late. Bubbling gently both gunwales sank below the surface. We were sitting just as before the disaster, the rowers neatly side by side at the oars, Erik in the bow, facing Jean and me in the stern. But the boat was nowhere in sight.

"Bail everybody!" Jean shouted.

"Where?" Erik shot back. A round Dutch cheese bobbed disconsolately past his chest.

When many hours later we crawled back onto the beach, half drowned, hanging onto the oars, the dunes glowed in the early light of yet another day.

* * *

After this, we were all somewhat disenchanted with the North Sea. I gave it one more try, this time alone. Scheveningen Beach Club owned a dinghy, which the lifeguard used to float around in among the swimmers. Apparently the Germans did not consider it seaworthy, for they allowed it to stay halfway up the beach at night. To me it looked pretty good. Erik, who knew about boats, wouldn't touch it. I decided to risk it and set the date for August 19, three days after the Noordwijk flop. It didn't take much organization. Kobus, peeved by the fate of his mighty contributions, sold me a greasy little outboard and two containers of gasoline, cash on the barrel head. Jean and Erik volunteered to help push the dinghy to the waterline. On the morning of the nineteenth I put the gas cans in some cartons, hid them in our private cabin at the Club ready for use that night, turned the key in the lock and put it in my pocket. Now nobody could get in except Dirk, the beach attendant.

Once again at ten in the evening I said goodbye to my parents. Nobody cried anymore. With the motor under one arm and the usual cheese under the other, I arrived on the beach. My two friends were waiting for me by the cabin; could I please hurry up a little, they were late for their dates. I turned the key in the lock - the gasoline was gone!

Later that week Dirk told me that in the heat of the afternoon the lids had popped off the cans. The entire solarium had smelled of gas, and the guests complained. Possession of gasoline was illegal and could get you into serious trouble. Dirk, no fool, put two and two together, and meaning to be helpful had taken the cans home for safekeeping. He winked at me. "Any time you need them..."

Erik and Jean rushed off to their dates. Suddenly I felt utterly, endlessly weary. Tiny engine in one hand I wandered aimlessly across the sand, then north along the water's edge. The tide was out. I walked to the end of a stone breakwater and turned around.

A tepid breeze brought scents of summer from far over the land. Above Rotterdam, as usual, spattered the delicate lacework of antiaircraft fire, soundlessly. Scheveningen lay in moonlight like a gray cardboard cutout: the row of hotels on the boulevard, the beach alongside cluttered with summer structures, the promenade pier like a gingerbread mass stretching far into the sea, the darkened lighthouse and the jetties of the fishing harbor just visible at the southern tip of the boulevard. A single strand of surf whispered rhythmically - curve, hiss, silence, curve, hiss, silence. Somewhere a train whistled; the impatient sound died, the surf sang on.

I lifted the motor high above my head. "Okay then," I growled. "To hell with it. They'll have to do without me in England. Tomorrow I am going to lie on this beach, in the sun, together with the Germans like everybody else."

It was the second engine I threw in the North Sea that week. With a splash it disappeared in the black water. Specks of phosphor whirled after it like fireflies. I watched them die, then walked back along "the little stone pier by the North Boulevard", as it came to be known later in the reports of the British Secret Service.

CHAPTER 6

Under German Occupation

One of the wonders of World War II was the Renewal of the Dutch people. The holy flame of patriotism melted away all internal differences, all columns, all class distinctions, all pigeonholes, wiped away a history of dissent and welded the nation into unity forever more. It seemed too good to be true, and of course it was. But not to some of us, including the Queen of the Netherlands. Renewal was a myth that created a good deal of confusion, for which I and other young idealists were responsible.

To those who actively fought the Germans under the occupation, Renewal was a fact, a dream come true. The fearsome dangers of the Resistance left no room for petty distinctions of social background, class and religion: we stood together, we fell together, we died together, brothers and sisters in the classic sense. We had risen to a higher level of citizenship, and truly believed that the invasion had effected this renewal in most Hollanders, while in reality we constituted a mere sliver of the nation. However, our Queen was part of that sliver.

Wilhelmina, Princess of Orange, descendant of William the Silent who led our country to independence from Spain until his assassination in 1584, was pear shaped and small of stature. She had an iron will and commanding presence, which led to Winston Churchill's famous admission that "he feared no one in the world, except Queen Wilhelmina." When World War II broke out, she had been on the Dutch throne for 41 years, and although both her mother and husband were Germans she had consistently refused to do business with the Third Reich, "an immoral system", or accommodate its leaders, "those bandits". Clearly, she interfered with the Führer's dream of a greater Germanic society, and his parachute attack on The Hague had as one of its main objectives the capture and elimination of this proud and stubborn woman. For her part, she had publicly vowed that, rather than fall into Hitler's hands alive, she would kill herself first.

Queen Wilhelmina of the Netherlands; Princess of Orange-Nassau

The invasion, without declaration of war, enraged her, and when the tide began to turn against her country she had to be restrained from going to the frontline "to die with the last man in the last trench" as she put it, quoting her ancestor, William the Third of Orange, Stadholder of Holland, King of England. That same night she telephoned King George to insist on the help the British had promised, but could not possibly supply.

Next morning the Netherlands' commander-in- chief informed her that she must leave the country or risk falling into Nazi hands. Queen Wilhelmina, tough, dignified, almost sixty years old, burst into tears. But she never hesitated. Ordinary Dutchmen, like myself, left behind in optimistic ignorance, were appalled by her departure. True, we had learned by the grapevine that Crown Princess Juliana and her two little daughters, Beatrix and Irene, had been taken to safety in Canada by her husband, Prince Bernhard; that made sense. But the Queen?!

"I knew that many people wouldn't understand it," she commented later. "But it was the right decision for Holland. Besides, everybody knows I'm not a coward."

She arrived in England despondent, yet the very next day breathed fire over the BBC, and some of the names she called Hitler and his henchmen surprised and delighted me. Her spirit was the same as ours, fearless, ferocious, and sadly lacking within the lukewarm Dutch community-in-exile that surrounded her, including a government of which the first Prime Minister, shaken and defeated, escaped in reverse, back to the Occupation.

Passionately involved, she was focused not on London, but on the Netherlands under the Germans. The arrival of an escapee created great excitement. He or she was immediately received by the Queen personally, who hung on every word they spoke. In those early years only the most militant of patriots made it across to England, and we believed in Renewal. On the basis of our reports Queen Wilhelmina renewed herself with alacrity. She called the escapees "our new nobility, the true ambassadors of my people", yet we represented only those who fought in the Resistance, estimated at 45,000 out of 12 million. The first free election after the war confirmed our misjudgment: the Dutch were once again at each others' throats, with a vengeance. Renewal had been a myth.

In reality the pressures of the Occupation enhanced the idiosyncrasies of everyone's character, and if character is destiny it wasn't surprising that our little group of extreme individualists fell apart rapidly.

Its first and most shocking defector turned out to be Aad Robertson, although for one trembling moment on the eve of the invasion, in my room on the Rapenburg, I had clearly foreseen his peril. The following morning found him marching east to defend our country against the Nazis. During a short rest at a roadhouse on the edge of his hometown, Hilversum, he got permission to call his parents. The phone was answered by a policeman who informed him that Mr. and Mrs. Robertson had been arrested "for security reasons."

As his mother was German, his worst fears had come true. After finding out where they were being held, he left the café by a back door and visited them at the police station. They were huddled on a bench along the wall with other suspected collaborators, indignant, scared and vengeful. They had been roused from their beds in the middle of the night and given ten minutes to dress.

For half an hour he sat hand in hand with his mother, then kissed her and walked out, leaving his rifle behind. Through streets and alleys he sauntered to a little park where he had played as a child. There he sat down in the grass with his back against a tree and smoked a cigarette. Being Aad, he quit the army there and then. Also typically, in the chaos that followed he got away with it.

I received this detailed information from Aad himself in a telephone call, two days after the capitulation. At first I felt for him, badly. Then he made a mistake. He asked me to come and stay with them for a few days, in Hilversum. Me? Stay at a house with a couple of suspected collaborators? Two days after the surrender? He must be nuts. He was my friend and it wasn't his fault that he had the wrong parents, but war had warped our old concepts, this was a new world. "No thank you, Aad,' I answered coldly. "If you want to see me, you'll have to come to Wassenaar."

He didn't come to Wassenaar. I didn't hear from him again, and vice versa. Several months later some one sent me a magazine, anonymously. The front page showed Aad Robertson, looking absolutely smashing in SS-uniform. I was deeply shocked. Why had he become a traitor? Then I realized that I really didn't care a good goddam why. He had been my friend and one of the most delightful human beings to grace my life, but as far as I was concerned, he had now ceased to exist.

* * *

Even before the autumn storms brought the long, beautiful, deadly summer of 1940 to an end, I returned to Leiden.

England had been a dream. My academic career was falling apart. My life had been shunted onto a dead track, I must get it rolling again. After hanging a "Do not Disturb" sign on the door I dejectedly gathered my law books together.

But whatever the capitulation had aroused in me, grew steadily in the gloom of the lengthening evenings. With methodical thoroughness the Germans imposed their authority, and every day the Dutch had to bow a little lower. It was sickening. For hours on end I sat bent over my texts with unseeing eyes, stewing in impotent rage. How long could I keep this up?

Not surprisingly, Jean Mesritz was the next member of our little group to leave, but in the opposite direction. Again, my foresight had been accurate.

At about the time when our dinghy sank off the coast at Noordwijk, the RAF had parachuted Holland's first official secret agent into a bulb field behind the dunes, a few miles to the south. He was Lodo van Hamel, a navy lieutenant whose destroyer, heavily damaged in the battle for Rotterdam, had managed to reach England at the time of the capitulation. We knew him from high school in The Hague, and inevitably he and Jean, both under false names, ran into each other sometime, somewhere.

Lodo's mission was to lay the foundation for a Dutch espionage network, after which he was to return to London in order to become its chief. Capture would mean the firing squad, so he remained holed up and operated through go-betweens, mostly Leideners, soon including Jean. After accomplishing his task in less than two months he contacted London with his secret transmitter, built into a suitcase the size of a weekend bag, and was informed that his superiors would send a plane to bring him back. A Fokker T8 amphibian would try to land on the Tjeuke Lake, in the province of Friesland, as close as possible to midnight on October 13, 1940. In case of bad weather, it would try again on either of the following two nights.

Jean, pressured by a number of recent anti-Jewish proclamations,- suggested that there would be plenty of room to take a few extra people along. After all, firsthand knowledge of the Occupation should be valuable in England. Lodo agreed and consented to take three additional passengers. Jean put himself at the top of the list, understandably, but passed me over as devoid of military experience and, furthermore, "blind as a bat". I was furious, but not for long.

On the agreed night the little group sat in a rowboat on the Tjeuke Lake. That first night, nothing. Nothing but silence and cold, and an occasional slap of a fish's tail on the misty lake. The second night, ten minutes past midnight, they heard the plane approach. It made three passes, first high, next lower, then very low. But the group was wrapped in heavy ground fog,surrounded by a luminous world of water and vapor and air, with no way to tell where one ended and the other began. The airplane circled for twenty minutes in the moonlight above the mist bank; then the drone disappeared in the west.

Obviously others had heard the noise and come to the right conclusion. Lodo, Jean and two representatives of Resistance groups were arrested as they stepped on land, and taken straight to the Orange Hotel, the SS-jail in Scheveningen. The interrogations were tough and one of the passengers - not Jean or Lodo - gave away the show.

On the third night, October 15, the weather was perfect and a bright moon poured its tricky glow over the scene. Almost on the dot of midnight commander Hidde Schaper, Royal Netherlands Navy, himself a Frisian, eased his Fokker T8 onto the surface of the Tjeuke Lake. But after the events of that day, the Germans were ready for him. Two infantry regiments, dozens of cannon and several searchlights ringed the lake, a police launch armed with a machine gun awaited him in the water. They signaled with a flashlight that the coast was clear and the plane could approach.

However, on this point Lodo had tricked his Gestapo interrogators. He withheld vital information, with the result that the light flashes aroused the commander's suspicion. Taxiing very slowly, keeping the boat between himself and the moon, he ordered his gunner to take it in his sights and fire at the first hint of trouble. When the Germans opened up at short range, they were blasted out of the water in seconds. Pandemonium burst loose around the lake as guns and searchlights sprang to life, but Schaper pushed his throttle all the way forward, got off, and made it back to England, with forty holes in the fuselage and a wounded gunner. Several German soldiers were killed.

Lodo stood trial before a military tribunal. The officers of the court expressed admiration for his courage and bearing throughout the ordeal, then ordered him executed in the dunes of Waalsdorp. Jean, in his cell in the Orange Hotel, must have heard the shots at sunrise.

* * *

Then, when the university closed, Chris Krediet threw in the towel.

In the morning of November 26, 1940, a fearless and principled professor, one of the few left, gave a scathing speech in the main lecture hall in protest against the firing of a Jewish colleague; in the afternoon the Germans shut down the academy and locked the speaker up in Scheveningen; in the evening Chris dropped by at 56 Rapenburg. He was accompanied by Herman van Brero, generally known as Count B, a dashing romantic whose recommended solution to the war was "to challenge Hitler to a duel and settle this undignified brawl like gentlemen."

Chris and I had drifted apart. Always hard to fathom, he had gradually become inscrutable. Long since retired from anti-German activities, he nevertheless showed no signs of studying either. Most of his time he spent alone in his little room under the attic, where even I felt unwelcome. Once, barging in unannounced, I caught him surrounded with heavy tomes by obscure philosophers. Whatever they provided him with, it wasn't happiness; even his cheeks, always a barometer of his moods, were fading. He seemed adrift, rudderless, and resented my well-meant intrusion. That was weeks ago, and now he came to say goodbye in the company of Herman van Brero, the elegant, swashbuckling Count B, tips of his pointed mustache quivering with determination. They were leaving the Netherlands the next day.

"Where to?" I poured them another drink.

"Any place where I can breathe freely and think straight," Chris proclaimed. "Perhaps even England."

Irritable, morose, he had become a shadow of his whimsical former self. His unlikely teammate suddenly jumped up, strode to the mirror, inspected himself and saluted smartly.

"Which way are you going?" I asked.

"Petsamo."

I sighed. Finland's arctic harbor, mysteriously hidden in the mists beyond Europe's North Cape, always came up after three or four genevers. "Any idea where it is?"

"I have it on good authority that it's somewhere near the North Pole," Chris snapped. "The German army has yet to occupy it and American ships still go there."

"And how are you going to get to it?"

"Dutch coaster to the Baltic. Jump ship in Helsinki, then trek northwards; turn right somewhere. - Rumor has it that the coasters are short of cooks."

I had to laugh, in spite of everything. Count B abandoning his duel with Hitler to sail forth as a ship's cook and Chris trekking north to turn right somewhere near the Pole - what next? I felt sorry for Chris. The closing of the university could well be temporary. You had to stick to your guns and not dance to the Germans' tune. And then Petsamo, for Christ' sake, and Count B to boot! I got up. "Why don't you guys drop in for a drink, say, Sunday? You'll feel better."

But on Sunday they had disappeared. Ten days later a postcard arrived from Helsinki. At about the same time the Wehrmacht occupied the port of Petsamo; poor Chris, poor Herman!

But then I got a card from them, mysteriously, out of Moscow. After a week or so another one from Vladivostok, then one from Tokyo. Two weeks later, January 1941, a picture of the Golden Gate bridge in San Francisco, and finally the Empire State building in New York. The last postcard read, "Next week we're off to see Little Will and Big Julie", irreverent allusions to Queen Wilhelmina and her daughter, Princes Juliana. Chris and Herman, the most unlikely team of escapees with the lousiest plan, had made it to England, one hundred miles due west, by traveling east, all the way around the world.

The rain whispered against my window. Dusk was falling.

The academy was still shut, its somber hulk huddled deserted across the water. The Empire State card lay in front of me between the legal tracts on my desk. I burst out laughing. I laughed till my guts hurt. Then I grabbed my "Laws of the Netherlands" and hurled it right through the glass panes of my bookcase.

* * *

And then there were two, Paul Erdman and I. Two extremists, ostensibly similar, intrinsically opposites. So much in common, like love of country, anti-German sentiment, humanist ideals; so much in conflict, about methods and attitudes and ultimate goals. We read Law side by side, Paul out of conviction, determined to realize his legal future come what may; I from desperation, frustrated as a cat in a cage. The Occupation put us on a collision course.

Leiden remained closed. After our failure to escape last summer, another road to the future appeared blocked. Even so, I continued to study. I locked myself in my room and doggedly plowed through volume after volume. As the months passed, I began to get somewhere. But where? Sometimes the sheer immobility of the somber building across the canal overwhelmed me, all three hundred and fifty years of it, as if Paul and I stood still while life rushed by. But I knew my Germans. The empty edifice on the Rapenburg was a monument to their failure at keeping the Dutch in line. They would never stand for it. Sooner or later they would reopen the academy, one more try. I intended to be ready.

First the authorities tried blackmail. They offered to restore Leiden to normalcy if we meekly submitted to the Numerus Clausus, an ordinance which required Jewish students to register as such. Not only was this clearly against the history and tradition of our proud alma mater, but I and a few others saw it as a first fatal step on a steep path to disaster for our Jewish colleagues. Besides, William the Silent would turn over in his grave. We had to stand firm on this.

The danger was the student council. By now all professors with any guts had long been fired or jailed, and many of the worthwhile students had disappeared into the Resistance. The rest, the usual jelly-bellied majority, held the power, and most of them were desperate to resume their studies. It hardly surprised me to learn from an reliable source that the council, in private session, had decided to accept the German terms. Leiden university would reopen, with the Numerus Clausus in effect. This disgrace had to be prevented, by fair means or foul.

Seconds after the curfew ended at four a.m. on February 14, 1941, six teams of two men each, all old stalwarts from the Pieter's Church area, hit the icy streets of the blacked-out town. Every team carried a bucket of glue, a brush and a stack of hand bills, and apart from scaring each other half to death whenever their paths crossed, they spent a cold but relatively uneventful night. The next morning every wall in town, including the door of the Gestapo headquarters, displayed its copy of the "Leiden Manifesto", as it came to be called later. Nobody, not even the bucket brigade, knew who was behind it.

The manifest, beautifully printed on heavy paper by an unsuspecting little shop in Katwijk, contained a list of demands, including a ban on racial discrimination, as conditions for the reopening of the university. It was brazen and provocative, and meant to be. After writing it, I tried to think of someone who would share the secret responsibility for its contents with me, but in vain. So I signed it flatly: "The Leiden Students."

The German High Command, including Hitler's top henchmen in the Netherlands, received their copies through the mail. As expected, they exploded with rage and promptly declared that the academy would remain closed. Their fury was matched only by that of the Student Council, especially those members who were hauled off for questioning, vainly protesting their innocence. As far as I was concerned, it served the bastards right. So much for the Numerus Clausus. William of Orange could rest easy.

Paul Erdman, who suspected my involvement, reacted with bitterness, not about the substance of the demands as much as their method of presentation, which precluded any compromise. Of course, representing the majority he had a point, but what would have been the alternative? The jelly-bellies were always in the majority, and sometimes an issue was too important to let them have their way. Not very democratic perhaps, but neither were the Nazis. The authorities would try again, and perhaps next time they would lower the ante. Paul went home to The Hague to concentrate exclusively on the study of the Law, Leiden or no Leiden, occupation or no occupation, war or no war.

Our paths crossed one more time. The little printer in Katwijk had made a mistake. Proud of his handiwork, he had left his name and address on every eighth copy of the Leiden Manifest, which in the dark had escaped our attention. Somebody warned me that he had been arrested, and not knowing my real name he sauntered through Leiden all day under orders to point me out to his two companions, both of them Gestapo officers. His nights he spent at the Oranje Hotel.

I did not dare to go home, not the Rapenburg nor Wassenaar. They were after me, at any time they could knock on my door. I had to "go underground", but where? My father approached four of his rich friends who lived in big houses with plenty of room. Of course they were staunchly anti-German, but sheltering a fugitive? Too risky. "These heroics are all fine and dandy," one of them protested, "but hell, those boys have nothing to lose."

"Nothing but their lives," my father answered, dryly.

Finally I decided to try Paul Erdman in The Hague. True, we did live in different worlds, but first and foremost we were friends and fraternity brothers. Furthermore, I couldn't think of anybody else. Maybe I could hide in his attic for a few days, until a more permanent solution turned up.

When I rang the bell at his home, one of his girlfriends opened the door. I remembered her vividly from the beach in Scheveningen, tiptoeing daintily through the masses of humanity in a little yellow bathing suit, all male heads both Dutch and German turning to follow her progress. Erdman liked them beautiful, and young. Her name was Sari, tall, chestnut hair and huge dark eyes, and she remembered me, too. She gave me a quick, flashing smile.

Paul, after hearing my request, expressed his regrets: his mother suffered from headaches lately and furthermore they had no room, large as the house may seem. "Very sorry, old boy. But you know how it is.."

"Why don't you come and hide at my place?" Sari suggested innocently. "They'll never find you there. I live in a flat in Amsterdam."

Her boyfriend immediately offered to discuss my case once again with his parents, but I assured him that, really, Amsterdam was much safer. We left together, Sari and I, as if it were the most normal thing in the world, with my former roommate buzzing about us nervously. When I happened to look back, he was staring after us with a puzzled expression.

We took a bus to the station and an hour or so later walked silently down a deserted street in Amsterdam South, two inconspicuous figures in raincoats through the gray afternoon. In a narrow old building we climbed three pitch-black flights of stairs to the top floor. Sari's "flat" consisted of one room under the eaves, sharing kitchen and bathroom in the hallway. It contained a table, two chairs, a sofa and a hide-a-bed. The first night I slept on the sofa. The next morning I turned all pictures of Paul with his face to the wall. When by evening not one had been turned back, I moved in properly, hide-a-bed and all.

Sex is fine, but war must reject love. It spawns ties and worries about the future, involvements I had to avoid at all cost. Sari and I were made for each other, at least physically, and one wild week we barely left the room. In the end I kept my head and returned to reality. If I had hopes of making it to England, or else graduating, or both, then I could not stay in bed forever with a girl, no matter how delectable. I took a cold shower, finally put on some clothes again and said goodbye. The stairs were endless and my knees buckled. Outside the streets looked lonely and hostile. And then there was one.

* * *

Nobody believes in his own death, or, for roughly the same reasons, in his own arrest by the Gestapo. Two friends of mine, who had helped put up the manifests, were off to England and invited me over for a farewell drink. Erik Michielsen, heavily involved in the Resistance, asked me to hand them a roll of film for delivery to British Intelligence, a reasonable request. "It will save me a long walk," he smiled.

As it turned out, it saved him a great deal more. When I got to the front door below the Pieter's Church, two gentlemen arrived at the same time. They rang the bell and courteously let me enter ahead of them. Once inside they pulled out pistols, and for the first time in my life I found myself face to face with that little black hole and the devastating authority it carries. Minutes later we were on our way to the Orange Hotel. It was as simple as that.

To fail at escaping is one thing, but to be unjustly arrested as an accomplice to someone else's misfortune struck me as unreasonable. I tried to make my point on the way to the police car. When the rear door opened for us to get in, I wished everybody a pleasant afternoon, turned left and walked off. The barrel of a pistol was rammed into my ribs and I squeaked with pain. "Next time, boom!" the Gestapo man said. He spoke with an atrocious Bavarian accent, but I understood him perfectly.

My real worry lay in a different direction. The printer from Katwijk still roamed the streets of Leiden, but the nights he spent in the same jail where I was now headed. Obviously I had to get out of there before our paths crossed.

All the way to Scheveningen I argued my case, staunchly supported by the two Leideners, on either side of me in the back seat. The German next to the driver kept us covered with his gun, grinning amiably at my efforts. We stopped at a tiny door next to the main gate of the Orange Hotel. The high, blind wall of red brick ran the length of the entire block and around both corners. When we entered the building through a second gate, I still could not believe it. All those long corridors, deserted, the shiny, tiled walls, rows and rows of green cell doors in absolute silence - were there really people behind them? The momentary pride I felt on entering the honored ranks of inmates of Holland's most infamous SS prison, did not sustain me for long.

We were taken to a room bustling with activity, like a precinct police station. Secretaries worked behind crowded desks, typewriters rattled, sergeants and corporals walked in and out with papers; I could smell real coffee and Egyptian cigarettes. We were lined up with our faces to the wall and nobody paid much attention.

After fifteen minutes or so a sergeant at a large table called for one of us. The first Leidener went, and from the corner of my eye I watched him being registered, told to empty his pockets and dump his possessions on the table. After that he was searched by a corporal.

At this moment a sudden intimation of certain death shattered me. The roll of film I was carrying! The jarring arrest had made me forget all about it, I could feel the little box in my righthand pants pocket. Erik Michielsen's reputation guaranteed some thirty negatives of the highest quality secret intelligence material, likely to include some German bunkers, antiaircraft emplacements, invasion barges, camouflaged factories and to top it off probably a few secret documents for good measure. The hairs in my neck bristled. This meant the firing squad, absolutely dead certain, and all the torture required to get to the source of this material.

The second Leidener was called over and began emptying his pockets. Cold sweat trickled down my spine. Looking around desperately, I spotted an electric junction box on the wall above me, just within reach if I stood on my toes. It took me all of one second to implore divine intercession, whoever was interested; then I put the film on top of the box, in full view of the room behind my back, and waited for the outcry. Nothing came. The next moment it was my turn to sign in. I emptied my pockets on the table, submitted to the search and smiled weakly at the sergeant on leaving. From all the way across the room and with every step backI saw the bright yellow Agfa film box stand out against the drab wall. Nobody else did, nor noticed when I snatched it down and slid it back into my pocket. The cell door had barely clanged shut behind me when I exposed the roll to the light and flipped it out of the barred casement window onto the roof.

I spent seven days in jail, including my twenty-fourth birthday. By and large treatment was reasonable. The first moments were tough, but after a few hours of confusion and despair I was back on track with a single target: how to get out. Every guard who stuck his head into my cell I belabored with my unjust arrest, and one appeared susceptible. He agreed to take a letter of mine to the prison commandant, an SS colonel, and although lack of choice forced me to write it on three feet of toilet paper, it did the job. The guard came reeling back with the news that at any repetition of the insult, the colonel would have us shot, both of us, at dawn. Even so, probably because of overcrowding, he returned the next morning to yell, with obvious relief: "Raus! Get out!"

What was jail like? It's been told many times. Once you know one SS-establishment from the inside, you know them all. The walls of the Orange Hotel were thick, you rarely heard the screams. There were compensations. Sometimes, after a long, fearful day, I felt the warmth around me of the best of my countrymen. I saw my name scratched on stone in the courtyard, with furtive greetings from lost friends. Once someone whistled the Io Vivat!, Leiden's Corps song, very far, very soft in the lonely silence. I remember the cheerful "Thank you!" from cell to cell, mocking the guard who bolted the doors at sundown; and, from the women's block across the way, the sobbing of a girl in the night. Occasionally, the thought of the printer and his diligent Gestapo escort endlessly combing through Leiden for me, while I was safely hidden in their own jail, cheered me when I needed it.

The greatest moment came at the very end. I had already left my cell and was scurrying through the connecting hallway to the main exit.

Suddenly somebody called my name. There, at the end of corridor C, broom and bucket in hand, stood Jean Mesritz. There was no one else in sight. He put his bucket on the floor, leaned the broom against the wall, and stretched both arms into the air as wide as he could, hands open, fingers spread.

Like that, he stood motionless between the cell doors, a warm smile on his emaciated face, in silent, unbelievably exuberant greeting. I waved and rushed by in my headlong dash for freedom.

It was the last time I ever saw him.

* * *

The end came in the summer of 1941. Both the university and Minerva remained closed. Leiden's powerful intellectual flow had been polluted and finally stalled in the ooze and slime of political compromise and oppression. Its bizarre social adjunct, the Student Corps, had lost its purpose and withered away. Professors continued their studies in private, students had scattered across the land either in the Resistance or at parental homes. The Rapenburg curved deserted on both sides of the canal; now and then a furtive figure could be seen leaving or entering one of the old houses. Behind its little balcony on the corner of the Kloksteeg, number 56, first floor, stood empty.

Ever since my release from the Orange Hotel the Germans had put my room under round-the-clock surveillance. For a few days I watched the plainclothes agents hanging around patiently, mostly across the bridge, sometimes pacing up and down the Kloksteeg. Meanwhile, as far as I knew, the printer of the manifesto and his Gestapo escort still combed the town in hopes of arresting me. All in all, as the last of the Mohicans, I felt that I had outlived my welcome in Leiden. I moved back to Park de Kieviet, Wassenaar, taking my law books with me. With nothing better to do I studied and studied.

Then a very strange thing happened. Suddenly the authorities reopened the academy, without fanfare nor any strings attached. Nobody knew why. It stayed open for ten days, after which, just as mysteriously, it closed again, this time for good. As it happened without prior notice, no one could take advantage of it. Except me. Through circumstances beyond my control I knew more about law than any self-respecting Leidener would normally concede. I applied for an immediate examination, which was granted.

On the big day, June 10, 1941, I refused to give in to the temper of the times. The Leiden Student Corps required its members to take exams dressed in white tie and tails, into which I changed at home. My parents didn't quite know what to make of it, after all those Edam cheeses the previous summer. My mother knotted the white butterfly and my father brushed the little silk hairs of my black hat in silence. Next came forty-five excruciating minutes in the streetcar to Leiden, under the amused scrutiny of the local hoi polloi, after which I could be seen in top hat slinking furtively along the Rapenburg. With a nervous glance at the Gestapo stakeout in front of my abandoned room across the canal, I finally sneaked into the iron gate of the university. Then, like a phoenix rising from its ashes, I strode straight and solemn from the gray Occupation into the past glory of my old alma mater.

Five hours later I stepped from the examination room, closed the door behind me and loosened my tie. Now it was up to the professors. The old building around me, which once rang with laughter and cheers for the graduated, oozed silence like a mausoleum. According to tradition, I took a seat in the "Sweat Room", where after examinations students await their fate. It took only a few minutes, then the beadle appeared and motioned me to follow him. Opening the door to the chamber he rapped the floor three times with his silver plated staff, called out my name and accompanied me inside. Thirty seconds, and I was back in the hall, a full-fledged Doctor of Law.

It was the only recorded action at Leiden University in these ten days. There is no explanation, even today. As the Javanese put it, "The bird of luck prefers to alight on a well prepared perch." I felt deep gratitude and a sense of awe, but no desire to speculate. We do not have to know our benefactor to acknowledge our debt.

Someone came at me through the gloom, arm outstretched. It was Paul Erdman. He shook my hand endlessly, beaming and smiling. "My dear fellow, congratulations! A great occasion, a great occasion."

"My God, Paul, don't tell me you bicycled here all the way from The Hague? For this?"

"Of course I did, old boy. First doctor of our year. Greatest day of your life. Let's go celebrate!"

I stared at him, fascinated - the earnest, decent face, the fine features, the immaculate suit. In spite of everything I found myself admiring his stubborn refusal to change. He had set his course through life, no inconveniences like wars, surrenders or enemy occupations would budge Paul Erdman from his chosen path. In the empty hall he stood like a remnant of the old Leiden, lost, yet somehow indestructible.

We went back into the Sweat Room together, its walls covered from top to bottom with signatures, some very old, back to the 16th. century. While Paul held my top hat, I carefully wiped a small area clean and wrote the happiest words in the life of a Leiden student:

HIC SUDAVIT SED NON FRUSTRA

(here sweated but not in vain)

Erik Hazelhoff Roelfzema

10 June 1941

* * *

Nobody knew where she came from, nobody knew where she was headed. She lay moored in Schiedam at pier 5, a grubby hunk of mystery. From the middle of her rusty eighteen-thousand ton hulk rose a single smokestack, tall and thin. Below it, from deck to waterline, the center section of her sides was painted bright red with an enormous white cross, the flag of landlocked Switzerland. From her stern flapped the bizarre banner of a Central American republic: two stars, one red, one blue. On the bow, in dirty white letters, her name, St. Cergue. German soldiers guarded the gangway.

Jean de Kuyper, of the famous De Kuyper distilleries, had given me the tip that a ship, caught in Rotterdam by the German invasion, had been cleared to sail for New York in order to bring back grain for neutral Switzerland. I had no reason to trust or even believe him, but prior to the war and her subsequent return to the USA his stepdaughter, Barbara Huttig, member of a prominent Missouri family, had been my girlfriend. Perhaps his unexpected helpfulness was on her behalf. It seemed worthwhile investigating.

I started in Café Sterrebosch, a local bar of some repute in Schiedam harbor, and the general attitude was negative.

A landlocked Swiss captain? Yodeling on the bridge? Yes, he was looking for a crew; no, the official version was bullshit. Nobody knew anything for certain, but the diverse rumors floating around all agreed on one point: if she sailed, the St. Cergue and every man aboard were doomed. It was the end of June, 1941. Hitler had just assaulted Russia, and most of the regulars saw us disappearing around the North Cape in a white arctic night, laden with explosives for the advance on Leningrad. No self-respecting Hollander would sign up for this, so now this cuckoo-clocker was trying to crimp a crew together.

And what if the official line were true and the ship, a neutral vessel, had been cleared for sailing to the USA? Wouldn't the crew be subjected to a full-scale identity check, in which case I might just as well report directly to the Orange Hotel? On the other hand, thanks to my Seaman's Indentification Card from the ss. Spaarndam I could legally sign on...I decided to bet on De Kuyper, take my chances, as usual, and mustered as cook's mate.

At eleven sharp on the day of departure the Gestapo marched up the gangplank. I was sitting on hold 3, between galley and bridge, with two sailors and Toon, the bosun's mate. From their reactions to the hated uniforms I gathered that only Toon had nothing to worry about. The police detail that stepped on deck consisted of a lieutenant and two sergeants, customary in cases of "arrest with possible violence". At the foot of the gangway stood a car and a paddy wagon and half a dozen guards. The Nazis had come loaded for bear.

I went into the galley, filled some mugs with chicory coffee and followed the policemen to the bridge. I meant to keep on top of the situation. Our captain, a handsome Swiss mariner, stood talking with two German Navy commanders. The Gestapo lieutenant was studying the crew list.

"Well then," he said after a while. "Thirty-four men. Captain, First officer and bosun, Swiss. The rest Hollanders... Thirty-one. Right?"

"Right."

"Identity check. All crewmembers on deck, immediately. Have 'em bring all papers and identification." I was seriously considering slipping overboard and hiding in the water for a while.

The captain didn't blink an eye. "Officers and bosun are aboard. The rest -" With a wave of his arm he indicated the little group on hold 3. The Germans stepped to the railing of the bridge and stared down on the three Hollanders, who pretended not to notice.

"But... three men? And this one here, and four officers and the bosun... and you..." The lieutenant counted on his fingers."Where are the other twenty-four?"

"Hey!" the captain called down. "Where are the others?"

A certain amount of discussion took place on the hold. Then Toon got up. "In café Sterrebosch."

"In café Sterrebosch," the captain repeated politely.

For a few moments the Gestapo officer stared at him, dumbfounded. Then he pulled himself up to his full height, which wasn't much. He had a round, vicious little face and in talking focussed his eyes on a point several inches above the captain's head. "Did you not get orders to sail at noon?"

"Yes." The captain looked at the ship's clock. It showed eleven thirty-five.

"Did you not get orders to the effect that nobody was to be allowed on or off the ship twenty-four hours prior to sailing?"

"Yes"

"Did you not communicate these orders to the crew?"

"Yes, I did communicate them."

It was quite true. Forty-eight hours ago I had stepped aboard, after another uncertain parting from my parents. In the course of the afternoon the rest of the men had come trickling in. At noon the next day, twenty-four hours before departure, we had been called together amidships. They looked like a tough bunch, except for some dubious types who, in spite of their rugged garb, carried a faint air of Minerva or some similar establishment. The captain had addressed us from the bridge in a voice like an alpenhorn, first reading the Gestapo order restricting us to the ship, then promising damnation to anyone who failed to comply. We smoked and listened, trying to decipher the avalanche of Swiss intimidation that rumbled over us.

"What's the old man saying, except verflucht and verdammt?" Sjakie, a wiry little Rotterdammer with grey hair, had no time at all for the German language

"Mostly verflucht and verdammt. And that we have to stay on board," Toon translated. "Compliments of the Krauts."

"The Krauts can stuff their compliments," Sjakie snorted. "And their orders too. What do you say, Squint?"

"I say screw 'em," answered my boss, the cook, squinting his left eye which had a life of its own.

When at ten the next morning I did the rounds with coffee for the officers, apparently a cabin boy's principal occupation, I found the ship all but deserted. Led by Sjakie and Squint the entire crew had sneaked off to café Sterrebosch, no doubt to toast an uncertain future. They still had not returned.

The captain shrugged his shoulders at the German officers: Hollanders and orders... His eye fell on me, standing quietly in a corner. "Beat it," he said, not unkindly.

The Gestapo lieutenant threw up his hands. This was a situation for which his brain had not been programmed. Conscious of his sinister powers, he felt he had a right to expect everyone aboard the St. Cergue to be in a state of acute anxiety. Instead, half an hour before departure, the crew was absent drinking genever in a local café. Against all orders. He paced up and down, muttering to himself. The two Navy commanders put their heads together, then called down some instructions to the pier. We heard soldiers start the motors and drive off.

I left the bridge reluctantly and positioned myself at the railing near hold 3. Ten, fifteen minutes went by. No one spoke. The bridge radiated tension. The harbor was silent, dismal, dead. Only the gulls wheeled against the grey sky. Then I heard singing, softly in the distance, suddenly loud and rowdy as the paddy wagon careened around the corner of a warehouse. With its brakes still screeching the doors were flung open, and out spilled the crew of the St. Cergue. I could almost smell the genever.

The police lieutenant jumped to the railing and shouted at the soldiers, who quickly blocked the way to the gangplank. In the resulting confusion Sjakie stepped forward and started arguing, waving his arms, to no avail. The Gestapo officer looked down on him with unconcealed satisfaction. He'd show these pesky Dutchmen!

After a few minutes Sjakie realized that he was barking up the wrong tree. He turned around and walked to a crane which towered between the ship and the warehouse and began to climb the iron ladder. About sixty feet above the pier, a platform stuck out towards the St. Cergue, some four feet square. On the extreme tip of it Sjakie balanced himself, swaying gently. Now he stood level with the Swiss and German officers, in line with the bridge, on the edge of a dizzying void.

"Good morning, Captain," he said with dignity across the precipice, politely tipping his hat. And then pleasantly to Toon, spotting him on the hold. "Good morning, Toon."

"You're drunk!" the lieutenant shouted in German, visibly reddening. "Besoffen! Ganz besoffen!"

"What says the gentleman?" Sjakie asked Toon down below.

Toon beamed. "He says you're pissed, Sjakie. Verrrry pissed."

"That's correct," Sjakie confirmed, with satisfaction. He rocked slowly back and forth, at any moment I expected to see him plummet to his death. Apparently the rest of the crew had come to the same conclusion: the more sober ones had pulled a canvas cover from a stack of crates and held it like a fireman's net over the spot where he could be expected to land. With every sway the noisy crowd in the abyss moved faithfully with him, whooping with expectation.

"Captain," Sjakie continued, disregarding the German. "When do we sail?"

"Silenz!" the lieutenant yelled. To be ignored was the ultimate insult. "Silenz!"

"The gentleman says: Silence!" Toon translated, helpfully.

Sjakie looked into the void and tottered. Expectant shouts greeted him from below. "Silence!" he called down. "The gentleman says Silence!" "Silence yourself, or we won't catch you," a voice came back. Sjakie steadied himself indignantly and looked past the Gestapo man at the captain.

"You have wilfully disobeyed the orders of the German authorities." The Swiss tried to speak sternly, but didn't do too well.

The Rotterdammer understood his predicament. He shrugged his shoulders in sympathy. "Aw captain, those Krauts..."

The icy hush that descended on the bridge was broken by the police lieutenant. He banged the railing with his fist. He was puce with fury. "Nobody comes aboard!" he yelled in German. "Niemand!"

"Now what's on the gentleman's mind?"

Toon grinned. "He says, as far as he is concerned, you can all stay in Holland." He grinned some more - he was getting his own back for missing the party in the Sterrebosch

"We're not allowed on board? Really not?" For the first time Sjakie sounded taken aback.

"Nein!" the lieutenant barked. "No!" His round eyes glittered. He would show them. He would have to be persuaded. He strutted up and down the bridge. Now he had them where he wanted them. He waited.

Sjakie digested the news, wobbling gently to and fro on the tip of the platform, sixty feet above ground. Then, with a heart stopping stagger, he turned around and pointed imperiously in the direction of Schiedam. "Men!" he proclaimed, grandly. "Back to the Sterrebosch!"

A roar of approval rose from the quay, where the Hollanders fell over each other to get back into the paddy wagon. The lieutenant froze - for such eventualities Gestapo training had failed to provide. The two Navy commanders, who had kept in the background, now took over. They came to the railing and shoved the lieutenant aside. "Halt!" one called down to the pier. "Everybody board, immediately!" Then he turned to the captain. "No more delays, you sail now. We are in charge, orders of German Naval Headquarters. There's a convoy waiting for us three miles out of Hook of Holland. Not a moment to lose. All aboard and cast off!"

The Gestapo officer did not interfere. I watched him get into the car with his two sergeants, sick with frustration. If an identity check ever took place, I saw no sign of it.

It wasn't always easy to be a Kraut, especially in Holland.

The captain clapped his hands and motioned me up to the bridge. He pulled me into the chartroom an closed the door against the German Navy men. He whispered like an accomplice. "Get your ass down the stokehold right now. Two of our three fires are out. Damn stokers are so drunk, they can't stand up straight. Keep that last boiler going, or we won't get away. Allez, down, shovel the coal, shovel it in as if your life depends on it!"

It may have, at that. I rushed below decks. One of the sailors, in better shape that he had pretended, ran down with me. I had met him at the party, a slender, dark boy, obviously Indies, with a thin gold chain around his neck. His name was Peter Tazelaar, and he seemed just as eager as I to get away. When we stood side by side shoveling coal into the remaining fire, half naked, black and sweating in the flickering heat, he suddenly started laughing. He laughed so hard, I couldn't help joining in.

We leaned on our shovels and we roared, and our laughter bounced around the hot iron plates in the bowels of the old freighter.

On one boiler the St. Cergue limped down the channel to the sea.

The St. Cergue–a grubby hunk of mystery

CHAPTER 7

Escape to England

François van't Sant, Major General, Head of the Central Intelligence Service, Private Secretary and confidential adviser to Her Majesty Queen Wilhelmina of the Netherlands, stood by a window in his study at 77 Chester Square, London S.W.1, and watched a sparrow. It sat on the rim of a stone birdbath, freshly filled, outside at the foot of a lime tree. It turned its head left and right, dipped it in the water and shook itself with a whirr of feathers, spattering droplets like pearls in the sun.

Van't Sant watched, motionless, every muscle in his face relaxed, no expression in his light blue eyes. Evidently he had forgotten all about Peter and me; he was observing a bird and naturally gave it his full attention. Without turning he pressed an ivory bell on the desk behind him. Almost immediately there was a knock on the door and in came a corporal of the Dutch Military Police, in khaki battle dress.

"Oh, Tepper, bring me a piece of bread or something?"

The order was given in the tone of a request, as if van't Sant regretted the necessity that for the corporal, as for many others, his word was law. For a robust six-footer his voice was surprisingly gentle.

Tepper seemed entirely at ease. He moved to the window for a look at the bird, drying itself in the sun. "Sparrows don't go for bread in the summer," he stated with aplomb.

"This one does," the general answered dryly, without taking his eyes off the little creature. The corporal left, stymied. When he returned with a bread crust, he stayed for the outcome. Van 't Sant opened the glass doors to the balcony, which protruded low above the square, walled garden. He stepped outside and scattered some crumbs around his feet. The issue was never in doubt; the sparrow flew to an over hanging branch, from there to the wrought iron fence, and presently hopped about unconcernedly between the general's shoes.

"Rascal," van't Sant muttered approvingly. "Bold as the hangman." Tepper grinned and retired to his post in the hall. The bird made off with an oversized bit and disappeared into the tree. General van 't Sant pulled the doors shut behind him, put an arm around our shoulders and walked us away from the window.

It was an ample room, furnished with taste verging on luxury. Books covered an entire wall to the ceiling, sofas and armchairs surrounded a wide fireplace, in one corner stood a grand piano. Yet, for all its brightness and comfort, something was lacking. Not a cushion was dented, not a volume out of place.

All the ashtrays were emptied and on the shiny black piano the gladioli creaked with freshness. Something that could have been warm and alive had succumbed to an icy influence, which had frozen it into order. Van't Sant, passing his desk, paused to shift a letter opener and a ruler an inch or two, arranging them symmetrically on either side of a spotless blotter. Then he picked up the telephone, rotated it one half turn and placed it back in the cradle with the cord hanging straight.

The Chief of the C.I.D. - Centrale Inlichtingen Dienst, the Netherlands Secret Service - might have been anything from forty-five to sixty years old, but whatever his age, General van't Sant in 1941 was clearly at the peak of his powers. Trim in his dark suit, a pearl under the knot of his gray tie, his face smooth and tanned, the thin strands of gray hair carefully brushed back over his spacious cranium, he moved trough the room as an integral part of it, decorative, impeccable. He softly hummed the Andante of Tschaikovsky's "Symphony Pathéthique."

Van 't Sant was thinking.

Suddenly he stopped at the couch where Peter Tazelaar and I sat waiting for an opening. He bent down, bringing his head very close to us. "This is where we do some real talking," he said, his voice soft and confidential, as if he had arrived at some conclusion that escaped us. He smiled unexpectedly, all charm.

I came straight to the point. In an instant his face tensed around watchful eyes. Every feature seemed focused on a distant point, like the motionless head of a tiger who out of a thousand stealthy jungle sounds has picked up the one meaningful rustle.

***

All at once life was moving at breakneck speed. After getting my law degree on June 10, 1941, and sailing from Schiedam on June 30, my escape on the St. Cergue turned into a fairy tale.

We had barely cleared the channel when the sun broke through to stay with us for the entire trip, beaming from an azure sky. At dark, the moon drew a silver path across the glassy sea, night after night. Over starboard the grim European continent, plunged into the gloom and blackout of occupation; on the port side death and destruction in Britain's cities, on sea and in the air; and in between, in its own lackadaisical little world, this strange duck: an old freighter with the flag of Switzerland painted on its sides, flying the colors of Panama, with a Swiss captain and German navy officers on the bridge and Hollanders before the mast, including a lawyer, a midshipman and a fighter pilot, all three hell-bent for England, plowing along northwards on a journey that had the makings of a delightful summer cruise. Gilbert & Sullivan could not have done much better.

My job consisted primarily and in about equal parts of serving coffee to the two German officers on the bridge, who were in fact in charge of the ship, and looking after a stowaway in the engine room. The latter had popped up from underneath the floor plates, close to where Peter Tazelaar and I were shoveling coal, with the words, "Well, hallo Erik!" He turned out to be Bob van der Stok, a classmate of mine from high school as well as a Leidener, and more recently a fighter pilot in the Royal Netherlands Air Force. Later in the war he was to be shot down by the Germans and captured, but tunneled his way out of Stalag Luft III in an epic adventure, which Hollywood made into a film called "The Great Escape". Out of 82, he was one of the three escapees to make it back to England, where he became commanding officer of No. 322 (Dutch) RAF Squadron, flying Spitfires. After one week aboard the St. Cergue he felt so at home that, when our rambling cruise took us into the Norwegian fjords, he could be seen sitting on the poop deck, stowaway or not, sunning himself and taking in the glorious view.

Of course, we never knew our destination. We steamed steadily north, and as gradually the sun clung to the horizon and nights turned gray and luminous, the dire predictions in the bars of Schiedam about the North Cape and Leningrad appeared about to come true. Where else could this course lead? But the sea beyond the coastal waters was

British, and when we dropped anchor off Ålesund, a mere four degrees below the Arctic Circle, I suggested to Peter that the next day we should overpower the two German officers who stood between us and freedom, turn the ship west and make a run for it. He agreed without a moment's hesitation. By now I knew his strength, or weakness: the plan was romantic, it was dangerous, what more could a man wish?

Midshipman Peter Tazelaar, Royal Netherlands Navy, was born in a village on Java, less than fifty miles from my birthplace as the toucan flies. As soon as I saw his brooding black eyes under the high forehead, the sudden exuberance of his smile across his chiseled features, I wondered what wild blood stirred his soul. Probing, I asked him for the story behind the thin, gold chain around his neck. He shook his head and did not answer. The glorified memento of a dull love? A princess's reward for saving her life? A Sunday morning bargain at the flea market? He glowered - take your pick. Who wants truth if it's commonplace? Who wants reality if it's boring? Truth has a thousand faces, and behind reality loom larger concepts. He stirred vague memories of my native island, and one thing I knew positively: he was bad news for Hitler and his cronies.

As Fate would have it, we did not need to go through with our wild scheme. We hauled anchor very early the next morning and when I arrived on the bridge with my mugs of coffee, there was no sign of the German officers. Overnight they had left the ship, and judging by the Norwegian coastline, rapidly fading in the distance, the Swiss captain had wasted no time in setting a new course: west. Jean de Kuyper was right: the St. Cergue had been cleared by the Nazi high command to get grain for neutral Switzerland and was heading for New York, in the process becoming WW2's largest mass escape from Occupied Holland. Behind us Europe slid away in the morning mist.

Within half an hour flashes of light signaled from the Western horizon. A gray speck grew with stunning speed into a warship. It looked huge. It bore down on us and turned out to be a British cruiser, the H.M.S. Devonshire. After she cut across our bow, we both hove to. They lowered a sloop which was rowed across by sailors in unfamiliar uniforms, and minutes later a baby-faced midshipman stepped on our deck. So this was my liberator - for I knew that the English welcomed any and all escapees from Nazi Europe. I stared at the little gold crown on his white cap, and suddenly saw it dissolve in my tears. I was free.

In spite of our captain's protestations about losing part of his crew, Peter and I clambered down into the sloop; Bob, the stowaway fighter pilot, was already there, huddled together with Toon the bosun's mate. "Can't you wait till New York?" the skipper yelled, furiously. "The war won't go away, you know!"

We weren't so sure. A terrible sense of urgency drove us along. New York? Who had time for New York? Yet, as we cast loose, the "cuck-oo-clocker" waved us goodbye, a gesture warmly returned by his former stowaway.

When we reached the Devonshire, looming up before us like a steel mountain, I looked back, just once. In the distance, grimy under a plume of black smoke, the St. Cergue churned away out of my life, a last bizarre link with Holland, Leiden, security checks, false names, Gestapo, treason, Orange Hotel, firing squads, the whole dirty, lawless, heroic, despairing world of the Occupation.

Two weeks later we sat on the sofa in General van 't Sant's study, and offered to go back to it all.

* * *

Transitions of freedom create changes of pressure in the soul. You must regulate yourself, consciously, otherwise you suffocate within your prison walls, or conversely explode like a diver who rises too fast from the deep. We had enjoyed three days of decompression among goats and Danes on the British-held Far Oer Islands where the Devonshire deposited us, two days aboard a Polish freighter in small convoy steaming to Edinburgh, one under guard in a troop train rumbling south, and two hours driving through endless suburbs in a prison van. When we finally reached our destination, a counterintelligence camp oddly named "Patriotic School" on the outskirts of London, we had adjusted sufficiently to prevent our exuberance from embarrassing innocent bystanders.

On August 12, 1941, British Security released us, and within twenty-four hours the Dutch authorities and I were at each other's throats.

Our first act as free men was a bus ride to Piccadilly, what else? We climbed to the upper deck and sat down in the front seat. Here you still had a view; the other windows had been covered with glue against bomb blasts. An official notice pleaded with passengers not to remove the opaque substance:

> *I hope you'll pardon my correction, This stuff is here for your protection.*

Underneath was written in pencil:

> *I thank you for the information,*
> *But I can't see the bloody station.*

After fifteen months of Verboten! we recognized this lighthearted interplay between the ruled and the rulers as a root cause of Hitler's problems.

London sparkled in glorious sunshine. There had been no bombing for weeks, and under the antiaircraft barrage balloons that sluggishly nuzzled the balmy breezes, the city seemed to be catching its breath. England was still in desperate straits, but almost a year ago the RAF had decisively beaten the Luftwaffe in the "Battle of Britain", stopping the threat of invasion.

Then came the bombings, night after night, yet London survived and now, after the slaughter of the past winter and spring something stirred in the air, shyly, a germ of hope that perhaps the struggle had entered a different phase. New names covered the front pages - Kiev, Smolensk, Sidi Barrani, North Atlantic - no less critical, no less deadly, but farther away, farther away! People still slept in the subways at night packed together like sardines, and yet, in August 1941, the old capital of the British Empire breathed the free air more deeply, and lovers in the parks once again smelled the flowers and heard birds sing in the shrubs.

At Piccadilly Circus we got off. The statue of Eros was boarded up and a fearful gash gaped in the storefronts down the road, but the sidewalks were jammed with people in uniform, clean, fresh and trim. We felt like bums in our filthy clothes, the same in which we had stepped off the St. Cergue. But proper attire was second on our list of priorities. First of all I had to find the headquarters of the Dutch secret service to check out a disturbing statement: one of my interrogators in the Patriotic School, a British major, had maintained steadfastly that no contact existed, secret or otherwise, between occupied Holland and the Allied war establishment in England. Considering the risks and casualties which the Dutch Resistance incurred while supplying the Allies with military information, mostly by wireless, this infamous rumor had to be tracked down immediately. Now I ran into a brick wall.

The most important function of the Dutch government, which had left Holland one jump ahead of the German army in May 1940, not without some arm twisting by Queen Wilhelmina, was the maintenance of a principle: the uninterrupted legitimacy of the State. This required no activity of any kind. Being a government in exile where Britain ruled, its characteristic feature was that it had nothing to govern but itself. Except for some administrative detail, all ministries stood by for better times. Apart from the navy and the merchant marine, which played a vital part in Allied shipping, it was difficult to imagine, in the summer of 1941, what kept the Dutch authorities in London busy, apart from making sure that everyone got his paycheck on time.

This forced inactivity was being administered by hundreds upon hundreds of Netherlanders in Stratton House, Arlington House and other impressive government buildings. It did not seem to bother them in the least. Why should it? They lived in a world of jobs and salaries, promotions and raises, which to us escapees, after fifteen months of Occupation, was as illusory as to them the cell and the firing squad. Because they were all in the same boat, they were unaware that reality had left them behind, since for their tired old act no audience existed anymore across the North Sea.

Until the escapees, soon named "Englandfarers", came trickling in and challenged their world. To us, Holland's mystique was safeguarded in the person of the Queen - from the government we expected action. We found none. The Occupation had made us unfit for any society based on respect for rank, title or position, we judged by one touchstone only: What is their record against the Nazis? They had none. In a matter of days we were after each other's blood.

"Unbalanced adventurers," the Minister of War called us. "Fossilized old farts," was one of our more restrained allusions to His Excellency and his colleagues. Like supercharged particles flung from the cauldron of the Occupation we crackled around the arid Netherlands colony, and wherever we made contact sparks flew. Genuinely bewildered, the authorities tried to neutralize our onslaught by sticking us in uniform and tucking us away as far as possible from London. Since we all arrived penniless and had to fall back on the government to eat, this ploy usually succeeded. I was determined to defeat it, at least until I had checked out the contacts between London and our intrepid Underground operators in Occupied Holland.

It wasn't easy. After a week of unceasing effort, I hadn't even located our secret service, let alone asked those vital questions. From building to building, from waiting room to waiting room, from excuse to excuse I was shunted around, and slowly felt myself suffocate in the porridge of bureaucracy.

Whether it was me or my dirty clothes, the subjects I raised or the intensity of my arguments, I made everyone visibly nervous.

If I merely touched on money or replacements for the rags I was wearing, they got rid of me politely. But if I used words like "Resistance" or "secret contacts", they recoiled as if I showed signs of advanced leprosy.

Finally, after half a day's wait, I managed to attain the presence of the Minister of War. Here the buck stopped. But His Excellency opened with a statement that he was really too busy to see me, at which I blew up and smashed my fist on his desk, which upset his teacup. Greatly alarmed, he hastily terminated the audience by calling in the MPs and having me thrown out of his office and Stratton House.

Peter Tazelaar stood at the entrance waiting for me. When he saw me being escorted into the street, he burst out laughing. Bizarre situations always delighted him. "Come on," I fumed. "I'm through with these bastards. Austin Reed is just down the road, and we need some new clothes."

We turned left into Piccadilly, left again into Regent Street and admired for a while the solid, British creations displayed in the windows of London's famous men's store. Then we went in and each selected a suit, a couple of shirts, a tie, underwear, socks, an elegant pair of shoes and a raincoat, the works.

"May I charge it for you?" the salesman asked, ignoring our smelly togs with regal aplomb.

"You certainly may." Rags or no rags, underneath still beat the heart of a true Leidener. I wrote my name across the bill, big and clear, and instructed him to send it to Mr. Pieter S. Gerbrandy, Stratton House, Stratton Street, London W.1.

Professor Gerbrandy was the Dutch Prime Minister, and in Stratton House he kept his office. It was my declaration of war to the Netherlands government-in-exile.

* * *

As things turned out, I never did find the Dutch secret service - it found me. Shortly after Peter and I got some decent clothes, I received a telephone call in our wretched little hotel in Victoria Street. A feminine voice, warm and cheerful, invited us for tea with Queen Wilhelmina. "Would tomorrow be convenient?" It was a question nobody had asked us for a long time. The Queen? Sure, it would be very convenient. At her town residence, three o'clock.

Chester Square, behind Buckingham Palace, used to be one of the best addresses in London. Now most of the houses stood empty. Windows, blown out or boarded, covered in spider webs, stared darkly out into the street on both sides of a narrow, neglected park, its wrought-iron fencing long since removed for contribution to the Metals-for-War drive. Here and there shrapnel had pitted a graceful façade, as by a giant hurling a fistful of pebbles. In two places a direct bomb-hit had punched a gap in the row of houses, exposing dingy back alleys. The rubble had been cleared, the foundations showed the layout of the vanished homes. A chunk of wall still stood upright, its wallpaper intact: little bears and monkeys. From the barren stone, like a miracle, grew grass and moss and a weed with blood-red flowers.

Number 77, Queen Wilhelmina's London headquarters, stood in a corner with a garden tucked behind it. On April 16, 1941, while she spent a few days in the country, it had been hit by a bomb. The damage was patched up, but the front looked shabby and badly in need of a coat of paint. However, since paint jobs required a special permit not available to ordinary citizens, Wilhelmina would not hear of it.

The moment I set foot in the building, I sensed the essence of the place, an alternate focus of power, not as broad and blatant as the government, but fiercer and more awesome. I instantly identified with it, as if my every move and emotion since the invasion of our country had sprung from this common source. Whatever fed it, also nourished my undefined goals in life, or anyway in war. In this house my rage would be shared and understood, my sacrifices - if any - welcomed and put to good use. Here I could serve, if they would have me; and to hell with Stratton House.

Peter must have experienced similar sensations. Instead of "unbalanced adventurers", we were suddenly treated as exceptional people. After fifteen months of enemy occupation, but even more these last few weeks of humiliation by our own countrymen in London, we hardly knew any more how to accept respect, even admiration.

Queen Wilhelmina expected us at her country home, near Maidenhead, and as we got into a green camouflaged Buick a tall young man in RAF uniform stuck his head through the window. "I'm Bernhard," he said simply, shaking hands with us. "My mother-in-law told me you are having tea with her today. I just wanted to say hello and welcome. If there's anything I can do for you, let me know." He smiled and left.

"Boy!" Peter muttered, staring after Prince Bernhard, husband of Crown Princess Juliana. "That sure beats getting thrown out of Stratton House."

General van 't Sant, impressive, suave, but not known to us at that time, sat down next to the driver, then half-turned to talk to Peter and me sitting side by side on the back seat.

"Things are different here," he said, with his soft voice. "In this house, it's the Dutch people that matter, not the government. Holland, not London. Especially as far as She is concerned." For security reasons he never referred to the Queen by name or title, always as She or Madame, or even "there." ("There will be no staying in town the next few days," meant that Queen Wilhelmina would remain in the country).

"What is she like?" I asked.

The woman we were about to meet had already reigned twice as long as I had lived. Yet, like almost every other Dutchman, I did not know much about her, the way one knows little about the moon. There it is, as usual, forever. Distant and strange, close and familiar. God only knows how it got there, or what it's for. Yet it obviously belongs where it is, and fulfills its function whatever that may be. And the bare fact of its existence seems somehow right.

My entire life, as baby, as child, as student, in the Indies, in Holland or anywhere, Wilhelmina had sat on that throne, and twenty years before. She was part of my existence, focal point of my patriotism. As a boy I saw her once a year in person, on her way to open Parliament, riding through The Hague in a golden carriage drawn by eight black horses, surrounded by all the pomp and glitter, scarlet and splendor our long history prescribed. There she came, you could tell by the cheering. Even from my usual perch high up in a lamppost, somewhere along the way, I couldn't see much of her, but what I saw fascinated me.

She was small and round, and bounced back and forth against the velvet backrest of her seat with amazing energy, back, forth, back, forth, waving and bowing to the cheering crowds, back, forth, loose in the wrist, back, forth, like a well- oiled windup puppet. For one moment she always looked in my direction. Then I waved with both arms, balancing precariously, yelling "Long live the Queen! Orange and Wilhelmina!"

The fact that she was a human being, like me, had never entered my mind. That's the way she wanted it. The concept of public relations was alien to her, and she detested publicity.

Never in all her life had she given a press conference, all journalists to her were "press-mosquitoes", and she glowered into cameras as if they were deadly weapons. She was used to communicating with her people through appropriate channels, and considered her private life nobody's business but her own.

An only child, she was raised in the iron protocol of a nineteenth century royal court. The little girls who, on rare occasions, were admitted to the palace as playmates, addressed her as "Madame" at the age of six. As she grew up, no boy was permitted near her, and her partner at the prescribed dancing lessons was a countess. She loved skating, but when she arrived at a suitable pond, it was immediately cleared of the merry crowds, and she had to amuse herself all alone on the deserted ice.

No wonder her character took an imperious bent, both publicly and in private. We all knew by rumor that you should never say "no" to her, resulting in answers like "Yes, Your Majesty, my name is not Jan"; that you must walk backward out of her presence, until you are out of her sight; that you must never offer her physical assistance, even if she trips right in front of you; that there is no smoking at any time in any of her palaces. And finally, unforgettable, that cabinet ministers faced by her displeasure, were absolutely, definitely known to have wet their pants. If any of these tales were true, and at some point in time they must have been, it hardly seemed conducive to a jolly tea party.

"Just be yourself," Van 't Sant answered, sensing the real purpose behind my question. "Address her as Your Majesty and behave like you always do towards a refined old lady."

When we arrived at the charming but modest country home, we were ushered into a study full of portraits and pictures of family groups. Dogs were much in evidence, and there was a silver-framed photograph of a horse. Within minutes the door opened wide and on the threshold stood Wilhelmina Helena Pauline Maria of Orange-Nassau, aged sixty-one, in the forty-fourth year of her reign as Queen of the Netherlands.

She held herself so straight that, in spite of her small stature, she conveyed an impression of height. Her gray eyes, set close together, looked at us in silence with guarded intensity, while a shy half-smile appeared on her lips. Then she did a curious thing. She made an awkward bow in our direction, stiffly inclining her upper body from the hips while looking slightly over our heads, as if her solemn greeting and gesture of respect concerned not so much ourselves as our nation behind us, lost in darkness. Peter and I stood petrified.

Tea was being served on the terrace. The conversation followed a predictable pattern of questions and answers, all about the Occupation, showing the Queen's appalling factual ignorance on the subject and an almost pathetic desire to correct this. We did our best, yet we must have disappointed her. All my life I had seen her image, on coins, stamps, posters, in magazines and newsreels, even for a few magic moments as a puppet in a golden coach, and now suddenly face to face I needed time to get back to earth. Instead of talking intelligently, I felt an urge to pinch her arm, to see if she was real. Furthermore, I simply couldn't bring myself to destroy the fairytale by hitting the good fairy with all kinds of negative news. One doesn't emerge from the galley of the St. Cergue to tell the Queen of the Netherlands that her government is a bunch of fossils - how was I to know that she would have agreed? We were guests of royalty, it was a lovely afternoon, and every disagreeable subject that somehow raised its head we killed off on the spot.

"It's not easy for me to meet new people," Wilhelmina once confided to me, later, when we had become friends. "I must never forget that it's an important occasion for them. So I always have to be at my best, in order not to disappoint them." She meant well, but it contributed to the sense of unreality that surrounded our first meeting with our royal hostess.

The conversation, difficult at best, faltered. Shadows of clouds drifted across the grass to a mighty cedar at the end of the lawn. The table looked cheerful, homey and Dutch, with sandwiches and fruitcake and the sun chipping sparks from the silver. Her Majesty was involved with Peter, who darkled beside her like a stray buccaneer. General van 't Sant, humming under his breath, stared unseeing in the distance. The lady-in-waiting imperturbably poured tea. It was a charming scene, full of late sun and ripe colors and the sad evanescence of an English summer evening. Involuntarily I glanced down the table for the Dormouse and the Mad Hatter.

* * *

On the way back to London General van 't Sant gave himself away, no doubt purposely.

"Did either of you two happen to know Lodo van Hamel?" he asked innocently, referring to my former schoolmate who was dropped by parachute near Noordwijk as Holland's first secret agent. He said "did," not "does," so obviously he knew that Lodo was dead, executed in the Waalsdorp dunes, information that could only have reached England through some secret contact. With the driver present, I hesitated to pursue the matter, and waited till Peter and I were standing with him in his office at 77 Chester Square. There the vital question, raised by the British major in the Patriotic School, finally got asked.

"Is there contact between the Resistance in Holland and intelligence services in Britain, or not?"

I was naïve enough to expect an answer, unaware that the general was an old hand at the Great Game. As head of the Rotterdam Harbor Police in World War I he had walked a fine line of neutrality and managed to keep both British and German spy masters satisfied, although his sympathy lay with the former. At their request he had traveled to Paris to arrest Mata Hari, the Great War's famous super-spy. In 1940, when he accompanied his queen to freedom, the British intelligence community had welcomed him to London as an old friend.

Van 't Sant's reaction to my inquiry was rigid silence. After repeating the question and getting the same stony treatment for an answer, I began to squirm. Without a word the general got up and gave his attention to a sparrow, outside the glass doors to the balcony, while Peter and I watched. He fed it some bread crumbs, and on the way back put an arm around our shoulders and walked us to the sofa. There I got even with him.

"I am only asking that question," I said, "because Peter and I have a plan. By sea, at night. To the beach at Scheveningen."

Now I had his attention.

CHAPTER 8

Contact Holland

"Give me a well placed spy," one of Napoleon's generals supposedly stated, "and I'll give you a regiment of Hussars." Modern militarists have frequently upped the ante to a division.

One way or the other there's no doubt that in any conflict, military or otherwise, the secret agent can be the most telling factor in the equation which determines victory or defeat. When operating behind enemy lines, he is also the most vulnerable: of the 145 Dutch agents who were dropped or landed in occupied Holland in World War II, twenty-eight survived. They must be regarded as the ultimate warriors.

During the fifteen months since the German invasion, General van 't Sant's C.I.D., in cooperation with Britain's renowned espionage agency MI-6, had infiltrated six agents into the Netherlands, including Lodo van Hamel. When we arrived in England in August, 1941, only one of them, Aart Alblas, was still in operation. Even I, in total ignorance of these facts, needed less than a week to discover the shocking lack of communication between Allied Intelligence and the Dutch Resistance. Nobody in London, including our own Queen, knew anything about the situation at home. To Peter and me, this seemed both unacceptable and unnecessary.

The plan that we presented to the head of the Netherlands' Secret Service and which in principle he promptly accepted, did not look like a big deal to us, Englandfarers; just more of the same, but now in reverse. An MGB (Motor Gun Boat), one of the British navy's super fast little warships, would take us across the North Sea to Holland at night, to be transferred to a dinghy and rowed ashore. Peter would stay to organize one pole of the new contact ("Contact Holland"), while I returned to

London to manage the other and lead additional infiltrations of agents and their equipment into the Netherlands. If this division of tasks seems somewhat skewed, neither of us wanted it any other way, because each was unsuited for the other's assignment. We both had a romantic streak, but on the ship of our dreams Peter saw himself before the mast, I myself on the bridge.

In that position I needed assistance, a trustworthy alter ego, someone like my old buddy Chris Krediet who, after circumnavigating the globe to get to Britain, seemed to have sunk away tracelessly into the mire of Dutch bureaucracy. After days of probing I dug him out of an army camp near Wolverhampton, where he had been hanging around ever since his arrival seven months earlier, waiting for God only knows what. General van 't Sant let himself be persuaded to arrange that both private Krediet and midshipman Tazelaar would be assigned to me "on confidential duty." To make this militarily possible required my being commissioned as an officer. Fortunately no departmental records had made it to England, so I conveniently forgot about my "shortcomings" and military discharge, and was duly sworn in as a second lieutenant. Chris, carrying a duffle bag with all his worldly possessions when he arrived in London, spat demonstratively on my new officer's boots and refused to salute. He was as feisty and red-cheeked as in the old days.

To make everything perfect the general put a small apartment at our disposal above the garage of 77 Chester Square, the Queen's residence in London. No.4 Chester Square Mews looked out over the garden onto the little balcony in front of his own office and, above it, Queen Wilhelmina's quarters. Peter, Chris and I, from then on usually referred to as "the boys of the Mews", or "the Mews" for short, moved in and promptly resolved to lead spotless, or at least unfathomable, private lives. From this stronghold we would wage war, and apart from picking up my paycheck I never set foot in Stratton House again.

One critical piece in the jigsaw puzzle was still open: who could authorize this odd and risky operation? Not van 't Sant, nor even the Queen. According to the Netherlands' Constitution it takes a cabinet minister to accept responsibility for anything, as a chosen representative of the people. Who, among this weak-kneed group, most of whom detested General van 't Sant and Englandfarers, was the most promising candidate? Unfortunately the choice was obvious: it had to be the Prime Minister himself, Professor Pieter S. Gerbrandy, whom we had recently saddled with the Austin Reed bill for our new clothes. With heavy heart I set out to persuade him.

Of the entire Dutch government, only Gerbrandy had stayed in the heart of London in spite of the blitz. I called him from the lobby of his wartime residence, the venerable Brown's Hotel in Brown Street, and bluntly asked him if I could come upstairs - my experience with cabinet ministers had taught me that you had to jump them fast and press them hard.

"Come up in ten minutes," he answered. "Room six." He didn't sound a bit alarmed.

I went into the bar, ordered a whiskey and planned my approach. The professor, a minuscule Frisian from the town of Sneek, deserved his reputation of uncompromising hatred of the Nazis, but it was his outsize mustache that had made him famous, drooping from his small round face like the whiskers of a seal.

Winston Churchill, who called him Cherry Brandy, was known to be fond of him. The story of their first meeting still did the rounds. After crossing a vast lobby on his short legs, the Dutch Prime Minister, who had rarely been abroad and hardly spoke English, put out his hand to greet his British counterpart and said cordially, "Goodbye."

"Sir," Churchill is reputed to have answered, "I wish that all political meetings were as short and to the point."

When minutes later I stepped into his room, Gerbrandy was invisible. The door to the bathroom stood ajar, and to judge by the splashing the Prime Minister lay in the tub. From there he conducted a spirited discussion about politics in prewar Holland with two gentlemen, apparently journalists, who lounged about in the bed/sitting room.

Suddenly the bathroom door swung open and before me stood His Excellency Professor Dr. Pieter S. Gerbrandy, Prime Minister of the Netherlands. He was naked except for a towel around the waist, which fitted tightly over his tiny potbelly. From between slight shoulders his little head, held high, rose round and bald as a cannonball. Above the massive mustache his pale blue eyes looked out fearlessly into the world. This entire apparition, four feet eight inches tall, could have passed under my outstretched arm. He was a firebrand in miniature. He looked angelic.

"Gerbrandy," he introduced himself, with a true Dutch rasping of g's and r's. He shook my hand, entirely at ease. Then laughter closed his eyes to slits and he added, slyly, "The clothes make the man, eh, lieutenant?"

When the others had left, our conversation lasted into the small hours of the night. On so many subjects did we find ourselves in agreement, that I resolved to revise my negative generalization about cabinet ministers. After discussing the landings and getting his support, I knew that in "the Walrus" - as Van 't Sant called him - I had a fully committed ally.

He walked me to the door and we said good night. Then, just as I was about to step outside, he took a lapel of my jacket between thumb and forefinger and rubbed them together, testing the material. Even before he said anything I blushed - it was indeed the suit for which I had stuck him with the bill.

"I say!" he exclaimed, in his flat Frisian accent. His little eyes glittered. "That's one hell of a fine outfit you're wearing."

* * *

To all of us Continentals in England - Dutch, Poles, Norwegians, Czechs, Belgians, Danes, even some French - Great Britain was our big brother in the best sense of the expression.

We liked and admired the British, and were well aware of the fact that without them our world would have ceased to exist. We watched the interminable intrigues of our own governments-in-exile with disgust, while England worried about survival and the ultimate defeat of the Third Reich. To us, foreigners in uniform, Britain competed in the Big League to which we all aspired.

In spite of their tact and forbearance, and the many diplomatic niceties, the English remained very much in charge of their own country and kept tight and exclusive control of every military action emanating from their shores. Nothing happened until it had Whitehall approval, least of all secret operations on enemy shores.

On September 3, 1941, a slight, beautifully dressed Englishman walked into Chester Square Mews and rang the bell of no. 4. I pressed the release of our gate and watched from the kitchen window as he crossed the courtyard with precise steps and entered the garage. We heard him mount the stairs, then he came down the short corridor. I was standing in front of the kitchen stove, wearing an apron, holding a frying pan with slightly smoking scrambled eggs in my hand. Peter and Chris lay draped across the couch in pajamas, reading the morning comics. The man took off his hat, revealing thin, reddish hair shot through with gray that partially covered a dent the size of a silver shilling in the front of his head. For a moment or two he looked us over with keen, brown eyes, thoughtfully stroking his tiny mustache. Then a disarming smile totally rearranged his face. "Rabagliatti," he said in an impeccable accent.

"Awfully nice to meet you."

The arrival in our humble flat of Colonel Euan Rabagliatti MC.AFC., Head of the Secret Intelligence Service (MI-6), section Holland, could mean only one thing: the British, prodded by van 't Sant, had decided to take us seriously, and come to the conclusion that we had something valuable to offer. The Mews was in business.

Colonel Euan Rabagliatti MC.AFC

Chris made us all a cup of tea, and before we knew it we were discussing a timetable for the first secret landing on the coast of Occupied Holland to establish contact with the Dutch Underground. This revolved around the curfew which the Germans enforced rigorously, especially in coastal areas. Consequently we had to land before midnight or after four a.m. Since in addition we had to cross the North Sea in both directions, we needed long, dark nights. The moon calendar set the date: October 12, 1941.

One provision in my plan raised a lot of British eyebrows: the location of our landings. I had picked Scheveningen, not for sentimental reasons. To me, it was the key to success. We were sure to recognize it even on a dark night and knew every inch of the territory, an important practical and psychological advantage. Also, our old stamping grounds had become a leading R&R resort for the Wehrmacht, and we remembered from observation that the night life was pretty lively and by no means restricted to Germans. Even in winter revelers could be seen reeling along the boulevard, or sometimes catching a breath of fresh air on the beach. The zone of greatest danger to us lay between the surf and the first row of houses, so I planned to put Peter ashore in full evening dress, reeking of liquor. Then, if he were stopped on his way inland he could fall back on his considerable experience and pretend to be drunk, an innocent partygoer sobering up.

Specifically, I wanted to land at the little stone pier by the North Boulevard, where the previous summer I had dumped my final outboard motor into the sea. This also caused concern, because it was located smack opposite the Palace Hotel, which housed the headquarters of the enemy's Coastal Defense Forces for Northern Europe. To me, the advantages seemed obvious. Aerial reconnaissance had shown extensive mining of the Dutch coast, but even the Nazis might hesitate to booby trap their officers' own stretch of beach in front of the HQ. Furthermore, wasn't it the last place where the Wehrmacht, not known for its imagination, would expect Allied secret landings? "De l'audace, toujours de l'audace!" I quoted Frederic the Great, and won the day.

Five weeks to go, and we needed every minute of it. We worked for the British, yet in some mysterious way General van 't Sant remained at the core of the enterprise. From the living room of our apartment, where day after day we labored on the operational plans, we saw him pacing around his study, endlessly, back and forth, back and forth. Occasionally he would step out on the balcony, facing us a bare sixty feet away, sometimes in the company of Prince Bernhard who always gave us a big wave. On clear days he strolled with the Queen along the geometric paths in the walled garden, below our bedroom windows, down to the end and right and left and back and down again, always half a step behind her. Apart from them we saw nobody, except Rabagliatti, "the Rabbi" to us. It seemed as if we were involved in an important family venture, a Cosa Nostra, of which the General, discreetly in the background, was nevertheless the Godfather.

The Rabbi proved a tough taskmaster. At times we practiced nocturnal small-boat landings off England's south and west coasts. One moment we were thrashing about in the pitch-black sea off Cornwall, hanging on for dear life to a capsized dinghy in the fierce Atlantic surf. Another night, barely in time, we found Peter bobbing upside down like a float in the icy waters off Devon, because air had collected in the boots of his experimental watertight suit. We dined as guests of honor in the headquarters of Britain's Submarine Command at Portsmouth, where candlelight glowed on polished mahogany and the after-dinner port circulated clockwise in a crystal decanter. Then again we rolled on the floor of a secret pistol range under unsuspecting crowds at Baker Street Station, blasting away at cardboard Hitlers, who popped up maniacally from behind the concrete girders. We also studied code and other esoteric subjects, taught by a purple-nosed genius in a school with many exits, like a rabbit warren, where students using many languages moved like specters through unseen corridors.

After all our frustrations, operating in the Big League was a heady experience. When on one occasion, discussing air cover, I suggested that a flight of Spitfires would come in handy, Colonel Rabagliatti with a mere nod of the head agreed to provide them. All I had ever requested from the Dutch authorities was a steel cabinet to secure our secret papers in the Mews. After three months we gave up on it, and our confidential documents remained stashed in a hole behind the bathroom mirror.

Nobody followed Contact Holland with more interest than Queen Wilhelmina. As the weeks went by she sent for me several times to inquire about our progress and discuss conditions in the Netherlands. We began to get used to each other. This did not always prove to be a blessing, for when we got down to business Her Majesty could bore into a subject with unbelievable tenacity, particularly if she sensed weakness on my part. Before long, in sheer self-defense, I always told her the truth, good or bad, in straight language. It must have played havoc with prewar court traditions, but she never seemed to mind. On the contrary, I got the impression that she enjoyed our informal, democratic relationship and liked to experiment with the ways of common folks.

One day, direct from Baker Street Station, I found a message in the flat inviting me for afternoon tea. As always, she got up to greet me as I stepped into her room. She poured our cups in silence, something on her mind. I never took the lead in our conversations, as much from caution as courtesy. She looked at me speculatively, and just as I was preparing for some devastating question she pulled a pack of Woodbines out of a drawer, cheap cigarettes, terrible stuff. "Would you like to smoke?"

Everybody in Holland knew of the Queen's fierce dislike for cigarettes, which from time immemorial had been banned at her palaces. I must have looked surprised, but she held the smelly pack right under my nose, as if to say, "That was the past, I've done with it. I know how to behave like ordinary people and respect their rights, however deplorable their habits."

Touched, I accepted my role in the little ritual. I took the pack from her hand and offered her a cigarette first.

After a moment of confusion, she smiled. "No, thank you", she said primly, obviously pleased. "I don't smoke."

I brought her up-to-date on my score against the Hitlers under Baker Street Station, a favorite subject, and then we got serious. She was passionately in need of better contact with occupied Holland. Her instinct as Queen of a dynasty that had served the Dutch nation since its inception half a millennium ago, alerted her to the mood of the people and the stirrings of something new, a Renewal, brought to her by the Englandfarers, something tremendously exciting born from oppression and defiance. With the bearers of that spark she desired to plan the country's future, not with a tired old government about which she once remarked, bitterly, "When the chips are down, they all hide behind my skirts." For lack of alternative, she put her chips on Contact Holland.

As the date drew nearer, tension grew. Ever since the British had approved our plan and we faced the certainty of our risky venture, we had felt a hot urge to live it up. We weren't exactly scared, in fact we could hardly wait to get going, but our horizon had suddenly contracted to the moment of departure. There wasn't much time. The Rabbi seemed to consider this perfectly normal and improvised a generous extra allowance to finance our nightly escapades.

Around nine in the evening, duty permitting, we emerged from the Mews resplendent in our new uniforms, bathed, shaved, pressed and polished, with just one thing in mind: girls. Chris, wholly revitalized since his liberation from boot camp, made even a private's battle dress look elegant. Almost by instinct we made our way through the blind London night to our favorite haunts, excitement stirring in our loins long before we burst miraculously from darkness into the blast of light and noise and humanity at Oddenino's or the Gay Nineties or the Cracker Club, for cocktails and a first glance at the talent in town. Then off to Hattchett's, La Speranza or the Chinaman for dinner with whoever of our friends were around, on leave or waiting for orders, an ever-shifting group of Hollanders on the make. Finally off to a night club, the Suivi, the Embassy Club or the Coconut Grove, or one after the other - bodies pressed together on tiny dance floors, English, Canadians, Norwegians, Hollanders, Poles, Australians, arousing each other in a whirl of khaki and blue and color and music and laughter, everybody high on booze and war and sex and the tenuous miracle of life. Lastly, if all went right, the mating, sweet or wild, warm or casual... Why not? We felt we deserved it.

For Peter it wasn't enough. He was about to return to the Occupation and stay put, a secret agent behind enemy lines. The colonel had warned me to keep an eye on him. Every man (or woman) who volunteered to take the lonely plunge into hostile territory was a special case. He elected, in fact, to spend what would in all probability be the rest of his short life in solitary, unremitting terror, knowing that barring extraordinary luck his end would come after agonizing torture, violently, desolately and without the balm of public recognition.

Sustaining him was a superiority complex that strengthened his natural inability to believe in his own death, but he also possessed sublime courage and patriotism of the highest order, as well as a sense of private glory. Beyond the humdrum, fearful fate of the spy, beyond reality, he was attuned to vague, exaggerated visions bordering on fantasy. These kept him going. They also made him unfit to be measured by ordinary yardsticks, which - particularly in his own opinion - were too puny to be applied to individuals of his caliber.

More and more, as time grew shorter, Chris and I had to take Peter in our stride. He did as he pleased, slept whenever he felt like it, ate and especially drank whatever he could find, and spent every cent he could lay his hands on, by fair means or foul. He became more and more uncommunicative and it was impossible to guess what went on behind those dark eyes. Not that we ever asked; by his sullen secretiveness he indicated that it was all entirely too tremendous for discussion. We found ourselves humoring him, and even Rabagliatti treated him gently, as someone whose time was running out.

Four days before our scheduled departure I walked into his quarters with an early cup of tea, but he was gone. His bed had not been slept in. I barged into Chris' room, who sleepily tried to hide a sizable blonde. "What gives?"

"Peter has disappeared."

"Try the Coconut Grove." Chris sat up and lit a cigarette. "There's that hatcheck girl. He wants to marry her."

Other men had girlfriends, Peter only True Loves. We didn't hear from him for three days. Rabagliatti, whose men combed the West End but couldn't find him, suspected a collapse of morale, not uncommon under the circumstances. We knew better: somewhere in London flourished a Great Romance. Yet we did not worry, Peter would never let us down.

The night before our scheduled departure for Felixstowe, a naval base on England's east coast where we would board the MGB, I was confidently going over some last minute details. At four in the morning I saw Peter climb over the wall around the garage. He had lost his key and didn't want to disturb us.

"Well?" I asked, the moment he stepped into the room.

"Let's go!" he said, grinning from ear to ear. "What are we waiting for?"

We woke up Chris, who happened to be alone, while Peter sneaked into the cellar of no. 77 and came back with a bottle of Veuve Cliquot '29. We drank and toasted, laughed and slapped each other on the back. The Mews was ready.

But under the bravado something stirred, a distant memory. At first I could not place it. An oppressive dream that I had banned resolutely from my consciousness, forever, now seeped back into our friendly, free little house, frame by frame - the silent roads, the tense faces, the gray cars, the stone wall, the empty corridor, and in the back, all alone between the green doors: Jean Mesritz, arms above his head, fingers spread, a smile on his emaciated face.

* * *

On October 12, 1941, Peter, Chris and I were put on standby in London to await favorable weather for our action. On October 20, 25 and 30 we traveled to Felixstowe, a British naval base from where we were to cross over to Scheveningen. On each occasion we returned to London after two days because of deteriorating weather conditions. Meanwhile the new moon period expired, and no further operations could be contemplated until the next one. And that was that.

Only Peter's remarkable composure throughout this ordeal kept Chris and me from exploding. Every morning he braced himself for the fateful move, only to be let down. Yet he kept his sanity, so we had something to live up to. In Felixstowe this was not so difficult. The officers of the MGBs and MTBs (motor gun boats and motor torpedo boats) whose quarters we shared, mostly peacetime yachtsmen, were a lighthearted lot who cheerfully whisked around the North Sea in search of action. At night, when they weren't prowling around for "Jerries", they kept the nearby Felix Hotel jumping. But the Rabbi was afraid that our continued presence there would attract attention, and when Peter's pistol, an awesome cannon of German origin, clattered onto the dance floor during one of his torrid tangos, we had to concede the point.

So we returned to London, three times in a row. Nothing was more depressing than to step back into the Mews, where the signs of our high-spirited departure for Holland lay all around.

Every time, after a few days in London, the next start seemed a little more difficult.

At the beginning of the next dark period, on November 13, we pushed off again, this time to Great Yarmouth, north of Felixstowe. It was much of the same. The weather turned bad and the crossing had to be postponed. We went to bed disgusted. The following day we finally put out to sea for the first time.

The MGB 320, captained by Lt. Peter Loasby RN, a slight, gentle Englishman with a black beard, turned out to be a sleek little warship, not much bigger than a tug. Three Rolls-Royce - Packard engines drove her to a top speed of about fifty knots. The center motor, used singly, could push her along in complete silence at about eight knots. Behind the narrow bridge stood two multiple machine-gun towers, on the tiny front deck an Oerlikon 20 mm rapid fire all-purpose cannon. The entire cabin downstairs measured six feet by ten.

We rumbled smoothly across the little harbor, Chris, Peter and I proudly on deck, and I later reflected that this was the only sane part of our journey. The moment we stuck our nose outside we found ourselves in a hostile world, and by the time we got out of it I was convinced that the execution of our plan exceeded our powers. The bewildering violence of the sea on the fast, slender vessel, the murderous blows of the waves, the blind darkness, the gushing water everywhere, the numbing inescapable cold, the stuffy, bouncing, tumbling cabin where we blundered about, deathly ill, retching and shivering, trying to prepare for a delicate landing action - must we cope with all this, in addition to the threat of sea mines, enemy aircraft and gunboats?

And then get into a dinghy, jump into icy water and swim through the surf, cross a beach in the line of fire, possibly mined, outwit the Nazis, and finally go through all this once more in the opposite direction?

Impossible, even though these bloody British navy boys smiled through their beards and pretended everything was just dandy.

Five hours out, an estimated twenty miles from the Dutch coast, a wave cracked the inch-thick window of the chart room and the operation had to be abandoned. We got back to Great Yarmouth at six in the morning. "Awfully sorry, old boy," the captain remarked cheerfully, as I took my leave thanking God for creating solid earth. "Better luck next time."

We returned to London. Next time? I really couldn't see it. Yet, after a couple of genevers at Oddenino's and half a bottle of Bardolino in La Speranza, I already remembered the experience somewhat differently. We visited the Embassy Club and the Coconut Grove, and by the time we arrived at Le Suivi I was ready for the next trip. Four days later we were back on the 320, in relatively good spirits.

We tried two more times, but never got closer to the Dutch coast than thirty miles before something went wrong, either with the boat or the weather. Once again we returned to London, sorry we had ever started the whole damn business. On paper our plan looked fine, but obviously too much could go amiss. Seven times we had failed to make it, and we hadn't even come near the difficult part of the operation: the landing. Never had Holland seemed farther away than that night, as we sat in our usual corner of the Embassy Club, pouring whisky from our carefully marked bottle, waving to friends across the room, listening to the music of Harry Roy, cozy and at home in the warm, noisy cocoon of wartime London.

Yet the following midnight we lay at anchor off Scheveningen, in dark and deadly silence, a stone's throw from the promenade pier.

* * *

At eight in the morning Rabagliatti had called us out of bed with the news that the weather had unexpectedly improved; his deputy, captain Charles Seymour, was on his way to fetch us. We shrugged our shoulders and got our things together. We didn't even inform van 't Sant. In Great Yarmouth we drove directly to the harbor. When we boarded the 320 it struck me, in spite of everything, how much I had begun to feel at home there - the cheerful greetings, the bearded smiles, the sound of our footsteps on deck, the nautical smells, even the miserable little cabin where we had gradually learned to organize ourselves. Captain Loasby winked at me gingerly and I slapped him on the shoulder. Shortly after two we rumbled past the outer jetties.

The calm weather held, no cause to worry this time about seasickness, but I decided to play it safe and went below to dress for the landing. After taking off my clothes I covered myself with a thick layer of sheep's fat, cold and smelly. Then I struggled for ten minutes to force my sticky limbs into long woolen underwear. Over it all I put on battle dress. Now my stomach told me it was high time to hurry on deck, into the fresh air.

It was a still, dreamy afternoon, drained of color. The sea, a glassy mother-of-pearl, lost itself in the distance where, somewhere, it became sky. The 320 streaked along easily, leaning into a lazy swell now and then, due east into evening. A soft, peaceful world enveloped us in shades of gray, until suddenly, fifteen feet away, a mine rode the water surface, its horns protruding from the monstrous round body higher than our deck, jet black in the dusk.

When night had fallen it became unthinkable that we were not alone in its blind emptiness, but after several hours a light appeared over starboard. A fierce buzzer hummed through the MGB, calling the men to action stations. The eerie glow turned out to be a German buoy. Our captain had never been this close to the enemy coast and switched to the silent engine. At eight knots we stole towards Holland.

Peter, Chris and I decided to turn in. We still had an hour to go and fell asleep instantly. In my dream I played soccer for HVV and was just about to score, when Chris shook me awake.

"This is it," he whispered. "Scheveningen."

We went on deck. Lying stationary in the water, the ship flopped from side to side unpredictably. I positioned myself on the upper rung of the steps to the bridge, holding on to the hand rail, Chris and Peter in front of me huddled together against the cold. The outline of Scheveningen, rigorously blacked-out, loomed against the sky, unmistakable, darker even than the night.

Our distance from shore, difficult to estimate, could not have been more than a few hundred yards. Everybody whispered, and the sailors wore socks over their shoes.

Suddenly the 320 took an unexpected swerve and I was thrown against the ledge above the steps, where with typical British logic the button of the ship's siren was located. A wail built up which ripped the silence apart. We looked at each other, stunned, unable to grasp the meaning of the hellish racket that continued undiminished. Finally someone pulled me away from the ledge and the howl died down. It was the captain. He put a finger across his lips and said, amiably: "Shh."

Fifteen minutes later we boarded the dinghy, together with first officer lieutenant Bob Goodfellow, a thin, quiet, unflappable yachtsman who was to row us in. I had helped Peter into a brand new set of evening clothes, black tie as planned, once more going through his instructions to act drunk and confused if anyone stopped him on the beach. He flashed me a quick smile, as if to acknowledge that for this part of the operation he'd had plenty practice these last weeks. I adjusted his tie for him - even for this occasion the Leidener in me scornfully rejected the use of a clip-on bow - and surveyed the end result. In the dim little cabin Peter looked like a teenager all revved up for his first formal. He grinned at me, but his eyes sparkled feverishly. I quickly hoisted him into his watertight overalls.

Seconds after pushing off we lost sight of the 320. From the black mass ahead of us came not a sound, not a pin prick of light. And yet, surely, that hump there was the dome of the Kurhaus, and that long straight line the roof of the Palace Hotel, with those dark bumps on the left the summer houses where we used to have parties with out-of-town girls? No doubt about it, this had to be Scheveningen. But the nearer we came, the stranger the outlines behaved, and when we reached the edge of the surf the big seaside resort had vanished like a mirage. Nothing but ragged dunes rose up before us.

We turned around, bitterly disappointed, and headed out to sea again, black water sloshing off the oars. Where was that damned MGB? After ten minutes rowing we took a chance and waved Bob's flashlight around. A short stab of light cut through the dark, less than a hundred feet away. Many hands helped us aboard.

The time was eleven fifty, just before the curfew. Now we had the choice between going home or executing the landing after the curfew. The big difference was the moon: it would rise shortly and be well up in the sky, illuminating the scene of action. However, having come this far, nothing could be worse than returning to England with another failure. We agreed unanimously to take the risk. Of course, we first had to find Scheveningen.

Bob Goodfellow thought that we were too far south and decided to start out in a northerly direction. The captain kept the 320 close in, prowling along the coast on the silent engine.

After a few miles we saw two colored lights. We crept even closer inshore, I could clearly hear the surf. As we nosed in between the two pinpoints, they turned out to mark the entrance to a harbor. We stopped to take a good look.

"It's Scheveningen," Chris whispered. He had the sharpest eyes of us all. "The entrance to the fishing harbor."

"In that case, let's get the hell out of here," was my immediate contribution. I knew this place, we were lying smack in the channel between the jetties, and I vividly remembered the rows of E-boats, the German equivalent of MGBs, jamming the outer harbor all last year. Would skipper Van der Zwan have chugged home through here tonight? We heard a church bell chime, the first sign of Dutch life, and it brought a lump to my throat. Then slits of blacked-out headlights came towards us from the left, cars driving down the boulevard, and Chris said he could make out the sea wall. We pulled back and continued north just offshore, to make sure, and minutes later almost crashed into the promenade pier.

Well, now we knew. All we had to do was wait until four o'clock. The captain took his ship a few hundred yards out to sea in order to stand by. The men remained at action stations, dark, formless humps around the guns. When they smiled at us as we came by, their teeth always gleamed with a speck of light from somewhere. The three of us, in great spirits now, made ourselves comfortable below and slept until Bob woke us at three thirty.

Falling asleep was never a problem; nor was my sea sickness, which invariably disappeared in sight of the Dutch coast. When we came on deck, a bright half moon hung low above the horizon.

Once again we bundled Peter in his clumsy waterproof suit, boarded the dinghy and shoved off. I tied one end of a long line to my belt as a means of communicating with Chris, who would stay in the boat with Goodfellow outside the surf. From there, with his range of vision, he could cover us with his Sten gun.

Glancing back at the 320, I realized for the first time how miserably light the night had become. The MGB stood out against the pearly sea like a sketch in India ink and took forever to fade from sight, although Bob rowed strongly and steadily. With every stroke a green pool of phosphorescence whirled around the oar blades.

Taking a bearing on the promenade pier, we aimed at our planned landing place in front of the Palace Hotel. An offshore breeze kept the waves down and, with the temperature around freezing, I cherished a momentary illusion that we might make it all the way by boat. However, when we approached the surf we decided not to take any chances. Bob stopped the dinghy, Chris cocked his Sten gun, then Peter shook hands with both men while I slid into the sea to catch him coming over the side.

I could just stand on my toes. When the water streamed into my clothes I gasped for breath, but only for an instant. Peter landed smack on my head, pushing me under water, but the air in his suit kept him buoyant, like an inflatable giant panda.

Coming up for air and remembering Devon, I held him meticulously upright. All at once the surf caught us, and for a few minutes I had to struggle to pull him through. Then we waded ashore, hand in hand. Puddles of light clung to our legs and the communication line glowed like a green ribbon leading to the dinghy, which stood black against the sea, so sharply drawn that I could see the barrel of Chris' gun.

While we were still wading I pushed Peter in front of me and began to work the zippers on his overalls. Suddenly he stopped, holding me back with an outstretched arm. Someone or something was standing at the water's edge, barely visible against the land. Did it move? I drew my Mauser pistol, but Peter waved me on. It turned out to be a sign on a pole. From very close up we could read it: "Ladies Only". We had landed in the women's section of the Scheveningen Beach Club. It was November 23, 1941, 4:35 a.m. Dutch time.

A stuck zipper at this moment would have been the margin between success and failure, but modern technology did not let me down. In thirty seconds Peter stood before me in sartorial splendor, tuxedo and black tie, dry, immaculate. I doused him with brandy from a hip flask to strengthen the image - only Hennessey XO would do, at his special request. It was low tide, the wide beach looked endless. We walked across to the ramp of the boulevard, still hand in hand. Here we both took a swig from the brandy flask for luck and said goodbye. Actually, we didn't say anything, we sort of patted each other on the back, mumbling, and suddenly Peter turned and walked away toward the black buildings.

The night swallowed him.

I stood quite still for a moment, feeling very much alone. These were Peters' most dangerous moments. I cocked my gun and listened till my eardrums hurt. Every moment of quiet was a gift from God. I waited. Silence...

Then, like a revelation, I realized that nearby my parents lay asleep. And my sister, Ellen, with her new husband. And Paul, and dozens of Leideners. And Jean Mesritz and all those other poor bastards in the Orange Hotel, a few hundred yards away.

This deadly stretch of land that we were stealthily assaulting was not only enemy territory, it was Holland. The grim Palace Hotel like a lump of rock, the Kurhaus there, dark and dismal, this cold, deserted beach - yet it was Scheveningen. I heard a church clock chime the quarter hour, then the whistle of a train.

A dog barked, an unbelievably normal sound. Under this black crust something lived, and it wrenched my heart. Last year, from the tip of the little stone pier behind me, I had hurled a motor into the sea, despairing of deliverance. Now, returned from freedom, I stood like a ghost amongst everything I loved, invisible, reaching out in vain, cut off by the curse which Adolph Hitler had cast over Europe.

When all stayed quiet I finally tore myself away and rejoined the dinghy, which lay bobbing about peacefully just outside the surf. We rowed back to the 320 in complete silence, our thoughts with Peter. Once aboard, Chris and I turned in immediately, while the ship crept out of hearing range. As soon as the big engines cut in, we passed out and slept soundly hour after hour, until the sudden silence awoke us and the MGB, losing all forward movement, settled back heavily into its element. The morning mist lay in patches on the water, beyond which loomed Great Yarmouth rigid in the icy dawn. Slowly we approached a jetty that reached out into the sea, deserted. On the very tip stood a small, solitary figure, motionless, immaculate in British army uniform, rising straight and tough from the wisps of fog around his feet. Colonel Euan Rabagliatti MC, AFC, Head of the Secret Intelligence Service (MI-6), section Holland, was paying his respects to the boys of the Mews.

Chris Krediet

Peter Tazelaar, London 1942

Erik in Dutch uniform – 1941

The boys of the Mews

CHAPTER 9

Secret Landings and Exile Intrigues

The dark prince, whose presence bothered me so much in Finland, never got a grip on me in World War II. Even in moments of the greatest peril I felt I was his match, provided I never gave up. Our relationship, farcically out of balance at the time of my Finnish caper, grew into one of mutual respect, based on my demonstrated commitment to a worthwhile cause. Recognizing his superior power, I never had the arrogance of facing him alone but always counted on support from equally powerful allies, unknown and mysterious, who took over once they were convinced that I had reached my limit. Whatever their motivation, I responded with blind gratitude. Some nights, like January 18, 1942, they had to work overtime.

It was our sixth trip to the Dutch coast. Peter Tazelaar and I, with Chris' help, had made progress in consolidating the poles of Contact Holland on either side of the North Sea. We had also infiltrated two more agents behind enemy lines, both of them wireless operators, to handle our communications; one, called Johannes, by parachute somewhere behind the dunes, the other, known as Fat Willem, per MGB 320 on the beach of Scheveningen during the previous moon period.

Unfortunately, their secret transmitters, packed in shockproof, waterproof, unsinkable suitcases the size of weekend bags, had both been destroyed on landing, respectively by impact from the air and because our dinghy, putting Willem ashore, had capsized in the surf opposite the Palace Hotel. How this happened, I'm still not sure. The waves suddenly grabbed us, God knows why, and as the first breakers hurled us landwards I knew what was coming. Instantly Goodfellow and I jumped overboard and seized the boat fore and aft, in a desperate effort to keep it from capsizing. We could just stand, and struggling in the roaring foam it looked for a moment as if we might succeed. But then the nose went straight up, Bob was yanked out of the water and dangled in midair like a bearded catfish, Fat Willem tumbled from the bow with a pained expression on his face and landed smack on top of Chris, who squeaked under the weight. The entire craft overturned and all three disappeared in the waves. It looked like a staged farce, and in spite of the disaster I couldn't help laughing. The next moment I too went under, still laughing.

Coming up for air I only saw Goodfellow, still hanging on to the dinghy. A strong undertow pulled us northward, but when Chris and Willem reappeared we managed to drag the empty hull onto the beach. Everything else had been swept out to sea, leaving us hopelessly stranded within sight of the German headquarters, with a wet spy and a British officer in uniform sulking around a waterlogged vessel without oars. I managed to get the shivering agent across the beach onto the boulevard and, as it later turned out, safely into Holland. Then, reaching the waterline on my way back I stumbled in the dark over the two oars, in spite of the northerly current lying neatly side by side south of the dinghy. This minor miracle, to which I reacted with my usual unfocussed but profound appreciation, enabled us to get away through the surf and rejoin the MGB. But the wireless set was lost.

Direct communications were obviously essential, so I had instructed Willem to inform Peter that we planned a special crossing for the purpose of delivering two replacement transmitters. We would meet him during the next dark period at the usual place and time, the little stone pier by the North Boulevard after curfew, and signal the night of our arrival via Radio Orange, the Free Netherlands radio station in London to which every good Dutchman under the Occupation listened secretly. If our national anthem, which opened every evening's broadcast, was recited instead of sung as usual, we were on our way to Scheveningen.

On January 18 of the excruciatingly cold winter of '41-'42, Chris and I set out on our mission. But in Holland someone had talked. A notorious informer, George Ridderhof, intercepted the rumor in detail and reported it with remarkable accuracy to his Nazi boss, including the planned tip-off on Radio Orange. He in turn passed the information on to his colleague, Major H.J. Giskes, Head of Military Counterespionage in the Netherlands.

Giskes didn't take it too seriously but, as a proper German officer, took his precautions. He instructed Coastal Defense to place two heavy machine guns halfway down the promenade pier and start patrolling the North Boulevard. Then he ordered close monitoring of the Dutch radio from London. On the evening of January 18, in the arranged manner, Radio Orange dutifully informed friend and foe of our approach, and both prepared us a warm welcome.

From here on in, the night unfolded like a carefully scripted shadow play, in which sightless characters in mutual ignorance perform simple acts which in fact are totally interdependent and, when fitted together, establish an ingenious pattern. Being one of the blindest myself, I must credit my ghostly allies for masterminding this production which kept the dark prince at bay, under almost impossible circumstances.

Aboard the 320 Chris and I, like unsuspecting lambs,   rushed towards Scheveningen straight into the wolves' den. But on one point the diligent Dutch traitor had misinformed his boss: he insisted mistakenly that the landing would be executed between 11:00 p.m. and 1:00 a.m. Of this Giskes informed Coastal Defens, who manned the machine guns on the pier, accordingly and reluctantly, for a sharp northeaster cut across the beach and temperatures had dropped to minus 20 degrees Celsius. Nothing happened, because we were not scheduled to perform until 4:30 a.m., after the curfew, when we would meet Peter Tazelaar at the usual spot opposite the Palace Hotel. On the dot of 1:00 a.m. the shivering soldiers packed in, put the canvas covers on the guns and hurried back to their warm barracks. Just in time, because two hours later the intrepid new captain of the 320, Lt. Hall, determined to be in the right spot at the right time, scraped so close past the Promenade Restaurant at the end of the pier that we could see the icicles hanging from the gutters.

To Chris and me, blissfully unaware of all this, everything seemed to be rolling along fine. With an hour to spare the MGB anchored off the North Boulevard. Shortly afterwards Bob Goodfellow, unflappable and taciturn as always, took us aboard the dinghy, together with two new sets for the wireless operators, and pushed off. The surf was light, rustling the icy mush in the sea like cornflakes. I went overboard and swam to the tip of the little stone pier, just before Bob decided that it was safe to row in all the way. We unloaded the transmitters, Chris rejoined Bob and cocked his Sten gun, and I, covered with icicles and tinkling like a Christmas tree, walked down to the foot of the pier. We were in place, on time, ready and waiting for Tazelaar.

At just about this moment Peter was looking into the muzzles of two Luger pistols, aimed at his head.

* * *

When earlier that evening Radio Orange had alerted Peter Tazelaar, and just about everybody else, that we were on our way over to meet him, he had seriously considered staying home. Scheveningen was in turmoil. Rumors about covert landings, machine guns on the pier, increased patrol activity and such, came out of nowhere and whispered in the wind, creating a mood of nervousness and tension which spells mortal danger to the secret agent. Yet it was precisely this element which ultimately motivated him to venture out all the same.

Together with his sidekick, midshipman Gerard Dogger, he donned his tuxedo and black tie under a heavy overcoat, and sneaked out into the cold: Chris and Erik had to be warned. In the dark dance that Peter and I executed around each other that winter night, he tiptoed to disaster, right into the arms of a German patrol, a stone's throw from the spot where I stood waiting for him.

At 4:45 a.m., when he and Gerard were fifteen minutes overdue, Chris came up behind me. "What in God's name is the matter with Peter?" he whispered. His teeth were chattering audibly. "Where could he be?"

"Probably at the movies," I growled.

"Shall we beat it?"

"Not yet." It wouldn't solve anything, and establishing direct communication was of critical importance. "At the very least, let's leave the transmitters here for Johannes and Willem. Somehow we'll get a message to them, then they can pick them up later." A sudden vision of a telephone booth behind the Kurhaus, often used for making dates on warm summer days gone by, floated through my mind.

"How? Where?"

"Bury them in the sand. Some spot easy to identify."

"Bury them with what?"

I thought for a moment. The MGB lay no more than ten minutes' rowing behind us. "Listen. Go back to the 320 with Bob. Pick up a shovel, I know they've got one, somewhere downstairs in the closet with the sheep fat. Come back as quickly as you can."

He had already turned away when I added, "And bring me something else, a British Navy greatcoat and cap. Goodfellow's fit me." Apart from transmitters, my mind was on clarification.

I must know the reason why we had missed each other this night, or else it could happen again. Too long we had pirouetted around each other, we had to come to grips. I knew the name of Peter's local girlfriend, in his case an infallible connection. She should know a thing or two and could pass along some pertinent instructions.

Suddenly Chris was standing next to me again, with a steel shovel and his Sten gun. We each grabbed a transmitter, not much bigger than a fat briefcase but unexpectedly heavy, and crossed the beach to the northern tip of the boulevard, Krediet ahead with the gun, I a prudent ten paces behind in case of landmines. We picked a spot right against the wall, easily indicated over the radio or by phone. Chris positioned himself a few feet up the dunes, from where he could cover both the strand and the street. I took a firm grip on the shovel and drove it into the sand with all my might. You could have heard the clank all the way to the Kurhaus: the beach was frozen and hard as a rock.

After all the effort, the cold, the disappointment of Peter's absence, this was the last straw. I simply lost my temper.

I attacked the sand furiously, the steel shovel ringing through the icy silence, making a racket that even startled Goodfellow in his dinghy at the end of the little pier. Finally Chris rebelled.

"Quit it!" he hissed. "You're damned lucky the Jerries aren't on top of us."

Luckier than we knew. The Coastal Defense detail of four men and a corporal which was patrolling the North Boulevard that night, well within earshot, was right at this moment elsewhere marching Peter and Gerard into captivity behind the Palace Hotel. Harmoniously the dance pursued its intricate pattern. However, at last the precautions that had raised so many British eyebrows, paid off. The two immaculately dressed prisoners not only reeked of liquor, but once in the guardhouse they also produced a precious crock of genever, which they generously passed around. On such a miserable night the Germans found it hard to resist. The mood mellowed progressively, and when a Dutch policeman appeared who vowed for their innocence - being Gerard Dogger's boss in the Resistance - the German corporal saw no further reason to prevent these jolly revelers from rejoining their party. Peter, carried away by the dramatic potential of the situation, insisted on staying with his new pals, but the corporal was more interested in the gin. He dismissed them out of hand; protesting convincingly, Peter and Gerard vanished in the night, without the crock, a small price to pay for life and liberty. The German unit immediately resumed its patrol of the North Boulevard, which Chris and I had just vacated.

Glumly we carried the transmitters back to the dinghy, where Goodfellow greeted us with a rare smile. He held up a greatcoat and a Navy cap. "What, pray, are these for?"

My mind was made up. "I have to make a phone call in Scheveningen."

Despite the startled silence I did not find the plan all that crazy. I had to contact Peter, or at least speak to his girlfriend for some explanations. The phone booth behind the Kurhaus stood within easy walking distance, assuming it was still there. British naval uniform did bear a slight resemblance to its German counterpart, particularly in the dark, at least more so than my soaked, stiffly frozen Dutch togs, and it might save me from the firing squad in case of capture. Lastly, no Jerry would be on the lookout for a uniformed enemy officer in his own military base town - de l'audace!

Chris easily went along with the idea, as if he regretted not having thought of it first. Bob finally shrugged his shoulders. "Always knew the Dutch were balmy," he said, not without respect. "Just remember, I pull out of here at five forty-five. On the dot. With or without you. Captain's orders." That left me with forty minutes for my sortie.

As soon as I hit the boulevard I swallowed hard and switched from our usual stealth to the heavy stride of a German officer. It struck me as the most difficult moment of the whole action, a commitment, although the arrogance of the noise gave me confidence. I chose the inside pavement, remembering guardhouses along the outer sidewalk from our shipwreck with Fat Willem. The boulevard, deserted, stretched away into the dark. Now came the walk past the entire, endless length of the Coastal Defense Headquarters, with sentries on the roof, as one could tell from the flashes when they lit their cigarettes.

At the Kurhaus, in front of Serbán's bar, I turned left into the square, meeting my first German soldiers, four men and a corporal, on their way to the North Boulevard; had they passed me any closer, I would undoubtedly have gotten a whiff of Peter's genever. It was just light enough to notice each other's uniforms but not to recognize them. I began to feel good. I crossed the square diagonally, and here the town was awake. Dark figures in heavy overcoats hurried through the icy dawn; nobody paid the slightest attention to the British officer in their midst. A streetcar slowly approached screeching through a curve, line 9, Scheveningen - The Hague; I touched it with my fingertips. The cars were full of laborers, dozens of men huddled together, their faces leaden under the faint blue lights.

Everything around me seemed gray and sallow and sad, like a memory bled to death.

The phone booth stood exactly where I remembered it, a glass cubicle, dimly lit. Once inside, I pulled the door shut and found the directory for the number of Peter's girlfriend. But my cup that night was not full yet: I couldn't read the stupid small print, not even when holding the pages above my head against the blue lamp. What else could go wrong? Pondering my plight I gradually became aware of a figure across the street, on the sidewalk in front of my mother's favorite Indies' restaurant. He caught my attention because he was the only person standing still in the biting cold. Besides, he was looking at me. He had positioned himself on the very edge of the sidewalk, facing me squarely, motionless. Suddenly I felt screamingly visible in that cell, with nothing but glass around me and a light, however weak, smack above the telltale gold crown on my British hat. Well, there was nothing I could do about it, except hope that he would go away.

I decided to call Paul Erdman, of all people, mostly because I still remembered his telephone number. My old Leiden roommate would probably have a heart attack, but I trusted him.

He could look up the girls' number while I held the line, and then forget that he had ever heard from me. I fumbled in my pockets for some Dutch change, without which we never left England, lifted the receiver off the hook, dropped the coins into the slot and turned my back on the dark shape across the street, who faced me like a statue in the cold.

When I stepped out of the booth, the man was still there. No doubt about it, I was the object of his fascination. Had he recognized the uniform, or was he just puzzled, not sure of his case? Under the circumstances, it seemed best to brazen things out and call his bluff. I crossed the road boldly, straight at him, but he had a surprise for me. Before I had gone halfway, he switched on a powerful flashlight, right into my eyes. Only public authorities carried flashlights. In the next thirty seconds a bizarre scene unfolded, the climax of the shadow play.

I walked blindly into the light cone. He, in his own German-occupied town, saw a British officer come at him, gold stripes, crowned cap, unmistakable in the glare. Inside my coat pocket I held my pistol aimed at him, as he undoubtedly covered me. We waited for each other. Every step brought us closer together. I looked straight ahead, as if unaware of the blinding light in my eyes. By acknowledging it, the spell would have been broken. But he knew that I knew that he had recognized me, and this deadly knowledge existed between us two alone, in the whole world, binding us together in the silence and the darkness and the cold and the human misery of the war, until the idea of shooting each other dead became unthinkable to me, pure madness.

Only my steps sounded through the hush. The light cone, pulling me to him, shrank and sharpened until my sleeve brushed his uniform. I must have moved by him like a ghost, from the blinding glare into sudden darkness. The beam flipped around, I saw my shadow on the pavement ahead of me, and suddenly I smelled the dank threat wafting from the Black Cave, and me without a pebble in my mouth. Don't look back, I thought, keep going.

You've got to trust him; if you don't, you die. No shot, no word, no sound followed me. With every step my shadow lengthened, then the light went out. I marched off the square, down the street, along the boulevard, across the beach, up the pier and into the dinghy. I never looked back.

And what about my telephone conversations, with Erdman, with Peter's girlfriend? They fitted admirably in the general pattern of the night. Public telephones in the Netherlands had just been fitted to accept only new, zinc, larger coins. Mine were the old, tiny, silver ones. They tinkled prettily all the way down and out again.

* * *

"Take van 't Sant," Colonel Rabagliatti said. A spark of admiration glinted in his small, hard eyes. "Now when the general takes you out to lunch, he would really prefer to sit at separate tables, with his back turned to you, and talk through a tube under the carpet." The thought evidently tickled him, for he clapped his hands together with little wooden movements, looking like a pleased puppet with a dent in its head.

For the Rabbi this was a long and exceptionally candid statement, so we nodded our heads in appreciation. We were winding up lunch in the Ecu de France, in Jermyn Street, where he would occasionally invite Chris and me for a meal when he had something on his mind. Observing him thoughtfully, it struck me that, for someone to whom I entrusted my life several times each month, he had managed to remain a complete stranger. Of Rabagliatti as a person I only knew with certainty that he was a Scot of aristocratic background whose ancestor, a forerunner of Garibaldi, had been forced to flee Italy; that he handled his superb Jaguar like a racing driver; and that in the annals of human conflict he had earned his place as the first man to destroy an enemy in aerial combat: on August 26, 1914, the fragile flying machines side by side like a pair of dragonflies above the warm summer green, the pilots aiming hasty shots with rifle and pistol, dropping their guns to fly the planes, wobbling and tottering, until the German airman collapsed on the stick, mortally wounded, and screwed himself into the lush French soil below.

More than this we did not, nor really wanted to, know about him. His sinister anonymity, the dent in his head like a thumbprint of his violent past, the clever eyes, the total self-assurance that radiated from the dapper little figure, even the sudden charm of his smile, like an ambush - all contributed to our fond conviction that when the chips were down, Rabagliatti, like van 't Sant, would be tougher, meaner, dirtier and deadlier than his counterpart in the Gestapo.

"Straightforward?" he sneered. "In this business there is no such thing. Honesty and all that, splendid! But in this game, it kills people." He slowly swirled his brandy. "If you want your war to be straightforward you should sign up with one of those hairbrained services, where you lose your life to a dumb piece of metal that happens to be flying through the air."

He snorted. "Like the Marines."

Chris and I chuckled. The unthinkable had happened.

Exile politics had forced General van 't Sant out of Intelligence by implying a conflict of interests between his job as Head of the C.I.D. and his position with Queen Wilhelmina. For the general the Queen came first, and now the office for which he had been so eminently suitable had devolved upon a colonel of the Marines, a complete neophyte in the espionage business. The Rabbi predicted disaster; it wasn't long in coming.

From the moment the Marines entered the picture, they and the Mews were on a collision course. Colonel M.R. de Bruyne, a big, brawny regular soldier, obviously Indies, was idolized by his men; I might have been in their vanguard, had I been a Marine instead of a secret agent. He exuded the appeal of an honest man in a wicked world, and when we met face to face for the first time I knew instinctively, with very mixed emotions, that he didn't have a mean bone in his body. His innocence charmed me as a person and scared me to death professionally. Before me stood the perfect Marine: handsome, bold, and above all - dammit, man! - straightforward. In the world of secret intelligence, he was a bad joke.

The timing could not be worse. Ever since our ghostly night around the Palace Hotel, the Mews had prospered. Following the hard lessons of early winter, both we and the Navy had settled down. We abandoned Scheveningen as a landing site and switched to Katwijk, Noordwijk and a succession of alternate locations on the Dutch coast. During every new-moon period the 320 sailed from Great Yarmouth or Felixstowe, weather permitting, and generally put us on target with time to spare. Goodfellow handled the dinghy routinely and we went ashore like veterans, infiltrating a steadily rising number of agents and transmitters. Meanwhile Peter Tazelaar, whose arrest however short had jeopardized his career as a secret operator, once again eluded the Germans and was on his way back to London, now via Spain. The Mews had come of age and felt secure in the growing strength of Contact Holland.

It took Colonel De Bruyne and his Leathernecks less than a month to reverse the trend.

Mostly it was a matter of security. The first time Chris and I reported for duty at the new C.I.D. headquarters at 4 North Row, we almost had a fit. The outer office area was open to visitors and full of military personnel, with secretaries buzzing in and out, and there on the wall before us, in lonely splendor for all to admire, hung three charts showing lots of sea and a tiny chip of land, the three sites on which we were operating: Katwijk, Noordwijk and a new, experimental site in Zeeland. There and then we began to look nervously over our shoulders, a habit that never left us during our dealings with the Marines.

Next our most promising agent, baron Louis d'Aulnis de Bourouill, quit. Three times a week we labored together in a bare little room in Hans Place, under the guidance of our old friend the purple-nosed genius, to master an exceptionally complicated letter code. In the next moon period we were scheduled to land him at Noordwijk, but one evening he unexpectedly dropped by in the Mews. "I'm pulling out," he announced flatly."I'm not going with you chaps."

I poured him a Scotch and waited. You had to give Louis time and room to elaborate.

"Absolutely delightful, these Marines," he went on, after a long and appreciative swallow. "Marvelous chaps. And the coffee they serve at the

C.I.D., the real stuff. Delicious. And then, all you have to do is listen. They'll tell you everything that's going on in Holland. With names. First names, middle names and last names. And cover names."

He roared with laughter, jumped up from his chair and paced round the room, gesticulating. "Yesterday they gave me a marvelous reception. 'Good heavens, Louis, you still here? We heard you had gone back to Holland. But you're leaving shortly, aren't you? By boat, isn't that right? Well, old boy, have a good trip. Say hello to the old place for us. While you're still alive.'"

He gulped down the rest of his whisky and poured himself another. Then he flopped back in his chair, suddenly subdued, barely hiding his bitterness. "Ah, the romance of it all! No wonder it goes

Pierre Louis baron
d'Aulnis de Bourouill

to their heads. Imagine being a Marine - a Marine mind you - and all of a sudden you're plunged into all this delicious, secret stuff. How can you possibly keep your mouth shut? Well, the point is, they can't. So count me out. I wish you chaps luck, but I'd rather stay alive."

A few days later the North Row office handed over a complete list of our agents in enemy territory, names and cover names, to an employee of Stratton House. A diplomatic telegram had arrived from Switzerland concerning an execution in the Netherlands. The Department of Foreign Affairs had difficulty in deciphering the name of the victim, so they turned to the C.I.D.

"Could it possibly be one of your fellows?"

"Here's our list, why don't you take a peek yourself?"

When I learned about it, I stormed into De Bruyne's room to protest this murderous idiocy. He was frankly puzzled by my fury. "But lieutenant, they are good people, there in Foreign Affairs. Fine people. Good Hollanders. We should trust them." I felt like throwing up. On behalf of every agent in the occupied Netherlands I yearned for the muddy, distrustful safety of Rabagliatti and van 't Sant.

It was only a matter of time. The final confrontation came when the new Head of the C.I.D. solved a difference of opinion between us with the words: "That's an order."

A what?! He did not say it in anger or irritation, or even with emphasis. To De Bruyne it seemed the most elementary thing in the world. He was a colonel, I a second lieutenant; he gave me an order, that's all. The thought that I might not obey him undoubtedly never entered his mind.

I, from my side, hardly believed my ears. I had never received an order before, nor given one. Orders might be fine in the Marines, but in my opinion a secret service, staffed by the type of individuals who make good agents, operated on intelligent relationships based on mutual confidence, not on dumb discipline.

The game was the thing, there were no rules.

The point at issue was whether to put our agents in direct contact with the established Resistance organizations. The Marine colonel wanted quick results, but my experience under the Occupation had shown these bodies to be too large to avoid Gestapo infiltration; they posed unacceptable risks for our people. Right or wrong, this was my conviction, and only sound arguments - of which De Bruyne failed to produce a single one - could have budged me from it.

Van 't Sant and Rabagliatti might be ruthless secret service types, yet they had taught me to regard the trust of an agent behind enemy lines as a sacred responsibility. The men I had landed in enemy territory counted on me to protect them to the best of my ability. I knew the Occupation, De Bruyne did not.

As far as I was concerned, he could go fly a kite. I shrugged my shoulders and walked out the door, without even saluting. I never returned - except for my court-martial.

The very next day I was recommended for the Military Williams Order, Holland's Medal of Honor, and the knighthood which accompanies it.

* * *

Sustained research into Dutch history has failed to produce any other case of a soldier being simultaneously recommended for the Military Williams Order and for a court-martial. In London in World War II the combination was a natural. The court-martial originated in 4 North Row,

Navy headquarters of the Government and office of Colonel De Bruyne, while the MWO and knighthood had their roots in Chester Square, bastion of Queen Wilhelmina and seat of General van 't Sant. Behind both recommendations I recognized the moves and counter moves in a barren game of power. The struggle for control of Contact Holland had erupted at the highest levels. The Mews, caught in the middle, was paying the price of its success.

Above all else, unassailable, stood the Queen of the Netherlands. Every report from occupied Holland confirmed that the people, in their extremity, had turned to her, and her alone.

On the other hand, the cabinet ministers who made up the government, deprived of parliamentary support, had nothing to fall back on but their force of character, if any, and even the best of them was no match for the formidable Queen. As a result, Wilhelmina in London had more actual power than she could ever wield under normal circumstances.

From her side, the Queen's consciousness was entirely focused on her subjected nation in the Netherlands. Being an emotional woman, she let herself stray beyond the bounds of fairness in this respect, often barely bothering to hide her contempt for those who had missed the Occupation, as she would later be suspicious of anyone who had failed to get arrested by the Gestapo. The simplest escapee from Zwammerdam commanded more of her attention than the highest functionary of the government-in-exile. Anyone with news from Holland had her ear; anyone who based his position on information from occupied territory gained her support. As the war progressed, such intelligence became more readily available, but in the summer of 1942 Contact Holland was by far the most promising source of this politically powerful commodity.

All Europe lay under German rule and London became home base for many exiled governments. Intrigues flourished like toadstools in its hothouse atmosphere. One of these had cost François van 't Sant the job he loved, but Contact Holland and the Mews were his creations, behind which he stood with all the power and influence he could command. And behind him, solid as a rock, stood the formidable Wilhelmina.

Her Majesty the Queen took three steps forward, raised her right hand until she was bending over backwards and gave Bob Goodfellow a resounding smack on the left shoulder. Bob, even paler than usual behind his black beard, looked surprised. He was obviously unfamiliar with the ceremony, and while the Queen walked back to the piano where the next citation lay ready for her inspection, he whispered to me out of the corner of his mouth, "Bloody party's getting rough, is it?" - Robert Goodfellow, receiving the royal accolade, had thereby become the first British Knight of the Military Williams Order since the Duke of Wellington after the Battle of Waterloo.

We were standing stiffly at attention, Bob, Chris and I, between the couch and General van 't Sant's desk at 77 Chester Square. Late, wet light filtered through the lime tree outside, touched the leaf pattern of the curtains and filled the familiar room with a soft, green radiance like an aquarium. On the Steinway the documents had apparently gotten mixed up and the Queen, amiably assisted by her son-in-law Prince Bernhard, busily sorted them out.

Near the window the guests stood watching silently. Considering the circumstances, they made a curious group. The Netherlands Ministers of War and of the Navy were present. I had not seen the former since he had me thrown out of his office in Stratton House; the latter was Colonel De Bruyne's direct boss. I could well imagine van 't Sant's devil-ish delight in commanding their presence at this ceremony, in the name of Queen Wilhelmina. Between them stood Colonel Rabagliatti, savoring every minute.

The General himself, as always, hovered in the background, with an expression of such saintly innocence on his face that I almost burst out laughing.

Awarding high decorations for acts of courage in war is an unfair business, at best. For every man who wears the rare MWO or Victoria Cross or Medal of Honor, there are ten who, with a little luck, could have received the distinction with equal justification. Merely sticking out your neck won't do it. You also have to be noticed by somebody, ideally a general, who for reasons of his own decides to recommend you for the honor. Among the score or so of MWO's awarded in World War II ours didn't cut a bad figure, but as I watched van't Sant's sanctimonious expression I could just imagine the delight he must have felt in ramming this one down De Bruyne's throat.

Wilhelmina, documents in hand, stepped forward for the next pre-sentation. She positioned herself opposite me, waited for complete si-lence and, with the curious stridency that crept into her voice on official occasions, read out my citation. Then she advanced three paces, which brought us closely face to face, and suddenly the ceremony consisted solely of the two of us. She was about to grant me the decoration that, more than anything in the world, she craved herself. She looked into my eyes with the utmost gravity, and I became aware of her as a duality, both real and symbolic, a Queen, far removed from the petty intrigues represented in this room, performing the historic rites to invest me with the greatest honor of which she was capable. My knees began to tremble. The accolade fell and in that same moment her expression relaxed to a smile, so unexpected, so sweet, so human that tears sprang to my eyes.

After Chris's turn the guests came forward to congratulate us, Prince Bernhard in the lead. "Now every man in the Dutch armed forces has to salute you first," he said. He grinned from ear to ear, digging van 't Sant in the ribs. "Even generals." "Even colonels of the Marines," van 't Sant responded icily, in his gentle voice.

* * *

After this honor, Colonel De Bruyne had no choice but to terminate the court-martial proceedings, which had entered the preliminary hearing stage. But he fired us anyway. We paid no attention; as long as we had van 't Sant and Rabagliatti behind us, we could operate, with or without the CID. Security did not improve, of course, with enemies both in front and behind us, as the German Kriegsmarine enthusiastically demonstrated by their presence in force at the next landing operation. Our fifteenth, on May 11, 1942, turned out to be one to remember.

We set out routinely for the Dutch coast, where we were to land at Noordwijk this night and pick up a passenger for England. In spite of calm seas and lovely spring weather, Chris and I hung around the cabin of the 320, where we had lived through so much in the last year, and worried about the Marines and the unpredictable dangers the chaotic situation in London presented. The Germans we could handle, but we felt threatened in the back. We sat and dozed and tried to hide our mis-givings, until the roar of the engines changed abruptly to the hum of the silent motor.

"I only wished that De Bruyne hadn't stuck that map of Noordwijk on his wall," Chris sighed, getting up. An hour later the dinghy was head-ing straight for that little chip of land so blatantly displayed on the wall of 4 North Row. We were sitting as usual, Goodfellow at the oars, Chris and I side by side on the rear seat. The night was dark, the sea smooth, all seemed quiet and peaceful. The hotel Huis ter Duin, scene of so many Leiden parties in the distant past, loomed in front of us, blacker even than the sky... Plop! I heard the sound of a champagne cork, saw a little rocket shooting up into the air and poof! there lay the Huis ter Duin before me bright as day, steps, terrace, restaurant, windows, balconies, flagpole. The boulevard, the beach, the surf, the 320, the dinghy, we ourselves, everything bathed in the flat white glare of a parachute flare. At the same time tracer shells began to flash by overhead, red and white, in low trajectories between the hotel and the MGB.

Motionless we stared each other in the face, dumbfounded.Bob leaned casually on the oars, as if we were boating in the sun on Serpentine lake in Hyde Park. Chris' expression hovered between shock and amusement, and I was suddenly struck by the incongruity of seeing him sit there with his pleasant face and apple cheeks,C. Krediet Esq. of Sumatra, Wassenaar, Leiden and more recently the Embassy Club, London W1, sitting in a dory by flare-light under tracer bullets before Huis ter Duin in Noordwijk.

All at once Bob came to life, turned the dinghy around and started pulling out to sea with grim determination. A second, then a third flare exploded into dead-white light. Two other MGBs, which had accompanied the 320 to gain experience, opened fire close behind us. Colorful tracers crisscrossed over our heads like monstrous party streamers, machine guns and cannon chattered and barked. One burst would have blown us out of the water, but apparently nobody saw us. In the middle of the ruckus we bobbed about forlornly, as if it were all none of our business.

Suddenly a ship cut past from an unexpected quarter, white foam hissing around its razor-sharp bow. It turned away, then came straight at us. Men crouched on the fore deck and along the sides; I was about to jump into the water when it occurred to me that they might be ours. They pulled us aboard without stopping, abandoning the dinghy. Then, rearing up under its full power, the 320 roared out to sea.

In a short time we had left the glow behind; flares wobbled to earth and abruptly it was dark. Just as I began to breathe normally again, a dozen specks of light pricked through the night in a wide circle all around, followed by two stupendous searchlights between us and the open sea. Our engines stopped and we lay dead in the water. I pushed myself into the wheelhouse.

"German E-boats," Bob explained. "They all flick on a light at the same time and keep an eye on each other. If a light disappears, it means that we've come in between. Then they know more or less where we are, and everybody and his grandmother comes plunging down on us. So we've stopped." He sounded like a tour guide, counting aloud the E-boats. "...seven, eight, nine. Those bloody great searchlights are destroyers, two of them."

One of the blue-white beams came slowly sweeping across the water, hesitated, groped back, halted, then moved on again. As it crept inexorably towards us, the 320 started to maneuver on its silent engine, very carefully, until it presented the destroyer its narrowest profile, the bow. When the beam touched us, we found ourselves in bright daylight for the second time that night. It was so powerful that I could read the spidery scribblings in the log book on the chart table. At this distance we had felt fairly secure, but the glare seemed to pull us close to the enemy, and we cowered in the wheelhouse as if a twitch of an eyelid would give us away. How could they fail to see us?

At last the beam slid by, but the grim game continued. The sea would seem deserted except for the searchlights while the E-boats changed position in darkness, then all at once a circle of white pin pricks popped up around us, a noose tightening little by little around our necks. During the dark periods we motored westward as fast as the engine could push us; when the lights flicked on we stopped dead instantly, wallowing in the swell, hoping we weren't blocking some fatal line of vision. When moving we nipped through the searchlights time and again, but twice more one grabbed us while we lay motionless in the noose of E-boats, pawing and feeling for the 320 until, incredibly, the beam passed on. How were we ever to slip through before daybreak? Already it was possible to tell where the sky began, just barely gray against the black sea. An hour at the most, and that would be the end. How would it come..?

I did not stick around to find out how. I went below into my bunk. Sometimes in life we're forced to place our fate in more powerful hands, which to me comes easier asleep than awake.

Once again, they did not let me down.

CHAPTER 10

The Wild Blue Yonder

I want to state unequivocally that in the winter of 1941-1942 I had the time of my life. There were moments, of course, when I was frightened, cold, exhausted, frustrated or seasick, but these did not affect my overall mood of exhilaration and joie de vivre.

Occasionally I felt that I would burst from sheer happiness.

Did I feel guilty about this? Not at all! True, there was immense misery in the world around me, but isn't that always the case? Not the matter of degree makes the difference, but whether we do something about it. In peacetime, unless it hits home or next door, we look the other way, or at best give money (tax-deductible). Admittedly it took the invasion of my own country to get me into the war, but now I was involved to the maximum extent possible, time and again, in a battle against the root cause of all the new suffering of mankind: Adolf Hitler and the Nazis.

To risk one's life for the common good creates self- respect, an essential element of contentment. Whenever in the course of that winter I stepped out of the Mews for a day in the country or a night on the town or simply a walk with a friend under the barrage balloons in Hyde Park, it was the previous crossing to occupied Holland that made it right and enjoyable. So did the thought that the agent whom I had ferried across was now busy undermining the power of the bastards who kept Europe, including the Netherlands, under the heels of their well-polished boots.

With Contact Holland as the source of our inner peace, we lived life to the maximum of our youthful capacity. For us, if there had to be war, it had come at the right moment. We were old enough to fight, but not yet burdened with commitment towards family and career. If we survived, our war experience, rather than an interruption, would be an extension of our education and forming of character. Moreover, we were of an age which looks for dragons to slay, and in Hitler fate had certainly provided us with a prime specimen.

Focused as we were, the stupendous developments of World War II barely penetrated the narrow parameters of our own area of consciousness: London, Holland and the North Sea. In December 1941 the Wehrmacht was fighting in Moscow's suburbs, within sight of the Kremlin, unbeknownst to us. Japan struck Pearl Harbor, bringing America into the war; we hardly noticed, because just about then we were tumbling around in the surf off Scheveningen, trying to land Fat Willem. A few months later, the banners of the Rising Sun were unfurled over the Dutch East Indies, wiping my father's proud "emerald girdle" off the map, with Java surrendering on March 9, 1942. I didn't hear about it for days, but it left a strange void inside me; somewhere far away a taproot to old, deep wellsprings had been severed. Yet, at all times in London, while crossing a blacked-out street or necking in a park, we kept our eye on the waning moon, judging the brightness of its reflection on the beach below the Palace Hotel.

When the first signs of internal trouble had appeared, they barely scratched the surface of our confidence. Unfamiliar with the bureaucratic mind, Chris and I could not conceive of the possibility that the vital role of Contact Holland would be affected by quarrels concerning competence and procedure. Immediately after General van 't Sant's resignation as Head of the CID, his successor, Marine Colonel De Bruyne, had ordered us out of the Chester Square sphere, with instructions to find an apartment close to his office near Marble Arch. Suddenly it was all a matter of rank, a colonel, a second lieutenant and a private. There was nothing we could do about it, so we said goodbye to our beloved Mews and peevishly rented the most expensive flat we could find, 23 Hyde Park Place, the prewar pied-à-terre of Douglas Fairbanks and Mary Pickford. We installed ourselves in these august surroundings and viewed the future with misgivings.

For a while nothing much had changed. We executed our operations under the guidance of Colonel Rabagliatti, who faithfully provided the CID with copies of our agents' reports. Life resumed its routine, except for the preposterous luxury of our new quarters.

The first visitor to enter our stately salon was Ernst de Jonge, who five years previously, as President of the Leiden Student Corps, had exploded a soup tureen on my bald head. Colonel Rabagliatti had requested us to take in some new agent, code name Ernst, so that we could get used to each other prior to landing him in Holland. Chris and I weren't too keen on the idea; the average spy about to disappear behind enemy lines is usually not the ideal house guest. However, operationally it had its use, and besides, you can't very well shove a poor soul like that into some hotel for his last week.

Poor soul? Ernst strode into our apartment as if he had rented the joint for the social season. In his gray pinstripe suit straight out of Bond Street, the onetime Student next to God halted a moment in the doorway and looked at me with his dark, intense eyes. To him, also, our meeting was a stunning surprise. "What the hell are you doing here?" we both said simultaneously, before we realized that the byways of fate had led us from Leiden and Minerva to this absurd flat in Mayfair, in order to have a go at Jerry together.

On the first night of Initiation, Ernst had entered the dining room of Minerva like a potentate; the intervening years had not dampened his self-confidence. He didn't exactly underestimate the Germans, "but you know, old boy, they really, totally lack any semblance of style." That he would make it to England was a foregone conclusion, as was his choice of the riskiest job in the Allied forces: secret agent. There and then I knew that he could play a key role in our organization.

His confidence did not prevent him from preparing himself with grim thoroughness, but he could play as hard as he worked. The evening prior to our departure for occupied territory we celebrated in Le Prunier, a renowned French restaurant in Lower Regent Street, where we astounded waiters and patrons alike by devouring the Menu Gourmand from beginning to end - twice.

With the cigars Ernst ordered a bottle of Armagnac, which I immediately recognized as the same brand that we had demolished together in my room five years earlier, to toast our friendship after the bloodbath of the tureen. He raised his glass and we drank in silence. Never had the future of Contact Holland looked more promising. In the night of February 22, at 4:30 in the morning, we safely landed him on the beach at Katwijk as successor to Peter Tazelaar.

* * *

Shortly after Ernst's departure, Peter had returned to London. With a bang, literally. In the middle of the night a shot thundered through our apartment. I dived out of my huge, round bed on the raised sleeping platform, stumbled in the dark across my palatial bedroom into the blacked-out corridor and switched on the light. I listened - dead silence. A sick feeling swept over me; Tazelaar, just escaped from Holland for the second time, was staying with us at 23 Hyde Park Place, and the noise had come from his room.

With my heart in my throat I pushed the door open. Light flooded in from the hallway and there he stood, in the middle of the sumptuous room, an enormous, blue steel Browning in his hand. A wisp of smoke curled from the muzzle, just like in the movies. When I flicked on the chandeliers I saw that the mirror, which covered one entire wall, was pierced by a neat, round hole at about stomach level.

"Oh boy!" he said. His tongue seemed to give him trouble.

"Awfully sorry and all that. I came in here, couldn't find the bloody switch, and the next thing I see is this creep coming at me." He pointed the gun at his own reflection. "So...boom! You can't be too careful these days." He grinned happily, teeth flashing in the dark, handsome face. "Do you think De Bruyne will pick up the tab?"

He hadn't changed a bit. After his arrest with Gerard Dogger on the boulevard in Scheveningen, in the early hours of January 19, Peter had called it quits. During those long minutes of captivity his mind's eye had looked down the barrels of the firing squad. He also concluded - rightly so, according to Rabagliatti - that considering the circumstances, he had outlived his usefulness along the coast of Holland. He decided to escape once again and made it back via Belgium, occupied France, Switzerland, unoccupied France, Spain and Portugal. Whatever hell he raised in London, he had a right to it.

For a few days everything had seemed like old times. The Mews - the name stuck - was complete again and strolled along Park Lane, pressed and polished, descended noisily on La Speranza and the Chinaman, swiped girls from British officers in the Embassy Club and le Suivi. We were joined by other new arrivals from the Netherlands because, as Peter's trip had shown, the overland escape routes across Europe had begun to function. Queen Wilhelmina came up with the idea of a club for "her" Englandfarers, now steadily growing in numbers. The ground floor of 23 Hyde Park Place, in our view an eminent location, became available, so we had rented it on her behalf and called it "Orangehaven", a name she picked. It provided a living room to all those homeless Dutchmen who came to London on leave, staying in rundown hotels on the top floors at a twenty percent discount thanks to the Luftwaffe, whose occasional bombs added spice to Mayfair's night life.

But the Marines were on the march and I overestimated the protection General van 't Sant could still provide to us. He had successfully stymied De Bruyne's clumsy attempt to court-martial me, but our dismissal from the CID stood. After all, the colonel was our commanding officer and had the right to fire the Mews, whatever the cost to our country. However, the old fox van 't Sant, still stewing about his forced exit from the CID, had the last laugh.

Our operation at Noordwijk on May 11, 1942, to bring out a passenger, had been planned weeks in advance. It promised to be of great strategic importance, but in the wake of our dismissal De Bruyne had canceled it. We paid no attention and set out for Holland on the 320, as usual, backed by the British and Colonel Rabagliatti. As described, we almost did not make it back, and later learned that we owed our lives to one of the accompanying MGB's which had blocked a fatal line of vision. While the Germans pounced on him, the 320 had slipped through the noose. When, much to the chagrin of the Marines, we returned safe and sound to London, all hell broke loose. A military action executed by an officer under his command after being fired and all but court-martialed, placed Colonel De Bruyne in an untenable position. He had no choice but to resign regretfully as Head of the Central Intelligence Service (CID), much to his predecessor's delight.

It turned out to be a Pyrrhic victory. De Bruyne's departure from the CID created a war of succession of such intensity, that the Dutch government suspended all intelligence activities. Candidates buzzed like flies around the exotic emanations of the secret service, studies were ordered and reports written, behind every door hid an expert, sudden stars shot up like meteors and plunged back down below the horizon, documents disappeared and popped back up in compromising places, Dutch officialdom plotted, conspired, insinuated, denounced and accused, and in this pea soup of exile intrigue the Mews gradually disintegrated.

Midshipman Tazelaar was the first to fall. Officially he reported directly to 4 North Row, Headquarters of the Dutch Navy and the Marines, who made short shrift of him. Before we knew it, he had disappeared tracelessly from London and, in fact, from the United Kingdom.

Chris, never one for half measures, went out in style.

In June, 1942, President Franklin D. Roosevelt invited Queen Wilhelmina to America for an official visit, including an address to the joint Houses of Congress. As a symbolic gesture she wanted to be accompanied by an Englandfarer and chose, on the advice of her private secretary, Chris Krediet. Fittingly bizarre, it was the crowning moment of his military career. To arrive in Washington D.C. with a buck private as her aide-de-camp might have shocked the U.S. hosts, so he was quickly commissioned and promoted to second lieutenant, to the chagrin of the brass who had just fired him.

In Washington, where the Queen appeared on the front page of TIME magazine, a photograph was published on which Chris, surrounded by American congressmen, was clearly visible behind Her Majesty. Someone, at the peril of his life, smuggled it into Dachau concentration camp, where Chris' father had been taken after his arrest in Wassenaar for having assisted Contact Holland through Peter Tazelaar. According to a fellow inmate it provided a moment of great emotion and pride to a brave Hollander, who did not survive the horrors of the camp.

And I myself? Whoever is dropped by a secret organization, instantly finds himself surrounded by a wall of silence. He becomes an outcast, his former world vanishes, his erstwhile colleagues avoid him or disappear. With nothing to do, I hung around London in endless boredom. I knew that our agents in occupied territory would continue to work with MI-6 and the British, but I was excluded. Landings on the beach had clearly become impossible since the disaster at Noordwijk; the Germans were on to us, not surprising considering the lack of security at 4 North Row. But surely there were other ways, by land, by air, via Sweden, Switzerland? My proposals to our government in this respect weren't even answered.

"Tell me honestly," Colonel Rabagliatti said when we parted. "Are you Dutchmen really interested in this war with Germany?" For a moment his warm smile broke through, but his bitter question hit home. We shook hands, and as abruptly as he had surfaced into our lives a year ago, he faded back into the murky world that had spawned him. Gradually the truth dawned on me: I was wasting my time.

Contact Holland had slipped out of my life, for good, and unless I wanted to become part of the mess in London, I'd better find a new mission. I had escaped the Occupation for one reason only, to fight the Nazis as a free man. If this was made impossible for me in Dutch uniform, then any other would do. Didn't I always want to be a pilot in the RAF?

Chris Krediet returned from the USA, dressed in a brand-new lieutenant's uniform of superior quality. "Just in time," I greeted him, as he
stepped into Orangehaven. "How about flying in the RAF with me?"

"Out of the question," he answered indignantly. "I just bought this
very expensive monkey suit on Madison Avenue in New York."

"We'll sell it in Stratton House, London. You should be wearing
blue, anyway, with your red cheeks."

He never hesitated; Chris had seen the end coming well before I did.
That same afternoon we took a bus to the British Air Ministry, and from
there to its Dutch equivalent in Arlington House. The prospect of getting rid of us drove our countrymen to paroxisms of efficiency. Within
hours we were registered for transfer to the Netherlands Air Force, on
detachment to the Royal Air Force as flight crew trainees. We concluded
the preparations for our new career at Jones, Chalk & Dawson, Tailors,
in Sackville Street, a match for Madison Avenue any day.

We still had one melancholy duty to perform. On a fine July morning we put on our Dutch uniforms for the last time and walked through
Green Park to St. James' Street. The Rabbi wasn't in his office, but we
handed his deputy, Charles Seymour, a message, with the request to trans-
mit it to any agent in the Netherlands. Of course he was totally noncom-
mittal, but I knew he would do it, and he did. It twittered, heavily coded,
into an operator's earphones in occupied Holland during a few perilous
moments of contact: "Mews bust good luck goodbye."

Contact Holland survived the Mews. Ernst de Jonge, in cooperation
with two other Leideners, laid the groundwork for an espionage network
which functioned throughout the war. Its contributions to Allied intelligence gained public recognition from Winston Churchill. Ernst himself
was arrested by the Gestapo in Rotterdam at the height of his success,
and disappeared. Others took over and continued to build on his foundations. Many of them were caught and executed. Their successors carried on and expanded the operation. They also suffered severe casualties.
Others always took their place, until of the original Contact Holland not
a trace remained under the generations of agents and Resistance fighters
who gave their lives for the link between occupied Holland and England
in World War II.

* * *

Prince Bernhard banked the little plane on its ear, pointed to a meadow somewhere in the English countryside below, and shouted through the speaking tube, "OK now, just put her down... there."

Never having flown before, I grabbed the stick with desperate determination. The field, surrounded by a fence, looked about as big as a postage stamp. The De Havilland 82 "Tiger Moth" began to buck towards the earth, wobbling and slipping like a drunken camel. The Prince, whose head was sticking out of the open cockpit in front of me, looked around unconcernedly, as if nothing were wrong. Only when all seemed lost he would give the stick a shove, or pull us back on an even keel.

At the very end of our sickening descent we had to pass between a tree and a haystack, a very tight fit. Frozen with terror, I forgot about the fence. This time my tutor reacted too late. The wheels hit the ground hard, the nose went up, we sailed over the barbed wire, Bernhard closed the throttle and kept the wings level, and the aircraft sank to earth like a pudding. The bang vibrated in my molars, but there we were, right side up in the middle of the meadow.

We clambered out and lined up side by side for a leak against the haystack. "A Hollands boy," the Prince quoted a common Dutch saying with a slight German accent, "never pisses alone." He smiled. "By the way, did you ever fly a plane before?"

I shook my head, still trembling from the experience.

"Well," he went on, casually. "Now you know. There's nothing to it. Piece of cake."

As soon as Prince Bernhard heard that the Mews was aiming for the RAF, he had offered to teach me a thing or two about flying. I promptly accepted, of course, but with mixed feelings. The dashing young prince, barely thirty years old, slim, handsome and charming, exuded an aura of action and adventure that had earned him the reputation of a daredevil. A fast car buff all his life he had almost killed himself in a 1938 car accident, which in no way slowed him down. He knew no fear, danger attracted him - admirable qualities which however I preferred to admire from the safety of solid ground. Nor did the knowledge that he had himself only recently earned his pilot's license bolster my confidence.

I need not have worried,he was also proverbially lucky. For Bernhard, the Prince of the Netherlands, son-in-law, husband and father respectively of three consecutive Queens who reigned Holland for the entire 20th. century, World War II was a frustrating experience. Born a German, he had married Queen Wilhelmina's only child, Princess Juliana, and in record time made a conscious and meaningful transition of loyalties to his adopted fatherland. Because of this, and in view of the doubt his background initially evoked among some Britons, he longed more than anyone for a personal crack at the enemy.

By nature no less adventurous than his mother-in-law's Englandfarers, he shared with us the zest for combat and revenge from which his position excluded him. Instead, he had to burden himself with marginal military affairs such as liaison and representation, which left him unsatisfied. The irritations of the London scene, for us mere interruptions at a time of maximum fulfillment, were his daily diet. Like us, he was separated from his family, who had gone on to Canada, but while we blew off steam in bars and nightclubs, often getting gloriously drunk in the process, the royal image at a time of national distress precluded his presence in public places of relaxation. In his heart he envied the lowliest soldier who saw action in the field, but best of all he would have liked to change places with an operational pilot. He got his wings with the RAF, yet it was the U.S. Army Air Corps that helped him fulfill his dream. Queen Wilhelmina pretended not to notice, but after the arrival of the Americans her son-in-law secretly flew a number of missions in B-17s, B-24s and a P-47.

Prince Bernhard shared with us the zest for action

Perhaps because of his own restrictions Prince Bernhard understood, better than anyone else, the desperate finality of my situation. After Contact Holland, what? In 1942, Dutch units in action outside the Netherlands were limited to the navy and the merchant marine, for neither of which I was suited nor wanted.

The army stationed and trained some troops near Wolverhampton and in Canada, but informed opinion maintained that they were being saved for victory parades in the Netherlands. The Dutch air force had fought itself into oblivion and ceased to exist by the second day of the invasion. The only alternative was foreign service, the British Royal Air Force (RAF) which, in need of air crews, had agreed to train foreigners in exchange for aerial combat. Most Englandfarers, unwilling to spend the war marching back and forth on parade grounds or wasting time behind desks in London, had availed themselves of this opportunity. It was the only way out - if you could pass the proverbially tough physical examination for air crew. I, who had flunked my prewar test for the Netherlands infantry and needed glasses even to drive a car, looked into the future with my nearsighted eyes and stared calamity in the face.

There was no choice. If I failed to get into the RAF, I would have done better to stay home. To improve my vision I had eaten so many carrots that I was turning a ghostly orange. It wasn't unrealistic optimism or heroic determination which spurred me on, but sheer desperation. Passing my physical was just as important to me now, as escaping from Holland had once seemed. Only seen in this light does the rest of the story make sense.

It started on the eve of the critical day, in front of the Wings Club in Curzon Street. I ran into a group of England-farers who insisted on buying me a drink to wish me luck. They were pleasant company and together we walked up Park Lane past Marble Arch to Orangehaven, our new club. Purely out of curiosity I stuck my head around the door. Chris was there, and Gerard Dogger, and onetime agent Louis d'Aulnis and a couple of newcomers fresh from Holland - it seemed a shame not to have one small beer together. It tasted great, so one became two or three, after which I lost count. The conversation drifted around to fighter pilots and eye tests and we started comparing vision. I became the laughing stock of the party. What difference did it really make how many beers I drank?

About two in the morning we all moved to the Embassy Club and switched to whisky. A bunch of Polish RAF officers occupied their usual table on the little balcony above the band. The mood was playful, and when we began to snipe at them from the rear of the room, using little balls of silver paper from Player's cigarette packs and an occasional beer coaster, they went on the attack. You know the Poles! They jumped over the railing a full ten feet down on top of Harry Roy and his Band, which scattered in a explosion of crashing brass and cockney curses, and stormed our corner where we frantically overturned tables and chairs to throw up a barricade. Later all I remembered was agent Louis high up against the wall in a flower pot, but according to eyewitness reports the Polish charge against the Dutch position in the Embassy Club must be counted among the more memorable actions of World War II.

I got home around seven in the morning, just in time to brush my teeth and take a taxi - very gently, please - to the RAF Medical Building. Apart from my passing out in the waiting room, the physical proceeded smoothly: most doctors simply recoiled. Finally I wafted into the eye section.

"Christ!" said the doctor, a huge, shaggy squadron leader. He seated me on a wobbly bar stool in the middle of the room. "When I turn out the lights, read the letters."

As soon as he flicked the switch, the chair and I crashed to the floor. The second attempt achieved a measure of success, in so far as our remaining upright. But letters? What letters? Looking around me in the pitch-black room, I might as well have been blind. This was obviously the end, so I decided to go down fighting; after all, never say die, until you're absolutely stone-dead. I took a deep breath, yogi-like, and began to recite, leaving the door open for a last minute miracle from whatever powers felt so inclined: "B... MZ...OHF... UVRT... PNXASL... - how many lines to an eye chart? No matter, the lights came on. The medical giant stared at me, fascinated.

"Quite remarkable," he mumbled, shaking his head. I looked up, startled, buoyed by faint hope and my usual unfocused confidence. "Considering that the letters weren't turned on yet."

It was almost noon. Without another word the doctor exchanged his white smock for a blue jacket, put his RAF hat on and walked me out of the building, down the road and into a pub, where I made a speedy recovery. Then, over a light lunch and a bottle of Chablis, I told him my whole story, starting with Leiden. He had studied in Oxford, and I must have touched a sympathetic nerve, for back in his office he gave me the highest possible medical qualification: A1B.

"Tell me, doctor," I asked him. "What made you take me out to lunch?"

"When you started quoting that imaginary eye chart in the dark, you really got my curiosity going." He smiled. "But do me one favor. Stick to single seater aircraft, so you only break your own neck." - If there are more ways than one to skin a cat, my mystical allies obviously knew them all.

On September 19, 1942, I became No.128292 RAF cadet air crew, with the rank of pilot officer. I picked up my new uniform in Sackville Street, complete except for what really mattered: wings. Around the corner in Bond Street I bought six pairs of eyeglasses, three with tinted lenses to fool my instructors by day, three to wear secretly at night. I also had my standard flying goggles fitted with lenses, on the black market.

Nine more times I had to pass eye examinations before arriving in the blessed medical indifference of an operational RAF station where, in contrast to American squadrons, all rules and regulations are more relaxed. Eight of these presented no problem. While testing one eye, we were required to screen off the other with a hand. For this purpose I had smashed one of my glasses and selected a few triangular slivers of lens, which fitted invisibly between the base of two fingers. Looking through one of these, I could read the charts faultlessly.

The ninth and last time, do or die for getting my wings, I had to contend with a sergeant in Medicine Hat, Alberta, Canada, who prided himself on his efficiency. He got it into his head to screen off my eyes with a sheet of cardboard. Forewarned, I had spent much of the previous day in a bramble bush outside with a pair of binoculars, learning the letters by heart through the sick bay window. At the critical moment I recited my lesson full of confidence, but the bastard had hung a new chart over the old one. Predictably, the result was startling. He left triumphantly to inform the squadron leader of his catch. When they returned, they caught me with my nose on the new chart, studying madly. With a slimy smile the sergeant put the chart away... behind the old one!

I was back in charge and made not a single mistake. He gave me a dirty look, but it was nothing compared to the snarl he himself got from the squadron leader.

I had finally passed my RAF medical, once and for all.

* * *

The notion that one should never make a pass at another man's girl has always bothered me. It assumes that a person can be someone's property, and therefore out of bounds to others. To me this seems an insult to the woman, who is thus denied the opportunity of making her own decision on the matter. A girl should know who wants her, apart from the boyfriend, so she can make up her own mind. She has a clear choice of remaining faithful to the status quo, but equally a right to change partners and, well, dance. Unless married, she should be approached and propositioned as a free person, without regard to previous entanglements. This is especially true in wartime.

In Northern Europe, particularly Holland, England and Scandinavia, the above is a relatively safe philosophy. In other parts of the world, surprisingly including the USA, many men still consider their women property without rights of decision, and frequently draw pistols to prove their point. When, while waiting in London for my first RAF posting, I was informed that the fiancé of my brand-new girlfriend was looking for me with a gun in his pocket, I tracked him down first and invited him by telephone for lunch in the Dorchester Grill.

The girl in question, Midge, was a worthy apex to the triangle. Blonde, blue-eyed and radiantly pretty, she was also gifted with that basic toughness and marvelous sense of humor under pressure that makes the British, as a nation, irresistible.

She had come in from the country for a career on the stage, more gifted with looks than Thespian talent, and in the George Black revues and similar West End productions of that time she ranked tops in the chorus, always either floating down endless stairs as the Pretty Girl who is like a Melody or smiling down from the Bowl of Cherries like Life itself.

We met at a party and fell in love, promptly rented a cottage in Maida Vale along London's only canal and set up house. Much of our time we spent in bed, to the musical accompaniment of Richard Addinsell's "Warsaw Concerto". Midge was an air force girl, happy and at home with pilots and aircraft since the beginning of the war. She had recently volunteered for national service and been assigned to the

Midge

Ministry of Aircraft Production, as a truck driver. Now she awaited orders, just like me. Permanence was the last thing on our minds, which did not make our relationship any less exciting.

Contrary to America, where thousands jumped into hasty matrimony when war was declared, the number of marriages in England dropped steeply at the outbreak of hostilities. Instead of trying to cement the impossible, the British loosened formal bonds, as if to make it easier for individuals to lead an existence adjusted to the uncertain era. To saddle a girl at home with years of unfulfilled loneliness when she could have had a perfectly normal existence waiting for circumstances to change, did not seem to me like an expression of true love. Life in wartime should be lived now, not in times to come. In my experience even the dark prince thought so, picking his victims by choice from many whose minds were on the future instead of on the grim job at hand.

Midge's fiancé, she told me, was a flying-officer rear gunner with a Distinguished Flying Cross, obviously a man to reckon with. He was also handsome, amusing, generous and Irish, not a foreigner like me. He had it over me in every respect, except one: I happened to be stationed in London and he in North Africa, which put him at a grave disadvantage as Midge's suitor. Until he got back on leave, in September, 1942.

"He's really awfully nice," she assured me, as I left the cottage for the Dorchester. "You'll like him."

"I'd like him a lot more if he didn't have a gun in his pocket," I answered.

Flying-officer Jack Cowper, DFC, unmistakable after Midge's descriptions, was waiting for me in the lobby. Despite the seriousness of the occasion we established immediate contact, mostly from curiosity. With the girl as focus we weighed each other for the role we shared, or at least had shared. We were not disappointed in each other. A charming Irishman, he couldn't help smiling when I asked him to identify himself by showing his revolver. This done, I ordered cocktails and confronted him with my theories, which he considered carefully. As we sat down to lunch he agreed to leave the decision up to Midge, whom we called directly from a phone the waiter brought to our table. In an unpleasant situation she did not hesitate, at which Jack, with a nice Gaelic touch, whipped out a pair of dark glasses to hide the tears and gave us his blessing. After this we dined on excellent roast beef and Yorkshire pudding, with a bottle of Indian Ale apiece.

A month later I was posted to Cambridge; Midge decided to accompany me. On a misty autumn afternoon the two of us boarded a train in Liverpool Street Station, and suddenly Jack Cowper stood outside the window. Informed of our plans, he had come to say adieu. He waved at us as we slowly puffed out of the station, all the way, a lonely figure behind his dark glasses.

Jack I never saw again. Midge, in due time, became my wife.

CHAPTER 11

Pilot, 139 squadron, RAF

Generally speaking, pilots in wartime fall into two categories: the happy and the dead.

In the course of two and a half years of service with the RAF in World War II, I can truthfully say that I never knew an airman who was not eager to be posted to an operational squadron and, once there, did not feel an emotional high whenever his name appeared on the battle order of the day. Their ranks were fairly balanced by those killed in action, but the latter cannot bear witness to their dark fate. Harrowing accounts of calamities at sea give testimony that a sailor's lot, whenever his ship sinks, is not a happy one. The soldier's demise in trenches and jungles, grim deterrent to all war, has been minutely recorded by their comrades of the Press. Not so the sudden, lonely death of the airman.

The nature of air warfare is such that everything seems marvelously right until it goes terribly wrong, at which juncture all witnesses are usually wiped out. Consequently, only those who return to base, unscathed and victorious, are left to tell their tale, without any offsetting testimony by those who paid the price. As a result, combat flying is invariably depicted as a glorious game - which, for those who survive, indeed it is.

Chris Krediet and I emerged from the murky responsibilities of Contact Holland as two slightly tarnished novices into the pure, innocent world of airmen and their flying machines. The skies of England, as once her playing fields, seemed to promise victory in a lighthearted, gentlemanly way wholly unlike the caldron of Dutch intrigue in London. We were ready for it.

On the first day of November, 1942, in the gray light of dawn, B Flight, No.2 Initial Training Wing, RAF-Cambridge, marched smartly through the old university town. The narrow, curving streets lay deserted in the early silence. A freezing drizzle draped the spires and arches like fog, deadening the alien din of our boots. We could barely maintain regulation pace, a ridiculous 117 steps a minute, almost two per second, as if to demonstrate that we'd rather fly. Even so, we shivered in our greatcoats. As officer cadets - officers in rank, cadets in every other respect - Chris and I brought up the rear behind a multinational group of noncommissioned trainees. When we passed a row of giant beeches on the Common, I slipped out of the column and hid behind a tree, turning with the movement of B Flight to keep the trunks between me and the sergeant in charge. Chris took the next tree, and we listened as the troop marched off, left, right, left, right, away into the fog.

We came out of hiding, lit cigarettes and strolled back to St. John's College, hands in our pockets, collars raised over our ears, caps down on our eyebrows. Through gateways and arches and up three flights of stairs hollowed out by countless generations of Cantabrigians, we came to the tower where we were billeted. Everything around us looked as if the RAF had spared no effort to make us Leideners feel at home. And so we did. We got out of our uniforms as fast as possible and dived back under the blankets. Cold, early church parades did not fit in our concept of aerial warfare.

Our superiors did not burden us with excessive discipline. Recognizing the fact that we had already seen more of the war than they would probably ever experience, they made concessions in that spirit of flexibility which typified the Royal Air Force. Contrary to Americans, who are paranoid on the subject, the British grew up in a culture of social inequality. As a result, they more easily accept differences in rank, also on a personal basis. The enlisted man's resentment towards commissioned officers, so prevalent in the U.S. armed forces, was largely unknown among England's Tommies. The reverse was also true, especially in the RAF where rank did not always carry the day. The pilot commanded the airplane under all circumstances, even if he was a sergeant and his crew included officers as high as captains and majors, who during the flight would their orders from him without question. This constituted a victory for democracy never equaled by the U.S. Army Air Corps.

However, Chris and I were well aware that the concessions in discipline came at price: we had to be the best. This was not too difficult.

Navigation, meteorology, theory of flight, aircraft recognition, signals, in everything except marching drill and PT - which we ignored - our Dutch education helped us post high marks in all exams. All the same, it wasn't always easy to get fired up about reading morse flashes across a village green when a few months ago we worried about the lives of agents.

Around nine o'clock we reported as usual at Jesus College, where meanwhile the other cadets had arrived. In its medieval surroundings RAF instructors lectured us the rest of the day. After dinner we were dismissed and descended on the pubs, the Blue Boar, Mitre, Bath, Eagle... Around us the night throbbed with airplanes. Cambridge lay in the heart of bomber country, a giant complex of airfields from which the "heavies" - Stirlings, Wellingtons, a few new Halifaxes and Lancasters - slowly got the night offensive against Germany off the ground. The bars were blue with RAF, except for a sprinkling here and there, almost shyly, of the first American khaki. Surrounded by wings and DFCs, next to which our foreign decorations meant nothing, we felt painfully inadequate. Yet sometimes in the midst of all the noise and laughter, screened off from it by silence he himself seemed to generate, a man in blue would sit, sipping beer. From the stripes on his sleeve, usually flight lieutenant or squadron leader, our envious looks would slide upwards to the wings and the purple/white slashes of a DFC. Then came the shock: the schoolboy face, the acne, the grayish skin, the old lines around eyes that stared vacantly from dark, deep sockets. Not all flying was fun and games.

When the pubs closed, at eleven sharp, we stumbled out into the black night on our way back to the tower of St. John's.

Sometimes, all of a sudden in ghostly silence, the sky would light up, bright as day. For five, ten, fifteen seconds the streets lay before us, pale, drained of color, wet with drizzle hanging like smoke in the glow. In Cambridge everyone knew - a plane had crashed on takeoff, crammed with bombs and gasoline, and five or six of us had just "bought it". No one spoke. The glare faded to orange, then red, and slowly died away. Darkness settled once again on bomber country.

Just before the end of the year we graduated from no.2 ITW and checked out on a De Havilland 82 "Tiger Moth". After 8 hours 55 minutes of dual instruction, I flew solo in the same type of airplane that Prince Bernhard had dropped like a pudding into a local meadow a few months before. Chris and I, proud as peacocks, set out for London on leave and arrived in Liverpool Street station around eleven on New Year's Eve. We made it to the Embassy Club in record time, only to find the doors closed on a full house and the entrance funnel packed with people shoving to get in before midnight.

When all seemed lost, a lady in front of me fainted, practically into my arms. Chris, not one to miss a trick, picked her up by the legs, and yelling and pushing we made our way through the crowd and kicked against the door. The bouncer, peeking through a crack, recognized the emergency and let us in. Dumping the woman in his arms we ran inside, where Harry Roy had just launched into "Olde Lang Syne". We joined the circle of revelers, swaying arm in arm on the dance floor, in time to sing along with the happy crowd, "Should auld acquaintance..." On the dot of midnight, when the drummer's roll culminated in a clash of cymbals and a roar rose up to welcome 1943, Chris and I gave each other a big wink.

It had been a hell of a year.

* * *

Our switch to the RAF brought unexpected consequences. When we returned from Cambridge as pilots, however green, I discovered that London had become my home. Throughout 1942 it had sheltered me as a Dutch exile, but now, as I roamed its familiar misty streets with Chris or Midge or alone, waiting to go overseas for my next posting, it was my town and the Hollanders in it had melted into its polyglot citizenry. Instead of a beer in Orangehaven I drank my mild-and-bitters more and more at the Inn on Shepherd's Market, traditional meeting place for officers of all nationalities on leave in London from afar, Tripoli, Scotland, Canada, Tobruk, Washington, even Cambridge. Beyond the world of Dutchmen, with which I had so passionately identified, a wider brotherhood emerged and received me with open arms.

Around the noisy bar at Shepherd's, with its friendly Irish girl at the tap and every other allied nationality cramped into the tight little room, my life expanded. No matter our varied origins and uncertain futures, in the crush we stood shoulder-to-shoulder, even if only for a beer. In the past I had fought for my country, only for Holland, but now, didn't I fly for England as well? And just as much for the embattled Poles, and the Norwegians and the Czechs, and even the Russians and the Americans, God bless them? Perhaps for all of Western civilization in its life-and-death struggle against the Nazis? My core is Dutch, forever, but like a snake I felt that I was shedding my nationalistic skin to make room for more generous emotions. I was on my way to becoming a citizen of the world.

Meanwhile the war news disturbed us. General Montgomery had finally brought Germany's Desert Fox, Field Marshal Rommel, and his Afrika Korps to bay near El Alamein. At the other end of the Mediterranean the Yanks, fighting in Tunisia, were finally getting the hang of it. The Russians had turned the tide at Stalingrad and in the process, to our intense satisfaction, wiped out Hitler's Sixth Army, which had crushed Holland and Belgium in 1940. Now one Nazi defeat after another made the headlines - Rostov, Rhez, the retreat to Smolensk... Would there be any war left for us, when we were ready for it? Would we make it in time? Were we missing the boat? It was our one constant obsession, the only cloud to darken the year it took us to become fighter pilots.

At last our orders came. Under the Empire Training Scheme all flight instruction had been moved outside the United Kingdom, to the British dominions and later the USA. RAF brass kindly allowed cadets to express their preference of overseas location, so the Dutch contingent, after endless deliberations around maps and atlases, opted for Rhodesia, in Africa. With predictable military logic, we were posted to Alberta, in Canada. Midge and I, as befits lovers in wartime, had a brave little dinner, closed down our love nest in Maida Vale and entrusted our joint fate to a cloudy future. The next morning Chris an I took a train to Liverpool and boarded the Queen Mary. Together with 15,000 other troops including ten Hollanders, most of them Englandfarers, we set sail for Halifax, Nova Scotia.

It would have made no difference wherever we went. For seven days we played nonstop bridge in the officers' lounge rather than go below decks, where the next torpedo might hit. Most of the time Chris and I got clobbered, until we found out that our opponents, a couple of Polish officers, had studied bridge and chess as courses in their military academies, after which we designed a system of eye-signals which put an abrupt end to this advantage.

From Halifax we chugged due west on the Canadian National Railway along a straight and seemingly endless line. Here and there on a deserted platform of some Godforsaken prairie town a few civic-minded ladies offered us coffee and doughnuts through the windows, obviously with the best intentions, but their shy smiles and skittish glances suggested a certain doubt as to which side in the war we were on. Anyway, they waved goodbye with obvious relief. We were a self-contained contingent of foreigners on a military mission, welcome guests of the Royal Canadian Air Force, but totally cut off from civilian society. To my knowledge no one of us, during the six months of our stay, set foot in a Canadian home, not through lack of hospitality, but because we carried our own alien world with us.

Course no.78 at RCAF-De Winton, consisted of some eighty cadets of whom twenty-two were officers, veterans with war experience, judging by their decorations for valor, including three DFCs. These "supernumerary officers" represented eight nationalities, British, Norwegian, Czech, Dutch, Polish, Belgian, Irish and one Swede, and constituted as sophisticated a group of Europeans as any Canadian instructor would ever fear to tangle with. Yet as pupils their shortcomings were minor and of a national nature. To our RCAF hosts, the British talked funny, the Norwegians could drink anybody under the table except the Dutch, the Czechs were moody and impossible to make out, the Dutch could drink anybody under the table except the Norwegians, the Poles had to be scrapped from bomb practice because they sneaked away to dive-bomb a nearby German POW camp, the Belgians quarreled in two languages at once, the Irish would get homesick after three beers, and the Swede no one could understand. And all declined to participate in drill and PT.

These were carefree days for mature men who lived their boyhood dream of learning to fly. We rarely thought of the war, as we shared the magic of bright lights without blackout, half- forgotten delicacies like corn flakes and cream and fresh eggs with bacon. The staggering beauty of the Rocky Mountains rose like a surrealist backdrop to our airfield just outside Calgary, Alberta, a sleepy little prairie town in the foothills. At times we wondered where the gas came from that kept burning day and night on top of a single, solitary chimney on the outskirts. Somebody should catch and sell it and make some money, we figured, which in due time was more or less what happened and brought me back there fifty years later as a director of Barnwell, an oil company.

Our air base lacked runways, and in our little "Tiger Moth" biplanes I had a constant notion that we were one war behind. World War I must have been like this, my father's war, in which he worried about the honor of our country; Colonel Rabagliatti's war, in which he was the first man ever to shoot down an enemy in aerial combat. His flying machine must have looked like ours, oilcloth stretched over flimsy frame, double wings stabilized with struts, round open cockpits connected by simple speaking-tubes, two heads sticking up one behind the other, leather helmets with goggles, white scarves flying in the wind... I felt like Richard Arlen in "Wings", with all the little boys, brown and white, cheering on both sides of the transparent movie screen, in Surabaya, a lifetime ago.

After two months the course divided, bomber pilots to Moose Jaw, Saskatchewan, and the rest of us, including Chris and me, to Medicine Hat, Alberta, to train on the Harvard AT6 for fighters. Immediately on arrival we found ourselves lined up on the parade ground. From the flagpole, more ominous than skull and crossbones, fluttered the efficiency banner, awarded to the station which produced the most flying hours. The short word of welcome confirmed it: our new commanding officer, an old time group captain, was a spit-and-polish man, who would stand for nothing but model military performance.

At first the supernumerary officers didn't worry too much; after all, the British had always left us alone. But things were different at no. 34 SFTS (Service Flying Training School), and to our consternation we were ordered to participate in early morning PT and Sunday church parade. Our barrack buzzed with indignation in English, Dutch, Norwegian, Czech, French and Flemish, as we called one emergency meeting after another. The Poles had meanwhile left us for some training post of their own, from where they presumably resumed their onslaught on the hapless German prisoners.

Everybody caved in, except the Dutch. We promptly professed our allegiance to an imaginary religious creed which, in defiance to the Church of England, we christened the Church of Holland. Clearly this was tricky ground in Canada, where obscure denominations flourish like prairie flowers, and even the group captain fell back before the danger of getting entangled in foreign ethics.

Our sect was governed by stringent rules that forbade its members all early morning activities, particularly on Sunday, and when the other nationalities marched off on church parade the Dutch had to resign themselves to staying in bed and snoozing a little longer. Spurred by these successes, our fervor gradually assumed fanatic proportions, to the extent that we solemnly proclaimed an occasional holy day. Then all Hollanders were grudgingly awarded special leave and departed, with sanctimonious faces and thirsty gullets, to congregate at Banff or Regina for ancient ceremonies involving yeast and hops, followed by the wistful stares of the Norwegians, Czechs and Belgians.

Finally, on October 1, 1943, proud and desperately hung over from the previous night's end-of-course celebrations, the cadets stood lined up under the efficiency banner for the wings parade. The Netherlands, in spite of everything, won the "Prix des Nations" for the best national result, which always alternated between the Dutch and the Norwegians. If I report, not without pride, that I received a pair of gold RCAF cufflinks as the best overall fighter pilot of course no. 83, I do so mostly because later circumstances prevented me from putting this honor to the test in practice. One Dutch cadet had celebrated so severely on the previous night, that he failed to make it to the parade. True to tradition, the commanding officer appeared at his bedside and pinned the wings on his pajamas.

On the last night, by special permission, I went up one more time in the AT6 Harvard II. It was pitch dark, except for a sliver of moon in the east separating sky from prairies. I climbed to ten thousand feet, aimed the right wingtip at the silver crescent, firmly clamped on my glasses, turned the Harvard on her back and let the nose drop. The needle of the speedometer crept to the red line. I gently pulled the stick towards me, executing a big vertical curve until we shot up straight into the heavens on the other side of it. I kept the aircraft vertical, revolved her ninety degrees to the left around her longitudinal axis, pulled her on her back at precisely the right moment, and rolled out to normal flying position. The nose pointed straight at the moon, the altimeter once again read exactly ten thousand feet.

From sheer exuberance I gave a mighty shout into the night. It had taken a year, but I was back in the war.

* * *

"To arms!" the tall lieutenant called out, as soon as he saw us. He took off his cap, made a sweeping bow d'Artagnan-style and beamed up at me. "Up and at'em! Welcome aboard!"

"For Christ' sake, if it isn't Count B." Six thousand soldiers swarming like ants over the ss. Aquitania in New York harbor and who do we run into? The unlikeliest of Leideners, Herman van Brero, who used to dream of challenging Hitler to a duel. After escaping from occupied Holland with Chris Krediet as cooks on a coaster, they had made it to the USA the long way around, via Moscow. Chris had gone on to London and war, Herman opted for Washington in the safe and comfortable position of Netherlands Assistant Military Attaché. Now he was on his way to eradicate this disgrace and get into the fight. Tugboats hooted goodbye as we steamed down river past the Statue of Liberty.

After getting our wings Chris and I, with three weeks in hand, had taken the Canadian Pacific to Vancouver, hitchhiked down the West Coast through Seattle, Portland and San Francisco to Los Angeles, then taken a plane east for some fun and games in New York City before returning to England. My Rendez-vous in San Francisco days had seemed like a mirage, and walking across the Golden Gate Bridge from San Francisco to Sausalito I had felt like a ghost stepping back into a dream. For old times' sake I telephoned the siren who had lured me on that improbable pilgrimage in 1938, but the directory was ancient and the number disconnected.

The USA, too large and powerful to be visibly affected by even this war, disturbed the casual visitor from Europe. Of course, the hospitality was superb, in some cases bizarre. On our way from San Francisco to Palo Alto, we hitched a ride in a Buick whose driver stopped before a house in San Mateo, about halfway there. "This is where I live," he said, handing me the car keys.

"Return it here when you're through with it and drive carefully."

We did both.

Yet the raw power of its economy, its undiminished traffic, its unabashed abundance and shops bulging with goods, were not easy to accept for us who were used to life on a smaller scale, to rationing and blackout and the daily wear and tear of an uncertain future. Particularly the unrelenting commercialism and advertising made us feel hunted, targeted by radio, newspapers and billboards every second, everywhere, until we longed for the privacy of a murky London night. In New York war seemed absent, glimpsed only through occasional cracks in its vast, crusty surface. We accepted dinner one night at the Park Avenue mansion of a banking magnate, and when we arrived the news of his son's death in action on Kiska Island had just reached him. Somehow the two did not seem to fit.

Most upsetting to me was the realization that American hospitality, always startlingly generous, in our case was laced with pity, as if we deserved compassion for being pilots about to enter combat. Even when we assured our hosts that we would not change places with them for all the money in the world, it was taken as heroics instead of the simple truth. All this did not prevent us from being profoundly touched by everybody's kindness, and having a marvelous time while staying free of charge at a luxurious suite in the Waldorf Astoria.

On board the Aquitania Count B took us in tow. We settled in an empty lifeboat and watched the skyscrapers of Manhattan fade to unreality in the autumn haze. Looking forward to a beer together, we sent our old friend on an expedition to the bar. To our dismay he returned half an hour later with, of all things, three bottles of Coca Cola; apparently, on any ship with even a single U.S. soldier aboard, everybody had to teetotal it for the duration of the journey, undoubtedly the worst American public relations slip of World War II.

"By the way," Herman said, after deflecting the brunt of our ire. "I have a corporal in my unit who says he knows you. Tazelaar. Corporal Tazelaar."

"Peter Tazelaar?" We stared at him, perplexed. "Where is he?"

"Down in the hold." Count B pointed at the deck under his feet. "Straight down. As far as you can go without getting wet."

We immediately set out for the bowels of the ship. The deeper we went, the hotter and fouler the air. Row after row of bunks, bulging with sweaty bodies, crowded in all directions, four high right up to the ceiling. It was difficult to imagine that we all served in the same war. In the farthest corner of the bottom hold, where our sun-drenched deck seemed a distant memory and only the ship's skin separated us from unimaginable amounts of cold, black water full of U-boats, Herman stopped at a bunk with the canvas tightly laced around it.

"This is it," he announced, as if we had arrived at the cage of the rare white gibbon in the zoo.

"Peter! Hey Peter!" we called, slapping the sides. I felt the same anxiety as when I was standing in the hall of 23 Hyde Park Place, the night he shot himself in the mirror.

"Fuck off, all of you," someone inside growled. "Everybody, fuck off!" He had trouble with his speech. No doubt whatsoever, it was Peter, and he was looped.

For Peter Tazelaar everything had gone wrong since his second escape from Holland. On his arrival in London, he landed squarely in the middle of our fight with the Marines. It didn't take Colonel de Bruyne long to get midshipman Tazelaar bounced out of the navy. With the demise of the Mews, the reorganizers of the CID, all rank amateurs, considered it prudent to rid themselves as quickly as possible of this experienced Resistance fighter. They offered him a charming choice: corporal-draftee in the army or an indefinite stay on the Isle of Man, Britain's concentration camp for quislings. He chose the former.

But corporal Tazelaar knew himself to be a respected member of the Dutch Underground, a status he refused to relinquish. Frustrated at every turn, he broke all rules and regulations, until in the end nobody knew what to do with him. Finally he was bundled off to a Netherlands army camp in Guelph, Canada, as far from London as possible. There he totally withdrew into himself and, unpromoted, undecorated, unbelieved, unknown and bitter, he was generally regarded as a nut. Until June 30, 1943, when Queen Wilhelmina visited the camp.

The royal inspection had been minutely planned. On the stroke of noon Her Majesty entered the mess hall to greet the soldiers assembled for chow. Dutch, Canadian and American generals fluttered around her, and the hall swarmed with lesser officers. But Wilhelmina, who never forgot a friend, had prepared her own little plan and knew exactly where to go. To everybody's consternation she walked right through the crowd straight to a corporal, shook his hand, and said, "Good morning, Mr. Tazelaar.

I'm glad to see you again. I hope that things are all right with you." From that day onward corporal Tazelaar was treated with nervous but universal respect.

Also, Peter saw his chance. He'd had enough, he wanted to get back to the war for which he had twice escaped from the Occupation. Not above a little blackmail, he threatened to give his story to an American newspaper if the next boat to England sailed without him. The Dutch authorities capitulated. London...

Canada... New York... our shadow dance continued to pursue its mysterious pattern, not for the last time. That next boat happened to be the ss. Aquitania.

Even at this nadir, his proverbial luck held out. When one bottle of whisky was discovered on the otherwise stone dry ship, the commanding officer, a Kentucky colonel, decided to raffle it off among the six thousand soldiers. No million dollar sweepstake could have aroused greater excitement. Peter won. He locked himself in his cage and finished the entire quart before the ship had cleared the Hudson River. He opened up for no one, not even for us. Once during the journey we ran into each other, but he seemed ill at ease. When we entered Liverpool harbor, standing high on the sports deck I saw him way below me on the poop. He looked up and I waved, but Peter pretended not to see me.

* * *

After a week's leave in London, I knew we were in trouble. The West End swarmed with aircrews, trained and battle- ready, who would cut each other's throat for an operational posting. Bomber crews were relatively better off, due to the increasing air offensive over Germany - U.S. Air Corps by day, RAF by night - but the plight of the fighter pilot appeared desperate.

It was more than a year ago that the Luftwaffe had ventured over England in force, except for some pesky night fighters, and Spitfire sweeps across the Channel became increasingly unproductive.

Air cover and ground support action picked up after the invasion of Normandy, but Britain's factories concentrated on "heavies" - Lancasters, Halifaxes - and some twin-engined Mosquitoes for fast, fancy jobs.

Single engine pilots however, once in hot demand, now greatly out-numbered available aircraft. Even Germany's secret weapon, the un-manned V1 flying bomb that had meanwhile made its debut, was be-ing adequately confronted, and with little loss of life, by existing fighter squadrons. Was there room for us? Had we sweated a year for nothing? Were we too late, after all?

In our absence, London had changed. No more roly-poly barrage balloons nuzzled the chilly breezes overhead, no crash of bombs shat-tered the quiet nights. After New York the blackout was stifling, but if ever the guns in Hyde Park fired on some lonely intruder, everybody went "Aaaaah!" like kids at a fireworks show. Hotels dropped their low rates for top floors, and where "Taxi!" had sounded through every dark West End street, now American voices yelled "Cab!" The evacuees had returned, every restaurant and bar was packed, and head waiters began to get cocky again. "A few little bombs now and then," I grumbled to Chris, standing in a queue somewhere, "would do this town a lot of good."

In Orangehaven we had become strangers. Its clubroom, once enor-mous for its purpose, bulged with recent Englandfarers.

They were a different breed. They drank sparingly, worried about money and called each other Mister. The conversation, in our days a mix-ture of inspired nonsense, flying talk and abuse of Stratton House, now bored us with topics like pensions, insurance and the future. It was back to Shepherd's Inn for me, with Midge who - lo and behold, never under-estimate the ingenuity of True Love! - had met me dockside in Liverpool, in her Ministry of Aircraft Production half ton little pickup van.

That's where it happened, at Shepherd's one evening, as we were having a few pints, gloomily discussing the interminable subject of squad-ron postings, agreeing that is wasn't what you knew, but whom. Outside, Hitler's "buzz-bombs" flutter-farted their way along inky skies. As long as we heard the noise, nobody paid any attention, although sometimes we had to raise our voices over the din. When the motor cut, indicating that the bomb had started its steep glide to earth, conversation faltered while everyone waited, five, ten seconds, for the explosion. "Midge, m'dear," a voice spoke, when the glasses had stopped rattling on the tables. "What a delightful surprise."

"Hamish Mahaddie!" In front of us stood a short, square wing commander whose face looked familiar, as if I had seen it in the newspapers. Under his pilot's wings he wore just about every decoration obtainable through combat flying, as well as the gold eagle reserved for Pathfinders. Midge jumped up and hugged him.

"Just the man I want to see. I've got a pilot for you." As she introduced me and pushed the wing commander into a chair at our table, I wondered how she could have gotten drunk so fast. This was a preposterous proposition. Pathfinder Force (PFF) consisted of a mere dozen squadrons in which the best and most experienced air crews had been gathered to lead the night offensive against Germany. With just a handful of planes they would fly ahead of massive air fleets, guide them to the target, mark the aiming point with target indicators (TI's) and often stick around to supervise the attack. On nights when the weather was considered too fierce for the rest of the RAF, PFF squadrons took off and used their special radar to stage raids on their own.

Pathfinder crews, responsible for the precision of attacks carried out by hundreds of heavy bombers, were recruited almost exclusively from personnel who had completed thirty or more night mission on major German targets. With an exclusive gold eagle under their regular wings as a sop for the high casualty rate, they formed an elite that was the envy of every RAF officer. I myself had often eyed them with awe in the Blue Boar or Mitre at Cambridge.

Of what possible use could I be to this phenomenon at our table with his DSO, DFC, AFC and DFM? Pathfinders flew bombers; I had trained for fighters. They were experienced; I had just left school. They flew twin-engined Mosquitoes and four- engined Lancasters; I had only flown singles. Their element was darkness; my solo night-flying totaled seventeen hours, not to mention the five pairs of glasses I carried with me on those occasions. But Midge kept on talking and flashing those big, blue eyes, and finally Mahaddie said, "Well, m'dear, on occasion we do take above average pilots with somewhat less experience."

"There we are." Midge smiled, kicking me under the table. "Then he's just what you're looking for."

Two weeks later, not without misgivings, I reported to the Mosquito Training Unit at RAF-Warboys. So much for being a fighter pilot, for dogfights and victory rolls, for Spitfires and...well.. Spitfires. But the trick in life is not to waste time over inevitable setbacks. Accept them in a hurry, and - as they say in the RAF - press on.

For a month or so I flew twin-engined Oxfords and Blenheims to familiarize myself with multi-engined aircraft. Then, one fine morning, came the moment when I took off in a De Havilland Mosquito, the fastest plane of its day. It was like stepping from the family Chevy into a Formula One racing-car, and they can keep their Spitfires. Somehow I

Group Captain "Hamish" Mahaddie

survived, and after thirty flying hours I completed the course with the predicate I needed: Above Average.

Mahaddie, of course, was as good as his word.

* * *

In the morning I reported as Pathfinder pilot to 139 (PFF) Squadron, RAF-Upwood, Cambridgeshire; in the afternoon my name appeared on the battle order for that night, pinned to the green plush notice board in the hallway. Target: Hamburg.

I walked out of the officers' mess for some fresh air. In the flower beds around the entrance a few late roses still bloomed. Over neatly paved paths I wandered into the gray morning, between low brick buildings, cutting across the parade ground where an RAF flag, red-white-blue concentric circles on a light blue background, fluttered in the misty breeze, then along the back of an enormous, camouflaged hangar. The grass verges had been trimmed, the hedges clipped. The few sergeants and corporals I met saluted me cheerfully, except for a sergeant-major who all but dislocated his shoulder.

The sound of airplanes was everywhere: the flat, stationary rumble of a test-run close by; somewhere above ten thousand feet a far, smooth drone; the controlled, high whine of a landing approach; now and then the roar of a takeoff. On the other side of the hangar a concrete apron stretched out into the grass. Beyond it, lonely and deserted in spite of all the audible activity, lay the airfield. Mosquitoes stood parked in clusters of three in widely separated dispersal areas, their slick lines squat on the ground. I tried to locate Q-Queenie, the aircraft I would be flying tonight, and found her on the apron in the hands of the ground crew, like a patient horse being curried. From time to time a plane taxied by along the perimeter track, wagging her tail for better vision, pulling to a stop downwind to rev up the engines. Then she swung onto the runway and took off in earsplitting thunder, slim and graceful as soon as the wheels had retracted, skimming the green, flat land - bomber country!

A Mosquito landed, taxied on to the apron and cut the engine. A ground sergeant approached, opened the nose hatch, placed a narrow aluminum ladder into it and handed up an artificial leg. Moments later the crew, pilot and navigator, came lumbering down the steps. They walked by me, helmets loosened, white silk scarves waving in the wind. The navigator- Johnny Day DFC, SAAF - a tense, thin man, leaned on a stick and laboriously kicked his left leg before him with every step - no need to worry about my "shortcomings" in this place. We nodded at each other. Squadron mates, yet worlds apart.

Why? - Suddenly I knew. In spite of my many months in the RAF, all the training, the wings, the psychological preparation, the books, the films, the lectures, the stories, the jokes, I still didn't have the vaguest notion of what it would be like tonight. He did. He knew exactly. And yet, even if he had wished to, he couldn't help me. It was a threshold that every man, when the time came, had to cross alone. What lay beyond was not so much frightening as totally unimaginable. Like the hereafter.

Tomorrow, if it ever came, would be different.

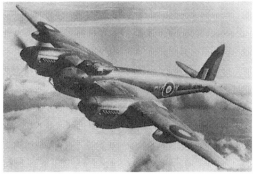

The de Havilland Mosquito—fastest aircraft of its day

CHAPTER 12

Target Berlin

Ben Hein is late. He's always late, but never too late. How many times now have we been over Germany together? Fifty-eight? Sixty? Still, every time he's late, I worry.

Actually, it's more a case of my being early. He's a cool one, old Ben; he likes to fiddle around until the very last moment with his maps, his pencils and dividers, his wind directions, bombing runs and ETAs, talking to the little computer strapped to his thigh as if the bloody thing were alive. Myself, I prefer to sit in the cockpit of our Mozzie for a while before takeoff, nice and quiet. It's so small, even for a crew of just two, that you've got to get used to it every time all over again.

I adjust the harness straps across my chest, tight but not too tight; wiggle back and forth on my parachute, which acts as the seat in the metal chair, until it feels comfortable enough for my tail to survive some five hours of continuous contact; reach out to various knobs and levers, first with my eyes open, then blindly, until I can find my way by touch in the confusion around me. Then I just sit, staring ahead. After a few minutes I begin to feel better, less awkward. It's very important to me, especially when the weather is bad. The weather is always bad.

Outside, the winter evening smothers our base, RAF-Upwood. Drizzle spots the windshield, distorting everything. Hangars look like battleships; runway and perimeter lights fuse into a muddled mess. The De Havilland "Mosquito": Rolls Royce engines, revolutionary construction, the latest in electronics, but simple windshield wipers - forget it. Typically RAF. The most sophisticated aircraft of World War II, I swear by it, but we never leave the ground without an ample supply of rubber bands and chewing gum for essential small repairs in the cockpit.

Darkness reaches down from the sky. It's cold, you can be sure there's ice up there. Cloudbase below three hundred feet when we get back, five hours from now, I'll bet on it. Bloody Met- blokes and their forecasts. Night fighters, flak, rockets, I'll take them all in exchange for some decent weather. But I guess we'll manage. Survive the first five missions and you'll be all right, they say. After my very first one, with flight lieutenant Ray Snelling DFC to Hamburg some eight months ago, I never thought I'd make it.

Of course, as a Pathfinder flying a Mosquito you have to get used to some odd ideas; mainly, that your plane is made of wood and carries no guns whatsoever. The wood is pressed and strong, but operating un-armed we are supposed to survive by being smarter and luckier as well as fast. To help us do so, we have a gadget in the cockpit called the Boozer. It's secret. It starts to glow when the Jerries pick us up on their radar: red when they track us, bright red when they lock us into the aiming mecha-nism of their heavy guns, yellow when we have a nightfighter on our tail.

From the moment we crossed the Dutch coast, the Boozer glowed. Every time it jumped to bright I threw the Mozzie wildly off course, once when the yellow came on - most likely through static electricity - yanking her into such a steep diving turn that I almost lost her. All this in solid cloud, pitch-black, hour after hour. It was a miracle that we ever found Hamburg, or even England on the way home. We reported no sign of the enemy, but the following morning Q-Queenie was under repair, with seventeen fist-size holes in her wooden fusilage.

After ten operations with Snelling I ran into Ben Hein in the Blue Boar, Cambridge. His short frame firmly planted on the ground, pugna-cious chin in the air, dark eyes under black bushy brows fiercely blazing into the world, he looked loaded for bear. He was wearing a navy blue uniform with Dutch navigator's wings and patted me approvingly on the chest, where under the Williams Order my brand-new Pathfinder's eagle gleamed.

"Hazelsnout," he declared over a pint of Watney's, "with you I'll fly. We may fall flat on our asses, but we won't turn back when the going gets sticky. There's more of that in this war than people think."

My desire to fly with Ben was based on less heroic considerations. As a lieutenant in the Royal Netherlands Navy Air Service he had to be a superb airman. Also, we were old high school friends and I knew him as a typical Hollander: more than ready to risk his life for freedom, totally immune to discipline.

Ferociously fearless, he had taken on everybody in the Dutch camp from the admiral down, before escaping to the RAF. So we'd make a fine pair.

He ordered two more pints and told me that he had just been shot down over Berlin. Somehow his Canadian pilot managed to crash-land in neutral Sweden, where two days later Ben had talked a British diplomatic courier into smuggling him back to England in the bomb bay of a Mosquito. So here he was, in the Blue Boar in Cambridge, looking for a pilot. He requested and obtained transfer, Ray Snelling and I parted friends, and the first and only all-Dutch Pathfinder crew in World War II was ready for business.

Our maiden trip together, on 12 October 1944 to Berlin, almost proved to be our last. The problem was discipline, believe it or not, but now the shoe was on the other foot. To begin with, we couldn't understand each other. With both Dutch and English at our disposal, the mixture of multilingual flying terms proved unintelligible over the intercom. Confused and unhappy we flew to Hitler's capital, where Ben dropped our target indicators (TIs). We were in cloud all the way and saw no sign of activity over the target - no diffused glow of searchlights, no night fighter flares, no flak, nothing. Under those circumstances it takes a lot of nerve to mark an aiming point for hundreds of approaching bombers.

But neither was there any trace of our own squadron mates, who were supposed to mark the target with us. After several minutes on the way home I looked back once more. Our cluster of red flares hung in utter solitude, while underneath the clouds a series of silent flashes reflected the bomb bursts of the main force behind us, dropping their 4000-pound blockbusters... on what? A meadow, killing some hapless cows? Ben sat in surly silence. Finally I could stand it no longer. "Ben, are you sure that was Berlin?"

This time he heard me perfectly. "Christ!" he exploded, grabbing his maps and flinging them through the cockpit. "You can kiss my arse."

That I couldn't take. "And you can kiss mine," I shot back, letting go of the steering column.

There we sat, two stubborn Dutchmen side by side, grim and furious, as if we'd never heard of Germans. From thirty-eight thousand feet we tumbled down. Out of Ben's sight I kept my hand on the trim-wheel and the tips of my toes on the pedals, but even so the Mosquito plunged like a brick. Every so often Ben cast a sidelong glance at the altimeter and when we whizzed by eighteen thousand feet without letup, he snatched a map out of the air.

"Aw hell, let's go," he mumbled sheepishly. I was happy to comply. It was just the beginning. We had forgotten about Jerry.

After leveling off we found ourselves smack over Magdeburg at fifteen thousand feet, ideal range for the gunners below. Ten seconds later we felt a sharp blow, and our starboard engine was on fire. It didn't exactly blaze, but all the same the flames flickered frighteningly in the cloud around us. I quickly feathered the prop, closed the petrol cock, switched off the ignition, increased power on the port engine, reset the trim, pushed the extinguisher button, and hoped the fire would go out. Ben, the microphone cover protruding from his round, helmeted head, stood out against the glare and looked like an unhappy pig.

"Did you press the tit?" he asked peevishly.

"What tit?"

"The whipped cream tit." The extinguisher was built into the motor to produce foam.

"Of course I did."

"Then why isn't the fire out?"

"Ben, I didn't invent the bloody thing, I only pressed it. If you let me fly, I'll let you navigate. Okay?" And that's the way it's been ever since.

The fire did go out, but we still had to fly home on one engine. With difficulty we maintained an altitude of twelve thousand feet. Having lost the generator, we ran out of juice which knocked out all lights and electrical equipment, including the radio. Increased gas consumption forced us to take the shortest route, and everyone along the way celebrated our unannounced arrival overhead by blasting away at us: the Germans in the Ruhr, the Americans near Aachen, the Canadians around Antwerp, and finally, with particular gusto, the British navy off Sheerness. When at long last we rolled to a stop at the end of Upwood's runway number two, completely unobserved by the control tower, we had pretty well jelled into a team. There was never any doubt again who was in charge. Hazelsnout or not, I was the captain. But you had to give credit to my navigator: only Q-Queenie that night had found and marked Berlin.

There's Hein, I can see from here that he's in the mood for a fat target. But then, he always is. Navigation board under his arm, chin out, he strides pugnaciously across the dispersal, around Mosquitoes that stand silently in groups of three and four, slender as wasps. He stops at

T-Tommy and says something to Dave Groom and his navigator, Rosie O'Grady, who are about to climb the little ladder to the hatch in the nose. They move like bears in their parachutes and Mae Wests. They laugh, jab Ben in the ribs, and hoist themselves up the steps and through the hole. The ground crew slams the hatch cover and locks it. Now they're no longer Dave and Rosie, only T-Tommy.

"Hello, skipper!" Ben 's head sticks up through the floor of the cockpit, round and smooth in the leather helmet except for the ear-phones. He squirms through the hole like a giant beetle, into his seat to the right of me. We both face forward, shoulder to shoulder in the mass of instruments. While he struggles into his harness, cursing con-tentedly, I switch on the wingtip lights. The ground sergeant holds up his thumb and shuts the hatch. He scurries off, wheel chocks in one hand, pitot-head cover in the other. I look at my watch - from now on until we have marked the target for the bomber fleets following us, we live by the second hand. Two minutes and twenty seconds till takeoff. It's almost dark now outside, all around glow the little red and green wingtip lights. Ben sits silently beside me; everybody and everything is waiting and it's very quiet everywhere, very quiet...

Behind us an engine sputters, immediately followed by two, three more. One catches and roars, then another, then four, six, eight, all of us, and within seconds the whole dull, dismal evening, the bleak field and miles of sleeping English countryside have sprung to violent life. All around us engines thunder, flames blast from exhaust pipes, propellers whirl, tailplanes shudder, airframes tremble. Now they move, nosing left and right, little red and green lights starting, stopping, stirring, Mosquitoes like black shades turning and twisting toward the perimeter track, then running straight for the takeoff post as if eager to get airborne.

I move in behind T-Tommy. The noise swells dramatically and there goes the first one, dimly lit by the runway lights, carefully feeling for di-rection, then faster and steady, roaring down the field, and up, away into the gloom. Now the next, and the next, and the next, one every thirty seconds. T-Tommy off and gone. Our turn, final check. "Check petrol cocks!" "Petrol cocks set." "Check booster pumps!" "Booster pumps on." The green flash from the control tower hits my eyes, hurry, hurry! We swing onto the runway and instantly, miraculously, the muddle of lights resolves itself into a wide avenue leading straight into the night. I slowly push the throttles forward.

"Ice," I inform Ben, as soon as I have a moment. Barely off the ground and already we're in the soup; cloud, rain, hail, ice. Queenie feels sluggish and wobbly. Outside the dim little cockpit the night is solid black.

"None of my business," he comes back cheerfully. I turn up the intercom, the better to hear him. "You're the bloody pilot, it's your job to keep her flying. That's what they pay you for. - Set course, zero nine three."

"Zero nine three. Okay." I adjust the giro compass, turn slowly onto course and start our climb through cloud four miles thick. Ben, oblivious to everything except the navigation board on his lap, double checks his calculations. Queenie drones along steadily, and just as I resign myself to another blind journey, we burst breathtakingly from the gloom. We have outclimbed the setting sun and caught the day in its last golden moments.

First I look around quickly; as usual, there are no other aircraft in sight. We all take off together, fly the same route at the same height to the same target to arrive at the same minute, yet we hardly ever see each other. Except when one of us is caught in enemy searchlights; then everybody sees him, often for the last time. Still, they are around us somewhere, eight pairs of friends, packed tightly in wooden boxes brimful of fuel and dynamite, covered in ice; and behind us, also invisible, follow hundreds of heaviesto aim tons of destruction at our "Christmas trees."

We level off at thirty-six thousand feet. I adjust the trim until Queenie all but flies herself, check that the exterior lights are out, and stretch my legs beyond the rudder bar. Ben, figuring out the time for his first route marker, is talking to his computer again, a sure sign of well-being. I nudge him and point outside. We seem to be sailing a scarlet sea crested by golden waves. Behind us, Queenie's tail fin stands like a black dagger against the sunset. Pink lace curtains of cirrus hang beyond the brute profile of our port engine and through a gash in the clouds below I glimpse a rose-colored abyss. Dead ahead, most majestic of all, comes the night in steely shades of purple.

There, in the dark, lies the Third Reich. "New course. Zero eight four." Ben's voice crackles over the intercom.

"Zero eight four. Okay."

We sit so close together, I have to turn my head almost at right angles to see him. It's getting dark now; he is lit from below by the clip-on light of the navigation board and looks like Dracula. Out of the corner of my eye I see the Boozer come to life, glowing red. We must have crossed the Dutch coast. I peer through the port blister, past the blue exhaust flames. Obliquely below us - Wassenaar? Scheveningen? - an orange speck appears, hovers for some seconds, then suddenly streaks up in jerky gusts of speed, passes us and disappears at stunning height:

Hitler's latest secret weapon, a V2 rocket on its uncertain way to London. To the south, where Allied armies are sloshing ahead in the Battle of the Bulge,I can follow the front from the Dutch rivers through the Ardennes well into France, a line of flickering reflections underneath thin cloud. From time to time streams of tracer bullets break through the cloud cover, whizzing back and forth. I would not like to changes places with those guys.

Ben stares at his watch, his finger on the trigger of a Verey pistol to fire a route marker. Plop! For a split second I see our wings, ghostly gray, as the flare shoots up and away. I bank the aircraft and look at the red ball hanging motionless in space, and imagine the main force behind us, like a pack of wolves, wheeling at full tilt to follow our lead. A second ball suddenly floats in the dark, out of nowhere, to port and slightly lower, then two more to starboard, very close, and another. After the hard, lonely brilliance of the stars, it's good to feel our buddies all around us.

We're barely over Germany when the Boozer jumps to bright red. I nudge Ben. "Hey! What are you pulling on me now?"

"Osnabrück," he answers calmly. "We're just a teeny- weeny bit close to Osnabrück."

I can't fool around, we've got to get to the target on time, two minutes before the main force. If the Pathfinders are late, the entire attack falls apart; bombers milling around in the searchlights and flak without an aiming point on which to drop their load - very bad show. I decide to ignore the Boozer, the gunners of Osnabrück aren't so hot, anyway. Soon it returns to dull and that's how it stays, because from now on the German Air Defense tracks us every foot of the way on radar, trying to guess tonight's target in time to crank up their guns and put their night fighters in the air. We try to fool them. We are routed to approach a city menacingly, turn away at the last moment toward another one, then veer off again to pounce suddenly on the unsuspecting victim - we hope. Sometimesit works, sometimes it doesn't.

We're approaching the heart of Germany. The night is moonless, but the weather has turned clear, right down to the ground. All around us lie the fat, juicy targets; legendary, awe- inspiring names that have bounced around in our subconsciousness ever since we put on Air Force blue. Now they're getting it, by day from the Americans, by night from the RAF. This morning it was the Flying Fortresses. To starboard the sky glows; below it, rivers of fire run into four orange pools: Brunswick. Far to the north a trickle of amber sparks drips down, then more, hundreds, thousands, a rain of golden flares that quickly knit themselves into a brilliant canopy over the unfortunate city below: Hamburg.

Elsewhere also the big boys are on the prowl, Lancasters and Halifaxes; in several places I see the lacework of heavy flak spattering delicately. Here and there, close to the ground, climb the leisurely tracers of light antiaircraft fire. Everybody's in the act tonight.

The Boozer flicks to bright. Now it's serious. This is Hanover and here they know their business.

"Have we time for evasive action?" I'll go by what my navigator tells me.

"What kind?"

"Slalom."

"Plenty time." Had he answered in the negative, we would have plowed straight on. It's as simple as that.

I wait for the initial shellburst, they rarely score first time up. There it is, an innocent-looking little black cloud to the left of us, slightly high. Now the Jerries below start correcting the error. I know that it takes a shell about twenty seconds to reach us, so after fifteen seconds I change course five degrees to the left. If they are efficient down there the change will have occurred after they fired the next round, but before it gets to us. Poof! There it is, on schedule, to the right where it ought to be. Below they're correcting again.

Meanwhile I change course to the right, ten degrees this time to make up for the previous deviation to the left. Poof! Very nice, to the left of us. Ten degrees to the left. Poof! To the right of us. And so on, occasionally combined with a gain and corresponding loss of a few hundred feet of altitude. In this way we maintain our original direction of flight, while staying alive. But you must have reliable, capable gunners below, Jerries you can count on.

"Hey, Hazel, what time do you make it?" I almost jump out of my seat. I recognize the carefree, down-under accent of Rosie O'Grady, somewhere out there in the dark, but he sounds so close that I instinctively look over my shoulder. We always maintain radio silence, except for emergencies and irrepressible Aussies. I tell him the time, that's all. I'm acutely aware that hundreds of Germans are listening to these two enemy voices deep inside their country. They all know the game. It can't be long now. Ben is immersed in calculations.

"Last course into target." Everything now revolves around the navigator and his radar box, and the accuracy with which I follow his instructions, We want to be the best.

"Course one four eight. First lose two and half minutes. We're early."

I put Queenie into a specific turn. Exactly two and half minutes later the circle is complete, we are at the same spot. "One four eight... now!"

Ben checks his watch, grunts with satisfaction and fires off the final route marker. Before sticking his head back into the radar box, he pulls a stopwatch from his pocket and presets the duration of the bombing run. Since our radar will be useless over the actual target due to the angle, we have to fly the final, critical miles by dead reckoning; course, speed, height, time, all determined beforehand. Bombers weave into the target area and fly straight and level no longer than it takes to drop their loads accurately, but Pathfinders must maintain an absolutely steady bombing run, sometimes for several minutes, to produce the basic requirement for a successful attack: a valid aiming point. Now and then I wonder if it's worth the little gold eagle.

I lower my seat and turn up the instrument lights. Whatever happens outside, from here on in there's little I can do about it. We have penetrated so far east, surely by now the Jerries know what it's all about... Ah, there they are, and they are ready for us. Dead ahead, wholly unreal but bristling with menace, hundreds of searchlights pierce the cloudless sky, rigid, motionless, like quills of a giant porcupine: Berlin.

"Come and get it," they say. We're coming.

* * *

Someone has entered the frozen forest, and the searchlights have come alive. The blue-white beams begin to weave slowly, each in its own sector, long, slim fingers feeling their way, touching the inside of the transparent black dome above, unhurried, hesitating, but always moving on, searching. Over to port I see a speck of solid matter in this rarefied world. On the ground they have seen it also - ten, fifteen beams whip over to it and cross each other where the Mosquito holds them together like a clasp. White lacework begins to spatter around her. Undaunted, the little ship plows on, straight, steady - one of ours, 139 Squadron.

Suddenly I find myself staring at some tiny cracks in the paint of our port engine nacelle, which a second ago was invisible in the dark. As I look over the side an unblinking, glittering eye meets mine, bitterly hostile, so blinding that I quickly pull back. Wham-wham-wham-wham... four more beams smack in on us, then half a dozen more. We're tightly coned, down below pools of violet light surround us. Even Ben looks up from his box. I can see every hair on his unshaven chin. "This is what they pay us for," he says soothingly.

"How much longer?" We're well into the bombing run.

"Ninety-six seconds... ninety-five... ninety-four..."

I drop my seat all the way, only the top of my head sticks above the cockpit. Don't look, just keep going. We're droning along inside a light-ball of incredible intensity. Course, height, speed, everything solid, just the way Ben wants it: on rails. Next to me, parallel to Queenie and only a shade higher, five or six black puffs burst into existence. I can't help seeing them out of the corner of my eye. Twenty seconds until the next salvo. No slalom this time, straight ahead, level and steady.

"Sixty seconds coming up." Ben never takes his head out of the radar box, he wants this Christmas tree in the right place.

"Sixty seconds...now. Fifty-nine... fifty-eight..." Poof! There they are, corrected for height, still to the left but close enough to be heard above the roar of the engines. Keep going... keep going... Crrrack!! Very close, smack in front. We sail through the black cloud, I can smell the cordite. At the same moment a cluster of three yellow flares pops out of nowhere, right above us, German nightfighters. They are signaling to the gunners below:

"Hold your fire. We're here. This one is ours."

"Thirty seconds. Open bomb doors."

"Bomb doors open."

We're actually not carrying bombs tonight, only target indicators, reds and greens. I must remember to call them out to the main force, to offset the dummy TIs the Germans are shooting up from the ground. Final check: course - exact; speed - exact; height - exact. It should be a fine aiming point, if we make it.

It's ominously quiet around us. Where is the flak? Then suddenly the yell in our earphones: "Fighters! Look out! Fighters!"

"Steady..." Ben has one eye on the radar, one on the stopwatch, and his thumb on the bomb release. Does he give a damn that we are lit up like a showcase, visible for miles, an unarmed sitting duck in a shooting gallery for every night fighter around?

The yellow Boozer flashes on. Fighters, here they come!

"Steady." Ben's voice is rising. "Steady... five... four... three ... two... one... TIs gone!"

"Q-Queenie, TIs gone! Reds and greens! Reds and greens!" Shouting my message to the main force, I yank the Mozzie into a vertical turn, dropping the nose steeply.

"Hit them, you peasants," Ben growls to the heavies in the chaotic night around us.

We dive, twist, turn, climb. The Boozer goes dim. As we soar and flop about the sky in my best Medicine Hat style, one by one the searchlights lose us. Suddenly we're in darkness, safe.

In a warm, exulting wave, life floods over me.

* * *

Weaving slightly, we fly out of the target area. To our right, the attack is in full swing. The Pathfinders have done their job, now it's up to the main force. Six cones of searchlights move slowly over Berlin, each holding a bright little Mosquito in its apex, surrounded by flashing white dots. Lower down, some Lancasters and Halifaxes are having similar problems. Clusters of yellow fighter flares hang all over the sky, and there, motionless among the searching beams, float our Christmas trees in deadly splendor, brilliant red, luscious green, a late one cascading among them like a golden waterfall. Below the TIs two-ton blockbusters crash into Hitler's capital, billowing into fiery mushrooms.

A mile to the north a horizontal stream of tracers shoots through the night to the focal point of a cone. At its tip an orange speck appears, gradually increasing in size, then holding steady. Slowly it begins to circle down in tight turns, slowly, slowly. The searchlights won't let go, from all sides others whip across to join in the kill and follow the stricken Mosquito down. It takes a long time. Finally the beams are almost level, a sea of light in which the Mozzie crashes and blows up with a puny little flash. The beams sweep the sky in exultation, up, down, up, down, up...

It's like a movie, exciting and sad, but we're not personally involved. It bears no relation to life as we know it. RAF-Upwood is a peacetime station, central heating, hot running water, spacious mess room, well stocked bar, stewards and batwomen, all the comforts of home. The roses in the garden used to win prizes in local flower shows. Here Ben and I lead a bourgeois existence, very settled, very smooth, few emotions. Hein has been promoted to lieutenant senior grade, I am a captain. We have completed our first tour of operations and wear British and Dutch DFCs between our wings and our Pathfinder eagles. We share a private room with bath, and if ever the hot water runs out, we snort with indignation.

A WAAF-corporal wakes us in the morning and keeps the place neat; if you smile at her occasionally, she brings you tea in bed. It's not unlike Leiden, lots of activity at night and long, lazy mornings. When around eleven we sedately proceed to the bar for an early sherry, we are greeted with respect by the new boys, just like in Minerva.

Meanwhile we fly missions over Germany and some of our friends don't come back. We grab a pint at the bar, shake our heads and say: "Bad show." We may miss them, but we are incapable of connecting whatever happened to them with ourselves. Already they're no longer part of us. Their rooms may be empty, but not for long. The life we know goes on as before. In a recent two- months period our squadron lost forty percent of its crews; except for a touch of nervousness, it did not basically affect the rest. You come back, or you don't. There's no connection.

Old-timers like us don't even have to sleep on base.

Midge, resourceful as ever, has found herself a room at St.Ives, six miles down the road. After debriefing I often climb on my old bike and pedal through the soft, silent countryside, still high on oxygen and my ears ringing with the roar of a flight to Nürnberg or Cologne. My girl wheedles fresh eggs out of farmers, scrounges jugs of Bass' Ale from the Pike and Eel, and holds me close on a mattress of goosedown. And when afterwards we lie under the covers, safe, warm and happy, I think about tomorrow and hope my name will be on the battle order again.

It often is. On New Year's Eve 1944, instead of crashing the Embassy Club, Ben and I and a few others slipped away quietly from the mess in Upwood, shortly after midnight, champagne glasses in hand. Most of 139 Squadron and their ladies were standing around the piano, and when we got back we plunged right into the same old song - "Roll me o-o-over, in the clo-o- over" - and nobody but Midge had missed us. Yet in the interim we had clobbered Hanover. - Behind us the attack has run its course. Except for a few searchlights sticking motionless up into the sky, Berlin lies in darkness. The remnants of one burned-out TI still glow in the target area, and three orange conflagrations show where the city is on fire. They're a tough nut to crack, the Germans. D-day come and gone, Americans on the Rhine, Russians along the Oder, bombers pounding them around the clock, and still they fight on like tigers. You have to respect them, but pity? Impossible. They have gone too far, wronged too deeply. Now the rest of humanity, outraged, is at their throats.

The Soviet army, most feared of all, is clawing at the gates of Hitler's capital, so close that we have been issued little silk Union Jacks to identify us as friendly forces in case of bail-out. We wish him luck, our gallant Red ally, but the thought of parachuting out of German skies among our Russian buddies does not fill us with boundless confidence.

For England the day of retribution has come. Like a giant aircraft carrier it lies on the fringe of the European front, which has now moved entirely to the Continent. Streams of bombers take off from fields around towns once ravaged by the Luftwaffe. London, so long the main target, has become every soldier's city of joy. Hitler's unmanned buzz-bombs have been licked, and nobody pays much attention to his V2 rockets - if you can't hear them coming, you can't worry about them. Air raid shelters are deserted now that the blackout is coming apart, except as last resorts for lovers. One night, dropping from cloud after a trip to Stuttgart, we could hardly believe our eyes: circles of little white lights twinkled around the bases of bomber country and flashing red beacons showed us the way home. No doubt about it, victory is in the air.

I play a role in that victory, however small. Not gleefully, but with grim satisfaction. I rejoice for the British; the Americans still have their work cut out for them in the Pacific; as far as the Nazis are concerned, they signed their own death warrant when they placed themselves at the triggers of the firing squads, the levers of the gas chambers. I am an atom in the sword of the executioner, carrying out the sentence not just because of Holland, not because of Europe, but on behalf of all humanity. War has made me a citizen of the world.

"You can start losing altitude, if you like," Ben suggests amicably. We are making a beeline for home base and have just plunged into a solid cloud bank, choppy as hell. I put Queenie into a very shallow dive and watch the instruments. The tension has taken its toll, they make me sleepy. After half an hour they try to take over. Their intent little faces watch me right back, and as soon as I relax they change places. I sit up, rub my eyes, and they slide back to where they belong.

Outside, cloud hugs the ship like black cotton wool. We are bouncing around in a series of sickening drops and lurches, and suddenly a blinding ball of lightning envelops us. When I can see again, blue flames dance on the propeller tips and fiery, crackling rivulets of electricity run down the windshield. Next we seem to be underwater, as a thick layer of ice instantaneously covers all windows. Queenie wobbles under my hand and flies like a pudding. Just as suddenly the ice is gone. In flying, it's never over until it's over.

"Ten minutes to the Dutch border." Ben reaches across me. He has picked up a radio beam from England and sets our final course on the compass. He folds his maps, turns off the navigation light and, grunting and snorting, makes himself comfortable.

His job is done, he wants no part of mine. I don't blame him, the last twenty minutes are often the worst. Finding the airfield and landing in British weather, with cloud base zero and running out of gas, has cost us more casualties than anything the Jerries can put up.

Not this time. Over the North Sea the clouds disperse like magic, and before us unfolds the most beautiful - and rarest - sight ever to greet the night pilot of World War II: England, cloudless, fogless, clear as crystal. As far as the eye can see, hundreds of air bases, almost overlapping, cover the ground with perfect circles of soft white lights, like strings of pearls on black velvet. Scattered through them, little red beacons wink their welcome. No doubt, victory is in the air.

Let's see, dot-dash-dash, that's the W of Wyton. And there, dot-dot-dash, is the U of Upwood. Between Upwood and Wyton lies the road to St. Ives.

* * *

Often, in the course of 72 attacks on Germany, 25 on Berlin, I had difficulty taking myself seriously. A little man would be observing me from somewhere behind my right shoulder, and I would see myself through his critical, objective and not unhumorous eye, reminding me who I really was and where I came from. Somehow his presence seemed connected with my furthest past, my boyhood on Java, and gradually I came to identify him with old skin-and-bones with the red lips who had bewitched my young soul with its first intimation of a spiritual world. He was keeping an eye on me and put his perspective, whenever I felt the need for it, at my disposal. By him I was reminded time and again, caught in a searchlight over Bremen or after a particularly smooth landing in a snowstorm, that I might be acting like a hot RAF pilot, but that I was really a Dutch student with distant roots and a yen for writing. And by the way, when did you write last? Aren't you wasting a lot of time, a lot of marvelous material? Are you ever going to produce again?

At last I gave in. I decided to write the ultimate, definitive description of a raid on Berlin in World War II. In English. This was a commendable goal, as to all intents and purposes I had only learned the language since joining the RAF, and never written in anything but my native Dutch. Old skin-and- bones rejoiced, and obviously put his mystical powers behind the project. There is no other explanation.

During five consecutive missions on Berlin I observed Q-Queenie and its crew through creative eyes, with attention to detail and conscious memorizing. On returning to Upwood I made notes. When I considered my material complete, I borrowed a typewriter, wrote an article and in my innocence applied for a 24-hour leave in which to find a publisher, don't ask who or how.

In feverish spirit I took the train to London, where I arrived in time for a late dinner at Shepherd's Inn. However, traffic was heavy and as I walked in under the marquee the restaurant had just closed.

While I stood swearing and moping, making up my mind where to go at this late hour, some young Americans in civvies walked out and noticed my plight.

"Looking for something to eat?" one asked. When I nodded, he went on, "We're having a party, just around the corner. Lots of food. Just knock on the door, they'll let you in. Number twenty-five, Chesterfield Street."

I walked over to the place, a lovely little West End townhouse, and rang the bell. It was immediately opened by another American, a tall, well-built man, who looked somewhat surprised when he saw me. "Hello," he said. "My name is Roosevelt. Come in."

I mentioned the meeting in front of Shepherd's and as we walked into the exquisite hallway, a short, stocky man in uniform joined us. "And this is Colonel Hoover," Roosevelt introduced him. I said hello and shook hands all around, familiar with the names but unaware of the family implications of the two men before me, FDR Jr. and ex-president Hoover's nephew. "I'm here for the food," I added.

The party had not yet started, the house was silent. I was obviously the first guest, Roosevelt and Hoover were my hosts. Most graciously they led me to a totally empty room, except for a huge table creaking with the most opulent buffet that even I, as a spoilt Leidener, had ever seen, from oysters and lobsters to Oeufs-à-la-Neige and fresh strawberries. London in wartime had never before hosted a spread like that. But the room was devoid of any other tables or chairs.

The frontdoor bell rang and my hosts hurried away to answer it. Left alone, I stacked one of the enormous plates with all the goodies it would hold and, by lack of choice, sat down on the floor. Not wanting to be in the way, I installed myself under the table and started my sumptuous meal, not as strange a situation then as it might seem today. After a while other guests came by to load up, as I could see by their legs under the tablecloth, and I had just lit an after-dinner cigarette when a young man, also clearly American, crept down and sat next to me. We chatted a while, then I asked him what the party was about.

"It's a farewell party," he answered.

"Who for?"

"For me. I am flying back to the States tomorrow."

"And who are you?"

"My name is Bill Hearst," he answered.

Coincidences have meaning. They are a system of beacons set out by Fate. Some are tough to read, others easy, but they are always well worth attention and respect. Coincidence is Fate in action.

Even I recognized the name of the famous publishing family. I took the Berlin manuscript out of my inside pocket ("I happen to have with me," in truth) and handed it to William Randolph Hearst, Jr., with the request to pass it on to a publisher in New York the next day. He readily agreed, assuring me that, although he had no say about its publication, he would get it to the right person. Then, underneath the table, he started to read its opening lines:

Ben Hein is late. He's always late, but never too late.

How many times now have we been over Germany together? Fifty-eight? Sixty?... It was published in Cosmopolitan magazine, the September ssue of 1945, in slightly condensed form under the title Mosquitoes Sting at Night. I got seven-hundred bucks for it. After this "coincidence" I never again doubted that I was meant to write.

CHAPTER 13

The Outbreak of Peace

In 1945, at the age of twenty-eight, I was a warrior, no more, no less, superbly skilled in the art of combat, loyal to his cause, proud of his calling. Righteous and confident without ever a grain of doubt, I executed my grisly missions with cold dignity and gloried in the task. Time and place had spawned and nourished me.

I was also unprepared for anything else. From the benign follies of Leiden, the flow of history had thrust me directly into the deadly game of war. Here, also, there were lessons to be learned, but I sometimes wondered about their future usefulness.

Some would withstand the test of time, in spite of war's unique teaching methods. Stooging over Berlin one night, in the final bombing run, solidly coned by searchlights, the yellow Boozer warning me of nightfighters on my tail, I asked myself what kept me flying straight and level like a duck in a shooting gallery, instead of twisting away into the safety of the vast black sky.

Keep going... keep going... why did I always keep going, even as a small boy past the Black Cave, while my little six-year old knees were shaking with fear? Surely, I didn't have to, I could have turned back? - No, you can't turn back. If you turn back once, you'll never get past it again. Not past this, not past that, not past anything in life. If you turn back once, you are lost.

Old skin-and-bones used a crack in the rocks and a pebble to teach this wisdom to his grandson, Ahmed, and me in the bargain. Fear lives in the Black Cave, but you must defy him, and a pebble in your mouth will protect you. His vital lesson, which sustained me in war and peace, proclaimed that in Life, Fear is the enemy, but Faith will defeat him. Faith in anything in which you believe, under whatever name you may cherish it. From the silent jungle path on Java to the chaotic war skies over Berlin, the spark jumped. I did not shout Hallelujah or Allah Akbar or started humming Om, but I did keep flying straight and level till we had marked the aiming point.

Having solved and rationalized my childhood visions, I had to cope with some of the theories which the RAF rammed down its gladiators' throats. One, however unconventional in contemporary Western society, greatly benefitted me in the long, but especially the short, run. It was the Airforce's insistence that a warrior's life is now or never, popularly verbalized as "Stop thinking about the future, or you won't have one."

At the time, I found this statement to be generally accurate. The pilot who bought investments, inquired about post-war job opportunities or created family involvements, usually got himself killed on short notice; "went for a Burton", in RAF lingo.

Authorities ascribed this phenomenon to lack of concentration, but I knew better: the dark prince, when blatantly challenged, asserted himself.

For me, there was no life after World War II. When ultimately proven wrong on this point, I smoothly adjusted the RAF's philosophy to peacetime conditions under the slogan "carpe diem". It conclusively prevented me from ever worrying about the future, ever saving my money or ever buying life insurance, convinced as I am that every crisis carries the seed of its own solution.

As aircrews of Bomber Command, living like nocturnal hornets in their private hive, we did not pay much attention to the rest of the world. In June, 1944, the news of the Normandy invasion did penetrate our cocoon, but we followed the majestic Allied sweep across Europe only sporadically, as it affected our air offensive. In the fall, while American armies advanced along the southern and central fronts, British and Canadian forces in the north stood poised to break into Germany's heartland. Three rivers in eastern Holland lay astride the direct route to Berlin, and in September, in operation Market Garden, the Allies assaulted the crossings. The first one presented no major problem. The second, the bridge across the Waal at Nijmegen, fell to a combined attack by British and Canadian ground forces, supported by American paratroops, for which the U.S. 82nd Airborne Division was awarded the Military

Williams Order. The third, over the river Lek at Arnhem, was A Bridge Too Far.

The failure to break through the German line caused a national disaster for my country. Western Europe's major rivers, the Rhine - split into Waal and Lek - and the Meuse, divide the Netherlands in two by their converging flow to the North Sea. The part below these vast bodies of water had been liberated by the Canadians, but now the northern provinces, which contain most large cities such as Amsterdam, Rotterdam and The Hague, remained in Nazi hands until the last day of the war. The winter of 1944/1945, known as Holland's "Hunger Winter", cost the nation 30,000 lives.

I first heard about it from Queen Wilhelmina herself. In London for a few days of leave around Christmas, I dropped by 77 Chester Square for a cup of tea and was told that Her Majesty wanted to see me. Expecting one of our informal little chats, I stepped into her room with a smile on my face.

"Have you heard?" she exclaimed stridently, as soon as she saw me. She was sitting in a small armchair, wrapped in a blanket. For the first time ever she did not rise to greet me. An aura of great agitation surrounded her. "Have you heard? They're dropping dead in the streets."

Caught off guard, I stared at her in bewilderment. What in heaven's name was she talking about?

"The people," she repeated, with a gesture of impatience. "Our people are dropping dead in the streets."

By this time most occupied countries had been liberated - France, Poland, Belgium, even our own southern provinces - but the tiny little corner of Europe which held all I truly cared for, was caught in a trap. Living my limited, self-satisfied existence in the RAF, content to risk my life now and then, I had been unaware of it. Edema? Pestilence? Hunger Winter? I had no idea what it was all about.

"Don't you know?" the Queen kept insisting. "Haven't you heard?"

I was shattered and at a loss. Her grief and despair shocked me, and I thanked God when the meeting ended there and then. Something made me pause at the door and bow in her direction, but she had already dismissed me. She sat staring out of the window into the gray afternoon, huddled in her blanket like a wounded bird.

I fled back to Upwood, to the impersonal safety of my sheltered existence.

* * *

Four months went by. The Americans were across the Rhine at Remagen, the Russians at the gates of Berlin. At RAF-Upwood life, for those who still possessed it, continued its deadly routine. The first two months of 1945 had been murderous, now casualties were beginning to fall off. Spring was in the air.

In the small hours of April 23, on return from an early attack on Kiel, I found a message from General van 't Sant next to my traditional after operations meal, a plate of ham and eggs with a pint of beer. It was the second piece of mail I had ever received in Upwood. The first one had arrived months ago, but still raised eyebrows in the mess. It was a picture postcard, addressed to Erik Hazelhoff, Royal Air Force, England, and the stamps were Turkish. It read: "Kiev, Ukraine. Cordial greetings. Wish you were here. - Aad."

I burst out laughing. I knew that my former friend and fraternity brother, Aad Robertson, fought with the Wehrmacht on the Russian front, although it amazed me that he was still alive.

Evidently he had found somebody to mail the card from neutral Turkey, which maintained postal connections with England. But the message came from Kiev, from the crumbling German armies in southern Russia. "Wish you were here." Oh, shades of Leiden!

"Interesting people you know," remarked the wing commander opposite me, with a little smile. I turned the card over. It showed three idealized SS officers, shoulder to shoulder in super-Aryan glowing color, arms folded, legs astride half the globe, against a blood-red banner with a gigantic black swastika.

Yet it had been properly delivered, no questions asked, by the British Post Office and the RAF. Highly civilized; Aad would have approved of that. Suddenly I felt convinced that if I'd gone to stay with him in 1940, after the arrest of his parents, or shown even the slightest compassion for his predicament, he would have been sitting here next to me tonight, eating eggs and drinking beer in RAF uniform. Too late now. The date on the card was October 11, 1944, a few weeks before he was blown to bits on the Eastern Front.

Van 't Sant's note had been delivered by courier and requested me to report to Chester Square as soon as possible.

After obtaining permission from the squadron adjutant I took the first bus to Cambridge, then a train, and made it to London by noon. The city looked fresher, but no.77 still needed a coat of paint. The Mews was all locked up, dark, overgrown by the lime tree. I slipped into the garden by the little wrought iron gate. The general was standing on his balcony, deep in thought. Only the sparrow was missing.

"How is Mr. Krediet?" he asked, as soon as we had settled down in his familiar office. As a matter of manners some chit-chat had to precede the real discussion.

"Fine. Just fine," I answered, which was only partially true. Chris had finally obtained a posting with the new Holland Spitfire squadron, commanded by squadron leader Bob van der Stok, one time stow-away on the St. Cergue. Apparently the Dutch lacked the convenient flexibility of the British: after a few missions he had been grounded because of his tendency to black out.

"And how's Peter Tazelaar?" I countered.

"Doing the best he can," came the smooth reply, but the general's bland expression did not go unnoticed.

"And His Royal Highness?"

"He's back home in Holland." That came as no surprise. Prince Bernhard had finally obtained a position worthy of his talents, Commander of the Netherlands Forces, including the former Underground. He now spent most of his time in Brabant, a part of our country which had been liberated, trying to create order out of the hordes of ferocious Freedom Fighters.

"Any word from Ernst de Jonge?" Persistent rumors about the arrest of Peter's successor in occupied Holland had long circulated, but the former Head of the C.I.D. always feigned ignorance. Not this time. He confirmed that Ernst was in the hands of the Gestapo. "That is, if he's still alive."

"Is that... hopeless?"

General van 't Sant didn't answer my question. He looked at me speculatively, I couldn't figure him out. "Jonkheer de Jonge had great potential," he finally said, respectfully using Ernst' noble title. "What he did not have, was a little bit of luck." He kept observing me, with an expression of objective interest. "Not like you. You have been very lucky, and that's why you have survived this war." "Now, hold it a minute, General. The war isn't over yet."

"For you it is," François van 't Sant stated dryly.

* * *

The DC-3 Dakota landed on the airfield of Gilze-Rijen, between Tilburg and Breda, in the liberated part of the Netherlands south of the rivers. Peter Tazelaar and I jumped out into the wet grass, helped to push the steps in place, and stood at attention on either side.

After a minute or two Queen Wilhelmina appeared in the door of the airplane. She gazed over the flat, green land and sniffed the moist breeze with obvious approval. Then she looked down the stairs. They were steep and had only one hand rail, on the left, where Peter was standing in stiff salute. I put out my hand to assist her, which she pointedly ignored. The first step back on Holland's soil after five years of exile, leaning on somebody else? Unthinkable!

With a fine balance of determination and caution she subdued this last obstacle, seven shaky rungs, and with a sigh of satisfaction stepped back into the Netherlands. I participated in the historic moment with one hand at my cap and the other reaching forward, like a doorman expecting a tip. Peter, facing me five feet away, barely managed to keep a straight face. And suddenly I saw him leaning on his shovel, half naked, black and sweating, and heard our laughter bouncing off the rusty plates in the bowels of the St. Cergue, when we escaped together from the Netherlands. Together we had returned, as aides-de-camp to our Queen.

Of course van 't Sant was behind it. After his cryptic statement that my war was over, he had sprung the news of my appointment on me cold. It wasn't the only bombshell he had in store. Minutes later the door opened and Peter stepped in. I had seen him last on the poop deck of the Aquitania, docking in Liverpool, on his way to join the London fire department for lack of an alternative. But this was no broken-down fireman who walked into the office; I found myself staring at a smart soldier, a feisty paratrooper, purple beret, wings, lieutenant's stars and... the ribbon of the Military Williams Order.

"What the hell happened to you?" I finally managed.

"I seem to be Her Majesty's new ADC." He gave me his grin for bizarre occasions. "You and me both."

"God preserve our Royal House," I sighed, much to the amusement of the general.

It was van 't Sant's master stroke. After everything the Dutch exile community had done to him, his constant battles with the bureaucrats, the accusations, his dismissal from the C.I.D., Queen Wilhelmina was returning to the Netherlands with the boys of the Mews, his boys. No wonder the general was beaming, while Stratton House, Arlington House and North Row were spitting fire.

As far as the Queen was concerned, she just wanted to come home in the company of Englandfarers who had done their best. Tazelaar and I filled the bill.

The former midshipman in the Dutch navy had indeed been a fireman in Soho for several months. Nobody else wanted him, he had reached the end of the road. Only van 't Sant never gave up. His patience was rewarded when in the summer of 1944 an Englandfarer, who knew Peter as a Resistance hero under the Occupation, became Minister of Justice. At last the general had an ally in the Dutch cabinet. In a matter of weeks the former Contact Holland kingpin had been rehabilitated, commissioned and knighted. No victory in his war with Stratton House, except perhaps our appointments as ADC to the Queen, could have tasted sweeter to the old fox.

Now they had to find Tazelaar a job, but about this he had his own ideas. He wangled himself onto a parachutist course and persuaded the new Dutch intelligence chief, Major Somer, to drop him into occupied territory. He hated flying and assured me later that he had jumped out over Holland with a sigh of relief.

As a secret agent he once again proved himself more than a match for the Gestapo. When the Canadians entered Friesland in April 1945, he had missed out on his own liberation, sleeping off the effects of a premature victory celebration.

I returned to Upwood to pack my bags and say goodbye. News of my glamorous assignment had filtered down from the highest RAF levels, and action at the bar was brisk and costly.

Now that it was all over, I didn't feel the slightest urge ever to go up in a Mozzie again. Midge and I met for dinner at the Pike and Eel in St. Ives, in order to discuss ways for keeping in touch. The solution was simple. Next morning we took the train to London and a bus to the registrar's office, and got married. We weren't too sure of the long term effects of this bold move, but somehow the future would surely take care of it all.

A week later the two brand new ADCs departed from 77 Chester Square. "I must say," Peter remarked, grinning his crooked smile as he looked around the comfortable surroundings for the last time, "she has a lot of nerve, the old lady, plonking herself down in that mess over there with us two as aides."

"We can't hold her back any longer. You know how she is," the general replied. Then some final doubt crossed his mind. His last words to his protégé's were, "Now, please, don't forget, you've got to behave.

What the Queen says, goes." It started off badly. Peter and I arrived early at the airfield. It was miserably cold and we hurried inside for a cup of tea. From the counter we had a clear view of the runway, so we relaxed and took our time. Suddenly a Dutch general burst in and said, with icy sarcasm, "If perhaps the gentlemen would care to finish their tea? Queen Wilhelmina and Princess Juliana have been waiting in the plane for fifteen minutes." We had kept our eyes on the wrong runway.

We ran onto the field. Around the DC-3 stood all the highest Netherlands authorities, including the entire top of Stratton House, waiting in the icy drizzle to witness the historic departure. A snort of indignation went up, followed by an almost palpable sigh of relief when we raced up the steps, in part no doubt because at last they were rid of us forever.

Inside the cabin Princess Juliana, who was accompanying her mother home after five years of exile in Canada, gave us a smile, not without amusement. But the Queen, who was sitting in a special armchair way up front, did not look around when we clumped aboard. The total immobility of the small figure struck me as ominous, and I did not know what to expect. However, when we reported to her, she smiled good-naturedly.

"I know, I know," she said. "I suppose you were having a little snort to celebrate our going home."

The DC-3 bounced along the runway, pilot Rijkhof opened up and seconds later England, and the war, lay behind me. It was May 2, 1945, five years almost to the day since the Nazis invaded the Netherlands.

Arrival in Holland, May 2nd, 1945

* * *

In the woods of Ulvenhout, a few miles from Breda, stood a country house named Anneville. Is it still there? In my memory it materializes unexpectedly at the end of a noble row of beeches, a square structure, modest yet stately, its driveway curving around a lawn where stone steps rose to a small portico. Five rooms upstairs, an equal number plus verandah below, a dozen steps and you were across it, looking through high, glass doors over gardens at the back and the Brabant countryside. Here, where low walls around the terrace crumbled and moss pushed up between the flagstones, the proud little mansion could no longer hide the neglect of five years of Occupation and settled comfortably among wide lawns, huge trees and mounds of rhododendrons clustered around a pond full of croaking frogs. When Queen Wilhelmina entered the front door, Anneville became the center of the Netherlands.

Here we lived, the five of us: the Queen, Princess Juliana, Peter Tazelaar and I, and our female counterpart, Englandfarer Rie Stokvis. General van 't Sant had sent along half a dozen military police, most of them sergeants of retirement age, who set up quarters above the garage. After five years of exile, this was the entire Court that accompanied the Royal Family home.

World War II was grinding to a close in Europe. The gigantic vise from the Channel to the Volga was about to snap shut. Somewhere in the endless rubble Russians and Americans had embraced each other. Rumors persisted that in northwest Germany the Wehrmacht was about to cease its heroic resistance. In Holland above the rivers, still occupied and on the brink of total ruin, the RAF and USAF dropped food parcels to the famished population. Tremendous events were unfolding, in the midst of which Peter and I struggled mightily with problems varying from the safety of the House of Orange to the acquisition of toilet paper.

A few years before, the thought of living in a modest villa with the legendary Queen Wilhelmina would have made our blood run cold. All our lives she had been the symbol of our fatherland, how would it be to sit across from her at breakfast?

We need not have worried, our relationship which over the years, imperceptibly, she herself had molded, had radically changed. Her demands were clear, simple and few: do your best and tell me the truth. Besides, she had breakfast in her room.

It all suited us fine. We loved our new jobs, but knew ourselves well enough to realize that in the long run the restrictions and discipline of a Court were not for us. We had no axe to grind. As a result the bonds with our royal employer were those of free men, unencumbered by ulterior motives, in blessed contrast to the dignitaries who sometimes emerged trembling from an audience with the formidable Queen, pale around the nose and grateful for the snort of genever with which we quickly forti-fied them on the verandah. From us she always heard it "like it was", and many a time I had to report another minor disaster resulting from our honest efforts. Then she would look at me accusingly and state severely, with a gesture of despair: "Captain Hazelhoff, you make it impossible for me to reign" - and smile at my discomfort.

On this basis we tacitly arrived at certain ground rules to ease the closeness of our day to day contact. She allowed us to contradict her, as long as we didn't quibble or mope. On the other hand, her orders had to be executed, even if we disagreed; we could, however, register pro-test, provided that it never led to the slightest hint of "I told you so". A certain amount of tact was of course expected, and then it was wise to remember that the Queen's sense of humor, not her strong point anyway, simply did not exist in relation to Holland and the House of Orange. In particular she detested Leiden humor, known for weirdness, and if some unfortunate guest had crossed the line, she would call me to her room afterwards.

"Captain," she would say, with a chopping motion of the right hand, "as far as I'm concerned, this gentleman is through. Forever!" If you were through for Wilhelmina, it was always forever.

All in all, she clearly enjoyed the measure of intimacy that the snug villa forced upon us, although to me the house seemed too small on at least one occasion. On the first night, looking for the bathroom, I saw Her Majesty approaching along the corridor in her dressing gown. Not wanting to embarrass her, I opened the nearest door and dived out of sight, landing in a narrow cupboard full of cleaning equipment. With a mop in my hand and my nose pressed against the inside of the door, I barely fitted. But evidently the Queen was also on the prowl. Suddenly she opened the door. We stood face to face, perplexed.

"Good evening, Majesty," I finally said, for want of inspiration.

"Good evening, Captain," Wilhelmina answered, with a startled glance at the mop - and slammed the door closed again.

Immediately on arrival in Anneville, the Queen plunged into the business of running the country. For everything else - food, security, communications, transport, mail, laundry and all household details - Rie, Peter and I were responsible. Somehow we managed, but she didn't always make it easy for us.

Generous farmers from the area had filled our cellar with wholesome foodstuffs, but when Rie produced fresh strawberries for our very first luncheon, Wilhelmina refused to touch them. "I do not intend to eat anything that is not also available to the people," she announced.

That afternoon application forms for food ration cards arrived which she insisted on filling out personally - Name: Wilhelmina. Occupation: Queen. Age: 65. And so on. The meager diet this initially supplied seemed insufficient to me from a health standpoint; after all, I was responsible for the Queen's well-being. Consequently, I ordered a steak to be placed in front of her one evening. Deep in thought, she munched on one or two bites. Then she froze.

"Captain Hazelhoff, this is steak."

"Yes, Majesty."

"Is everybody in Holland eating steak tonight?"

This was a statement I simply dared not make. When I pleaded how hurt the farmers would be if she refused their offerings, the Queen kept a furtive eye on the juicy filet mignon. Which one of us finally persuaded her to resume dinner, is anybody's guess.

The news of Wilhelmina's return spread like wildfire and from miles around Netherlanders hiked to Ulvenhout to pay their respects. Throughout those early days endless lines of sober, silent men, women and children shuffled down the driveway, past the portico and out the other gate. At first Peter and I reveled in the processions, standing behind the Queen in our beribboned uniforms, but it soon palled. From the eyes of the crowd, sunken deep in pallid faces, something passed between the people and their Sovereign from which we were excluded. Besides, standing there for hours on end was just too tiring. Not for Wilhelmina. Her desk was piled high with urgent matters of state, but the people came first. Once, when I saw how close to exhaustion she was, I ordered the MPs to speed up the pace. Immediately I was called to task. "In my garden nobody gets pushed around," she snapped, although she could barely keep upright. "Don't you ever forget it."

From the moment we set foot in Holland and saw the chaos of war all around us, I worried about her safety. On arrival at Anneville one of the MPs warned me that the garden might still be mined. The report came from the local Forces of the Interior, who advised that only the paved walking areas should be considered safe. Consequently I all but begged Her Majesty to stick to the paths, until the garden had been checked out with mine detectors.

That very evening I saw her walking to the pond, right across the lawns. With my heart in my throat I ran out of the house, restraining an urge to shout a warning. She heard my footsteps on the path and watched with unconcealed amusement as I gingerly tiptoed the final yards through the grass, pleading all the way.

"Oh, come now, Captain," she chided. "Do you really believe I'll suddenly blow up? Boom! Just like that?"

Wilhelmina blow up? Boom! Just like that? Not on my watch! Still smiling she let herself be persuaded. Slowly we walked back from the pond, first through the grass and then, to please me, along the paved paths. It wasn't just the land mines; less than a dozen miles away a desperate SS division held the northern banks of the rivers. I wouldn't put it past them to try and kidnap the Queen of the Netherlands, perhaps as a hostage, and got little reassurance from the presence of the fatherly military police sergeants above the garage, our only armed protection. Involuntarily I glanced over my shoulder. Dusk lay across the land. Under the trees and rhododendrons black shadows lurked. Why had the frogs suddenly ceased croaking? Who had turned off the lights on the terrace...?

Abruptly the Queen stopped in her tracks, head high as if she were listening. I felt goose pimples rise under the hairs in my neck. "Ah!" Wilhelmina sighed, breathing deeply. "Nowhere does it smell the way it smells at home." For the first time during that long, confused day it sank in. I was back in Holland. I was home.

* * *

Lt. Peter Tazelaar, who happened to be drinking genever with the MPs above the garage at Anneville when the Third Reich surrendered, goes down in history as the person who brought Wilhelmina the great news. In the late afternoon of May 4, 1945, she was meeting with a general in the small salon, when without knocking Peter barged in and announced breathlessly, "The Germans have signed the armistice! It's all over! It's peace!"

"She got up amazingly fast for an old lady," he told me later, "and there we stood in the middle of the room, shaking hands endlessly, and with her left she was pounding me on the shoulder."

The news caught me by surprise in Tilburg, where I was trying to scrounge some soap from a Canadian supply depot. Suddenly a man shouted in the soft spring evening, "Armistice! Armistice!" People ran out of the houses with the news, calling it to their neighbors, writing it on the sides of trucks slowed down by traffic. In no time the streets were packed.

As usual on momentous occasions, my immediate reaction was a desire to be alone. To escape the crowds, I took a room in a nearby hotel. I left the lights out and opened the door to the balcony. An enormous full moon stood above the town, pouring its silver glow over long lines of revelers, arms around each other's shoulders, ten, twenty abreast, bouncing along the blacked-out street below. Holland south of the rivers, including Breda and Tilburg, had been liberated primarily by the Canadians, assisted by some Polish units, who were now swept up individually as heroes by the emotional masses outside.

I lay down on the bed, fully clothed, surprisingly alienated. The moon poured its rays into the shabby room, from below rose the rhythmic, inhuman din of carousing Dutchmen. Where did I fit into the picture, in my foreign uniform with wings and ribbons, relics of an already antiquated way of life? Once before history had taken me through a similar sickening lurch, on May 10, 1940, when Nazi parachutists dropped on Wassenaar, on Leiden, trampling all familiar visions of the future. I had wept in defeat, now the moment had arrived to exult in victory. However, never having doubted it, I dozed off instead and slept soundly.

Wilhelmina wanted to enter the provinces in the north without delay, but Allied security authorities would not allow it. Unknown to her, the German commander in chief in Holland had not immediately accepted the surrender. Rumors were rife about fully armed Nazi units roaming the countryside above the rivers and quislings sniping in the towns, but she dismissed all such reports as exaggerated concern for her safety. To pacify her I proposed that I should go to Amsterdam and lay a wreath in her name on the spot where in the final days a last, large group of Resistance fighters had been executed. When after my return I reported to her on my sortie, she calmed down considerably.

We had traveled by car, a driver and I, and as all the old bridges were blown we had to cross the Rhine over the pontoons at Arnhem before swinging back west. The roads, what was left of them, were packed with military traffic, until suddenly in a wooded area between Oosterbeek and Amersfoort I noticed that we were moving all alone along the deserted highway. It struck me as odd, then I saw troops swarming among the trees on both sides. They looked familiar, and by no means friendly.

"Captain," the chauffeur said. He was one of the MPs who had spent the entire war in England. "What kind of uniforms are those?"

"Pay no attention, just drive on," I answered reassuringly. It was too late to turn back, now I had to keep the driver calm. From where I sat I could distinguish the skulls and crossbones on the SS caps. "Must be one of those newfangled units from Stratton House."

The wrecked tarmac slowed us down. As we approached, groups of Nazi soldiers gathered by the wayside, armed to the teeth. They looked tough and sharp, and gave no indication of ever having heard of an armistice. Seeing their swastikas press in on us from all sides, I thanked God that the Queen wasn't sitting in the back, giving them hell and making things worse.

It looked bad enough, but just as I was ready to stop and point out that nothing could be gained by bumping us off, some of the soldiers began to wave. We inched along, and as they fell back to let us through, a mild cheer went up. There could only be one explanation: we were sitting in a large, gray, unmarked car and neither of us wore a hat. They took us for Germans of unknown rank, and were evidently pleased that at least some of the Herrenvolk were still driving around in a decent automobile. I didn't have the nerve to wave back and told the driver to step on it. After a while the last soldiers faded away like spectres in the forest behind us. In Utrecht, where we bought the wreath, military authorities confirmed that the road from Arnhem was still in the hands of an SS division, which up till now had petulantly blown up every Allied vehicle trying to get through.

The final stretch also brought its problems. We hit the remnants of a tank trap, which ripped two of our tires from the wheels. The council of Amsterdam had been notified of my imminent arrival, I could not let them down. Leaving the driver with the car, I stuck out my thumb in the best U.S. Highway 40 tradition and hitched a ride in a laundry van. At the city limits a large delegation, headed by the burgomaster, awaited the Queen's envoy.

They were wearing morning coats hung with all the regalia of their offices. Their solemn expectation turned to chagrin, when they saw Her

Majesty's ADC emerge from a mountain of dirty linen with an outsize wreath draped around his neck. - Wilhelmina couldn't help laughing at the story. We were home alone and had finished dinner. As usual, the food had been placed on the table in advance; we helped ourselves, there were no servants. A spring night, barely dark, enveloped Anneville in silence. It was getting late, even the frogs had suspended their concert.

"Well, Captain," she finally said, "if you are going to have another beer, I'll have one with you. But only one; so much to do tomorrow."

I fetched three bottles of Heineken's from the pantry and four glasses, of which I put three in front of me, one by the Queen. Now came the Beer Ceremony. From each bottle I poured a mouthful into one of my glasses and tasted it carefully. Wilhelmina followed my ministrations with rapt attention. When I had found what seemed to be the least gaseous one, I pretended a moment's hesitation.

"This one," I declared at last, pointing with great finality, and poured the rest of the bottle into her glass. While I watched with tense concentration she took a swallow and, as always, nodded approvingly. The clock in the salon tick-tocked through the silent house.

* * *

At last Holland north of the rivers was declared safe.

Now nothing could hold Queen Wilhelmina back. It was decided to celebrate the official liberation of the country by her entry into The Hague, seat of government and cradle of the Netherlands.

The great day dawned in glorious weather, and at the appointed time our little cavalcade of three cars halted at the city limits. The Queen and her lady-in-waiting, a wispy old countess, transferred from a closed car to the open Packard, in which she would be visible to all. They installed themselves on the rear seat.

It seemed Her Majesty just couldn't get comfortable.

"I know," she finally said. "It's much too drafty here."

Since the temperature hovered around ninety and we were standing still, we all waited for what would come next. I might have known that she had something up her sleeve.

The previous day she had suddenly asked me, out of the blue, "You are from The Hague, aren't you?"

Fresh from the Indies, we'd made it our home. I studied in Leiden and my parents moved to Wassenaar, but The Hague had always been my territory, the place where I had gone to high school, where I played soccer, where my friends lived, where I grew up: my home town.

The two old ladies got out again. Her Majesty pretended to study the situation. "I know, we'll sit on the little chairs."

When she and the now somewhat bewildered countess had finally arranged themselves on the small folding chairs, she still didn't appear entirely satisfied. She glanced over her shoulder at the wide, empty back seat and ordered, "Captain, you sit on the rear seat behind me. Otherwise the whole thing looks ridiculous."

Otherwise the whole thing looks ridiculous? She fooled nobody. The gesture of letting me come home in the Queen's car, in the place of honor, but even more the elaborate act to mask her generosity, was pure, unadulterated Wilhelmina of Orange-Nassau.

I took my place in the back seat. Up front the driver and co-rider, both MPs, composed their faces. Slowly the big Packard rolled into my old stamping grounds. As soon as she saw people waiting to welcome her, Queen Wilhelmina, on the little chair in front of me, began to bow energetically, back, forth, back, forth, bouncing off the backrest, waving to the crowds, the crowds growing into multitudes, among the pennants and the flags and the flowers and the bows, orange, everything orange, into the storm of cheers, Long live the Queen! Long live the Queen! the mass of humanity breaking through police lines, pouring into the streets, pressing closer, ever closer, waving, laughing, crying, cheering, the Packard

all but submerged, Wilhelmina barely visible, smiling, bowing, waving, bowing, back, forth, back, forth, like a little windup toy.

I broke protocol only once, when I waved back at a little boy halfway up a lamppost.

Accompanying the Queen on her entry into The Hague
July 6th, 1945

CHAPTER 14

Living with Royalty

Wassenaar, as always, smelled of flowers - lilacs, late hyacinths, Japanese cherry trees, a far whiff of sun-drenched dune shrubs. I told the chauffeur to stop the car short of our house, so I could sneak up the driveway unseen. If my parents were still alive, and this was still their home, they would surely be outside on such a beautiful spring afternoon.

The garden looked lighter, sunnier then I remembered, as did all of Wassenaar; most of the big trees had been cut down for firewood. Walking down the familiar road, my heart pounding, all at once I saw my mother standing near the wisteria, motionless, admiring its purple cascade. I turned into the drive and watched her awhile through the rhododendrons, to prepare myself for our meeting... how skinny she was! When a truly emaciated man in absurdly droopy clothes appeared on the terrace, it took me several seconds to realize that it was my father. He carried something that looked suspiciously like a bottle of champagne. After crossing the lawn to the little pond, he pulled up his right sleeve, got down on one knee and very carefully placed the bottle in the water. When I stepped out of the bushes, he didn't seem a bit surprised.

"Saved it through the whole war," he said, after we had all embraced each other and could speak again. "Just for this. And now that you're here, the damn stuff isn't cold." He put his bony arm around my shoulder and laughed through his tears.

We had little more than an hour together that first afternoon. Following her festive entry, the Queen was staying in The Hague for a couple of nights. Noordeinde Palace was a mess, a million problems had to be solved. I had barely managed to sneak out for a quick trip to Wassenaar, but it gave us enough time to discover how far we had grown apart. After the joy of finding ` each other alive and well, we rapidly lost touch.

For my parents, as for most Netherlanders under the Occupation, Queen Wilhelmina had become a mythical figure synonymous with liberty, pride and Holland's national heritage. They had joined the faceless crowd in the streets to celebrate the return of all for which she stood; to find their son in her company was a shattering experience. Now I was here, dressed in a strange uniform, decked with insignia whose meaning they did not know, a creature from an other, foreign world. And I? How could I possibly fathom what they had gone through? Our mutual ignorance was too stupendous to tackle in such a brief meeting. We settled for the few subjects we had in common.

The news that I got married, and that to an English girl, they received stoically, as a fitting part of my new, alien identity. They didn't seem curious about her.

"Your sister has three children now," my mother ventured shyly. Ellen had married a Leidener, a member of Dutch nobility, just before the war. "The youngest is called Erik."

"After me," my father quickly added, as if afraid that I might rob him of this one vestige of immortality.

We were sitting on the terrace, savoring a pot of tea brewed from Twining's Orange Pekoe of which I had swiped a can from the royal larders. It was my parents' first real tea in four years. Although barely past fifty, they struck me as old. No wonder, after a thousand mornings of setting out for Schiedam and back again at night, twenty miles each way through Dutch weather and darkness on a bicycle with wooden tires, and my mother alone in the chilly house waiting and hoping he would make it home another day. Then the Hunger Winter, and the desperate treks into the countryside with hundreds of starving city dwellers to barter anything, from family heirlooms to genever, for something to eat, some potatoes perhaps, or else sugar beets, or even tulip bulbs.

We searched for other things to say. The scent of white lilacs filled the garden, the water in the teapot sang, in the distance a column of military trucks rumbled by. Young people live on the sufferance of adults, but somewhere in the progression of time the helm changes hands and our parents become guests in our world. In this first, peaceful afternoon together, mine seemed to silently acknowledge the transition.

We limited ourselves to news about people, which mostly confirmed what I already knew, or feared. Ernst de Jonge had been arrested and was last seen near Breslau on transport to some concentration camp where he never arrived. He was listed as missing, and was never heard from again. Chris' father, Dr. Krediet, died in Dachau of typhus, Jean Mesritz in Camp Nueengamme. Broer Moonen, the policeman who had rescued Tazelaar and Dogger from their short captivity in Scheveningen, had been executed. Sabina Zuur, Peter's girlfriend - and future wife - whom I tried to telephone on that same bitter night, had been taken to Ravensbrück, the notorious camp for women. Lex Althoff, the would-be passenger whom we had failed to pick up in Noordwijk, was shot at dawn in the dunes of Waalsdorp. "And that friend of yours, that SS bastard Aad Robertson, well, he also got it in the end. Killed in action on the Russian front." My father rubbed his hands with glee. "Serves him right. Nice ad in the obituaries, black border and all. Dead as a doornail."

"Where? In the Ukraine?"

"That's right." He looked at me with surprise. "The Ukraine. How did you know?"

I didn't answer. Why should I tell him about the postcard, we'd had enough confusion for one afternoon. Some other day, perhaps. Besides, it was getting late and there came the royal town-car to collect me. I got up, distressed. "I have to get back to the palace."

We said goodbye like strangers.

$$* * *$$

Once the north was liberated, we found out how deep a chasm really separated us from those who had stayed in Holland.

"If they tell me one more time that they hid under the kitchen table when the Gestapo came to the door, I'll throw up," Peter exploded one evening, after an unauthorized foray north to Rotterdam. He had been getting increasingly restless. Germany had capitulated, but there was still a war going on in the Far East; then what the hell was lieutenant Tazelaar doing hanging around Europe? Furthermore, the position of ADC requires a talent for playing second fiddle, an instrument for which neither of us had ever shown much aptitude. More and more I saw him wander through the gardens of Anneville with a face like a thundercloud, or found him sitting on the verandah at any time of day with a crock of genever. Evenings he usually disappeared, and at night he rarely came home at all. It was an old story.

Prince Bernhard, who occasionally whirled through our little household like a fresh breeze from the outer world, only made matters worse. As Commander he spent his time by preference with the Forces of the Interior, all former Resistance Fighters, a wild bunch if there ever was one. He brought with him the smell of adventure, and when he roared out of the gate again in his Triumph or Ferrari, we stared after him longingly. Especially Peter, who now began to abscond across the rivers, where the breath of war still hung raw in the streets.

"They all ran out of the back door, when the Gestapo came in the front. And they were always in the Underground." He snorted. We were lounging around on the verandah after a hot, bright day, the stone crock much in evidence.

"Well, how about you? I bet you regale them with your adventures on the beach at Scheveningen."

"Like hell. I keep my mouth shut. Nobody's business but my own."

"Yeah, you know why? Because you don't have to tell them. It's damn easy to be modest, when all the time you sit there with a bloody great Military Williams Order on your chest poking everybody's eyes out."

We never expected a hero's welcome home, but in the cities of the north, still reeling from the Hunger Winter, we were actively resented. After the shock of the liberation, the people quivered with nerves. Every town throbbed with frenzied celebration, but underneath the boozing and the singing and the sex, times were sad. There had been too much suffering, too much destruction, too much death. The shrill flags and pennants could not hide the profound grayness of the hour.

Onto this scene burst the Dutch from England, like Peter and I, well fed, smartly uniformed, lavishly beribboned. They wore stripes, wings, stars, all kinds of insignia including at least one fascinating decoration. Those who had survived the horrors of the Occupation had nothing to show for it, nothing to fall back on but words, words, words. We nodded, and nodded, and nodded.

The Canadians and British and Americans who had liberated the Netherlands constituted the new élite. They had houses, cars, liquor, money, and little else to do but give parties. Why not, had they not just won a war? To those festivities we got invited, but not the Hollanders who had stayed behind, unless they were female, young and willing. The former Resistance Fighter bicycled home in the evenings past mansions resounding with music and gaiety, and sparkling with lights, long dresses and uniforms - on his homemade, wooden tires.

Bars and nightclubs shot up like weeds. The London Dutch had British pounds and could afford them. The girls, even the most stalwart, were sick and tired of all the drabness, all those years. They, too, wanted to go dancing, and perhaps to bed with a glamorous uniform spiced with ribbons and stars. But the Resistance hero, who had risked his life countless times under the Occupation, stood outside in the cold and gnashed his teeth.

"Had a nice war?" he taunted us.

"Guess you were in the Underground," we sneered back.

Our disenchantment was mutual. For us, also, the liberation had been a shock. Through the entire war one dream never left us, not for a single day: our homecoming, to Holland as we remembered it. We did come home, but the memory was crushed by reality and the dream exploded. Our country lay prostrate, unrecognizable, emaciated like a wretch from a concentration camp. We couldn't cope, we turned away as from a leper, sickened and uncomfortable. We felt more at ease with our Allied buddies, with whom we had fought the war in freedom, than with our old friends who carried the mark of the Occupation. Would I truly belong anywhere, ever again?

* * *

The day after seeing my parents I had the town car drive me to Leiden, not without misgivings. The university was still closed, of course, and the town untouched by war except for an all-pervading shabbiness. Minerva looked shut tight, as if it would never open again. I told the driver to wait, and as I wandered around the quiet streets my steps inexorably moved in the direction of my old room. What would have happened to my former roommate, Paul Erdman, once a beacon of stability in a crumbling world?

The Rapenburg, all its trees cut down, curved bare and deserted on both sides of the now filthy moat. When I finally stood on the humpbacked bridge leading into the Kloksteeg, it struck me that only two things had remained exactly the same: the massive hulk of the academy behind me, and the sagging old house with the silly little balcony on the corner opposite. While I gazed at it, slipping back in time, the sheer curtains above the balcony parted as if on cue and there stood Paul, like in a Punch & Judy show. He peered at me intently, then his face broke into a wide grin.

"Erik!"

"Good God, same old Erdman!"

I clambered up the stairs, burst through the door, and stepped straight into the past. Nothing in the room had changed, including its occupant. He seemed no thinner, no fatter, not even older; he wore gray flannel trousers and a beige jacket, and had just enough of a tan to look smooth, handsome and healthy. After seeing what the Occupation had done to others this immediately irritated me, of course, yet I was impressed. We greeted each other warmly.

As soon as we sat down he rapped the floor with a cane, a few taps to attract attention, plus two. The same landlady appeared whose bottom Aad used to pinch, and politely shook my hand. She put the cups on the table. The level of the coffee, or what had to pass for it, still slanted alarmingly.

"Lucky you found me here," Paul began, after she'd left.

"I only keep this place as a pied-à-terre. I got my degree, as surely you know?"

I nodded vaguely, not really listening. The ghosts were all around me. Chris, still in England somewhere; the compelling presence of Ernst de Jonge; carefree old Aad, tall and handsome; big, quiet, brilliant Jean Mesritz, and so many more. Did I hear canes outside, tapping on the cobblestones?

"Yes sir, you're not the only LLD anymore. I'm on the list for the Justice Department." Paul laughed happily. "Passed my finals at the professor's home, sort of underground. Quite risky, really. You have no idea what we went through here..."

"Did you hear about Ernst?

"Missing, I understand. Somewhere out east."

"And Jean? And Aad?"

He nodded. "I always said, it gets you nowhere, these heroics. Too bad, really, all those great guys. Lead a constructive life, much more important in the long run. Help this country back on its feet." He smiled at me blithely, not a shadow of doubt in his clear, blue eyes. "And you? There's just you and me left, you know. And Chris, if he ever comes back. Of the whole bunch. Now that it's all over, what are you going to do?"

I didn't have the vaguest notion. I finished my coffee and pushed off. Undoubtedly the future of the Netherlands lay in the hands of men like Paul, capable, reliable, trustworthy, solid, but right now he gave me the creeps. My parents, my friends, my nation, what had happened to us? It was all a matter of time, of course... But how long?

From the Kloksteeg past the Pieterskerk I wandered aimlessly in the general direction of the car, listening to the sound of my solitary footsteps in the narrow, stony back streets.

The grayness everywhere soaked into my soul. Around Leiden the narrow borders of Holland pressed in on me like prison walls. I wanted out. World War II was over, the unexpected eternity of a lifetime lay before me. To live it, whatever that might bring, I needed room, air, light, warmth, color. I'd done my bit, it's all yours now, Erdman. Take it away, Paul!

* * *

On August 6, 1945, an American Flying Fortress called Enola Gay dropped the bomb on Hiroshima which supposedly shook the universe. Even this thunderous message barely penetrated our small, focused world in Anneville, where we returned from our trip up north. The young princesses, Beatrix and Irene, aged seven and five, were flying home from Canada, which had sheltered Juliana and her children during the war. I went to meet them in England, and when their mother was slightly delayed, chaperoned them home in an antique DC-3 with ventilation holes in the windows.

They were three adorable little blondes, the two eldest clearly excited about their fairytale destination, Holland. Irene sat quietly looking out, clutching a shaggy bear and eating candies. Beatrix, very much aware and on top of the situation, kept asking every few minutes, "Are we over Holland yet? Are we over Holland yet?" Then, at long last, I could answer "yes." Irene was just about to slip another candy wrapper through the ventilation hole, but Beatrix stopped her. "We are over Holland," she said severely to her little sister. "Stop making a mess."

At the airport a small welcoming committee of authorities and their beaming parents, greeted the plane, and I thought it important to pluck the little girls from the awkward doorway. Helping them down, I lifted Princess Beatrix, our future Queen, high into the summer air and planted her, after five years of exile, firmly back on Holland's soggy soil, where she walked off forever with my heart.

Prince Bernhard welcoming Princess Juliana with their children;
Princesses Margriet, Beatrix, and Irene, on their return to the
Netherlands. August 2nd, 1945.

When her mother joined our little household at Annneville, she unwittingly created a problem. A warm and sensitive woman, Princess Juliana had been raised to follow in the footsteps of Wilhelmina, an old-style authoritative queen. She suffered through a lonely royal childhood, and when the upheavals of war liberated her, instead of plus royaliste que le roi she became more democratic than democracy. She craved human contact on a basis of equality and pursued it steadfastly, sometimes desperately, throughout her life, including thirty-two years as Queen. Occasionally it got her into trouble, but it also earned her the love of the people and the title "mother of the fatherland".

In 1945, at last back in the Netherlands, she clearly relished the informality of our bizarre "Royal Court". She was at her best in a small group, and on warm spring evenings that reminded us of the radiant invasion weather five years earlier, we would get together on the back porch for a glass of sherry - Juliana, Peter and I, and our female counterpart Rie Stokvis. At first the princess would remain on the edges of the conversation, flitting in and out with her devastating sense of humor which unraveled every subject until it lay stark and clear on the table. After conquering our mutual shyness, which took us less time than it did her, our talks grew into friendly, cozy, sometimes intimate gatherings that melted the distance between us in the heat of the exchanges. Then it happened: one day I heard Rie address our future queen informally, by her nickname "Jula."

"Rie," I said, after luring her into my office. "None of that."

"She gave me permission herself. In fact, she asked for it," countered Rie, with typical Englandfarers' pugnacity.

"Then you've got to decline the honor. With regrets. We can't have this sort of thing."

The problem did not lie with Rie and Juliana. The trouble was that, all desires for equality notwithstanding, a vast distance between royalty and its subjects still existed. If we reduced that gap for ourselves, we automatically put our own persons above the people, at least in their eyes. For this the Queen had not brought us from England.

After tenacious resistance Rie agreed to abide by a verdict from General van 't Sant in London. Via the military I sent him a cable which, while incomprehensible for outsiders, capsuled the matter in a few simple words: "Who may say Jula?"

A few hours later I received his response. He obviously harbored the darkest suspicions. It read: "Not you."

In the end even Wilhelmina relaxed her fierce prejudice against the Press and agreed to hold a press conference for a dozen Allied magazine photographers, the first one of her life. She hated the media and never spoke of journalists, always calling them "press mosquitoes", sometimes grimly repeating the word full of malice. She called on me for advice.

"Is it customary, you think, to offer press mosquitoes any refreshments?"

"I would think so, Your Majesty."

"What do you think those press mosquitoes drink? Tea?"

"I think whisky, Your Majesty."

"Whisky? Press mosquitoes drink whisky in the middle of the day?"

"American and British do, Your Majesty."

"Well, I suppose you'd better get some and let the press mosquitoes in."

The photo opportunity had been arranged on the terrace. Wilhelmina and Juliana sat down frostily in two rattan chairs at a coffee table. The photographers rumbled in as far as a rope that kept them at a safe distance from the skittish Queen.

Anneville: With Queen Wilhelmina and Princess Juliana

They complained to me that the table looked too bare, could I kindly dress it up a little. But in these moods my royal employer became unpredictable. As I was placing a handful of papers before her she suddenly turned on me and snapped, "Oh Captain Hazelhoff, in the name of God, get lost."

She glared at me, I froze in surprise, Juliana burst out laughing, the cameras clicked and the picture they took appeared in dozens of publications over the caption "The Queen of the Netherlands discussing matters of State with an Air Force aide."

After the North had been pronounced safe, we immediately moved across the rivers to Apeldoorn. Driving out of the gate for the last time, I looked back once more. Anneville had played its part, and over the stout little mansion at the end of the sun- speckled country lane already lay that hush which is an echo of historic events.

Once in Apeldoorn, Wilhelmina, in line with her new spirit of renewal and equality, refused to take up residence in her nearby palace "Het Loo", and installed herself in a town house close by. Prince Bernhard, who had no such qualms, promptly moved his headquarters into the vacant building. This irked the Queen, and over tea one afternoon she suddenly said, "Captain, those boys are not eating off my silver, are they?"

It took me some seconds to realize that "boys" referred to Bernhard and his staff. "Eh...I really don't know, Your Majesty."

"And they don't sleep in my sheets, I trust?"

The odds were ten to one that they did, but I considered it imprudent to mention this. "Eh... I am sorry..."

"I don't want those boys to sleep in my sheets or eat off my silver. Kindly see to it."

There was little I could do, except hope that the issue would die a natural death. It did. But when half a century later my wife and I spent a night at her granddaughter Irene's home, the mischievous Princess, familiar with the above story, had our bed made up with Wilhelmina's ancient sheets. They were still fabulous, but the Old Lady's ghost was not amused and kept me tossing and turning through a night of guilt-laden dreams.

Apeldoorn meant back to normal, the beginning of the end. With the passing of the weeks, then months, Anneville became a mirage, the war a page in history. We began to feel like relics of romantic times and as could be expected, Peter was the first to disappear, wrapped in his usual cloud of mystery. He sneaked off to London and wangled himself into a British commando unit bound for the Far East. Years later he was spotted in a rice paddy near Sukabumi, Java, in mortal combat with some Indonesian guerrillas in their war of liberation from the Dutch.

When summer turned to autumn, I felt that my time had come. However, my assignment included preparing a list from which the Queen would choose a permanent ADC, a splendid position on the ladder to a glamorous Court career. Once that was done I could leave, and even the army wouldn't be able to stop me: To everyone's surprise except my own, its records showed that I was unfit for military service, on the grounds of "shortcomings."

I waited a little too long. One afternoon Her Majesty and I went for a walk in the gardens of Het Loo, I half a step behind her, hands behind my back, exactly like van 't Sant along the paths of 77 Chester Square. We were discussing possible ADCs, and I was about to suggest my prime candidate, Robert Bergmann, Englandfarer, career soldier and pilot, when she said in a pleased tone of voice, "You may put yourself at the top of the list."

What now? The Queen of the Netherlands requested me to stay and work for her - could I refuse? The answer was yes. She herself had taught us always to put our cards on the table, always to speak the truth. Even so, I kept my fingers crossed.

"Your Majesty, I have other plans. In a little while I would like to leave your service."

She didn't answer. Gravel crunched under our feet. The grass, newly mown, smelled warm in the sun. From an open window somewhere a typewriter clattered. It lasted so long that I finally added, "I hope you're not angry with me."

Queen Wilhelmina pulled herself up to her full height.

Walking behind her, I could not see her face, but her voice was barely audible. "No," she said. "I'm not angry. It's been very kind of you to string along with an old woman for so long."

After Apeldoorn we saw each other one more time, before I left the Netherlands for greener pastures across the Atlantic: the United States of America. I came to say goodbye in Scheveningen, where she now lived in a humble, commonplace home, right on the street. We chatted a little and drank a cup of tea. It was cozy, but we didn't say much. I sensed that the war was on both our minds, all the way from that first afternoon in Maidenhead, full of ripe colors and the sad evanescence of an English summer evening. The living room shook whenever a streetcar rattled past, line 9, the same that had inched by me on that grim, magical winter morning in 1942.

Finally I got up to go. Queen Wilhelmina saw me out to the front door, as would any Dutch house wife. While we shook hands she suddenly smiled, that same smile I had seen once before in my life - when she had just reached up, whacked my shoulder and knighted me.

"Anneville..." she said. They were the last words I ever heard her speak. She died before I returned to Holland.

"Anneville... that was our fairy tale."

CHAPTER 15

America Here I Come

From the moment I set foot in the New World, my career took off - downwards. Considering my background it wasn't too surprising, and it undoubtedly did me good. Ambushed by peace and its sudden necessity of facing a future, I went through a five year shake- down after the war, more than some, less than others. It was a period of furious but mostly pointless activity - punctuated by some cruel quirks of history - that to my memory presents one vague blob of chaos, sometimes poignant, often bizarre, but always confusing. Don't ask me to translate it into sense, it would require more imagination than I can muster.

In my logbook, for instance, a pilot's most sacred and incontrovertible document, it shows that in 1946 I made eight transatlantic flights between Amsterdam and New York, apart from my clearly remembering a crossing by boat. Not bad, considering that I came out of the war virtually penniless and never touched my father for a single of his many guilders, as long as he lived. An open, undated travel pass from my glory days with Wilhelmina may have played a major part in this mystery, but what was the purpose of these trips, what their effect? Your guess is as good as mine.

In spite of living in Flatbush, Brooklyn; Forest Hills, Long Island; Mountain Lakes, New Jersey; Pacoima, Santa Monica, Brentwood and Burbank, all in California; and later Park Avenue in New York City and Rye in Westchester, I know positively that between 1946 and 1950 I had only one regular job, lasting five months, as salesman in Mathes Men's Store of Hollywood, California, located about a medium close-up from

Hollywood and Vine. What did I use for money in all those places, apart from a few fees for short stories in Esquire, Cosmopolitan and Argosy, some lectures, and three days' salary for my movie career? Perhaps it'll come back to me in the telling. And how did I get to California in the first place? As a matter of fact, by B-29 Super Fortress, that's how.

All times and places of these five years bear memories, some of which I shall describe with whatever rationality I can recapture. The jumble of their resurrection is perhaps the proper setting around a central truth. They were the frantic activities of a writer who failed to face the fact that he was wasting time.

For me and many other Hollanders peace was askew from its very beginning. The bomb on Hiroshima did not only end World War II, but in the process ripped apart the very foundations of our lives. As all over Asia the Japanese pulled out their occupation forces, many of the indigenous peoples they left behind tasted political freedom for the first time in centuries. It did not put them in a mood to welcome back their former colonial masters with open arms. No matter that it was our place of birth, our motherland, for some our home, for all of us the cradle of our spiritual consciousness - on August 17, 1945, after 300 years, a group of Javanese nationalists under Ahmed Sukarno closed the door on the Netherlands East Indies and proclaimed the independent Republic of Indonesia.

Modern history moves at a stunning pace, and already it seems inconceivable that any sane person could ever have been opposed to the end of colonialism. For those of us who were I do not seek approval or even sympathy, just understanding. The hostile separation between my motherland and my fatherland hit us, their children, like a grievous divorce in our immediate family. It was not just a matter of economics and power, more personal ties of mutual respect and, yes, love had to be severed, and many of us, blinded by sadness, lost sight of the majestic flow of events.

If nothing else, my immediate reaction stayed entirely in character. After deciding to shake the mud of Holland off my clogs, geographically speaking, I had wangled a diplomatic posting with the grand title of Director, Netherlands Government Information Service for Canada, which, come to think of it, accounts for several transatlantic flights before Midge and I were settled in Montreal.

At the time of our arrival, the developments in the Dutch colonies were headline news. Republic of Indonesia? Holland kicked out of Java, island of my birth? This was very much my business, it seemed to me, and I began to inform the Canadians about the situation, or at least what I thought of it. Unfortunately, this corresponded in no way with the cautious official position of our government.

After a few warnings from the Netherlands ambassador in Ottawa, which I ignored, I was ordered to shut up. This did not sit well with me. At a packed Kiwanis luncheon, covered by the news agencies, I made one last, detailed, unequivocal statement on the matter, after which I received a telegram from our Minister of Foreign Affairs, Baron van Boetzelaer, to remind me that "the foreign policy of the Netherlands government is made by me in The Hague, and not by you in Montreal". It also announced my immediate suspension.

"If you believe in something," my one-legged grandfather used to proclaim, "you must fight for it. Always." Right or wrong, he might have added. So instead of frolicking in greener pastures we returned to Holland, where I presented my views in a series of lectures and interviews, eagerly published by the opposition press. This helped to almost topple the government - but not quite. It did suggest, however, that perhaps I was not cut out for the diplomatic service.

So there we were, Midge and I, back where we had started from. My last stand in the "Canada Affair" had been much admired by some, particularly old colonials, but the majority of my countrymen considered me crazy for having returned to Holland. The Marshall Plan had yet to spread its healing balm - green, the color of U.S. dollars - over Europe. The Old World lay prostrate, empty and exhausted, while the privations of the recent past caused a unprecedented wave of materialism. The vision of a juicy steak, a car with unlimited amounts of gas, nylon stockings, chocolate bars and fresh orange juice, as well as an income in hard currency to pay for it all, drove hordes of onetime patriots to the promised land.

There was an other reason. In the second half of the nineteen forties an old nightmare spread across Western Europe.

I caught a whiff of it from my parents, who received us with open arms when we returned from Canada. Their clothes fit again, and the house in Park de Kieviet had been freshly whitewashed. We promptly moved in with them.

"We bought a boat," my father told me immediately. "Twenty seven feet overall, with a self-draining cockpit." And then, a little shyly, "If push comes to shove and the weather's right, we could get across the North Sea in it."

Self-draining cockpit? Across the North Sea? What was this all about? My sister, Ellen, had made a spectacular comeback into my life by joining the musical chairs of divorces that convulsed Dutch society after the war and marrying my old buddy Chris Krediet. So now he was family; perhaps he could explain things to me.

"It's for the grandchildren," he said, referring to the three kids he had inherited in the bargain. "Makes eminent sense. The old folks are planning to stay, but with this boat they hope to give us and the kids at least a sporting chance, when the Russians come."

The Russians? What was Chris talking about? America and Canada still regarded the USSR as their faithful ally; hadn't President Truman just recently referred to Joseph Stalin as "Uncle Joe?" But on this side of the Atlantic the tremors of conflict, in Berlin, in Vienna, already disquieted the furthest corners of the Continent, and rumors of unspeakable atrocities by Soviet troops revived the historic specter of Mongol hordes pounding out of the east. Some Americans sneered at his Fulton, Missouri speech, but Winston Churchill was right: an Iron Curtain had descended across Europe.

It was in the air. One afternoon, in front of the Ministry of Foreign Affairs in The Hague, I saw a familiar figure striding towards me across the square, hands in his pocket, chin in the air, black eyes gleaming with pleasure at our meeting.

"Hazelsnout!"

Ben Hein, my crusty navigator, Pathfinder par excellence, was enjoying peacetime as president of a shipbuilding yard. He invited me then and there for a delivery cruise on one of his new coasters, built for a brewery, Saturday next in the harbor of Rotterdam.

It turned out to be one hell of a party. We motored up the New Waterway to a smooth North Sea and back again, and then stayed moored quayside till the small hours of the morning. The guests, glass in hand, roamed around the ship, admiring in particular a twin suite complete with bath and dressing room, more suitable for a villa on the Costa Brava than a commercial coaster. "That's for the president of the brewery and his wife," Ben whispered into my ear. "For when the Russians arrive."

"What's the matter?" I asked perplexed. "Is everybody in Holland planning to get out?"

"Everybody who's got the dough. That's to say, they are quietly organizing back doors to sneak out when the Cossacks come roaring in, although they won't admit it. - Can you blame them? One Occupation per lifetime is the limit."

Now I got it. Likely or not, the mere possibility of a second enemy occupation was emotionally unacceptable, and thus created the Arctic breath of fear which blew across Europe.

"And what about the people who don't have the dough?"

"Genever. Nothing but genever." Hein waved in the direction of the rowdy bunch in the lounge. "As you can see."

When he finally drove me home, the fog lay wrapped around the car like a blanket. Ben, if possible even more sozzled than I, maneuvered the car onto the highway, took the white centerline between the wheels, and crawled in the direction of The Hague; as yet there was no danger of traffic in postwar Holland at three a.m. on a Sunday morning. Somewhere along the way a slight bump woke me up. From the window I could just distinguish the railing of a bridge to my right. I fell asleep again, but eons later, out of the corner of an eye, I still saw the railing next to me.

"Ben, either that bridge is moving with us, or we are standing still."

"Bullshit." Ben Hein kept driving, slow but steady, shifting a couple of times and listening. "The engine is running and we're in gear." He snorted indignantly and pushed the gas. It was just like old times, shoulder to shoulder in a Mosquito.

"Well," I announced, "You just keep going, I'm bailing out to take a look," opened the door and got off. The road stood still, so did the bridge. But the white centerline had led to a narrow, low traffic island in the middle of the highway, which we had very slowly mounted, until it had pushed the rear axle upwards and the wheels off the ground. They were spinning around obediently, but under Ben's firm hand we had stood still for hours in our foggy cocoon.

I got back on board and slept on. Let 'em come, those Ruskies!

* * *

Doubt and indecision are the termites of life, which if unchecked will destroy its foundations. Staying with my parents in Wassenaar, without a job, unsure where to turn, how to restart my career, slowly drove me—and all around me—nuts. For lack of alternatives I finally decided to tackle what I should have done immediately after leaving Queen Wilhelmina, and sat down behind my typewriter to produce a book about my war experiences. Finding a publisher proved no problem.

Theoretically, writing is no more than giving form to formless matter, the intellectual organization of a chosen subject for clarity and effect, occasionally flashed through by a thought or sentence of which the author himself does not know the source.

In reality, his total personality is involved. At first, it was smooth sailing, but after three months I foundered. My narrative had landed me in London, where I shipwrecked on my memories. They were too recent, the wounds too raw, I sat gnashing my teeth with vengefulness, by no means aimed at the Germans alone. It all had to settle, ripen and ferment before I could produce a balanced work... surely... Or was I kidding myself? In any case, I stuffed the partial manuscript in a metal cookie box, dumped it in the attic of my parents house, apologized to the publisher, and for the next quarter of a century burdened myself with the unfinished project in the pit of my stomach.

Meanwhile the Indonesian question churned along miserably, at least for the Dutch. The American press in particular pilloried us, day in day out, with sanctimonious lectures about freedom. I was appalled. Were these our pals, with whom we had just suffered through five years of war? Their historical motivations I understood and respected, but for a nation that had solved its native peoples problem by all but wiping them out and consigning the sorry remnants to miserable reservations, a more subdued tone would have seemed appropriate. After all, under the Dutch the population of Indonesia had increased tenfold, and all the intellectuals who now guided their quest for independence had studied at Leiden University, sponsored and financed by the Netherlands government.

"You must go back to America and explain things," Professor Pieter S. Gerbrandy implored me, poking his finger into my stomach. Holland's diminutive prime minister of World War II had telephoned and asked me to visit him, giving an address in a modest neighborhood in Scheveningen, close to the dour Dutch Reformed fishing families whose hero he was. I rang the bell to his unassuming home and waited, half expecting His Excellency to open the door naked, a towel around his little belly and his fierce whiskers drooping with bath water. It all seemed a very long time ago.

He opened the front door himself. He had hardly changed since our meeting in Brown's Hotel, except that he seemed even smaller. His head now reminded me of an ivory billiard ball with a fake moustache glued on, above which his eyes disappeared entirely in the wrinkles of his welcoming smile. We sat down in his parlor at a table covered with a Persian carpet, true to Dutch middle class tradition. Once tea had been served by a girl in a white bonnet, the old walrus wasted no time.

"They don't understand us, the Americans" he went on. "They don't realize what we're trying to achieve." The Dutch government had offered Sukarno all kinds of compromises in an effort to keep the Netherlands Kingdom together, some of them far-reaching for the times, but not enough to satisfy true revolutionaries. "You must go back and explain."

"And where will the money come from?" I looked dubiously around the spartan living room.

"You must go back and take a job," Gerbrandy elaborated helpfully. "And at the same time inform the Americans."

Strange as it may seem, that's exactly what I decided to do. Tired of Europe, dubious of its future, I would return to the USA, of which I had nothing but pleasant memories, make a fortune and create understanding for the Dutch cause on the side.

Emigrating to the United States right after World War II had to be more complicated and time consuming than ever. National quotas were under enormous pressure and waiting lists endless. My plan was simply to bypass these obstructions. In a nutshell it amounted to: let's go, and somehow we'll manage. As for sponsors and Green Cards - never heard of them.

So off we went again, Midge and I. Our diplomatic visas were still valid, and red tape was delaying the administrative implementation of my military discharge, with the result that although I had flown the coop, basic paychecks kept fluttering after me for a while. The future, while admittedly vague, once again looked rosy.

Our first address was Flatbush Avenue, Brooklyn. Well, why not? Rentals around New York, every European's starting point, were hard to find, the ad looked good and the price was right. There were some culture shocks, I must admit. Having been lured to Brooklyn because of the rustic charm of its Dutch namesake, Breukelen near Amsterdam, and to Flatbush on account of bucolic visions this name evoked, I found myself distinctly disappointed on both counts. The friendliness of its inhabitants, however, who clogged the streets in their thousands, more than made up for this. It appeared that they had their origins in a tribe called "Dodgers", and were usually on their way to or from an immensely popular ritual at a holy site named Ebbetts Field.

Two years later, when I understood enough about America to be lured to a truly global sports event, the World Series, I found to my astonishment that, in baseball, "world" meant the combined banks of New York's East River.

In these alien surroundings I immediately set out to make a living and simultaneously influence public opinion in favor of the Dutch, preferably by combining both. If you're ever looking for a job without a future, try lecturing Americans on the virtues of colonialism. I got one or two bookings, miserable affairs for civic clubs in high school classrooms, but mostly because my agent mistook Indonesia for a new fleshpot in the Caribbean. To further confuse matters I performed dressed up in my RAF uniform, and after taking a long look at me he booked me for a Women's Club luncheon in Mountain Lakes, New Jersey. It was such a roaring success, at least socially, that we promptly moved into the attic apartment of a large house on a lake, belonging to one of the Club members. From that day onwards, in spite of the hard-hitting political content of my lectures, I was in constant demand for weeks in advance.

While making some progress in the conversion of New Jersey, perhaps, my national impact did not keep pace. Apart from an occasional article I managed to place in mostly right wing publications, the American press kept clobbering the Netherlands position, capably fed by Dr. Tambu, a British-Indian expert who ran the Indonesian Information Service. We had never met, but we knew about each other. An almost personal rivalry developed between us, but I'm sure he didn't worry. The Indonesians had Washington and Main Street behind them, unlimited funds at their disposal and, let's face it, a better product to sell. It did not take Dr. Tambu long to wipe me off the map and think he'd seen the last of me. But Fate has a sense of humor, and three years later at the other end of the world it gave me the opportunity to pay him back. In spades.

* * *

So much for world politics. Nor did I do much better in the fortune department. Women's Club lectures are no gold mine, and my military checks, already truncated, barely kept us afloat and were doomed to be discontinued shortly. One day I noticed that the area where we lived smelled of perfume. Tracking down the source of the emanations, I came to a soap factory in nearby Boonton which must have been desperate for labor. When on an impulse I inquired about a job, all doors opened and I found myself sitting opposite Luigi, the vice president.

"Let's see your papers," he said with a spicy accent, after I told him that I was new in town. Then he added, "In the USA, no Green Card, no work."

"Well," I countered, after this alarming information, "where can I buy one?"

"You can't," he explained. "You ask for one, you get one."
That sounded fair enough. "Whom do I ask?"
"You go to the American consulate in Montreal, ask for Anna. She's my cousin, she works there. Give her this," he handed me his card, "she'll fix you up. Then come back, I give you a job."

This seemed excellent advice, considering the urgency of the situation. It struck me as somewhat informal, but what did I know about the intricacies of the United States legal system? I took an overnight train from New York City, and three days later was back in Mountain Lakes. With a Green Card.

I truly intended to join the great American workforce, soap division, New Jersey, but just about then Midge was entering the later stages of pregnancy. Naturally, to me at least, I would not hear of letting my offspring be born in the USA, or anywhere else for that matter except the Netherlands. Hadn't I been dragged from Surabaya to study in Holland for somewhat similar reasons?

Whatever life would bring, my progeny had to know where its roots lay in this world. And so, reneging on my career in the soap business in Boonton, we flew back to Amsterdam, Green Card in my pocket. As Anna had told me that it normally took two years to get one, I prudently did not say goodbye to Luigi.

When our baby was born, it wasn't nearly as scary as I had feared. The thought of becoming a father did not excite me, but I sensed that life would not be fully lived without the experience of procreation. Mostly I was curious: what would it be like to come face to face with one's very own flesh and blood? Well, let me tell you, it's a blast. After dropping off Midge at the hospital one evening in February 1947, I returned home to await developments. Around midnight the rain turned to sleet and covered Wassenaar with solid ice. By the time I made it back to her bedside after the urgent phone call, my wife had taken care of everything just fine. The baby, a boy, took one look at me and smiled his way to the core of my soul. The doctor tried to convince me that it was just a gas bubble, but he was too late. The arrow had struck, it never let go.

Six months later the three of us flew off to America, still followed by paychecks. Thanks to Luigi's Green Card we were legal immigrants, so now it became serious. The road back had been cut off, for if I did not make it this time I would be returning to Holland a failure, who would have to beg his friends for a job. Never, thank you very much.

After landing at New York's Idlewild airport we took a taxi and stopped at the first "Apartment for Rent" sign, in Forest Hills, Long

Island. It was a lucky choice. An early snap of frost had fanned the maples to flaming bouquets, which the dazzling Indian summer of 1947 gently wrapped in mild, motionless air. We walked the tree-lined streets pushing a baby carriage, a display of parental pride that got me jeers in Wassenaar, while here I felt like Rhett Butler trying to charm the citizens of Atlanta. In the distance, white against the pale blue sky, glinted the promise of New York.

Meanwhile the Indonesian question had gathered momentum and crossed an ugly line: in the summer of 1947, while we

With baby Erik – Born February 17th, 1947

were in Holland, Dutch troops had gone into action on Java. That same day I had visited Professor Gerbrandy and told him I quit. I'd done my best, for whatever it was worth, but wanted no part of a military situation. Slowly but surely I got inklings, more instinctive than intellectual, that I'd better take another good look at the developments in the former Dutch East Indies. Sukarno holding fiery speeches was one thing, but a young Indonesian dying in a rice field from a Dutch bullet... for what? For his country? For freedom? Whatever it was, he had considered it worth dying for. So what made him different from me, except that I was alive and he dead? And how about some very good friends of mine, who had been killed facing him in the same sawah?

I turned away from it all. Having recently survived my own war, I claimed the right to live forward, away from death and destruction. Pushing the carriage with my son through Forest Hills, I watched the skyline of Manhattan against the setting sun, like the gate to the postwar world. The place of my choice was here, and the future now.

* * *

During our months in Holland I had written a synopsis of Rendezvous in San Francisco and translated three chapters into English.

Now I needed a publisher. As far as I was concerned, New York City consisted of the area between Madison and Sixth, from Central Park to 42nd. Street. Walking down Fifth Avenue I saw "Charles Scribner, Inc." on the left side of the street, a name in publishing with which I was not unfamiliar. Inside I asked to speak to somebody, to which the receptionist answered, "I am somebody."

This I found hard to dispute, so I gave her my manuscript and telephone number. Within a week she invited me back. I was received by a middle-aged editor with pepper-gray hair and glasses, who introduced himself as Maxwell Perkins.

This, I am ashamed to say, meant nothing to me then, unaware of his reputation as one of the greats in the book business. He greeted me and turned me down with grace and charm, and one unforgettable consolation prize. "We are three editors here," he said, or words to that effect, handing me back my envelope. "We always vote on manuscripts. With yours, one of us voted to publish it, the other two found it too dated, what with the war and all. Thank you for letting us read it."

"Who voted for it?" I asked.

"I did," he answered. Only later did I realize the magnitude of this complement.

Nonetheless, it was a disquieting development. An advance would have seen us through, but what if my checks stopped coming?

On an impulse I crossed Fifth Avenue into Rockefeller Plaza, and as the sun was past the yardarm I poked my head around the door of the Netherlands Club, on the corner of 48th. Street. Holland being a small country, I knew half the people there. Apart from the regulars, mostly businessmen and consular officials who had spent the war in New York, half a dozen somewhat loud and clearly less established figures sat around a corner table overlooking the skating rink, sipping beer and genever. One of them, tall, dark and handsome in an expensive glen plaid suit, jumped up and greeted me with a sweeping bow.

"Welcome, sire! Always room for another half-assed immigrant." Herman van Brero, alias Count B, would-be duelist and around the world Englandfarer, in his usual sardonic way, had immediately put his finger on a tender spot.

Emigration is a precarious proposition. No matter how justified the criticism of one's homeland, he who tears himself away from his familiar surroundings opens a wound that heals slowly, if ever. In case of hunger or persecution it can be a bitter necessity, but whoever left Holland after

World War II did so of his own free will, without duress, fully responsible for his own decision.

Some, especially those who moved off with their whole family "for the children's future", resolutely challenged the past. They hurled themselves into their new surroundings, Dad joined the Lions or the Elks and the Voluntary Fire Fighters, Mom supported local charities and the PTA, the kids entered Sunday school and the Little League, at home they spoke English, period. And when after work Dirk was sitting in front of his brand new TV, trying to make sense of American football, a metal can in his hand with some weak fizzy beer, he would be sure to hide the longing for his weekly soccer game deep in his heart.

Others had bid their homeland farewell for less cogent reasons: they wanted to make more money quicker, the Russians were sure to come, or their lives had somehow become too deeply entangled abroad. Less motivated, they required time to make up their minds. They kept close contact with each other, continued to speak their own language even in the presence of Americans, and spent endless hours at Dutch clubs hunting through hometown newspapers for items that confirmed the wisdom of their move.

"I suppose you're an U.S. citizen now?" I asked Herman, after the first genever.

"Who, me?" Count B, whose objections to America, as well as Holland for that matter, were many and specific, looked at me aghast. "Are you out of your mind? These guys here freeze their beer and pour Coca Cola in their whisky. And they walk hand in hand with their wives through the streets. In broad daylight. Their own wives, mind you."

"Then why are you here?"

"Holland's flat on its ass. Did you see the Telegraaf this morning?"

Van Brero's syndrome was widespread. Thousands of Europeans - and a few Americans - found themselves emotionally stuck between the two continents. In 1950 it was said that more people lived in mid-Atlantic than any other place in the world.

The USA offered prosperity, admittedly, but the Dutch did not stay on their backsides for long either. Thanks to the Marshall Plan, drastic fiscal measures and much hard work by those who had stayed home, life in Holland improved steadily. And those tricky Russians let themselves be scared off by NATO, another worry gone. Now all that the newspapers presented to Herman and hundreds like him, as part of the daily problems, was the warm glow of the old, the familiar, the truly Dutch atmosphere which, naturally, you cannot get abroad. Had they made a mistake? Had they been wrong to leave? Were they really better off? And happier?

In their letters home they wrote exactly how much money they were making, carefully converted into masses of guilders, and enclosed pictures of villas and Buicks which proud fathers could show around to prove how well their faraway offspring were doing, without the slightest notion of the price these were paying for their material wellbeing. Pretty soon they came to Holland on vacation and bought a new car, tax-free, slightly more luxurious than the average Dutch family could (yet)afford, seeking an antidote for their self-doubt in the envy of their former friends. But nobody gave a hoot, they were much too busy.

"Well, what's it like being back in our little frog- pond?"

"Great! Great! - But I couldn't live here any more."

Damn right they couldn't. Life knows no round-trip. The family home, the soccer field, the musty café on the corner, old churches mirrored in canals, the blustering wind, hyacinth fragrance in the spring, a brown sail under scurrying clouds, the gray North Sea - the past, the past! Panta rhei. They had outgrown their fatherland, and partially relieved by this discovery, partially shaken, off they went again, to Canada, to America, to Australia.

I didn't give it much thought. Here I was, in America, by choice. Thirty years old, having never had a job before, except military service with temporary attachments to the Queen and the Foreign Ministry, I realized that I would have to start at the bottom. So be it. As I still did not consider writing a possible way of making a living, I would avail myself of other established methods for getting work, like the State Employment Agency. I entered the office with the sublime confidence of the ignorant.

"What diplomas do you have?" the friendly lady inquired, spreading an enormous printed form on the desk between us.

"I hold a law degree," I answered coolly.

"Which university or institution?"

"Leiden."

"Leyden, Massachusetts?"

"Leiden, Holland. - Europe," I added, to make sure.

"Not applicable," she stated cheerfully, and drew a line through an whole bunch of paragraphs. "Have you got a skill?"

It took me a moment or two. "Pilot. I can fly planes, I'm pretty good."

"What kind of license?"

"Singles. Multi-engines, most anything really. Military planes."

"Military? Only military?" She smiled. "N.A., not applicable." Once more the pencil traveled through a dozen sections.

"Do you have any specialized knowledge? Languages?"

"French, German, Dutch, Spanish," I started. She seemed genuinely pleased and got busy making notes, nodding her head in encouragement every time I mentioned another language. "A spot of Malay..."

"Any teacher's licenses? High school? Grade school? Translator's diploma?"

Another scratch across the form. By now we had arrived on page three. For a while we went on like this, but whatever I had learned or done in my life, all proved to be N.A. in the USA. The busy pencil whipped through one paragraph after another.

Finally the only thing left was one very small open space, at the bottom of page four. The lady hesitated.

"You're sure that's all?" She asked, gently. I nodded my head.

"Unskilled laborer," she wrote in the little square, and made it official with the Seal of Authority.

That far down the hole I was not prepared to start.

* * *

In the USA, there's always Hollywood. A common section of an unlovely city, shown up by posh neighbors, devoid of charm, undistinguishable from thousands of other American urban horrors, and yet a potent presence in the consciousness of the entire nation and much of the world. Apex of glamour and youthful ambition... - but I guess this is where we part company. Too much in my Dutch upbringing had conditioned me against the cult of the film star. Not that I had anything against fame and fortune, but in their place. I was raised to consider movies and sports as entertainment, and entertainment as the fluff of civilization, not to be taken seriously. Nor did I share the average American's passion for publicity, good or bad, anything as long as they spell your name right, as if it were a ticket to immortality. But hey! This was a new era, a new world, this was Hollywood, America, 1948! I would give it my best shot. As unskilled laborer, what did I have to lose?

First we had to get there. The blizzard of 1947 hit Forest Hills just before Christmas and buried it under three feet of snow, with drifts up to ten. Nothing could get through, not even the mailman. When finally he did, he brought us our usual government check neatly annotated to inform us that this was the last one - after two years of grace, implacable peace had caught up with us. One month's rent had been paid in advance, we had a few hundred dollars in the bank, if we meant to make it to California it had to be fast - and cheap.

My logbook reads: "1948. March 15. Lockheed C-45. (Pilot) Colonel Seal. Mitchell Field, Long Island - Wright Field, Dayton, Ohio." Followed by: "1948. March 16. B-29 Super Fortress. (Pilot) Captain Sylvester. Dayton, Ohio - Denver, Colorado - Ogden, Utah - Sacramento, California."

As was to be expected, getting out of Forest Hills we ran out of time and money; but in packing I came across my RAF uniform, wings, ribbons and all. It still fitted. Handing Midge what was left of our finances, just enough for one one-way train ticket to Los Angeles, babies free, I slipped into my war togs and set out for the nearest military airbase, Mitchell Field, Long Island. In 1938 I had made it across this continent for under ten dollars, it seemed worth a try adjusting my hitchhiking style to modern technology.

Nothing could have been easier. Within an hour two generals took me along in a staff plane, with Colonel Seal at the controls, and dropped me off in Dayton. The officers at Wright Field airbase received me like an honored guest, supplied me with drinks at the bar and a copious dinner in the mess. It turned into a delightful evening. No one asked for any identification or travel orders. As far as security was concerned, I could have been the head of the KGB or Joe Stalin's nephew.

The next day, after a good night's sleep in a private room and a stupendous breakfast, I flew across the rest of the USA in a Super Fort, captain Sylvester as pilot, with stops and meals in Denver and Ogden. Part of the time I sat in the cockpit, remembering the many times we had met, Fortresses and Mosquitoes, at dawn or dusk, the ones going out, the others coming home, over France or Holland or, mostly, the North Sea. What splendid times they had been, how great to meet again! - We parted in Sacramento, California, and I took some stupid bus to L.A.

A week later Midge and son arrived in Pacoima, a dusty little outpost of the never-ending city, where I had found a motel we could afford. Three days they had travelled by train, then rented a car somewhere, because I remember them driving up in an old, open jalopy piled high with suitcases, boxes, pots and pans, like a ghostly apparition out of

Steinbeck's Grapes of Wrath, Midge at the wheel with a bandana around her head, and little Erik, red as a beet, strapped in the seat next to her. With wife, baby, no job, no qualifications, no contacts, no transportation, I counted our pooled resources and came to 36 dollars and 14 cents. The next morning a child in the room next to us came down with polio.

Welcome to sunny California!

* * *

If you must pick yourself up for a comeback, ground zero provides the ideal starting place. The road ahead, though rocky, is one-directional, which reduces the risk of confusion. A look into the abyss, furthermore, offers a marvelous incentive for making sacrifices. Adjust or perish!

For a start, I needed a breathing spell to lay the groundwork, and fell back on an old ally. When in the war I had been hanging around London, out of favor with the Dutch authorities both before and after Contact Holland, I had temporarily kept myself afloat on the proceeds of a heavy gold cigarette case that my father pressed on me prior to every one of my escape efforts. "If you need money," he would urge me, "take it to the pawn shop. But always get it back." I had followed his advice, and did so now. It bought us time.

We left Pacoima in a panic, miserable about the sick little Mexican boy next door and dousing Erik with whatever antiseptics we could lay our hands on. We moved to Santa Monica to a typical motel of those times, five individual cottages under a large tree, until a raise in rent from $ 5.- to $ 8.- per night drove us out; then to a small hotel in Hollywood, where the paper-thin walls turned our nights into sex education classes; next to Brentwood, where instead of paying rent I had agreed to maintain forty rose bushes for the absentee owner, a never-ending battle against weeds which I lost; and finally to Burbank, home base for the rest of our West Coast initiation.

Circumstances could not have been tougher, but the rewards proved commensurate. Wherever we went, the people were a revelation, of all ages, all races and backgrounds, always ready to help, with young Erik, with our bags and boxes, with their cars, their food, their generosity and good cheer. Nobody had much, but whatever they possessed they were ready to share. In the middle of the twentieth century, in Hollywood, California, of all places, poverty proved the key to a compassionate America. For me, in 1936 as well as 1948, the most appealing way to experience the USA was from the bottom up.

Take Arles White, my fellow salesman in a men's shop on Hollywood Boulevard, where I snared the first job of my life. He came from Needles, somewhere out in Indian country, a small, wiry young man whose dark good looks and radiant smile betrayed some native blood. To me, raised with Karl May's image of Winnetou and his Apaches, this was a source of wonderment and awe, but to my surprise "Whitey" did not share my excitement about his lineage. Apparently in California to be a native American, even partly, was reason for embarrassment. He asked me to shut up about it, while quietly taking me under his wing.

As a retail salesman in "Mathes of Hollywood" I was a bust, naturally. I had never sold a thing and always congenitally looked down on the profession, which my father used to refer to as "counter jumping". My salary amounted to $ 175 per month, plus two percent of my gross turnover. I had one month to reach a daily sales level of $ 100.-, or get fired. Whitey did his best to teach me, but I proved a slow learner. At the end of the trial period, keeping fearful track of my progress, I knew that I was still well below the required amount. Yet I didn't get the pink slip. This remained a mystery for several weeks, until I found out that my fellow employee, without telling me, would each day write my number on enough of his sales slips to lift me over the dreaded threshold, at considerable cost to his own paycheck.

Ultimately I clawed my way to the magic level, and beyond, and life settled down. Our motel, a group of cabins, was built on a corner of the old Lockheed airport in Burbank, which made it noisy but cheap. The view was generally extensive, except when the engine nacelle of some parked plane all but stuck into our bedroom window. Here I departed every weekday morning plus Saturday at 7:30 in order to hitchhike to Mathes by nine, with one quarter in my pocket to cover all expenses for the day, including lunch in a nearby cafeteria - a slice of apple pie with cheese and a cup of tea. Both Midge and I limited ourselves to one bottle of beer a week with dinner, to which we looked forward all day.

Yet, the weird little cabin on the edge of the airfield breathed contentment. For both of us the days were endless, but at least they made sense, and a semblance of purpose and normalcy entered our lives. Young Erik thrived, and on evenings when I'd had an especially good day at work, we celebrated with chicken for dinner or an extra bottle of beer, and once even a movie. This last festivity backfired, as from our dusty, moth-eaten seats we watched the crowning of Wilhelmina's daughter, Queen Juliana, on the Movietone News, with Robert Bergmann, my successor as ADC, prominent in full regalia, striding in the royal procession from the palace in Amsterdam to the church next door.

As a salesman in a clothing store you never get rich, but you do learn a lot about selling. Watching Arles White's easygoing performance, his natural dignity and friendly smile, I gradually lost my frantic approach which scared the customer away, but actually grew from embarrassment about trying to get at his money. "Nonsense," countered Whitey, with whom I dared to discuss such matters. "He doesn't know what he wants, the peasant, but he wants something or he wouldn't be in here. You tell him what he wants. He'll be grateful to you. He'll be happy to give you his money."

Mister Blumenthal, our very tough manager, put it differently. Seeing someone leave the shop one day after buying a tie from me, he called me to his office, flustered with fury. "So you sold him a tie. What is he going to wear it with?"

"I don't know," I stammered. "A shirt, I guess."

"Right! And what does he wear over his shirt?"

Now I got it. "A jacket."

"Right! A jacket! And if it's cool outside, an overcoat. And if he's a gentleman, a hat. A first sale is like a first kiss. If you don't get any further" - here he made a very rude, explicit gesture - "it doesn't mean a flea's fart. But if you're a good salesman, you'll get a lot further, know what I mean?"

In the end I had a surprise for him. A man walked in, looked around shyly and asked, "¿Se habla Español aqui?" Only I at Mathes spoke some Spanish, thanks to Mauricio Pieper and his five hairy peones in Argentina. Reaching back a dozen years I called out "Si Senor, como no!" and sold him one cheap white shirt, nothing more. Mr. Blumenthal snorted scornfully, but the man came back the next day, asked for me, and bought a dozen. And the next day, and the next week, and the next, always asking for me in Spanish and buying cheap white shirts, sometimes six dozen at a clip, until I sold him shirts as fast as we could get them from the factory. Every sale put two percent commission directly into my pocket, not making me rich but, in comparison to the recent past, coming close to it.

We finally had a drink together, during which he confided that by smuggling and avoiding the import duty, our cheapest shirt cost him $1.65 less than what he could sell it for in Mexico. He liked dealing with me because I spoke Spanish, and Mathes of Hollywood was now his top source of trading goods. I drank his health, wished him continued success and assured him that in the USA we encouraged such private enterprise under the heading of the Good Neighbor Policy.

If nothing else, I was fast becoming an American.

CHAPTER 16

Hollywood

In the middle of this commercial fairytale, the crass reality of the movie business intruded. Shortly after our arrival in the Los Angeles area I had signed up with the prominent Darrow Agency in Beverly Hills, to represent me as an actor with the stage name of Erik Drake. Don't ask who brought me there, or why they were willing to take me on, I have a copy of the contract dated March 21st 1948 to prove it, to you, to myself. We're still not out of the woods, the era of chaos lasted five years, remember?

Heavily involved in supporting the Good Neighbor Policy with Mexico, I had given little thought to Erik Drake. He lived in a world that had no connection with the Hollywood I knew, where you could spend a lifetime without ever seeing a film star.

The magnificent mansions in Beverly Hills devoid of human life, the vast studio complexes guarded like alien fortresses, the entire movie universe functioning in secret behind a wall of publicity, did it really exist? Apparently, because it reached out and offered me a job.

My connection with Darrow had already produced some notable results. Having learned fluent English in Britain during the war, I naturally spoke with a British accent, evidently a potent recommendation in film society. The Agency arranged for me to meet some birds of a feather, actors from Britain, jolly nice chaps, really, and one day our conversation inevitably turned to cricket. Though less than brilliant at the game, I had played it for years in Holland, where it is popular as a summer sport. One thing led to another, and I was introduced to the president of the

Hollywood Cricket Club, veteran actor C. Aubrey Smith, who must have cut an imposing figure around the wicket with his huge nose and white moustache. He invited me to play in the next game, and although nothing came of this, I was accepted in the movie community. As with the Spanish speaking shirt smuggler, nothing you learn in life is ever wasted.

I entered the pearly gates, not without trepidation, through the kindness of movie director George Cukor, who asked me to his home for "an informal Sunday afternoon get-together". He had just finished shooting the intriguing thriller A Double Life, and it turned out to be a party for the stars of the picture, screen idol Ronald Colman and a very young up-and-coming Shelley Winters. It was a glittering company, many of whom I had watched on the screen innumerable times, including Greer Garson, fresh from her huge success as Mrs. Miniver, Alexander Knox and countless other world-famous actors and actresses, more than I can recall. Midge, as usual, was stuck with the baby in Burbank.

We sat on chairs, couches and pillows on the floor in a bright, casual room with big windows overlooking the garden, engaged in relaxed, wide-ranging conversations that surprised and delighted me, after my negative upbringing on the subject of film actors. Yet I felt as if I had entered a minimum security prison, where the inmates live in comfortable quarters, eat and drink copiously, play golf and sit around swimming pools, but are nonetheless incarcerated and cut off from the mainstream of humanity. In a society where fame is the ultimate achievement, they have become idols. In their exalted world they only have each other, and they cling together in their loneliness. Every one seemed pleased, even grateful, to welcome me as a visitor from a distant planet. I, from my side, felt totally out of place and kept an eye on the exit.

Another set-back to my movie career occurred two weeks later, when Mr. Cukor, a giant in his field who seemed to have taken a paternal interest in me, invited me to his house for supper.

Looking back, I still see the dining room, a jewel: French impressionists glowing against the cream colored walls, indirect lighting, a faultless table sparkling with silver and crystal, the small company in black tie and superb evening clothes. For lack of choice I was wearing my RAF uniform. As chance would have it, I was seated next to Lady Mendl, the grande dame of Hollywood at the time, who at ninety-two in a tight-fitting mauve dress reminded me of a lovely sprig of heather dried between the pages of a Emily Bronte book.

Had I been born American, grown up with New World values, that evening might have become a turning point in my career. Lady Mendl spoke of the film community with knowledge, love and wisdom, and in the process frankly offered to guide me, an aspiring actor, through its corridors to the centers of power. In dreamland as in the real world, it's not what but whom you know.

"If you want it badly enough," she said somewhere in our conversation, "Hollywood can give it to you." I rightly presumed that she meant fame and fortune. "But you must want it more than anything in your life. You must let nothing stand in your way. Nothing." Suddenly she looked tough as nails.

Well, that left me out, there and then. It wasn't just the fact that I was still a Hollander, first and foremost, a product of a different culture that considered movies, like sports, as the "fluff of society", but also because World War II had reversed my perspective on human existence.

Like many others after every war, I was secretly amazed to be still around. If you live while realizing that by all reasonable expectations you should be dead, everything further becomes a bonus, a continuing gift. Instead of a feverish race against the passage of time, life becomes a leisurely stroll. Rather than frantically chasing your ambitions and worrying about getting old, you pause at every milestone and gaze back for a moment or two, thinking, "Well, what d'ye know, here I am thirty-five, forty, fifty, and I'm still alive and kicking, I still have a roof over my head and clothes on my back. And if now and then I feel like enjoying a movie, a steak or a glass of champagne, lo and behold!, I can still afford it." - I considered this hard-earned spark of wisdom a major blessing. If making it in Hollywood required desiring success more than anything in life, anything, as my dinner partner assured me, well... bye-bye, Hollywood.

The Darrow Agency chose this fateful time to sign me up for a small part in a movie called My Dear Secretary, starring Kirk Douglas and Laraine Day. This was the moment of truth: would I stick to my guns, or wilt in the glow of fame and fortune?

On my first morning as a film star I left our weird little cottage in a taxi, Midge, hand in hand with young Erik who had recently learned to walk, waving me out at the front door. I arrived in style at the studio gate, grandly tipped the cabby and proceeded on foot to a building indicated by the guard. It was a working area crammed with lamps and cameras, but once inside the pace struck me as relaxed. After finally finding a live body, I reported for duty and immediately got the rest of the day off.

Still, here I was in one of the impenetrable movie fortresses, so I spent the morning snooping around. I roamed through studios larger than hangars, diffidently sniffed the scent of money and success, got a big hello from Robert Stack and a courteous nod from W.C. Fields, and slipped through soundproof doors from one fantasy land into the next. Nobody appeared very busy. On every set the director and his assistant were engrossed in continuous whispered consultations, while everybody else sort of hung around. On rare occasions a bank of lights flicked on, a voice called "Quiet!" and in a corner one or two persons spoke a few words in front of a camera, almost furtively. Within minutes everyone ambled back to his morning paper and Coca Cola, and the hours crawled on. Around noon I hitched a ride home.

The next morning was scheduled for serious business. I had to sign in at seven thirty to be dressed and made up. For this I left Burbank at 6:00 a.m., and puffing and panting made it with seconds to spare. The studio, however, was as quiet as the grave, with nobody there but a cleaning woman and some technicians. At nine o'clock the rest of the crew came trickling in. The director looked at me in astonishment, asked

Hollywood – As actor 'Erik Drake'

who I was and what I wanted, then ordered me back by two o'clock. At that time, finally, I was properly dressed and made up. However, nothing further happened that day and at five my makeup was removed and I went home.

The following afternoon, waiting around in the cafeteria, halfway through my sixteenth Coca Cola in the polite but somewhat mysterious company of W.C. Fields who drank something different, my name suddenly roared over the intercom: the big moment had arrived. Unfortunately, it took me forever to find my way back to the set, and just as some stage manager had carefully positioned me under a spot, it was five o'clock. The electrician turned off the light and every one went home. So what? I got paid by the day, $75.00 gross, $43.00 net, for me a minor fortune.

Yet, a day or so later, at last it happened. I portrayed a newspaper publisher, who awarded Laraine Day a literary prize.

Together we stood in the focus of lamps. She looked breathtaking, although under the make-up not a square millimeter of her own skin was exposed. Somebody yelled "Quiet!"

I got a signal. Laraine looked at me expectantly. "Ten thousand dollars," I began, with feeling. "Congratulations! The prize carries an award of..."

"Hold it!" the assistant director called out. "That guy's nose is shiny." A makeup girl stepped into the light circle and powdered my face.

We started again. Laraine looked at me expectantly. "Ten thousand dollars. Congratu..."

"Stop!" yelled the assistant director. Apparently something in the arcane proceedings had gone awry. An unhurried conference followed. The heat of the lamps blasted down on us.

"That guy's nose is shiny again," the assistant director called out, when the discussion was over. The girl powdered me hastily, then gave Laraine the full treatment. By the time she had finished, I was soaked right through my shirt. "Quiet!"

"T-t-ten dollar thousand..." I took off hastily.

"Stop!"

"Sorry!"

We started over. Laraine looked at me expectantly. "Ten thousand -" With a tremendous crash somebody knocked over a lamp.

"Hold it! Quiet in the studio, please! OK, once again from the top."

Laraine looked at me expectantly. "Ten thousand dollars. Congratulations! The prize carries..." Way in the distance, very softly, we heard an aircraft approaching. "...an award of ten thousand dollars, quite apart..."

"Hold it!" We waited patiently until the plane had flown over. "OK. From the top. Quiet!"

"His nose shines," Laraine said. I got powdered again.

She looked at me. "Ten thousand dollars. Congratulations!" and this time I managed to get through my entire little spiel without mishap.

"Terrific!" the director roared through his bullhorn, when we had finished the scene. "Sensational!" After which, just to make sure, he had us do it eleven more times, including the entire next morning. I liked making money, but this went too far.

With a sigh of relief I pocketed my check and announced my retirement from the movie business.

Every senior in the USA remembers the "Late Show," a TV movie after midnight, usually old and pretty bad. It was sometimes followed by the "Late Late Show," another movie, even older, even worse. Occasionally, when I couldn't sleep, I turned it on. Oh my God, there's Laraine! She looks at me expectantly. I smile, about to speak, then abruptly sit down on a couch, speechless. My immortal soliloquy had landed on the cutting room floor. By this time I can hardly keep my eyes open.

* * *

A logical consequence of my postwar views on human existence is the opinion that life is not, as always asserted, short, but on the contrary, long, with ample time to experience every aspect of it thoroughly without fear of missing some imaginary boat. Even so, with the spell of Hollywood exorcised for ever, I saw no reason to remain in California. Mathes and its trade in contraband shirts, however profitable, did not point towards an illustrious future, and for writing, which in view of an increasing lack of alternatives began to inch ahead as a career possibility, the movie world did not appeal to me. In making a wish at mystical opportunities such as shooting stars and clover leaves, my mind's eye never saw an abundance of money or glamour, but always, slipping away from me as time went by, the ever more unlikely vision of a magnum opus, fat and heavy, severely bound, and above all read, praised and ultimately renowned for the quality of its language.

For literary activities New York was the center of the English speaking world, in which I now aspired to become a factor. Our decision to return to the East Coast made eminent sense, the way we chose to get there somewhat less. At least this accounts for a few more plane trips and an otherwise inexplicable sojourn in the Netherlands.

It involved that darling of Holland's psyche, its symbol of national ego, KLM-Royal Dutch Airlines. Established in 1919 as the world's first airline, inaugurating commercial passenger service with daily flights between Amsterdam and London, it grew postwar into one of the largest—and, let's face it, finest—companies of its kind, in the process hiring practically every one of my friends who had flown with the Netherlands forces or the RAF. When I heard that they were taking delivery in Southern California of medium range "Metropolitan" passenger planes —the ones with the square windows—it didn't take me long to arrange a free ride for us via Chicago, Newfoundland, Greenland, Iceland and Ireland to Schiphol, Amsterdam, from where we could fly back to New York on my old, undated travel pass. All this to save the airfare of flying there directly from Los Angeles.

Once in the Netherlands, we must have stayed longer than we planned, for I recall the Eve of St. Nicholas, December 5th. 1948, in Wassenaar. Holland was in turmoil. When World War II ended in Europe and the country was liberated, thousands of young men and women had volunteered for military service in the Far East, to throw the Japanese occupiers out of the Netherlands East Indies and free some forty thousand Dutch (and part Indonesian) families from prison camps. Unexpectedly the atom bomb burst, Japan surrendered, Indonesian nationalists declared independence, and when the green troops arrived in Java they found themselves confronted not by the Japanese army but by their own onetime colonial buddies, whom they thought they had come to liberate. Half my friends and schoolmates, including Peter Tazelaar, were amongst them. And now, in a series of hopeless, ill-conceived "police actions" fighting was raging all over the Emerald Girdle.

The nation at home, so recently united by the Occupation, had once again split apart under this devastating blow. Hollanders called each other murderers, traitors, liars and hypocrites, depending on their political outlook. The only ones in favor of granting Indonesia immediate freedom were the Communists, hardly a recommendation at this point in time. They were matched at the other extreme by the Conservatives and right wingers, never much for liberty except their own, who opposed any change in the status quo. Most people in between supported some degree of independence at some future date, all too little and all too late. My own opinion I kept to myself, so as not to offend my family and friends - during three years in America my doubts had grown to grudging admiration for the Indonesian pemudas who were fighting and dying for their right of self-determination.

On the fifth of December we had gathered at my parents house for the traditional feast of St. Nicholas, a legendary saint with a murky past who arrives every year on this date, supposedly from Spain, seated on a white horse, wearing robes of red and gold and a mitre, carrying a staff and a bag full of presents for the children of Holland. When settlers carried the tradition to New Amsterdam, St. Nicholas - in the words of Count B van Brero - "converted to another half-assed Dutch immigrant and changed his name to Santa Claus."

My sister, Ellen, her new husband, Chris Krediet, and their three children had joined us, there were special cookies and sweet drinks, jolly rhymes and heaps of presents. Yet the war in Indonesia was never far from our minds. My father, whose pride in his career as an Empire builder was being shattered by the recent wave of vituperation, stood for no retreat, no compromise, not now, not ever. So when our neighbor, who thought differently, in the spirit of the occasion rode up our driveway on the milkman's nag, dressed in St. Nicholas' robes with a tall mitre on his head, my father ambushed him in the rhododendron bushes, waving a stick and shouting "traitor!" The horse spooked, reared up, turned around and tore down the road, old Santa hanging on for dear life, shedding staff, hat and ultimately even his beard. We spent the rest of the evening placating the neighborhood. Midge and I read the message in each other's eyes: It was high time we picked up the threads of our own destinies.

* * *

Early in the new year KLM flew us home (Home? New York! Where else?), and as we bussed across the 59th Street Bridge into Manhattan, that's exactly what it felt like - home.

How was that possible, after just these few years as immigrants? Of course, in areas that really mattered to me, like freedom and tolerance, my two countries had much in common. American liberty is not unique, and as far as melting pots are concerned, Holland matches the USA in miniature.

In a national sense, the Dutch have enjoyed as much freedom as the Americans, only longer. On January 30, 1648, the Spanish Empire relinquished its sovereignty over the Netherlands to the Republic of the Seven Provinces, after 80 years of warfare which the American historians Will & Ariel Durant proclaim to be "the longest, bravest and most cruel struggle for freedom in all history." From then on they ruled themselves by means of an increasingly democratic system, developing a culture in which all levels of society participated. Influence and treasures gathered not in palaces, but in town halls. Only in 1815 did the Low Countries become a constitutional monarchy, to consolidate their unity after the Napoleonic upheavals.

For more than three centuries in a Europe rife with persecution, Holland remained as much a haven of refuge as the USA across the ocean. Its borders were wide open to anyone in need of protection. First Jews from Spain and Portugal, then Huguenots from France and assorted Protestants from everywhere entered the country by the thousands and helped create the Dutch nation. The Pilgrim fathers lived in Leiden for twenty years before crossing the Atlantic, while practically across the street in Rijnsburg the first Mennonites and Quakers set up shop. By the end of the 17th century the Netherlands was the haven of choice for dissidents from all over Europe, political, religious and intellectual. To this, add floods of Jewish refugees from Poland, Germany and Austria in Nazi times, and after World War II, really stirring up our melting pot, fifteen thousand Melanesians from the Moluccan Islands who wanted no part of the Republic of Indonesia. To top it off, eight thousand blacks from our former colony in the West Indies, Suriname, recently chose the Netherlands as their home, and it's their talents that keep Holland near the peak of the international soccer world. No neighborhood in New York or San Francisco can claim to be more multi-racial, multi-religious, multi-everything than any of the famed canal streets of Amsterdam.

In the absence of compelling ideological differences, and after a spectacular social and financial dive from aide-de-camp of Queen Wilhelmina in Holland to third salesman at "Mathes of Hollywood" in America, why should I feel as light as a feather rolling across the 59th Street Bridge into New York, in the good old US of A? The answer had to lie within myself.

From the moment of birth, with babus Pih and Pah tending to my slightest wishes, I had been raised with a strong sense of class. Somehow it backfired, and in spite of my father's quiet objections little Ahmed became my first serious playmate, while his grandfather dripped alien wisdom into my young soul to sustain me when needed. I slipped away early from the old Dutch mold.

Holland, most notably Leiden, tried to recapture and assign me to my proper pigeonhole, which would have cut me off, safe and comfortable, from most of humanity, thus limiting my life's experience. And you only live once! This became my phobia, which drove me to the Wagenstraat in The Hague with a guitar, to the rocking little fo'c'sle of the KW 20, to Mauricio Pieper and his hairy gauchos, the roof of the 2412 pulling into Grand Junction, the frozen silence of Finland's tundras. Fate took over when World War II pressed me shoulder to shoulder with Dutch resistance fighters, whatever their background, and airmen from a dozen countries and national traditions. In the process I ripped the fabric of pigeonholes to shreds, to the left, to the right, up as far as royalty, down as far as bums riding a midnight freight, shattering all social restrictions. Should I now relinquish that hard-earned gain? Never! Life may be a one-night stand, but the world is its stage and all humanity the cast. Pigeonholes? Not in America!

In spite of its imperfections the classless society in the USA is a living fact. It creates a facet of freedom in which Europe lags behind, notwithstanding steady improvement since the war. Ask the foreign immigrants who speak English together to avoid the pitfalls of their native tongues, the vous and tu, the Sie and du, the tu and Usted, the revealing social and provincial accents; watch sellers and buyers in the New World, waiters and guests, employees and employers, most of them readily interchangeable to a casual observer. As Queen Wilhelmina put it admiringly in a private moment, after her visit to the USA in 1942, "When you shake hands with an American, you shake hands with an equal."

Bill Hearst, whom I had first met underneath a buffet table in wartime London with Hoover and Roosevelt in the wings, stressed a different angle. I owed him for taking my Mosquitoes Sting at Night to Cosmopolitan Magazine, so when we were living in Forest Hills I had paid him a visit one Sunday afternoon at his home on Long Island, a sumptuous place which promptly put me in an F. Scott Fitzgerald mood. He received me most cordially and for a while we chatted. A dozen of his friends and neighbors, young, beautiful people (jeunesse dorée, my mother would have called them) lounged around the vast room, sipping Tom Collins' and reading the Social Gossip columns of the Sunday papers, exclusively.

When our conversation touched on his father, notorious newspaper tycoon William Randolph Hearst, Sr., a controversial subject by any standards, Bill stated simply, "Whatever people may say about him, he was a great American." The ultimate, all-embracing, all-forgiving explanation, the great equalizing factor, understood and accepted from coast to coast.

We went out to dinner in a posh restaurant overlooking Long Island Sound. A truly obnoxious group nearby, noisy local yokels devoid of manners, got my goat. "Just because they've got the money," I hissed at Bill in disgust, "they think they belong here."

"You're wrong," Bill corrected me. "Because they have the money, they do belong here." I still had a lot to learn. - The only ones who seemed to have learned little in our two years of absence, were Herman van Brero and the other not-quite- yet immigrants in the Netherlands Club. Particularly Count B, who presided at their usual table one afternoon when I dropped by. He was at his strident best, and this time the Statue of Liberty and its welcoming words were his targets.

"Give me your tired, huddled masses, or whatever the hell it is," he snarled, turning his handsome, sardonic head in my direction, "and now it comes: the wretched refuse of something -or-another. Can you beat it? Wretched refuse they call us! And now I hear they've also put this garbage up at Idlewild Airport, in the overseas arrival building. The gall! Imagine, you've just arrived from some lovely place like Paris or London or perhaps even Amsterdam and before you know it you are refuse, goddammit, and wretched to boot. Arrogant bastards! Good thing I didn't see it when I flew in last week, I would have turned right back."

"That would have been a bitter blow for Uncle Sam," I grinned, pouring him another genever. And yet, looking around the table, I had to admit that the Dutch "refuse" made a strikingly non-wretched impression. Yearning to be free? They had just kicked the tyrant out of their own country - although, when hard pressed, even Count B would admit that the British and the Americans also had something to do with it. Huddled? Poor? They came from affluent suburbs like Wassenaar and Bloemendaal, and drove around in very presentable automobiles. Tired? Sure, after a game of field hockey with which they filled their weekends, or a hangover from the victory party. No doubt, at least in their own minds - the New World should be very pleased with their presence.

"Anybody take out citizenship papers yet?"

A general snort went up, but that attitude was about to change. The Dutch are world-class hockey players, and when it became known that the USA intended to enter that sport for the first time in the next Olympic Games, half of the Hollanders around the table were sure to qualify for the team - if they had the right nationality. By the time the games started they had all acquired citizenship, and proudly and successfully helped represent the United States of America in the 1956 Olympics. Now here was a goal worth immigrating for!

* * *

Back in New York, I finally had a clear vision of the future, for the first time in America. Not only were our papers in order, based on Luigi's Green Card, but the big decision had been taken - I was going to write, period. To tide us over I had managed to get assigned as correspondent for a group of Dutch newspapers, nothing that would make us rich but a welcome tributary to the fractured flow of money which supported us in this period. It took a fairy godmother to tie it all together.

Margaret Sangster, doyen of radio writers, mainstay of My True Story, lived in a classic townhouse on the northeast corner of Park Avenue and 77th. Street. Past stately mansions it had a fine view of Grand Central Station, which in those days rose up into blue sky instead of obscenely into the crotch of the present Pan Am building. Inside the house, the staccato clatter of Underwood typewriters filled the hallway and office area, where two full-time secretaries spent five days a week to process this single woman's output which supported the elegant ambience beyond: a large salon, exquisite dining room, kitchen, pantry, and a floor full of bedrooms with baths above. Miss Sangster wrote soap operas.

Our roads crossed somewhere in this time of confusion and, being totally involved in melodrama, she soon became entranced with a bizarre notion of adding the magic of a baby to her sophisticated lifestyle. When she invited us to move in with her until we had found a suitable place of our own, we were only too happy to oblige.

In New York, Park Avenue is the way to go. While Midge and young Erik spent their time in Central Park and the many fine museums around it, the creative energy which pervaded the duplex at Park and 77th carried me along. With a borrowed typewriter I settled down in the cellar, between the washing machine and the central heating pipes, undisturbed by the disconcerting flood of profitable human drama whirling around the ground floor. Not only did I feel like a writer, but a sense of pride began to flow through me, flushing out my inborn, insane social misgivings. The little man who used to watch me from somewhere behind my right shoulder, keeping me in contact with my real self on the beach in Scheveningen or coned above Berlin, had disappeared. Pulling myself into focus, he faded out of the picture. From then on, once behind the typewriter, I always knew exactly who I was.

While in awe of our hostess' prodigious output and the luxury it generated, soap operas failed to inspire me. I felt attracted to short stories, with their single punch in a classic beginning-middle-end format. Margaret got me an agent, Cap Shaw, and from my cellar under Park and 77th I produced some modest fiction and articles that were printed in various popular magazines. One in particular raised my hopes for the future.

Esquire had sponsored a contest for the best short story based on a picture of a bare-breasted Balinese girl, who inspired me enough to have my effort take third prize out of 1600 entries. It was published as the lead story in the next issue. But I still had my doubts: How often and how fast did one have to produce a masterpiece in order to make a living? And what happened to a writer who got tired? Or sick?

As if she were not busy enough Margaret Sangster, as part of the aristocracy of the radio age, also led a glamorous social life. She regularly treated us to intimate dinner parties with show-biz notables, including Mary Pickford, well in her seventies but still a little girl. America's Sweetheart was tickled pink - the color she happened to be wearing - to learn that 23 Hyde Park Place, her onetime love-nest with Douglas Fairbanks in London, had been our headquarters for secret operations in World War II. We also dined one evening with my second cousin, Hendrik Willem van Loon's son, Willem, and his boyfriend Ming Toy. My grandmother in Amsterdam - Willem's grand aunt - would have lifted one eyebrow.

After three glorious months on Park Avenue we moved to a place of our own, a proper writer's hideout in the country. Typically, it went like this. We set out for Connecticut, but didn't quite get there. I fell asleep on the train to Stamford, woke up in panic when we stopped after what seemed an eternity, and in the confusion that followed got everybody and our luggage off onto the platform. It turned out to be Rye, Westchester, several stops short of Connecticut. By the time I had located it on the map, the train had left. When a fellow passenger saw our predicament we got to talking, which led to the information that another Dutchman, a Mr. Oudheusden, had just put up his gate house for rent on his property adjoining Long Island Sound. There seemed to be nothing wrong with Rye, so why not live in Westchester? We loaded all our earthly belongings into a taxi, drove to Milton Point, saw, liked and rented the cottage on the spot. We were made for each other.

As 1950 approached, the era of chaos was about to expire. When it did, it almost took me with it.

CHAPTER 17

To Arms For Ambon!

For a few months of World War II a Dutch sailor, Admiral Conrad Helfrich, born in Semarang on Java, held the post of commander-in-chief of the Allied navies in the Far East, including the British and the American. When his submarines sank a number of Japanese ships in a row, the press gave him the nickname of "Ship-a-day Helfrich". It constituted the high point of a career which, like so many others, had come to an end with the fall of the Netherlands East Indies.

On a sparkling morning in January 1950, Admiral Helfrich stood in the exit of a KLM Lockheed Constellation from Amsterdam, pausing for a moment at the top of the stairs, and looked around.

I shoved my way through the noisy, always emotional crowd of greeters on the roof promenade of New York's Idlewild Airport, pushed a dime into the slot of a public telescope and maneuvered him into my sights. He didn't seem much taller than he was wide, a hunk of seaman, rock solid in the nervous bustle of travelers.

He walked down the steps and towards me, across the tarmac, and suddenly it hit home: This insignificant little link in the chain of passengers approaching the building under me, was Ship-a-day Helfrich, commander-in-chief of Allied fleets in a time of war. I hurried down to the arrival hall to greet him.

A few days earlier, after putting little Erik to bed, we had received a telegram. A pack of snow had wrapped Rye and the cottage on Milton Point in a cocoon of silence. I lay dozing on the couch after a steady stretch of writing, Midge sat reading magazines by the fire. The telephone ripped apart the gentle texture of the evening.

"Would like to visit you next week. Regards," the operator read from a telegram. "Signed Helfrich."

"Look forward to your arrival. Awaiting details," I wired back. Two things were clear: The visit spelled trouble, and it had to do with Indonesia. During the drive home from Idlewild the admiral filled me in.

It was all over. Under tremendous pressure from America, Britain and the United Nations, the Netherlands had ceased the "police actions" and on one of the last days of 1949, after several months of negotiation, signed a treaty recognizing "the United States of Indonesia" and its sovereignty over the former Netherlands East Indies. Internationally speaking, the problem had been resolved. Indonesia had won, Holland lost. Personally, apart from worrying about the economic future of the Dutch, I could live with it.

But that was not why Admiral Helfrich had come to Rye. The vast new country, a chain of islands 500 miles longer than the distance from San Francisco to New York, some of them twenty, thirty times the size of Germany or France, was inhabited by scores of nations with totally different backgrounds and unrelated languages. For many of them, the new leaders on distant Java were as foreign as an Eskimo to an Arab. To protect everybody's rights Indonesia had been created as a multiple state with far flung areas of local authority. The ink on the treaty was barely dry, however, when the first president, Ahmed Sukarno, and his revolutionary government scrapped the words "United States" and proclaimed Indonesia to be a unitary republic with all authority and power centered in Jakarta, Java.

"It's pure neo-colonialism," the admiral concluded. "People like the Ambonese, for instance, are never going to take it lying down."

He had picked the most glaring example. The inhabitants of the South Moluccas, a small archipelago just west of New Guinea with the island of Ambon at its center, differed from the Javanese in fundamental respects, racially, religiously, historically. They were mostly devout Christians, not Moslems, and as formidable soldiers they had traditionally served in the Dutch East Indian Army, much like the Gurkhas in British India. All this put them in a special category for which the United States concept of Indonesia was specifically designed. Sukarno's move left them in an untenable position.

"Well, what are we going to do about it?" I wanted to know. After all, Holland did not only owe the Ambonese a staggering debt for three hundred years of loyal service, it had also signed the treaty which safeguarded their future.

"Who knows!" Helfrich exploded. "But we put our signatures on it, so we've got to do something. Or the word of a Hollander, including the Queen, isn't worth a damn."

"And why did you come to visit us?" I smelled a rat somewhere. The old sailor observed me sideways in silence, but did not answer. Just then we reached Rye, turned off the Merritt Parkway and shortly afterwards pulled up at our cottage. Ship-a- day Helfrich was staying the night. After dinner we sat around the fire and talked into the small hours of the morning, severely denting a bottle of Bols' genever he had brought along as a gift.

"During the war I had an Ambonese on my staff," he finally came to the point. "He was our navy's highest non-white officer, Commander Karel Vigeleyn Nikijuluw. He's just arrived in this country. He may or may not contact you. I highly recommend him. If the Moluccans stick to their guns, they'll look for all the help they can get. You know America, he doesn't. See what you can do for him."

Before turning in, the little admiral lifted his glass and drank to Commander Nikijuluw and the Ambonese, "as brave a body of warriors you could ever hope to meet." I joined the toast not without misgivings. My life was finally beginning to get straightened out, I would have to be crazy to get involved in some dubious fracas near New Guinea.

* * *

On April 24, 1950, the Ambonese and other inhabitants of a group of islands west of New Guinea proclaimed the Republic Maluku Selatan (RMS) - Republic of the South Moluccas - and declared its independence from Indonesia. They had every right to do so. The preliminary Constitution of the United States of Indonesia, article 189, affirmed: "Each federal state shall be given the opportunity to accept the Constitution. In case a federal state does not accept it, they shall have the right to negotiate a special relationship with the United States of Indonesia and the Kingdom of the Netherlands." The same article appeared word for word in the Treaty of Independence between Holland and Indonesia, and as article 2 of the Dutch Transfer of Sovereignty Law. Both countries' highest representatives had signed these documents.

To remove any doubt about their status, the Ambonese brought the case before the International Court of Justice in The Hague, which pronounced the RMS legal. The Republic - formerly United States - of

Indonesia ignored the verdict and opened hostilities by throwing a sea blockade around Ambon and other major islands, vowing to wipe the new country off the map by military means. Meanwhile the RMS provisional government sent Karel Vigeleyn Nikijuluw, who had resigned from the Dutch Navy, to New York in order to seek support and recognition for the little republic from the United Nations Organization. Before April was over, Nikki, as his friends called him, appeared on our doorstep at Milton Point.

He was a small, dark brown man in his forties with a white flake in his otherwise coal black hair. It gave him a slightly roguish air, immediately forgotten once you looked into his eyes which, though friendly, were steady as rocks. Of compact build, immaculately dressed, he exuded a certain calm which at first I took for reserve, but which time and again dissolved in flashes of humor and a generous laugh. With his people in mortal danger, he showed no signs of anxiety. Here was a man completely at ease with himself.

In spite of the urgency of his situation we drank a leisurely cup of tea with Midge, as required by the civilized traditions of his nation, after which I led him through the back garden, pausing to admire the lilies of the valley, to where the Oudheusden property touched Long Island Sound. From the jetty we boarded a dinghy I had bought and rowed out

Karel Vigeleyn Nikijuluw

to sea - no better security in those innocent and nontechnical days than the wide views of open space. To satisfy his extreme demands for caution, we covered the expedition visually by bringing along bait and fishing poles.

It was a soft, radiant late afternoon. Bugs danced above the motionless water which reached hazily towards Long Island across the Sound. Where the two coastlines converged and touched, New York's skyline rose against the southwestern sky, the rectangular slab of the United Nations Building on the East River clearly distinguishable, unreal and vaguely hostile. After a look full of longing at the fishing gear, the Ambonese picked up where Ship-a-day Helfrich had left off. He held me spellbound.

Ideals are like your children, often a pain in the neck, but they are your very own, so you can't just dump them. You are responsible for them. The cause of the Republic Maluku Selatan, morally right, legally uncontestable, threatened by the overwhelming might of giant Indonesia backed by the limitless power of pragmatic, ill-informed Uncle Sam, was pure as gold and almost hopeless from the beginning. The Ambonese stood for everything that I had fought for in World War II, freedom, the right of self determination and national identity. All they had against them was the size and location of their country, and three centuries of loyalty to the Dutch. How could I not support them? Already in 1572 William of Orange, the George Washington of the Netherlands, re-marked during our desperate 80-years' War of Independence: "It is not necessary to hope in order to attempt, nor need one succeed in order to persevere." Well, what was good enough for William the Silent was good enough for me. I told Nikijuluw he could count on me, provided it left me time to write. In answer to more specific questions, he assured me that God would show the way.

From then on we met several times for conspiratorial discussions, always in the dinghy under cover of fishing trips. Staring at our floats on the gleaming water, under the distant spell of New York and its U.N. Building, we schemed, speculated and conspired about the fate of a few tropical specks of land in the South Pacific, half a world away. Meanwhile Sukarno's blockade of the islands, a few rusty corvettes and war surplus B25s, somehow sufficed to isolate them from outside contact. It was Nikijuluw's greatest fear that inside this ring of silence the RMS, sur-rounded by Indonesia, cut off from the international community, would be swiftly and secretly crushed without anyone knowing about it.

"One of these day they'll land troops," he would say, tensely. "More than we can handle. Then we must have proof and documentation, if we are to get any support from the U.N. Also, we've got to get our guys weapons and ammunition, you can't beat machine guns with klewangs, no matter how sharp. We have no choice, we've got to get through this blockade."

Underneath it all he was a fisherman, like most of his race, so that often the conspiracy broke up temporarily into feverish activity and cheers every time we landed a bass or an eel. But only for a moment, be-fore we took up once again where we had left off. "It doesn't take much. Just a stout boat with a sail, a diesel auxiliary and lots of cargo space."

"And money," I added. "And somebody who can sail the whole she-bang across five thousand miles of ocean."

Back on the jetty Nikki bundled our catch of the day in a paper bag, his dinner for the night in his one room apartment on 44th. Street, around the corner from the U.N. He shook my hand, silently and earnestly, as if we had just sealed a solemn pact.

Then, small, inconspicuous, he walked away serenely confident into the dusk.

* * *

Through my contact with Vigeleyn Nikijuluw and the cause of the Ambonese I seemed to be sliding back into the past. It felt as if I were partly relinquishing control over my destiny to powers that for the last five years - the era of chaos - had kept their distance from me. It was a familiar, reassuring sensation as good things began to happen for which I myself could not possibly take credit. Judge for yourself.

At the time of the Spanish Civil War (1935 - 1939), the proving grounds and dress rehearsal for World War II, a handful of British seamen in small ships regularly risked their lives - and made money - by sneaking through General Francisco Franco's naval blockade around Spain in order to feed and supply the Loyalists, including thousands of Americans who fought in the International Brigade. The two most renowned of these, Potato Pete and Dod Orsborne, were finally intercepted by the Fascist navy. The former reputedly paid with his life, but Orsborne, cut off from friendly territory and unable to return to England, alone and with no other provisions than some leftover raw potatoes and beans, kept sailing his little craft, the "Girl Pat", due west, until one fine day he hit the USA. Instantly famous, he later wrote a book, Master of the Girl Pat, that made the author with his red beard and wicked smile the darling of the radio talk shows. Through this he met, somehow but inevitably, Margaret Sangster. She telephoned us with an invitation "to meet this crazy Brit"; Midge took the call because I was out on the Sound discussing ways to sneak through to Ambon. That same night, the most celebrated blockade runner of the times and the world's only contemporary naval blockade were fused together at Park Avenue and 77th Street.

The affinity between the Dutch and the Scots is as mysterious as it is documented. In most places on earth, no matter how distant, you'll find one or two of each, side by side in a local bar, sharing their exile experiences. From my father's friends in Surabaya to Mauricio Pieper's buddies in Argentina to my own RAF pals in World War II, Scotsmen - and their lassies - abounded. The feisty little redheaded sailor with the Vandyke beard and a Scottish burr that could cut timber, proved no exception.

"Erik m'lad," were about his first words after we were introduced, "have ye got any money?"

Dod Orsborne, in his late forties, had made a living all his life from owning small ships and using them for a variety of singlehanded seaborne enterprises, some legal, mostly not. The problem was, apparently, that his latest vessel, several boats removed from the "Girl Pat", had recently been confiscated.

"What did they do that for, Dod?"

"Aegh, laddie, some bastard bloody bureaucrat could nae find anything better to do one day."

That came as close to an explanation as I got, but whatever the circumstances, to be stranded ashore clearly constituted the ultimate disgrace to my new friend. Captain Orsborne without a ship? Unthinkable! "And I got me eye on one, an absolute bargain. A former pilot boat, built in Belgium. Eighty-five feet of pure English oak. Sail and diesel. And all that for ten thousand lousy dollars, laddie. Well... perhaps a wee bit more."

Running blockades, winning battles, gaining independence, it's all a matter of money. Courage and determination the Ambonese had plenty, justice was on their side, but when it comes to winning in our international community, the intangible values always lose out against money. Time and again during our planning sessions, as Nikijuluw and I sat looking across the water at the sickening wealth of New York City, our discussion faltered on the question, "Where in God's name are we going to get the cash?"

In June I flew to England at my own expense, and offered a financial consortium an exclusive trade contract with the Moluccan Islands for thirty years, in return for 5 million dollars now. The bankers studied the map of giant Indonesia, picked out the specks of the RMS with difficulty, smiled condescendingly, treated me to an expensive luncheon at White's and paid for my cab back to the airport.

Amidst the eels and the flounders on Long Island Sound I reported to Nikki about the British flop. "Don't you guys have anything else to offer?"

"Ambon has the only deep-water harbor between Surabaya, Manila and Australia," he suggested.

Off I went again, this time to Washington, D.C., to offer the American navy the unlimited use of Ambon's harbor for fifty years, in return for a little discreet assistance now. The head of foreign liaison, Colonel Drexel Biddle, I knew from Queen Wilhelmina's days at Chester Square in London. But when it took me twenty-five minutes just to find his department in the endless, depressing corridors of the Pentagon, I realized that we'd never get through this bureaucratic heap of porridge.

Inevitably our dreams became ever more modest, and when Dod Orsborne was presented to me on a silver platter by Margaret Sangster, while that very afternoon Nikki and I had been staring at our floats without the slightest notion where to find a ship, let alone with matching blockade runner, the idea of an old Belgian pilot boat captained by a red-haired, middle-aged Scotsman seemed the obvious solution. Ten thousand dollars? A small sum to pay off a three hundred year old debt!

Our ship was called "l'Insoumise", the Untamed, a name that suited her disheveled appearance when I first saw her lying in Barstow's Shipyard, Whitestone, the Bronx. Not that her surly disarray necessarily made her unattractive, because her lines were clean and sturdy, and her build and size imposing. She was a two-masted vessel, 85 ft long by 22 ft wide, built in 1908 of 7-inch thick English oak, with a teak deck and copperplated bottom. Her problem was that she had lain moored there for four years, from the day that Bill Barstow had impounded her for unpaid bills. But Orsborne jumped aboard and strutted around her deck as if she were his very own, or at least some private super-yacht.

"A battleship. Solid. Indestructible. Admiral Cunningham sailed around the world in it, with his entire family. Twice." Dod," I interrupted, "something is missing." I don't know much about boats, but when I had clawed my way up on deck I noticed, amidst the staggering confusion of old iron and rotting cables, a gigantic oval hole. "Dod, we are missing a mast."

"There," He pointed to the quay, where the main mast was lying alongside, fully ten feet longer than the ship itself. "Finest Engelmann spar ever cut in Alaska. Specially for the famous racing sloop "Valiant", which has broken seven world records with it. Hundred feet long, brand new. Well, just about. Totally indestructible."

"How will we ever get that monster aboard? Upright, no less." The diameter at the base, oval, almost round, measured more than a yard.

"Details! Chickenshit!" The wiry little Scotsman waved his arms towards the massive tree on the quayside, the heaps of debris on the deck, and to the world in general. "Nothing but lousy details!" This much self-confidence deserved my respect. Dod was our man and the l'Insoumise our ship. Bill Barstow proved eager to get rid of her, in return for payment of outstanding charges of $ 10,000.- He agreed to give us the use of his quay and his tools, including a giant crane, to put her back in shape, free of charge, provided "you get it out of here pronto."

I presented the proposition by phone to former Prime Minister Pieter S. Gerbrandy in Holland. He had urged me to do something, well, here was his chance to help. Perhaps he worried that, like once before, I might stick him with the bill anyway, but the little walrus never flinched. He contacted some of his pals in the business world and within a week I picked up the full amount at a corporate office in New York. In June we took possession of the l'Insoumise, registered in my name. Now we had a ship, but Barstow had all our money.

"Now what do we use for buying arms?" Nikijuluw asked on our next fishing trip.

"Nikki, I haven't the vaguest clue. We've got to go one step at a time and then God will show us the way. Remember?"

I couldn't help rubbing it in from time to time. "Let's see how it goes."

As a matter of fact, it went better than I had dared hope. Dod Orsborne saw the miraculous turn of events since our meeting as a way to fabled riches, and the l'Insoumise as a kind of legendary East India trader, loaded with trinkets for which the natives would carry aboard their costly silks and exotic spices by the picul. "What do you think those fuzzy-wuzzies will be keen on over there, eh? Coca Cola?"

"Well, Dod, I would say... more likely hand grenades. And machine guns. Light ack-ack. Lots of ammo." And having gone that far, I explained the whole situation to him, except for the political details.

His reaction did not really surprise me. "Oooooh!" the blockade runner cooed contentedly. "That's the kind of stuff I know about. I know where to get it, and how to get it financed, too. Leave it to me, leave it to me."

We verbalized an oral contract on the spot by which I appointed him Commercial Director of the enterprise and owner of the cargo, and all profits thereof, on condition that on the outward journey we would be carrying arms and ammunition with Ambon as our destination. His task would be to obtain same, either before departure, anywhere along the way or in the Far East. Furthermore I also officially appointed him captain of my ship. Unsalaried, of course.

All this took place in a little hamburger joint between the pylons of the Bronx-Whitestone bridge, with the constant rumble of unsuspecting commuters roaring by overhead. As much as possible I kept Dod and Nikki away from each other, not only for reasons of security but also because of the vast difference between their motives. I was their interpreter, cutout and contact point. By this time I had become totally involved in the covert operation, like an amateur replay of Contact Holland.

Meanwhile Dod and I worked from dawn to dusk at Barstow's shipyard, within walking distance of our hideout underneath the bridge. After four years of neglect the l'Insoumise had to be overhauled from top to bottom, stem to stern. Orsborne, possessed of maniacal energy, whipped us along shoulder to shoulder in the murderous midsummer's heat, and as two, three months passed the old pilot boat rose like a phoenix out of rusting iron and rotting wood.

It was a race against time. The information which through some mysterious channel reached Nikijuluw out of the Moluccas clearly alarmed him. In his gentle way he put me under enormous pressure, while the Scotsman rarely missed an opportunity to remind me that the ship would shortly have to be outfitted, at the owner's expense, of course.

One morning I woke up with the answer. I instructed Dod to buy a green pullover that contrasted nicely with his red beard, dress up to nautical perfection in spite of the heat, carry a copy of Master of the Girl Pat and accompany me to the offices of Argosy magazine, an adventure publication which had recently bought one of my stories. I informed the editors that a historical expedition under the command of the famous Captain Dod Orsborne (slight bow towards Dod and his book) was about to set sail, with the purpose of retracing a voyage of Vasco da Gama, the 15th century Portuguese explorer whose travels (this left unsaid) had taken him into the same regions we were eager to reach. I planned to describe our adventures in a series of articles, the first of which I happened to have with me, richly illustrated with pictures of our stout ship and its intrepid captain. Furthermore, if they were perchance interested in carrying the series, we would consent to change the ship's name to Argosy.

The editors promptly accepted our proposition. A few strokes of a paint brush and l'Insoumise had been rechristened, our red-haired Scot adorned the cover of Argosy's next issue and we had 5000 dollars in the bank as advance payment. The publicity resulted in a flood of applications by would-be expedition members, from which Dod signed up a bizarre crew based largely on financial contribution. This further increased our bank account and also solved our labor problem - the gang of workers at Barstow's increased steadily, because Orsborne engaged dozens of muscular candidates on spec. One thing and an other made it possible to outfit our ship and get her ready for departure. "Nae bother," Dod defended our deceptions, as if to keep me pure, "we do sail in the wake of this bastard Da Gama, but down the route he would have taken if the Panama Canal had already been there. And if we do take a wee swing through the blockade to Ambon, it'll do your bloody stories no harm, laddie."

At long last came the crowning feat. From the end of the giant crane the 95 ft tall main mast of the l'Insoumise - as she will always be called by me - dangled against an azure sky, descending slowly, angling down, feeling for the hole in the deck and finally entering the guts of the ship vertically. The moment its formidable base gently slipped into the oval seat in the hull, settling with a hiss of air like a sigh, Dod Orsborne stretched both arms above his head in triumph, swore with excitement and burst into tears.

I drove straight to New York and burst into Nikijuluw's room on West 44th Street. "Nikki! We're ready, we can cast off at any time!"

The Ambonese leader was standing in his underpants, ironing a shirt. When he looked up, his eyes glittered. I knew instantly what was coming.

"They have landed on Ambon." He spoke calmly, with conscious dignity. "Three days ago. In amphibian LCIs under cover from corvettes and B25s. Six or seven battalions of Javanese infantry. On our north coast, at Tulehu and Hitu."

* * *

Dirty tricks are pulled in the dark. In the eight months that it took the Republic of Indonesia to wipe the RMS off the map, not one word about it - as far as I know - reached the American newspaper reader. At the height of the conflict 1800 Ambonese, armed with klewangs (traditional sabers) and captured rifles, battled almost 12,000 Indonesians equipped with rifles, light and heavy machine guns, field artillery, armored cars and a few light tanks, supported by reconnaissance planes, two B25s and four corvettes with 10 cm. cannon.

Captain Dod Orsborne

Only the extreme isolation of the war zone made it possible to keep a conflict of such dimensions out of the world press. Day after day Radio Ambon broadcast pleas for assistance, but its primitive signals were received only by the local population, by the Indonesians who did everything in their power to keep the campaign secret, and by the Dutch in nearby New Guinea who, mistrusted and discredited by their police actions, were not believed by any foreign journalist. The Ambonese were not only right, but also strictly on their own.

"Cast off." Karel Vigeleyn Nikijuluw carefully placed a wet towel over the sleeve of his shirt, spit on the underside of the iron which hissed back at him, and seemed to concentrate on ironing the cuff. "As soon as Captain Orsborne is ready, he should cast off. But without you. It is absolutely essential that you fly to the Far East immediately, get into the RMS somehow and report back to me on the invasion. No time to lose."

In the four months that we had known each other, and particularly during our long, intimate fishing expeditions on Long Island Sound, Nikki and I had become fast friends. It wasn't difficult; his inborn graciousness and impeccable manners, common to the islanders, made him easy company. I admired him and appreciated our mutual regard. It soon became clear that his serenity even in times of stress, was rooted in faith - God is Justice, my cause is just, so God is with me. His own fate left him cold, which allowed him to concentrate on his mission in good spirits, no matter how mean his room, how lonely his life. Whatever the news from the Moluccas, his confidence never flagged, never did he appear down or dejected. And even when it was all over and I close to tears, he consoled me and said, "You Westerners think short term. God has time, leave it to Him. We may not live to see the RMS, but our children will. And if not they, then our grandchildren."

His standards led him to expect much of others. Gently and charmingly he would confront me, hard as nails, with the most horrendous alternatives. This last suggestion went too far.

"Nikki," I objected, "are you out of your fucking mind?"

He did not flinch. "I cannot leave here, otherwise I would go myself. But my contact at the U.N., in the Secretariat-General, thinks we have a chance to get the invasion of the RMS on the agenda of the Security Council, under the heading "armed aggression". But only if we have eyewitnesses, or firsthand statements and visual proof, like photographs. I am entrusting this to you, if you are willing to do it. Very important, not a moment to lose."

"Thanks a lot! Goddammit, you yourself told me that everything is locked up tight there, that nobody can get in or out."

"Exactly. That's why we need your help." Nikki's logic could be devastating, and not above a touch of flattery if it served the cause. "Then you can also make some preparations for the arrival of the Argosy, alert our friends, arrange for a landing place, dig around for some more arms, in Singapore perhaps, or in Australia."

"And where's the money going to come from?"

"Why? Are we broke again?"

"Of course. We're always broke. Just enough left for a ticket to Amsterdam, if that. One way."

Nikijuluw hesitated. I knew what was going through his mind - in Holland there existed an organization that collected funds for the Moluccans for humanitarian purposes. "We have no choice," he finally said. "Go to our friends in Eindhoven, they must have some cash. Better not tell then about the arms. Not that they'd mind, but they must stay legal. They are working on a load of medical supplies for Ambon from Singapore, maybe you can tie in to that. When can you leave?"

"Christ, man, hold your horses." I had lost too much ground to withstand the Ambonese leader's determination; you can't say A for four months, then refuse to say B. But suddenly there were goodbyes ahead, partings from Midge, from little Erik, three years old and the apple of my eye. Get into the RMS, somehow ... on my own... would I ever see them again?

"Tomorrow? Can you leave tomorrow?" Nikki stopped ironing and looked at me fixedly. In his dark eyes I saw the tension between his friendship for me and his devotion to Ambon. Under the iron a whiff of smoke curled upwards.

"Well, all right then. Tomorrow." I gave him a poke in his ribs. "And your bloody shirt's on fire."

CHAPTER 18

Standoff in the Philippines

"Watch every little step you take, my friend." Nikijuluw's last words at Idlewild Airport buzzed around in my brains. "Remember Karachi," referring to a notorious crash of a KLM plane some years before, which killed seventeen international journalists who, as guests of the Dutch, had visited the front on Java, but mysteriously never made it home to write about it. "The Indonesians are a determined lot and stop at nothing. They will move heaven and earth to keep you out of the RMS, and the RMS out of the newspapers." - By pure coincidence, which I have learned to recognize as Fate in action, this task landed squarely on the shoulders of my old nemesis, Dr. Charles Tambu.

I distinctly remembered our 1947 publicity battle in the USA and the drubbing he had given me, as well as the obvious relish with which this British Indian had pilloried my country in the American press. In recognition of his admittedly outstanding services Sukarno had appointed him Counselor at the Indonesian Embassy in Manila, the Philippines. Now Fate had ordained a second round, and one cardinal factor had changed: Justice, which used to be on his side in our earlier encounter, now had switched to mine. As a serious opponent he had undoubtedly written me off, probably forgotten me altogether. Life rarely offers a second chance, but if on November 11, 1950, at ten-thirty in the morning Dr. Tambu had looked out of an upstairs window of the Indonesian Embassy in Manila, he would have seen me sitting below on the terrace of the Swiss Châlet restaurant, having breakfast.

Much valuable time had meanwhile passed. Before leaving Rye I had given Dod Orsborne his sailing orders as well as handed over my ship and everything in it. I didn't worry. In illegal circles, be it drugs, arms, finance or smuggling, everybody keeps his word and nobody cheats, not for ethical but for practical reasons. Promises are by word of mouth and cannot be enforced by law, so the entire system would collapse without universal trust. For that reason the rare transgressor of this code is brutally punished, often by death, because he endangers everybody's livelihood. Dod, as an old pro, would be sure to abide by the rules.

After long hesitation I had decided to keep Midge in the dark about my mission, not just as a matter of security. It would have robbed her of any vestige of peace, just like in old RAF times, only worse. I said goodbye to my family as if I were off on a business trip to Holland. It would have been a lot better had I told her - she found out soon enough through an item in the New York Times under the headline "Dutch Writer Missing in Philippines."

The Ambon supporters in Eindhoven did not fuss around. After setting aside the amount required for a shipment of medical supplies to Ambon - if feasible - they had given me every last penny in their coffers, for a total of $ 17,460. To carry this amount of cash, I had bought a money belt which made me look about three months pregnant.

Trying to hook into their medical scheme, which was being planned via Singapore, I flew off to that hornets' nest in blithe ignorance of the bitter fighting taking place just north of the city, where British Ghurkas battled communist insurgents. As a result security was so tight, that on arrival in my hotel two English police officers were already sitting in my room to interrogate me. After twenty days of frustration - and superb Chinese cuisine - I had abandoned the notion of basing anything even vaguely unusual, and possibly illegal, on Singapore.

What now? There wasn't much choice. West of the RMS stretched the huge area of the Republic of Indonesia, now hostile territory for me. To the east New Guinea was still Dutch, a last and temporary remnant of the old empire, where Hollanders, under threat by the USA of suspending Marshall Aid to their country, grimly and miserably clung to strict neutrality. In both areas I was known and suspect, and a sure shot for arrest. To the south lay Australia, separated from Ambon by unbridgeable seas. For lack of alternatives I had packed my bags and moved to Manila, 1700 miles of water and jungle north of the RMS as the albatross flies. Except for Dr. Tambu, I knew no one in the Philippines.

The terrace of the Swiss Châlet was deserted. I ordered another cup of coffee and stared pensively at the embassy, a bright, new villa from which the red and white flag of Indonesia flapped listlessly. For nine days now I had wrestled with a problem not uncommon to secret missions: how to get things rolling. When defying the authority of one established state, you are suddenly confronted by the entire internationally interwoven apparatus through which the world community tries to maintain order. You sneak into a foreign city, the nature of your mission blocks all normal channels, you don't know a soul, can't trust anyone - where do you begin? Finally you make a move in some arbitrary direction, usually a wrong one, but if you survive the consequences you're on your way. Action takes over, doubt disappears, your sixth sense reports for duty, every nerve supports the age-old game. And sometimes it rattles your opponent and drives him into making mistakes.

I lit a pipe and looked over Manila Bay. From its motionless surface, gleaming like molten lead, poked dozens of masts, smokestacks and superstructures of 182 Japanese ships sunk in WW2 by American planes. Across the bay Bataan Peninsula rose as a somber reminder of the infamous death march, shimmering in the early heat, and to the south the island fortress Corregidor lay like a scorpion on the water. The mad race of taxis and buses, all jeeps, continued uninterrupted down Dewey Boulevard along the waterfront, behind which Luneta Park resounded once again to the cries of the balut and Coca Cola sellers - balut! balut!

When I turned towards the rubble heaps of downtown Manila, with here and there the white splash of a new building, three tiny newspaper urchins caught my eye. They raced across the street, almost trampling the smallest one, from whom I bought my paper with a ten centavos tip. Gratefully he placed the Manila Bulletin before me on the table: Smack in the middle on the front page stood my picture, with the caption "Indonesians accuse Manila visitor of Plot". The source of the story: Dr. Charles Tambu.

I sent the little fellow to get the rest of the morning papers, took a deep breath and thought. Well, I guess we were off and running. What did it mean, where did it come from? Two days earlier I had made the first move by paying three hundred dollars as a down payment on the charter of a sea- going prau, by check after transferring my dollars from around my belly to a bank account. It was a risk; what would be my story if the owner of the ship, with my money safely in his pocket, reported the unusual transaction and aroused the suspicion of the authorities? This didn't take much in the Philippines, where in 1950 corruption and contraband was rampant and communist insur- gents, the Hukbalahaps, penetrated to the city gates at night.

Obviously, this was exactly what that bastard with his crappie boat had done. The police, after seeing on the customs form that I was born in Surabaya, had called the embassy for information, and the Indonesians with Dr. Tambu in the lead had flipped their lid. To make matters worse, for them as well as for me, their President Sukarno was expected on December 3rd in Manila for an official state visit.

When a covert operation finally gets rolling, it often takes off like a firecracker. The urchin returned with the other papers, featuring the story on every front page. This was an organized, formidable attack. What did Tambu hope to achieve with this salvo, where could it lead?

Suddenly I got it, and also knew what to do about it. But I needed time. I jumped up and raced back to my hotel room. After locking the door I called Philippine Airlines and booked a seat to San Francisco for that very afternoon. Then I sent two telegrams, one to Prince Bernhard and the other to Bill Hearst, the newspaper tycoon whom I had met underneath a table in London during the war. Next I burned whatever compromising papers I had in my possession in the bathroom and flushed the toilet. Lastly, without much hope, I called the bank, and hallelujah! the check had not yet cleared, so the bum could whistle for his three hundred bucks. I was just lighting my pipe to mask the smell of burned paper, when someone knocked on the door. I kicked off my shoes, shot into a robe and opened up. Two security agents walked in, searched the room and requested me to get dressed and accompany them. We left the hotel in total silence and got into a jeep.

Freedom has presence, I can smell it. In spite of the cat-and-mouse game I played with Philippine authorities - me as mouse, but a slippery one - I never felt concerned in Manila. Its air was clear of the stifling odor of a police state, its officers correct and polite, the press rambunctious and irreverent, the people open, unafraid. The rule of law, however lackadaisical, was the backbone of the land and protected its subjects, even me.

The stories in the papers of November 11th amounted to the following. Dr. Tambu had given a press conference, all very official in the embassy, to announce that I was in Manila to illegally make my way to Ambon in order "to kidnap the rebel leader Chris Soumokil." Meanwhile Indonesian ambassador Maramis had paid a visit to the Philippine Foreign Secretary, Felino Neri, to personally inform him of my sinister reputation and undesirable presence. They clearly wanted me out, through publicity, through political pressure, they didn't care how. As Nikki had said, they were a determined lot and stopped at nothing.

However, Tambu had made two mistakes. He had broken the silence around Ambon, and also made it impossible for the authorities to expel me in secret. In flushing me out he had provided me with the perfect cover: that of a newsman eager to 'scoop' the RMS story. Publicity became the key, not only for the Moluccans but also to my own position. Any press corps worth its salt rallies behind an underdog, and in spite of the Indonesian accusations I hadn't done anything illegal yet. Besides, wasn't I really one of them?

All I needed was time to rally my forces, hence my reservation to San Francisco. It was Saturday, and in the Philippines you don't fool around with the weekend. If the plane left without me that afternoon, the authorities wouldn't know about it until Monday. Two whole days...

The jeep drove to the headquarters of Central Security, where shortly afterwards I found myself seated opposite a police captain in a room without windows. The walls were severely pitted, as if the building had recently fallen in intense hand-to-hand combat. Against the ceiling right above my head a giant cockroach lurked, motionless. The three of us were alone, no witnesses.

The classic scene was appropriately lit by a bare bulb hanging from an exposed wire. The officer, a pudgy little man whose skull, round and shaven, blindingly reflected the harsh light, blew his nose and meticulously studied the catch in his handkerchief. With short, clumsy fingers he finagled some sheets of paper and carbons into an antique typewriter, then sat back and studied me silently through spectacles half an inch thick. The rigid eyes, enlarged to colorless blobs, brought memories of Danny Kaye portraying a Japanese officer in "Up in Arms" Finally he opened his mouth, but I beat him to it.

"Excuse me, Colonel, but would you please hurry up. I have to pack my bags."

His mouth stayed open, but emitted no sound.

"My bags. In a few hours I depart for San Francisco. By Philippine Air Lines."

He picked up a telephone and in a torrent of Tagalog, from which I could only pick out my own name and the airline's, he obviously got confirmation that I was indeed booked to ship out in six hours time. That saved him some trouble. He replaced the phone, laboriously unloaded his typewriter, and without a word pointed at the door.

That evening, behind a Gimlet in the roof bar of the Hotel Continental with the lights of Manila twinkling all around me, I read in the paper that I had left the Philippines that same afternoon. What a moment of glory for Dr. Tambu, to see his old enemy skipping town with his tail between his legs - too bad it wasn't going to last. I had the waiter bring a telephone to my table and called every news room in town. Now it was my turn to give a press conference.

* * *

The Monday morning papers showed that I was still in Manila and had mounted a counterattack. As expected, the feisty doctor lashed back, and the old mano-a-mano from New York burst loose with undiminished gusto. The conflict around my presence in the Philippines was fought out on the front pages of the papers. The readers followed the developments like crowds at a cock fight and the higher the authorities involved, the more delighted the audience. Finally I was summoned to the office of the Foreign Secretary, Felino Neri.

He was a slender, elegant man dressed in a white, long- sleeved Filipino shirt worn outside the trousers. He received me courteously. "President Sukarno of Indonesia is planning to honor us with a state visit," he said, waving a piece of paper in my face. "But he won't come as long as you are here."

He looked at me with interest. I shrugged my shoulders. This was one development I had not asked for.

"It's a difficult situation for us. As long as you are legal in our country and don't break our laws, I can't throw you out." He smiled, then added, "The newspapers won't let me. - Won't you leave voluntarily?"

The Manila Newspapers were on the job

"Excellency, if you give me the exit permit, I'll leave for Ambon tomorrow." Here lay my critical weakness. To leave the Philippines legally, one needed a permit based on entry into the country of destination. Would the RMS qualify as such?

"I cannot give you that without a visa from the Indonesian government." There was my answer.

"Sir, in that case I shall enjoy your hospitality a little while longer."

In Monday's evening papers Dr. Tambu labeled me "an agent of Moscow", a brutal accusation in a country where communism constituted a desperate threat. In 1950 Manila was a city under siege, only to be reached safely by sea or air, with the surrounding countryside largely in the hands of the Hukbalahaps.

The vicious swipe did not come unexpected, however, and Prince Bernhard's answer to my telegram arrived just in time for the Tuesday morning editions: "Dear Erik - gladly confirm outstanding war record highest decoration and one hundred percent democratic outlook cordial greetings - Bernhard, Prince of the Netherlands."

When the Prince helped a friend, he didn't fool around. Caught in a lie, Tambu was effectively eliminated.

The next day, Wednesday, my visitor's visa expired, normally a mere formality. One of the policemen who had searched my room kindly came to warn me that under apparent diplomatic pressures an extension would be denied. This could still knock me out of the ring. However, for just such an occasion I had another ace up my sleeve, a generous telegram from Bill Hearst in reply to my request for a recommendation. And nothing bothered the Philippine press corps more than the opinions of their big brothers in America.

At ten o'clock on Wednesday morning I stood before Immigration Commissioner De la Cruz in a building which should have been set aside as a monument to Manila's war damage. He told me brusquely that "for reasons of state" my visa would not be extended. Then he waited for my protest. I bowed my head respectfully. "Sir, you are the responsible officer. Of course I must accept your decision."

A cloud of suspicion settled on his brow; such reasonable foreigners he rarely met in his position. With a smile I stepped out of the office, sourly watched by my host. I went straight to the Times, the Bulletin, the Herald, the Mirror and the Chronicle, with De la Cruz' marching orders in my left, Bill Hearst' telegram in my right pocket. Headlined all across the front pages, the afternoon editions accused the commissioner of endangering the democratic reputation of the Philippines.

Within the hour I received a call from the immigration service, with the request that I come in for a talk. I replied that I was unfortunately too busy packing my bags. Ten minutes later a courier was standing before me with a personal letter:

"As the files of this bureau show that there exists no damaging information about you, we shall favorably consider an extension of your visa, if you would be so good as to sign the enclosed request form. - De la Cruz."

I was happy to oblige.

* * *

Secret agents are always waiting, for news, for orders, for money, a telephone call, a message, developments, somebody else; for inspiration, for disaster. The universal enemy is boredom. In the telling it seems as if I must have been constantly busy those days, in my memory I am sitting in my hotel room from morning till night with a book. From time to time someone drops by, occasionally I go out for a few minutes, now and then a short, dry talk on the phone, but otherwise I sit there reading, in a blue flowered aloha shirt, bare feet on the table: Thor Heyerdahl's Kon Tiki. With the white, dusty light streaming in through the open window comes the call of the balut vendors, the smell of copra on the quayside. Six, seven jeeps screech furiously at each other in the distance, then the silence returns, except for the gentle whir of the fan above my head, the tinkle of ice in my glass, the cozy jabbering of my pipe.

To cover all my options, the moment seemed right to visit Dr. Tambu. The Indonesian embassy occupied an attractive, whitewashed villa on Dewey Boulevard, overlooking the bay. The hall inside was cool and clean, with rattan chairs and flowers on the coffee table. I requested the young receptionist to announce me to Dr. Tambu and gave him my card, which created some minor consternation. After he had left I installed myself in a chair, lit a cigarette and pondered my situation.

My twelve days in the Philippines had not brought me one step closer to the RMS. For the time being I could consider myself safe, even popular, in Manila, but I was also saddled with the best publicized secret mission ever attempted. Everyone knew that

I wanted to go to Ambon, but that to do so I had to sneak out of the country illegally, while everybody and his aunt kept an eye on me. To top it off, Foreign Secretary Neri had informed me that, in connection with Sukarno's visit, he would under no circumstances allow a second extension of my visitor's visa. Two weeks more, and between me and the RMS still some 1700 miles of sea and jungle-covered islands.

"What is your business?" Tambu inquired rather crudely, as we sat opposite each other in his room. Frankly, I had come to see if a relationship of respectful hostility in the classical sense might be possible between us, although his recent tactics had made such a noble experience unlikely. It did not look promising. He turned out to be a tall, emaciated British Indian, cool, condescending, with an accent that would have blended in nicely at Buckingham Palace. His tone would not.

"I need an Indonesian visa to go to Ambon," I answered truthfully. Impudent dog, I heard him think, accent and all. "We have no objections to giving you a visa. The only feasible way to Ambon is via Jakarta. I shall book a passage for you."

"Thanks awfully, but please don't bother." The capital of Indonesia seemed like a very unhealthy place for me right then. "Just issue the visa, I'll make my own arrangements to get to the RMS."

"But why not? It's really much more comfortable."

"No doubt. But it's such long way around." We grinned, like a couple of wolves circling each other. Every embassy in the world, whatever its nationality, is bugged. In an effort to ease the tension the two of us, both pros, went downstairs to the Swiss Châlet for a cup of coffee. It did not help much.

"I met Prince Bernhard once," Dr. Tambu remarked unexpectedly. "In London. Charming chap."

"Watch out!" It was too good to pass up. "Another agent of Moscow. Just like me. You've got to be careful, we're simply everywhere."

With a sour face he got up and offered me a slack handshake. His small, coal black eyes glittered like a cobra's.

"As long as you understand one thing," was his parting shot.

"You'll never get into the Moluccas. Forget about it. By plane, we'll shoot you down. By boat, you won't get through. And once we get you..."

As far as I was concerned, he could leave that sentence unfinished.

*   *   *

Ultimately you have to trust someone. It's a moment you postpone as long as possible, but you rarely last all the way alone. It's a critical step, sometimes a matter of life and death. In the course of a long, venturesome career I have put my fate in the trust of some pretty rum characters; the fact that I am still around is living testimony to my intuition. When U.S. Airforce Intelligence in the person of Captain Allan Charak came nosing around this strange duck who had alighted in his territory, I took him into my confidence. Well, at least partially.

"Al, we're in the same boat, you and me," I opened up.

He was a lanky, lively Westerner from Searchlight, Nevada, with a net of laughter wrinkles around his eyes, more the cowboy type than a secret service officer. I liked him immediately, but kept my cover as newspaper man. "Something is going on there in Ambon. It's your job to know what's new in your bailiwick. I aim to go there to find out. When I get back, I'll tell you everything."

"If, not when."

"Why don't you give me a hand? I'll write a report for you which will make you a general overnight."

Another week had gone by without any progress. Tambu, knowing that I had to break the law to get away, had put two men on my tail who shadowed me day and night. One false step, and he would have me arrested. From my hotel window I could see them hang around, and when I went outside they slid in back of me, never more than thirty paces behind. They in turn were tailed by two agents of Philippine Security, at my request, to prevent them from wiping me out at some convenient occasion. Towards sunset this miserable little parade with me up front could be seen sauntering sadly along the waterfront, to catch some fresh air, or on the way to a few glasses of beer at three different tables in some lousy bar or other.

"What do you need?" Allan asked. "Money?"

I shook my head. "Transportation."

After a few moments he said, "Why don't you come to dinner tomorrow?"

At six thirty I walked up to his apartment in the Rehabilitation Compound, a temporary wooden housing complex for Americans, out of bounds to locals such as my usual escort of agents. Captain Allan Charak, wearing a plastic Popeye apron, stood by the door broiling hamburgers on a barbecue. Inside, in a rattan easy chair with a bottle of whiskey on the floor next to him, well within reach, sat Meyer Schwartz, a renowned Manila businessman with a face like a morose bloodhound.

"Just call him Mike," Al introduced us. "And be nice to him, he owns a sea plane."

After dinner our host disappeared on the obvious pretext that he still had some work to do. Mike brewed coffee, with which we installed ourselves on the steps to the strip of grass and banana trees between the buildings. The night was hot, a half moon beamed on the leaves and as if on cue the notes of Debussy's Clair de Lune trickled from an open window, somewhere down the lane. We smoked, somberly. There was little time, less hope, I had almost given up. "That plane of yours.." I mumbled, to break the silence.

Meyer sighed, belched discreetly and interrupted me. "I don't know you. I don't know what you're up to. I know nothing. But Al says give him your plane, so I'll give you my plane. But I know from nothing." He went inside and brought out the Scotch and two glasses.

After another drink or two we went into town, straight to a bar where Al was waiting for us with a former U.S. navy pilot, John Millington, who was going to fly me to Ambon. "Here's the deal," Al explained in a private moment. "You give me five thousand bucks for Mike, in case you bust his plane. I'll get you an official U.S. Air Force receipt. And don't forget the report."

"How about Millington?"

"You do your own deal."

We made a night of it and at dawn drove by a mooring off the harbor to take a look at Mike's flying machine. We dared not stop the car, but I did catch a glimpse of a neat little amphibian, something cheerful in red and white, as eye-catching as one could wish for a secret flight. On the way home Mike handed me the keys. "Have fun," he said, dryly, and as abruptly as he had arisen, sank back into his world of exchange rates, CIF and FOB.

* * *

The next two days I spent in the swimming pool of the Manila Hotel, in the back garden which was separated from the bay by a narrow promenade in the heart of town. That's where Millington flew the plane and tied her to a buoy, barely fifty feet from the public walkway, which of course in no time filled up with loafers who patiently observed the activities around the little machine. In this welcome diversion they were joined by my usual complement of four agents, who had followed me to the pool and shrugged off my sudden interest in water sports as the whim of a notoriously eccentric foreigner. It did not enter their minds that from this strategic position I once again meant to outwit Dr. Tambu.

She was a Republic Seabee, a jolly little flying boat ideal for fishing trips. A single 230 hp. engine, smaller than many a modern car, powered a push propeller mounted on the trailing edge of the wing; with a tank capacity of 75 gallons and gas consumption of 15 gallons per hour at a cruising speed of 100 mph, this gave her a range of 500 miles. Not nearly enough, so an extra tank had to be installed. Splashing around in the ample pool I watched as a chair was being removed from the aircraft, after which two mechanics lugged something that looked like a 50-gallon oil drum into the cockpit. John, who directed the operation from a dinghy, gave me the thumbs-up sign.

A number of points had to be debated,which required an occasional conference on the highest level. Then John came ashore, disappeared in the hotel and minutes later, unrecognizable in flowered swim shorts, plunged in next to me. Sitting up to our chins in the cool water, we discussed life jackets and spare parts, provisions, takeoff speed and emergency procedures. We also pondered an as yet unsolved problem: how could I ever get aboard without giving the show away to my agents?

On the night before our departure the solution presented itself. The Seabee lay ready for departure, all we still had to do was load her and get away unnoticed. Al, John and I were having an urgent session about it in some café; in the murky back room hovered our inescapable guard dogs at separate tables, drinking beer. The situation became even more bizarre, when a flashy oriental beauty came in and sat down right next to us at the long, totally empty bar.

"Careful," Al hissed in my ear. "Pure poison. Works for the opposition."

He needn't have told me, I had seen her often enough. Every time Tambu's boys took a break, for meals or whatever, she would hold the fort for them. When she was around, the agents disappeared. I looked in the back room, they were paying the tab.

Moments later they were gone, followed by their own tails. Would I stay clear of them as long as I remained in her company?

Al almost flipped when I ordered her a drink. As I started a conversation with her, he kicked my shin. He got ever more somber as the floozy and I warmed up to each other, and when I finally enlightened him in the men's room he still looked dubious. But I was sure that this was our chance - I would rather tackle one female agent than four male. If I let her go, the others would come back. There was no other solution: we had to stay together until the moment of departure, including the entire night. And when something is inevitable, you may just as well make the best of it. Tambu's girl and I left the bar arm in arm.

We started out in the Wintergarden, the luxurious dancing and restaurant of the Manila Hotel with, as is traditional in the Philippines, one of the best orchestras of the Far East. This was the "in" place to be, and that night all Manila had come. It was hot and through the open windows the balmy breeze brought exotic scents from far over the mountains. The sumptuous room sparkled with silver and crystal and under the chandeliers danced the haute monde of the capital, the ladies elegant in their dresses with puffed sleeves, the gentlemen cool in their white, jacketless evening clothes. My date, in a backless western dress, rapturously acted her Mata Hari role, with an accent on seduction. Tightly around us all lay the murderous Huks in their dark encampments, to the north raged the Korean war, to the south fought the Ambonese, just outside rode my little Seabee ready for departure, and who did I see there in high diplomatic company? Dr. Tambu!

I maneuvered my flamboyant partner towards him and as we danced by we displayed a few sultry steps while I bowed gravely in his direction, a little too deep as if I were sauced. My girlfriend, who undoubtedly knew him and probably smelled promotion, outdid herself and with a wanton wiggle we waltzed our way back into the crowd. The Indian had smiled and in his glittering eyes I recognized aversion, disdain and triumph, just a touch of each, and I read his mind: conceited Dutchman, thinks he's so bloody smart, a couple of schnapps and a willing broad and I'll wrap you around my finger.

I took a room in the Manila hotel and before midnight we turned in - I badly needed my sleep. It didn't work out that way.

She smelled ever so slightly of musk. Her skin, when dry, had the downy softness of untouched grapes, but under the shower she gleamed like an otter. Of course, it was all for a good cause.

Besides, it worked. November 28, 1950, dawned brilliantly over Manila. We awoke slowly, my little spy and I, and after breakfast in bed we dove into the pool at ten forty-five. Gliding through the soft water I carefully looked through the usual crowd... not an agent in sight! No doubt about it, she had been given full responsibility for me, every one else had the day off. The sky, the bay, the mountains of Bataan shone in shades of blue; the red Seabee with the white roof sparkled in the clear light like a toy in Indonesian colors, less than fifty yards away. John, working on the final touches, studiously ignored us. Two mechanics were working in the cockpit, on their stomachs, legs in the water both sides of the airplane.

We swam around a bit, then installed ourselves in lounge chairs under a palm tree. My playmate soon fell asleep, I kept an eye on the activities around the plane. The inflatable life raft came aboard, pity we couldn't find parachutes. Water bottles were being filled; that crate should be the provisions. Finally the dinghy came by with 5-gallon gas tanks; I counted sixteen, so we had one reserve. The main tank was filled through a funnel in the mid section, the extra tank required a complicated operation of which I could only see the backsides of the mechanics. When they were finished, a mysterious rubber tube hung out of the port window - a ventilation valve? At midday John gave the signal.

I immediately suggested to my guardian angel that we have a bite to eat in the restaurant. She still didn't smell a rat, or any other rodent. We walked to the dress cabins hand in hand. I shot into my clothes and called over the partition that I was going ahead to get a table; would she like a drink? She did, a dry Martini, perfect. In the restaurant I ordered two cocktails and told the waiter to serve them immediately; a lady was on the way to join me, but I had to make a telephone call. She could start, of course, and would she please have some patience.

I slipped out of the hotel through a side door and ran to the promenade, where the dinghy lay ready. The Seabee was waiting with turning propeller, held by the tail, John behind the joy stick. While I climbed aboard I looked behind me one more time, very sharply. There was no sign of either the girl or the agents. I whacked the door shut, and with an earsplitting roar we barreled down the bay.

CHAPTER 19

Running the Indonesian Blockade

Manila Bay reaches into the heart of the city. Office buildings, fine hotels, branches of government and many embassies look out on it. Dewey Boulevard runs along the waterfront, separating it from Luneta Park, where on this radiant November day thousands of citizens were enjoying their lunch break.

An enervating roar disturbed the peace, now close by, then in the distance, or tearing along the entire length of the boulevard, without letup. People looked out of windows and lined the quayside to discover the source of this irritating racket.

That was not difficult. On the open bay in view of all Manila a small seaplane buzzed around in spurts and circles like a demented beetle, fiery red in the midday sun, obviously desperate to get off the water and into the air. From the cockpit I watched the growing crowds - a fine start for a super secret flight to Ambon.

"What the hell's the matter with this crate?" I bellowed above the noise.

"Too heavy!" John Millington was heaving on the stick, a drop of sweat at the tip of his nose. A nerve twitched in his cheek.

You don't say, I thought. But you're the pilot and should have figured out how much weight this little engine can pull. Apparently not two people, an extra fifty gallons of gas and all the garbage for a trip to the RMS. By circling tightly he tried making waves to break the suction of the mirror like surface, but the Seabee seemed glued down. Finally he closed the throttle. We bobbed about aimlessly somewhere between the Indonesian Embassy and the harbor police. What next?

"Oof!" John puffed. He pulled a handkerchief from his cute little weekend case and endlessly wiped the sweat off his forehead. "No choice, we'll have to get back to the hotel."

"Over my dead body." I had a vision of my guardian angel behind her watery Martini. "That broad's likely to scratch my eyes out. And at least we're still rid of the other bastards. Come on, let's go! Out of here! Out of town!"

Millington taxied down the bay until Manila shimmered hazily in the distance and finally disappeared behind a spit of land. An hour later we came to a deserted beach, twelve miles further south. It seemed a good place to quickly make adjustments and take off. After anchoring in shallow water thirty yards out, we went to work. We were still at it two days later, when John quit and left me in the lurch. I couldn't even blame him.

The Seabee was an amphibian, with wheels that folded away into the body, turning her into a flying boat. The only effective way to reduce its weight was to remove this landing gear and transform her into a pure seaplane. It was murder. With minimal tools and up to our hips in muddy water full of black, poisonous jellyfish, we labored like coolies. Just getting the wheels off took the rest of the afternoon, and the entire next day we battled to detach the struts and elbows, with only partial success. The remainder of the mechanism refused to budge and henceforth stuck out unevenly on both sides of the plane like the legs of a crippled grasshopper, hardly an aerodynamic advantage. During daylight we worked in the flaming sun, watched from the shore by buffaloes of infinite dignity. At night we slept in semi-submerged, slime covered invasion wrecks alive with sand flies.

The Republic Seabee in the Bay of Cagayan

At sunrise on November 30, during our third try for takeoff, there came a moment that we felt the little plane tremble on the edge of flight. We gave it a few minutes rest. I decided to reduce weight even further, and in a wave of blind determination methodically threw everything overboard that would move, much to John's dismay: the life raft, spare parts, loose cans of oil and gas and finally all provisions except six cans of Spam and one water canteen. Now or never.

We braced ourselves and a sour-faced Millington opened up. While we roared along endlessly, John hanging on the stick, I happened to look in his direction. Sweat dripped from his nose and chin, and the twitch was back in his cheek. For one breath- taking second the Seabee tore itself free, sank back onto the bay in preparation for the next, longer leap, and at that instant something hit the hull with a sharp, dry smack. John throttled back and without a word turned towards the land. We taxied in silence. I lifted the floor panel and with a shoe started to bail out the water which was slowly collecting in the hull. Finally my intrepid pilot cast out the anchor and waded up the beach, his immaculate weekender in hand, carefully avoiding the jellyfish. Once ashore he turned around.

"I'm going home," he stated simply.

"At least let me have your identity card." I didn't argue, but in case I got caught I'd much rather be American than Dutch.

He agreed and we parted friends. Suddenly I was alone, as Lt. Comdr. John Howard Millington, US Navy (82539). What the hell, hadn't I always preferred to operate on my own?

All was well while the light lasted, but with darkness came the willies. After an endless search I had found the leak, a single rivet knocked loose by floating debris. I plugged the seam with a sock, saving the other for later service as a gas filter. Then, in order to conserve my drastically reduced provisions, I walked an hour for a meal in a warong, where I read a paper and learned that Sukarno had postponed his visit for another week.

When late in the afternoon I got back to my lonely beach, Bataan was a cinder against the setting sun.

I installed myself in a wrecked LST and lit a pipe. Sea and sky appeared to be the inside of a single shell, mother-of- pearl, held together by a tissue of land across the bay. Two water buffaloes ambled by. Simultaneously they halted, threw back their heads and stared down their noses at the Seabee in a long look of disapproval. Resuming their slow motion, they took the last sounds of evening with them, leaving me at the mercy of my worries.

My mission was desperate. I had not piloted an aircraft since World War II, and never a seaplane. I knew nothing about the Republic Seabee in general, and my specific machine in particular, with its giant extra tank in the cockpit, a rubber tube hanging from the window and those crazy grasshopper legs protruding on each side. I had no parachute, no emergency gear and hardly any food or water. We had no radio. The Seabee lacked blind flying instruments, for cloud or darkness. There were no maps, except for a minuscule sea chart on which islands appeared as blank spaces without mountains or altitude contours.

About our route all I knew with certainty was that the land below us would be covered by jungle and the sea devoid of ships, all 2500 kilometers of it. I had no access to weather reports or wind directions, by which I could calculate a course.

Without radio I could not call for outside help and on a clandestine trip no one would miss us if we got lost. The Indonesians, who controlled the major part of our route, were my official enemies, and their military air base on the island of Morotai lay smack across my path. And if all went well, we still had to land in a war zone with its preferred policy of shooting first and talking later.

Did I have to see it through? Couldn't I just turn back and go home? If I explained it, Nikki would understand. Anybody would. But not old skin-and-bones, and he seemed awfully close. Life had diluted my youthful conceptions and illusions with a healthy dose of skepticism, but his lessons had stuck. If you turn back once, you're lost. If you let fear guide your step, you'll fall. And, on the positive side, if you reach your limit while doing your utmost, something will take over.

Twice that night I got up to bail the aircraft dry. Wavelets tapped against the hull, a welcome sound; every wrinkle would help break the suction. When I awoke the third time, the morning of December 1st dawned exuberantly over the bay.

Action took over. I jumped out of the wreck and jogged down the beach to limber up, scaring thousands of tiny crabs who scurried away into the mud. I sloshed into the lukewarm water and found that the jellyfish had fled before the breeze. Touching the Seabee I felt no vibes of any kind. She was cold to me, foreign, except for something very familiar I had not noticed before: the number 320, painted in large white numerals on the tail, as it had been on the stern of MGB 320 which had ferried me back and forth safely across the North Sea for Contact Holland. Some friendly presence had left its calling card.

After ten minutes of bailing I used a sponge to suck up every last drop of water from the hull. Then I climbed aboard, pulled in the anchor and slammed the door behind me. 'Hora est,' the moment is here.

The engine took at my first touch of the starter button. Taxiing out I tried to get a grip on the switches, handles and instruments around me. They eluded me. I aimed the nose at Bataan in the distance and slowly pushed the throttle knob forward, all the way against the dashboard. The little boat jumped ahead with a roar, I knew immediately that we had power to spare. So this was it. Every second the Seabee gained speed. Then she started to pitch, nose up into the air, down into the water, up, down, up, down, stamping ever wilder, like a bucking bronco, crazily, until I thought we'd dive straight down to the bottom of the sea. I did absolutely nothing. There was no contact, we were not connected, miles apart, separated by everything I had forgotten about flying.

I just sat, immobilized by panic.

Suddenly something snapped in me. Chaos leveled out into conflict, a challenge, a personal clash for supremacy. "God dammit, you bitch!" I yelled at the top of my lungs. "That's enough!" and raging and swearing like a maniac I wrestled the wildly swinging control column into compliance, kicked the rudder bar straight and forced the little craft to my hand; immediately she acquiesced. The controls became my tools, the engine my power and the total confusion of gauges, knobs and switches reported for duty in quiet order. All at once I knew how to fly again.

I broke the pitching and within seconds the Seabee moved up onto the step, high in the water, nose aimed at the sky, loyal and obedient. When we hit a wave I hung back on the stick with both hands. She broke free, then sank back onto the smooth surface. "Come on, baby!" I yelled, sensing how hard she was trying. Again she tore loose with me pulling back steadily, gained speed in a long, light leap, touched the bay one more time with a playful tap and was airborne. Not yet one hundred feet high I caught myself humming, the sweat salty in the corners of my mouth.

We set course in what should roughly be the direction of Ambon.

$$* * *$$

Within ten minutes I was lost. While the Bay of Manila slid away below us, breathtakingly blue, I climbed to 400 feet, leveled off and looked out of the window, fully expecting the islands to unfold themselves just as clearly before my eyes as they appeared on the little chart in my hand. They simply didn't.

The neat arrangement which the map displayed turned out to be, in reality, a confusion of mountain peaks and ridges and patches of water - quite hopeless. I tried to climb above it, but 4000 feet was as high as the little engine could lift us. To make matters worse, clouds began drifting in from the south, forcing us down to a level where mountains blocked my view on all sides. As I lacked all wind information by which to figure out a course, I had no choice but to make for the nearest coastline. We would have to follow these from island to island, with an occasional hop over water, a harrowing procedure which consumed both far too much time and gasoline.

Our goal for the day was Davao on the far coast of Mindanao, some 900 kilometers from Manila. It represented the last fueling point in the Philippines before the long haul south over Indonesian territory. The next morning, December 2, my final visa expired, and I did not doubt for a moment that the immigration police, whipped along by an enraged Dr. Tambu, would be hot on my heels. By taking off at dawn in all secrecy I hoped to slip through their fingers. These first minutes of the journey had not improved my outlook.

We reached the sea in the narrow channel between Luzon and what I figured to be Mindoro. From the waterline the island rose up steeply and disappeared in heavy cloud. When we neared the coast, the first raindrops spattered on my windshield.

Visibility shrank as the clouds pushed me down, and finally we skimmed over choppy waves, the starboard wingtip lined up with hazy palm trees behind white surf. We almost hit a sand spit, but at least it confirmed that we were on the right track. For twenty minutes the coast ran parallel to my planned route, a few degrees east of south. Flying along it I made note of the compass heading that kept us on this desired track. The stupid thing pointed due east. Meanwhile Mindoro gradually turned away from my route, so that we ended up in a gray vacuum. I could do little else but maintain that crazy course.

When the cloud broke, we found ourselves over open sea. In the distance I saw mountain peaks which fitted nicely in about six locations on the map. I continued on the same course, if for no other reason than to see where that would get us. After a full hour I got my first positive identification, the town of Capiz on the island of Panay. It lay exactly on our route! I gave a mighty shout of satisfaction and promoted the experiment to our official navigational system: from now on, whenever we flew along a coast which more or less corresponded with my planned track, I took note of the heading on my temperamental compass and maintained it over long stretches of sea and jungle, hoping that meanwhile the wind would stay steady. It worked perfectly, except once and that was more than enough.

For the moment, life was great. We crossed Panay at a thousand feet, then Negros, next Cebu and finally Bohol, in glorious sunshine and always within sight of a coast. Where the sea neared the sand, dark blue dissolved into emerald green, veined with white like onyx. Behind the surf, palms waved in the wind along a narrow strip of arable land that gradually arched upwards into rugged hills, covered with rocks and tufts of jungle. The tallest trees pushed their branches, dripping with beard moss, at the jolly little flying boat a few feet above that purred along contentedly in the hands of a Dutch fugitive dressed in a flowered aloha shirt, striped underpants and bare feet, en route to the embattled RMS. What would old Orsborne be up to right now, and where?

After five hours in the air I aimed the Seabee through a cleft in a mountain ridge, and before us lay the Sea of Mindanao. A quick estimate put us in Davao at 13:30 hours. But in flying you can predict whatever you like, what happens is often quite different. The unlimited vista of water dissolving into hazy sky chilled me like a cold shower. Half an hour later a shadow on the horizon grew into a coastline and from that first moment I wanted nothing to do with Mindanao. It didn't improve when we got closer.

The island looked like a continent, a wall of mountains that disappeared in massive cloud cover. How could I possibly get through this? For a full half hour I flew along the north coast to find a passage, but as far as the eye reached, yellowish wisps of fog over thick jungle pressed down through the valleys almost to the sea line. This formidable barrier was 500 km wide. I checked my gauges and got the message. We had to get down for gas.

For my first water landing I chose the wide Bay of Cagayan de Oro. White streaks of foam lined its surface, but that did not faze me. After all, it was sea, and wasn't I flying a seaplane? I descended in a long, flat curve, straightened out neatly against the wind as I had always done, decreased the airspeed to 100 km per hour and waited confidently for the little craft to settle in her element. In the last few seconds it did strike me that the waves, which had looked insignificant from above, seemed to be thundering towards me with terrifying speed. One earsplitting bang, we were whacked back into the air like a ping-pong ball, and before I knew what hit us we staggered along at 100 feet with the throttle wide open.

It took me a good half hour to sufficiently recover my wits for another try. Meanwhile I searched for calm waters, but the bay lay open to the northeasterly trade winds, so I could forget about that. I felt lonely and shocked, betrayed by what I had considered a friendly element. But one thing was certain: I had to get down, the gauges were solidly stuck on "empty". I curved into the final approach with considerable less confidence.

It was horrendous. The crests of the swells, which close up turned out to be four to five feet high, raced towards me in the final seconds like mountains, flashing by below with dizzying speed. We first touched water right behind a ridge, which slowed us down a little, but instantly the first crest hit us a murderous blow and bounced us back into the air. This time I had no choice and pulled the throttle shut. The little boat wobbled down, straight into the brawn of the next wave, and the next, and the next. In an ordeal of violence, foam and noise we smacked in and out of the water and each blow I expected to be our last. When finally the machine flopped down, moaning and trembling, and held fast to the surface, I sank back into my seat, shivering with shock and exhaustion. I couldn't even swear, the water leaked in around my bare toes and I waited resignedly for the two of us to bubble down to the bottom of the bay.

It may have been the location, or the lurid drama he described so well, but while I was sitting stunned in anticipation of the end, a marvelous line by the English writer W. Somerset Maugham began to whirl around my numb brain: "Resignation is the virtue of the vanquished." It somehow made me pick up a shoe that floated around the cockpit and begin to bail. We weren't licked yet, and the Seabee, its engine still ticking over, responded by not sinking. The leak turned out to be no match for the shoe, so I began looking for a way to escape this wet madness. Measuring the distance to the nearest shore, I recoiled from its desolation.

However, across the bay lay the town of Cagayan, undoubtedly no great shakes either, but with more chance of harboring some gasoline, a glass of beer and a bed. Two or three miles, I estimated.

I set out on the assumption that nothing could be worse than the landing. I had not counted on seasickness. In the middle of the bay the waves were so wild that we cracked a windshield. For almost an hour I taxied through chaos, slowly to save fuel, the door next to me open, bailing, puking, dripping, and when at last we reached our goal I shoved the Seabee roughly onto the beach right between some bamboo pole houses and their terrified occupants. One owned a horse cart, and past purple bougainvillea and waving palm trees I bumped into Cagayan like a drowned rat. One thing was certain - nothing could ever get me back into that flying machine.

* * *

Next morning at nine o'clock the order for my arrest went out all over the Philippines. I turned over snugly in my little bamboo room, listened to the pigs and chickens outside the window and dedicated myself to making life complicated for De la Cruz and his immigration police. I should already be one move ahead. During the last waiting period in Manila I had flown by airliner to Pelawan and Zamboanga, towns hundreds of miles apart, and rented a room in each place, paying two weeks in advance.

Early today the police had first gone to the Hotel Continental, where they found my room undisturbed, clothes in the closet, toothbrush on the wash basin, cigarettes next to my bed, as if I would return at any moment. Only after lunch did they decide that I had flown the coop. When they checked, among others with Captain Allan Charak, he advised them to investigate rumors in Pelawan and Zamboanga, red herrings that thoroughly confused the authorities and gained me at least one full day.

My depression after the almost fatal landing the previous afternoon, had not survived the subsequent night. The tiny hotel in Cagayan, where I registered as John Millington, proudly possessed a bathroom, in which a giggling girl poured enormous kettles of warm water over my body, driving the tension out of my bones. After dinner my host produced a bottle of Haig & Haig, three quarters full. It greased the way to a game of chess with a local missionary who, smiling angelically, confronted me with some really devilish moves on the chess board. Whirling into bed around midnight, I just vaguely remembered the Seabee.

She was still there the following morning, a short ride away, my strange little craft with the grasshopper legs. I felt happy to see her. The wind and sea had subsided, and half the village stood on the beach to watch our takeoff, including my holy executioner of the previous evening, dressed in a white suit that would have pleased my father in Surabaya. A jeep with a dozen five-gallon cans was parked nearby, arranged by the hotel owner, 80-octane gasoline according to factory specifications. I bought eight, enough for the trip to Davao, and filtered the gas through my remaining sock into the main tank. There was still a little water in the hull below the cockpit, but that would undoubtedly drip away in due time. Again the engine started instantly. I slammed the door shut and taxied out onto the bay. Everybody waved. The moment I pushed the throttle knob all the way forward, the missionary solemnly lifted his white sun helmet.

Mindanao took one more swipe at me. Making for a narrow slit of clear sky above the mountain, I suddenly noticed that the cloud base was lowering rapidly, filling the valleys in front but also behind us. In minutes I was caught like a fly in a sandwich, except for a tiny blue triangle at the end of a long, steep gorge running southwestwards. At maximum speed we dived towards it, pressed ever deeper into the chasm. Here was primeval jungle as I had never seen it, ominous, impenetrable, green-black as if it had rained oil, swatches of cloud rising from the gloom, vertical rock walls on either side of my wing tips towering to where they disappeared in cloud. Never did my motor sound so puny. At last we burst out at sea level into unbelievable, brilliant sunshine. I thanked my protectors and looked around: the valley behind me was shut tight, but before us stretched Mindanao's south coast under clear skies all the way.

Having lost a day I could only look to the vast distances and primitive communications in the Philippines to protect me from arrest. Sneaking undetected in and out of Davao had become critical. When after a three hours and forty minutes flight we plopped down on a sheltered strip of water, carefully keeping the sun behind us during the final approach, I saw to my dismay that the only pier lay in the center of town. A stiff breeze blew across the harbor, and taxiing slowly I immediately experienced difficulties. The wind whipped around the tail planes, turning us time and again in totally unexpected directions. The lee of the quay, where people were beginning to gather, presented the only possible spot for mooring. In a series of foolish curves and circles, now left, then right, we managed to wag our way to the pier, which was in the process of collecting a nice crowd. We closed in to about thirty meters, but in spite of noisy encouragement from the shore I was unable to push the nose of the Seabee through the wind. Bitching and swearing I veered off to gain maneuvering space, felt a shock and we were stuck. Trying to pull loose, propeller roaring, I apparently dragged us ever tighter into the mud. Finally I turned off the engine. A tense hush fell over the audience, broken by cheers when I went overboard in my underpants and put my shoulders under the tail of the flying boat. On breaking free she drifted away so fast that I just managed to climb on the back, and sitting with my legs around the hull as on a horse we bobbed along the shore together.

Filipinos like to laugh. The crush on the pier had become so intense that people began to fall into the water fairly regularly, which only increased the fun. It did not seem proper to ignore their welcome any longer, so I waved to the wall of laughing faces, both hands above my head like a boxer. Then I indicated to a group of youngsters that we could use some assistance. They jumped into the harbor without a moment's hesitation, which was rewarded with a generous round of applause. After pushing the Seabee ashore and tying her up, they insisted on taking me off the hull onto their shoulders. In triumph I was carried up the shore and into Davao, surrounded by cheerful, friendly Filipinos. A small town circus parade could not have created more commotion, and at any moment I expected to see Commissioner De la Cruz.

They took me to a hotel, where again I registered as Commander Millington. Even so I spent all night dreaming of Holland and the Gestapo knocking on my door. At the crack of dawn many helpful hands bailed, filled up gasoline tanks and, with a twisted coat hanger, fished out my sock that had fallen in. I kept looking over my shoulder for Dr. Tambu to show up and drag me, in handcuffs, triumphantly back to Manila. Incredibly, nobody came. At last I cast off, taxied up the bay and with a sigh of relief pushed the gas knob forward. A short skip, a long leap and we purred into hostile territory.

* * *

As Davao slipped away below us, we seemed to cross a threshold into a silent world where the Seabee and I were the only crumb of life. The sky was wide and empty, the sea devoid of even the smallest craft, not a trace of man or beast broke the solitude of the islands. Here we were intruders on the elements - the fat cumulus above its purple shadow, the line squall with its veil of rain, a solitary rock pounded by surf, eternally, and behind it the jungle, dark and brooding. Yet, as later turned out, unseen eyes kept track of us every inch of the way.

The first stretch we flew parallel to the coast, which pointed roughly in the direction of the RMS. I took note of the course: 130 degrees, not unreasonable given northeasterly trade winds and a temperamental compass. As the land disappeared we found ourselves over the Laut Sulawesi, or, as I was taught to call it at school in Surabaya, the Sea of Celebes. I maintained the same heading and hoped devoutly that it would prove correct. An endless expanse of sky and sea stretched in every direction, five degrees off course and we'd disappear tracelessly, and no one would miss us. The minutes crawled, half an hour, three quarters, where the hell were these bloody Panhas Islands? Nothing but treacherous shadows of clouds on water, looking exactly like land, trying to lure me off track... fifty minutes and there they were, exactly where they should be! I yodeled with relief and took the next long leap over sea with considerably more confidence. When the Talaud group also turned up on time and in place, I sat back comfortably and lit a cigarette. With the smoke came the thoughts.

Below me lay Indonesia, until recently the Netherlands East Indies, the land of my birth. Had I expected a rush of nostalgia and childhood memories, I would have been disappointed. In fact, I felt little except curiosity and some concern for my life. It all seemed so long ago, so much had happened... but that was not it. Looking out at the empty sea, the rugged islands, I felt no connection with Java, my birthplace, a busy, bustling world a thousand miles away, inhabited by people totally unrelated to the tribesmen below, if any. In reverse, why should the South Moluccans feel kinship for the power structure in Jakarta, Java? From where I sat, in the cockpit of a Seabee, their cause appeared stronger than ever.

Did I really believe in it? Idealistically yes, realistically no, or rather not anymore. Nikijuluw, after seven months of unrelenting effort, had failed to make a dent at the United Nations. My own experiences in the Philippines had demonstrated the unassailable position of Indonesia in the common front of recognized nations. But most of all, the Dutch government had thrown in the towel. In disbanding the Royal Netherlands Indies Army, it had failed to discharge 4000 Ambonese soldiers, all superbly trained jungle fighters, at the place of their choice as expressly stipulated in their contracts. They all chose Ambon, naturally, but when Sukarno protested, knowing full well that this would make the RMS impregnable, the American government supported his position and forced the Dutch to either discharge the troops in hostile Jakarta or offer them asylum in the Netherlands. Practically all opted for the latter. This made the successful invasion of Ambon by Indonesia a foregone conclusion.

If I no longer believed in victory, why stick out my neck? - Because Nikki still imagined that eyewitness material of these events could turn the tide, and he could be right; never say die until you're stone dead. If he was wrong, then I hoped at least that my effort to reach the RMS would be accepted as a symbol; by the Dutch, on behalf of all those Hollanders who were painfully aware of deserting Ambon after 300 years of loyalty; by the Ambonese, as proof that in their moment of sorrow they were not totally forsaken by their old allies. As I quoted before, "it is not necessary to hope in order to attempt..."

From the moment we crossed the equator I got butterflies in my stomach. Search as I might, I could not find a reason. The Seabee? Absolutely not, we had become fast friends. Fuel? We had enough to get to Ambon and back to Misool, a Dutch-held island near New Guinea where, so I was told, we could tank for the return journey. Time? At the present rate we should reach the RMS well before dark.

Was it something inside me? For more than six hours now I had stared out over total solitude. When we crossed the island of Halmahera and the jungle reached up in silent menace, a chill breath had seeped into the cockpit. Heading out over sea again, no far shore could possibly limit the endless water. I felt utterly alone. Also, the light changed. A leaden hue tainted the blue skies and the horizon disappeared in a veil. Thunderclouds emerged from nowhere and filled the murky emptiness. I saw lightning spattering in their bellies, from afar like sparklers in a ball of cotton, from close up as artillery in the fog.

Then it happened: a checkpoint was late. I flew on for ten minutes. The island failed to appear. After an eternity I saw it, clearly, far to the left. I took a sharp turn north, where had it gone? There it was. Another ten minutes and I looked right through a cloud shadow on the water's changeless face. I tried to correct the mistake by flying south for a while and picking up my previous course. After fifteen minutes I acknowledged defeat, I was lost.

I lit a cigarette and realized to my great surprise that this might actually mean the end of me. It was a lonely feeling. The gray horizon shrank steadily, the light faded, the sea began to blend with the sky. Once or twice I had problems keeping the wings level. The thunderheads had come alive, stalking through the dusk like grim giants, forcing me into full throttle to escape their terrifying embrace. All thanks to Leiden's Professor Buys Ballot and his Law of Changing Wind Directions on Crossing the Equator, which lay at the core of my misfortune. Too late, every four minutes I spent a gallon of gas, it was just a matter of time.

Suddenly I saw a green ring lying on the water. Already our nose was pointing down. One side of the atoll opened to the sea, and through this gap we floated over a snow-white line of surf into an emerald horseshoe.

We landed soft as silk on the mirror-like lagoon, the water hissed underneath the hull, then we lay motionless, surrounded by trees. With a sigh I cut off seven hours and ten minutes of roaring engine - in the sudden silence a bird sang.

Motionless I listened to the silvery little voice, spellbound. The treetops around us whipped in the wind, but not a wrinkle touched the face of the lagoon. Below I saw white sand and waving seaweeds, close to the surface, but when I went overboard with the anchor I kept on sliding through the crystal deep without ever touching bottom. The water felt soft and cool, I took off my clothes and floated. In the light green abyss below me fish shot through the coral like flames, above me clouds hurried by endlessly. Out of a hostile world the ring of trees had carved a haven of peace, silence surrounded by whispering surf, rustling leaves and the singing of a thousand birds. A deep sense of futility flooded over me, for myself, for the tragedy that spawned my venture, for every folly of humanity at this moment, everywhere. Water stroked my naked body, I listened to birds, I looked through trees at the sky, and felt no inclination to leave this magic place, ever.

Out of a corner of my eye I saw an outrigger prau across the lagoon, coming at us a few hundred yards away. Clearly we had been under observation from below all along. Behind it another half dozen vessels rowed towards the Seabee. High up in the water, the paddles dipping irregularly on both sides, they resembled giant spiders pouncing on their prey. Some were covered with reed roofs, in others I saw groups of small, dark men with high, fuzzy hair.

I nipped back into the cockpit, put my pants on and waited. There was something sinister about the silence of their approach, more so when after a few minutes I could distinguish a formidable array of spears aboard, stacked in racks. As a first line of defense I brought out a carton of Chesterfields.

The praus surrounded the flying boat, and close up I saw women with babies and children under the roofs, as well as pots pans and sleeping mats. Clearly none of my guests had ever seen an airplane at rest on the water, and living in boats themselves they assumed the same of me. I had merely moved into their neighborhood. The men climbed aboard, pushed themselves in turn into the tight little cockpit with me and looked around enthralled.

"Ruma bagus. Bagus betul," they assured me. "Beautiful house. Really beautiful." This much Malay I could still manage.

And as a matter of manners, they promptly began to bail out my living room with half a coconut.

The rest of the afternoon was spent in courtesy calls. Two by two my new neighbors spent half an hour with me at home. I served cheese crackers from Cagayan, which were dubiously received. They were friendly and open, and courteously hid their faces when I convulsed them with my linguistic efforts. Our conversation consisted mostly of nodding and smiling, and helped along by a few words of Malay to at least establish the subject of our harmony, we got along famously.

Once I ventured into a serious subject. "Orang Indonesia?" I inquired innocently. "The Indonesians?"

"Baik!" they beamed. "Splendid!" Their approval was undeniable.

Easy now, I had to watch out. Carefully I probed on.

"Orang Ambon?" "The Ambonese?"

"Baik! Baik!" they assured me, with gestures of equal enthusiasm. "Terrific!"

"And orang blanda?" I rounded out the conversation. "The Hollanders?"

"Baik betul!" they declared with conviction. "Really great!" The inhabitants of the island of Boo, as the atoll turned out to be called, obviously had something better to do than get involved in world politics.

As the sun set garishly they accompanied me to an extra protected spot, where I threw out the anchor. Exhausted, I fell asleep immediately, but the visits continued unabated. Awakening from time to time I saw dark, silent figures sitting next to me in the cockpit, or heard them discreetly bailing the hull under the floor panel. The night was black, but we were surrounded by light, a wide circle of billions of fireflies in the trees around the lagoon, which trembled with massive explosions of green glowing phosphorus. Above, lightning flashed across the sky, and when the floodgates opened, the drops struck sparks from the water's surface. A bunch of tiny lamps on the praus gleamed in the distance, and the wind carried waves of wild, unconcerned singing through the thunder.

I had to admit, Leiden seemed a long way off.

* * *

On December 4, 1950, towards sunset, the red and white Seabee purred into the RMS, the first and possibly only friendly visitor from the outer world. A long shadow to the southwest evolved into a rugged coastline, sloping up to hills and mountains: the north coast of Ceram.

Arrival in a war zone always brings a chilling moment in which to acknowledge death as a legitimate presence. The tragedy of events behind
that white ribbon of beach dispelled any feeling of triumph on reaching
my goal. I pushed down the nose until we were skimming over the water
and suspiciously watched the silent coast approaching.

I had spent the day in the protection of Boo atoll, cozily surrounded
by my neighbors in their outriggers. The storm had cleared the sky, there
were only 150 km more to go. However, when I poked the dipstick into
the extra tank, it came out dry; we had wasted more time and fuel than I
thought. The main tank still contained gasoline for two hours maximum,
not enough for making it to Ambon and back to our fueling stop on
Misool. I had to settle for a nearer goal, Ceram, symbolically less effective than Ambon, but the largest island in the RMS and for all practical
purposes equally useful. At five o'clock I had taken off across the lagoon,
pulled up just before the gap right over the heads of the stunned Boo
community, and set course southwest. Fifty minutes later Ceram loomed
on the port side.

My plan was to slip in low, land under cover of dusk, spend the
night collecting material for Nikijuluw, and get out at the crack of dawn
to avoid possible Indonesian patrols at sea or in the air. Purring towards
the black land mass I had absolutely no notion of what might happen. I
aimed at the first bay that looked inhabited, a score of bamboo and frond
shacks below coconut palms on a narrow strip along the beach. The
moment I pulled the throttle towards me, we settled on the water. By the
time we had taxied in, a group of men stood along the shore, dark and
still. I turned off the engine and looked on my watch: 6.13 p.m., barely
readable.

There are situations in life that must necessarily end in total disaster
or complete success. These men, who were they, and on whose side?
Who did they think I was, with my weird plane painted red and white,
the Indonesian colors? Would there be time for explanations, would we
understand each other? I went overboard in the shallow water and pulled
the Seabee behind me up onto the beach. Nobody lent a hand. I noticed
that the dark figures were armed with knives, the fearsome klewangs, and
at least one rifle. When it seemed wise to stop, I called out the only two
words of Ambonese I know, the ancient battle cry and greeting of the
Moluccas: "Mena Muria!"

The magic formula worked. The ominous immobility of the gathering dissolved, some younger men rushed to assist with the plane, others
undoubtedly of higher rank stepped forward to greet me with dignified

reserve. These latter showed no surprise, as if in some mysterious way they were expecting me. A small procession with me in the middle formed behind a wiry, gray-haired man in a long, white shirt, and almost solemnly we strode to one of the bamboo huts. Two petroleum lights were lit, filling the little room with fumes. We had barely sat down on the floor when faces, many of children, filled the window spaces outside from top to bottom, never to leave us all night. Nobody spoke until the old gentleman, two front teeth missing, addressed me, of all things in perfect Dutch.

"What is the meaning of your arrival?" was the gist of his opening statement, well hidden in words of welcome and assurances of at least a fair hearing of my case. I put my cards on the table, explaining my mission with frequent mention of Karel Nikijuluw's name and stressing the pressure of time - so close to success I felt a rising sense of panic at the thought of daybreak catching us in this vulnerable position, not so much for myself as for the invaluable material which should shortly be in my possession.

It did not take long to convince my host. A short conference followed, after which all but two of the men present left the hut, followed by some urgent discussions outside. The rest of the night the old man and I sat mostly silent in the smoky little room, our shadows huge on the palm frond walls, woken out of our fitful snoozes when something was brought in, a useless shell casing, a valuable firsthand witness statement, a photograph, a sketch of landing areas on a beach, all from my hosts and their many relatives in the vicinity. Shortly before dawn a young man, dripping with sweat, proudly handed us a fair-sized manila envelope brought over from a neighboring village. It was stuffed with more than thirty clear pictures of Indonesian soldiers and military equipment coming ashore, including a fully manned amphibian LCI and a B-25 in flight with discernible markings, just the kind of material to warm Nikki's heart.

It was still dark when I got up to leave. I planned to touch down in Misool at dawn, fill up the tanks in a hurry and make it back to Davao, Philippines, this very day in one long hop. Not that I looked forward to facing Commissioner De La Cruz, but I counted on Al Charak to keep me out of the slammer and protect the priceless documentation which I had collected. God willing, as Nikki would say, and properly presented it should suffice to convince the United Nations of Indonesia's military aggression.

The entire hamlet accompanied me back to the beach in total silence. Some youngsters helpfully pulled the Seabee into the water for me. A row of elders, headed by my white-shirted host, stood solemnly lined up for goodbyes along the soft rustle of the water's edge. We shook hands all down the line, and I was acutely aware of the fact that the precious envelopes under my arm carried the hopes of these unfortunate people. In spite of our shortage of fuel I made a farewell pass over the dismal little cluster of oil lamps that huddled below in the dusk. But when I looked up a new day glowed on the eastern horizon and suddenly this became my moment of triumph: I had done what I set out to do. Mission accomplished.

* * *

Not quite yet. After fifty minutes of euphoria I landed with bone-dry tanks in the Bay of Waigama, Misool, for refueling. Then came the blow - I had been misinformed, there was not a drop of gasoline on the island. At that time New Guinea and surroundings, including Misool, were under control of the Dutch, who were forced to maintain strict neutrality in the conflict. As this could still endanger the success of my mission, I once again hid my identity. When Netherlands Army soldiers reported my presence on Misool, the Dutch Royal Navy in nearby Sorong, New Guinea, sent a Catalina flying-boat to investigate this Commander Millington and his Seabee, who lost his way and needed help to return to Manila - a fabrication which just might generate assistance in the form of gasoline.

I stood on the beach with my new Dutch friends, chatting in English as we watched the Catalina land, totally at ease in my usual American disguise. The two-men crew in white uniforms, clearly Navy officers, left the plane and were being rowed ashore in a native canoe. I wasn't the only one taken aback when one of them waved at me from fifty yards and yelled, in Dutch, "Hi Erik! What brings you this way?" His name was Lt. Kanters and we used to play soccer together. Well, I guess I was home again.

That was just the beginning. They took me aboard their aircraft and on arrival at the base in Sorong I was recognized and joyfully greeted by two former HVV teammates, three ex-RAF pilots and five Leideners, the latter employed at the local Royal Dutch Shell headquarters. The authorities, however, under intense scrutiny from both their own and foreign governments, took a different view. They confiscated the Seabee, put me under temporary house arrest and finally bundled me off on a KLM airliner back to Manila via Djakarta and Bangkok. Fortunately I knew its pilot from the bar at Shepherds in wartime London, so he saved my life by skipping the scheduled stop at Djakarta, capital of Indonesia and Tambu's home base. Still, the mission had a worthy ending. We landed in Manila at midnight, and while the plane stood quietly at the end of the runway, suddenly cowboy Al Charak, six-shooter in hand, burst rambunctiously into the cabin and whisked me off into a jeep crammed with heavily armed secret service agents. Together we roared across the pitch-black airfield and through half the city to his apartment in the Rehabilitation Compound. There I sat for two days, well supplied with eggs, bacon and rye whisky, writing a report for him which, as I discovered years later, ultimately found its way to the desk of Allen Dulles, Director of the Central Intelligence Agency.

My reappearance in Manila made front-page news; I was still the pet of the disrespectful Filipino man-in-the-street. When Al finally released me, I paid my respects to Commissioner De La Cruz, who cheered up noticeably at the assurance of my imminent departure, this time for good. Dr. Tambu, next on my list, proved to be out of town and was shortly afterwards recalled. He was not the only casualty - one night six months later the stout little Seabee, her hull pierced and cut loose from the buoy, was found in thirty feet of water on the bottom of Sorong Bay. When I was told, I shed a tear.

Karel Vigeleyn Nikijuluw met me at New York's Idlewild airport on December 12, 1950, when I handed him the yield of my efforts. He assured me, perhaps out of friendship, that it would amply serve his purpose. All the same, later that month the city of Ambon was occupied by Indonesian forces.

For Karel this was no reason to give up. Day after day, month after month, and finally year after year he canvassed the U.N. building in New York, vainly hoping to create support for the cause of the South Moluccas. Everybody liked him, some listened, but nobody did anything. At long last, after twelve years of relentless disappointment, he tired. One icy night he dragged himself through the snowy canyons of New York from the U.N. building to his room on 44th. street and died, all alone, a martyr to a lost cause. - Or is it? I remember his admonition: "God has time, leave it to him... If not our children, then our grandchildren..."

And Dod Orsborne, and the l'Insoumise alias Argosy? Shortly after me they left The Bronx and set sail for somewhere. This I know for certain from a photo on the front page of the second section in the New York Times, sometime in November 1950, showing an impressive two-master under full sail against a background of the downtown skyline, with the caption "Argosy sets sail in the wake of Vasco da Gama." After that, silence.

Thoroughly involved with the business of living, it took until the spring of 1968 - eighteen years! - before I came across a yellowed receipt stating, "Received $ 10,000, (signed) Barstow, Whitestone, N.Y." Suddenly I realized that somewhere on this earth a Belgian pilot ship might be floating around with a mast almost a hundred feet tall, and that it belonged to me. Through tenacious inquiries I learned that the Argosy had reached Port of Spain in the Caribbean, where it was impounded for "the presence of contraband". Old Dod must have had enough arms aboard to conquer all Indonesia! The crew was sent home, but of the captain no news. About the Argosy the report read: "...swept off her anchorage during a hurricane. Missing, presumed sunk."

Missing maybe, sunk never. Not for nothing is she called "l'Insoumise ", the Untamed. I see her clearly, a worthy mate for the mythical "Flying Dutchman", sweeping along under billowing sails in the wake of Vasco da Gama, through all hurricanes unto eternity, with her insanely tall main mast and a swearing, red-bearded Scot at the helm.

CHAPTER 20

Early Adventures in Television

"You are just like an Italian," my old man, who thought in stereotypes, once remarked to me. "A fine father, but a lousy husband." While confirming the first, I deny the second. I loved my wife, protected and looked after her, and tried to make her happy. I just wasn't faithful. From someone whose passion was to experience life to the fullest, it would have been unreasonable to expect marital fidelity in a world so full of fascinating women.

My escapades, though always interesting and sometimes exciting, created little conflict, because they weren't worth it.

There was one notable exception. At a cocktail party in New York, shortly after returning from Ceram, I met Karin, a girl in her early twenties whose beauty stunned me. She was tall and fair, and part Swedish which may account for the fact that her eyes were blue flecked with yellow, and when they met mine across the room we were connected by a tunnel of silence. She had been married recently, my son was a toddler, and we both immediately recognized the danger. So we raised our guard and nothing happened - for fifteen years.

Those fifteen years I lived the exemplary family life, at least by standards generally accepted in Western society, based on job, wife, child, cat, dog, two cars and a home in the suburbs. Perhaps I wasn't cut out for it, for in the course of this period all these elements somehow vanished - my job evaporated, my wife took off, my son became a hippie, my cat was run over, my dog got heart worm, my cars were sold and I found shelter in the old Lambs Club on West 44th Street, New York. That was by no means the end of my story, but first things first.

After the Ambon episode I returned from the South Pacific yearning for normalcy. Our immediate problem was money, for as everyone knows, no good deed goes unpunished. Whenever you dedicate yourself to a noble cause and the funds run out, no one ever asks "what in Gods name did the poor bastard live on during that time?", but always "where the hell did all the money go?" Anyway, I emerged from the RMS struggle as poor as a church mouse. Once again it was time to rebound, and this time I meant business, no more freelancing, a real job with a paycheck at the end of every month until we were on our feet again. I did not have far to look.

Around 1950 television hit America like gold-fever. Every man, woman and child caught it almost simultaneously, and as the world opened up around them it engulfed the country in a tidal wave of excitement. The timing was perfect: a postwar boom had suffused the economy with money, everybody's pockets were bulging and the nation was restless with prosperity, ready for change, loaded for bear. Industry, eager to sell its accumulating products, shoved its wealth by the millions into advertising which funneled it directly to the new medium. TV sets rolled off the shelves across the nation, irrespective of price, and their slick commercials sold the cars that broke the bonds of city dwellers. They moved by droves into the suburbs, happy to stay in their brand-new homes and spend the evenings with fresh crops of entertainers on the screens in their living rooms.

On the flip side thousands upon thousands of the best and brightest abandoned promising careers to hurl themselves into the television gold-rush. Did they know much about it? Hell no, but who cares? Neither does anyone else, we'll learn when we get there. Often chaos reigned behind the little black-and-white pictures, slightly larger than a postcard, which shimmered on the front of a huge console; brave men and women trying things out for the first time in full view of avid audiences, live, always live because tape hadn't been invented yet. Remember the dog food commercial, where after the first bite Fido threw up all over the set (and screen)? And the motherly lady who, after finishing her kiddies show but unfortunately still on a live mike, startled cozy families everywhere with the p.s., "and that'll be all, you miserable little bastards?" So what, it's all part of the game, it's the future, it's what America's all about!

In these early days New York City dominated the television scene, and at the National Broadcasting Company the big story was Sylvester ("Pat") Weaver, just appointed the new Tzar of NBC-TV.

A navy man during the war, he had shared digs with Lt. Richard Pinkham, a thoroughly nice gentleman about my age whom he now picked to be his vice president and program planner. The next morning "Dick", who happened to be our new close neighbor in Rye, drove up in his station wagon and called out excitedly, "Come on, Erik, let's get into television!"

"What do you mean? Doing what?" As if I cared!

"Never mind, we'll find something for you. Hop in!"

Off we went to Rockefeller Plaza in New York and six great years at the epicenter of the American television earthquake.

From its inception in 1948 commercial TV in the USA went through three stages during the period of my involvement. The first few years were the era of creative minds, such as Weaver's and Pinkham's, who could envision and originate programs. They shaped the industry, but were no money makers. Their power soon devolved upon the super-salesmen, such as my colleague at NBC one-eyed Matthew ("Joe") Culligan, who opened the floodgates of big cash to the networks, but did not know how to hang on to it. They were supplanted in turn by the real business brains, the financiers and accountants who, as far as I know, are still in charge today.

I managed to survive one transition but, like most of my contemporaries - a very limited concept in American TV - struck out and moved on after the second. We were the lucky ones, for as far as sheer fun is concerned, nothing ever surpassed the first period.

In line with my history of comebacks I started at rock bottom, as a stage hand with the imposing title of Production Coordinator. On one of my very first days I stumbled into NBC's largest studio, 8H, during a production of the Kraft Theater of the Air. Touched by the sponsor's thoughtfulness in providing a table with refreshments for the lowly stage crew, I gratefully munched a few. They looked better than they tasted, perfectly pink meats, tempting cheeses, but somewhat waxy in the mouth. I found out why, when a furious advertising executive threw me out of the studio for eating the Kraft commercial.

The satisfaction of working for NBC was enhanced by its impressive ambiance in the majestic centerpiece of Rockefeller Plaza, compared to the dingy quarters which housed CBS on Madison Avenue and ABC somewhere on the West Side. Once inside, though, we never saw daylight again until evening, and in winter not at all. As lowly production coordinators, we spent our life learning our craft in windowless offices, corridors and artificially lit studios, blundering about confusedly like moles in a rabbit warren. The lengthy, three-Martini lunch became popular as an essential health break to counterbalance these unnatural conditions.

Occasionally a thought of the l'Insoumise, Dr. Tambu or the night in Boo atoll would interfere with my handling of the Howdy Doody Show or Mary Kay's Tips on Beauty, but by and large I enjoyed my work, particularly when it spread to more prestigious productions, such as Mary Martin and Cyril Richard in Peter Pan and, my all-time favorite, An Evening with Ray Bolger from some desolate studio in Brooklyn. That I, who never in his life had set foot backstage anywhere could perform my duties at all, let alone to the satisfaction of some very demanding producers, was due to Don Cash, an Englishman with considerable film experience. We shared a desk in our chaotic little office and he became the Arles ("Whitey") White of my television career.

As time went by, Midge and I blended in more and more with our American neighbors, who had welcomed us warmly. Early in the morning, together with thousands of respectable businessmen, anonymous as drops of water, I sat down in one of the commuter trains that feed like rivulets from the countryside into ever more powerful streams, which in the end roar like a mighty flood through the catacombs of Grand Central Station, from where we dispersed in all directions to get the insatiable turbine of Manhattan rolling. I walked with pride into the massive beauty of Rockefeller Center, scurried around our warren with my colleagues and reappeared for lunch at Toots Shore's or "21", never failing to pocket the bill, rightly or wrongly, for embellishing one's expense account. At the end of the working day, specially Friday, we all met again on the train home, in the bar car, for another martini or a scotch, a last minute sale or a date for next week, until one after the other we dropped off and disappeared in the night at cozy little stations, where our patient wives sat waiting for us in the family car. In this deluxe version of the American melting pot, Midge and I integrated painlessly.

Meanwhile Pat Weaver, a jug-eared, six foot four, super bright intellectual of the slam-bang-whizz type, did more to shape contemporary television as vice-president of NBC than any executive of his day. His irresistible drive grew from total self-confidence, which enabled him to try out new ideas without fear of fallout. Some stuck, and are with us today. One of these affected my life, temporarily but unforgettably.

Before Weaver, television programs were sponsored in their entirety, usually by a single client. On a national scale, this cost a fortune, freezing out the smaller companies. Pat invented the system, in force ever since, whereby an advertiser can buy into a program, like buying an ad in a magazine. This opened the gates to the networks for hundreds of smaller enterprises, and vastly increased the supply of money to the industry. The first TV show offered to sponsors on a "participating basis", hence dubbed a "participating program", was Today. When Pat appointed my friend and neighbor, Richard A.R. Pinkham, executive producer of Today, could I be far behind?

I started as a news writer and for eight months left Milton Point at 1:00 o'clock in the morning to join the night people of New York, a vast throng of great solidarity based on lack of sleep, overdoses of coffee and a generally patronizing attitude towards normal day workers. Driving along the Merritt Parkway in dreamy solitude, at about White Plains I would start to tingle with electrical energy emanating from the giant city, never asleep, crouched in the dark to pounce on the unsuspecting new day. After parking in a deserted area on 12th. Avenue and 45th. Street, I walked across the entire West Side including upper Times Square, never fearing for my safety, to arrive at the RCA Building by 2:00 a.m. for a first cup of coffee in Cromwell's drugstore before going up to the Today newsroom.

Driving along the deserted road at that magical time, it gradually dawned on me: a television production is like a bombing mission. This was confirmed when, later, I directed a modest number of programs from the control room. The myriad of pre-broadcast preparations are equivalent to ground-crew activities, the actual broadcast mirrors the execution of the mission itself. The producer runs the squadron, the director flies the aircraft and captains his crew in the control room. It is there that I found the parallel most compelling: the semidarkness of the cockpit, the panels, switches and buttons, human faces lit spookily from below, the absolute authority of the director, the smooth coordination of the experts around him, discipline hand in hand with mutual respect, every one's command in his specialized area, the crises and improvisations, lightning fast decisions without recourse from ever-threatening disaster - the only thing missing was Ben Hein to remind me "That's what they pay us for."

Night after night we put together the news package based on available film clips, which were prepared at our directions by a mysterious NBC editor on 125th street, who answered his phone at four in the morning with "Speak, oh Hot Lips!" We always gave the stories straight, except once when I was assigned to work on some footage about guano deposits off the coast of Chile. In protest I composed the text in rhyming Greek hexameter, which mortified our newscaster - Frank Blair - when he found himself declaiming a poem about bird shit.

We typed away through the wee hours, three men in a cloud of cigarette smoke, collating pages and running down corridors with last minute changes until airtime in the curbside studio on 49th Street. I usually stayed for the first hour's broadcast, from six to seven, enjoying the excitement of live television, the usual small crowd looking in through the windows, waving at the folks back home. Following the action on the monitor one dark morning, I saw a familiar face, tight smile, hat level on his brow - I could not place him, but pointed him out to one of our producers, Lenny Safir. "Christ!" Lenny yelled.

"President Truman!"

Someone ran outside and persuaded Mr. Truman to come in for a chat, on camera of course. This was big stuff for Today, the much maligned, first and only morning program in existence, "Pat Weaver's folly", struggling to survive. The former president himself was superb in his modesty, straightforwardness and unadulterated American integrity, rare commodities in Washington these days.

The stars of Today in 1953 were Dave Garroway and J. Fred Muggs, different in some ways but alike in others. As one was a highly erudite television host and the other a chimpanzee, they were intellectually distant. Emotionally, however, they had much in common, and if I had been forced to turn my back on one of them, I would have preferred Muggs. Underneath a folksy appearance they were both pathologically involuted prima donnas, mild mannered but sneaky, who could not bear sharing the limelight with each other. Amicable on screen, they

Dave Garroway and J. Fred Miggs

would bite and hit each other on the sly as soon as America's attention was diverted by the news or a commercial, to reappear smiling side by side when the red camera lights flicked on again. It was a love/hate relationship devoid of love, as illustrated by the Evil-Eye Finkle interview.

Evil-Eye was a modest but in certain circles well regarded entrepreneur, who got interviewed on our show because of his occupation, which was casting spells, at a price, on behalf of one of two opposing boxers. Dave Garroway, under his folksy veneer a sinister man himself, treated him with cautious respect.

"Tell me, Evil-Eye, what do your spells consist of?"

Our guest specialized in two kinds, both devastating, a single whammy consisting of fixing the opponent with a one-eyed stare through the fingers of one hand, at five bucks, and, twice as potent, a double whammy using both eyes and hands, at ten.

After one of these the unfortunate victim, depending on who paid the price, would collapse as if nailed on the chin by Joe Louis. Evil-Eye demonstrated his technique at length, carefully keeping us outside his field of power.

Dave, who could smell a good camera shot a mile away, ended the interview by putting a whammy on Muggs. But J. Fred, sensing that we were about to go into a break, immediately nailed him back with a double whammy, captured the picture and held it into the cutest and most talked-about fadeout in memory, stealing the show. One smart monkey. Garroway never forgave him.

Whenever possible, I tried to organize exposure on the Today show for anything to do with Holland. One of these rare occasions occurred when Dr. Joseph Luns came to town. Luns was not only Foreign Minister of The Netherlands but also the secretary general of NATO, and as such a political star of the first magnitude. A large, ebullient man with an offbeat sense of humor, he seemed good television material. I called him at the Plaza Hotel, which honored him by flying the Dutch flag. He promptly consented to appear on the program.

"Excellent," I wrapped up our conversation. "I'll pick you up tomorrow at five o'clock." That would give us an hour to rehearse and settle down.

"I doubt whether I'll be home by then," he answered.

My, my, I thought, quite some swingers these days in the Dutch Foreign Service. "In the morning," I added, to be on the safe side.

Over the telephone came a sound like the bellow of a wounded buffalo, but he did not try to wiggle out. Before dawn the next day he was full of good cheer, and beamed when the studio guard greeted us with, "Hello boys!"

In the course of the interview Dave Garroway, always well-informed, inquired why Holland had two Foreign Ministers simultaneously, a temporary political necessity of the moment.

"That's quite obvious," Luns answered seriously, as if putting Dave in his place. "Holland is a very small country, which makes the world around us very large. It's only natural that we need two Foreign Ministers to handle it."

* * *

When Today, the forerunner of all the world's early morning television, finally got into the black, where it has remained for the last half century, Weaver added two more participating programs, Tonight and Home. For the latter, starring Arlene Francis supported by a very young Hugh Downs, a special studio was created on Amsterdam Avenue, with the first ceiling camera for peeking into pots and pans. Many years later Tonight became world famous as Johnny Carson's show. Pat bundled the three programs into a department and appointed me manager. As one started rehearsals at 9:00 p.m. and ran until 2:00 a.m., the next got on camera at 4:00 a.m. and stayed on the air till 9:00, and the third neatly broke up the remaining time by airing from 11:00 to 12:00 in the morning, I finally had a round-the-clock job.

Try as you will, just working won't make you rich. It may bring you comfort, but wealth - never. Fortunes were being made in television, but not by me. What I lacked was the intense focus on money that this requires. The war years had affected my capacity for taking material matters dead-seriously; after landings in Scheveningen and attacks on Berlin it doesn't come easy to treat hemorrhoids ads with respect.

At a momentous sponsors' meeting the representative of a large advertising agency suddenly asked me, man to man, "Can we also bring her navel into the shot?"

"As far as I'm concerned, fine," I answered generously, although this went directly against the ethics of the television industry at the time. In the confusion that followed we lost the momentum of the sales pitch, the sale itself, the client and $ 82,343.78 per week. It did not do me any good, either.

Prior to Tonight's air date we flew to Detroit in the company plane to line up some big time sponsors out of the auto world - Richard Pinkham, producer Mort Werner, son of our top boss Bobby Sarnoff and I. We brought with us the future host of the show, Steve Allen, to add a touch of glamour. A brilliant but difficult man at best, Steve behaved abominably. While we gathered in the back of the cabin around coffee and doughnuts, hoping to break the ice with our new star, he sat stone faced by himself in the front row on the right, his nose buried in a newspaper just like Wilhelmina used to do in her worst moods. After a while the tension became painful.

"What do we do with this guy?" Pinkham whispered. "Do we all have bad breath?"

Mort Werner had the answer. "Let's throw this guy out of the plane," he suggested. "Turn around and get a new star."

Cooler heads prevailed, and for several years Steve Allen laid the groundwork for what became - and still is - an American institution. Yet, after Hollywood, after Dave Garroway, he also made me wonder what damage the magic wand of fame wreaks on the human soul. The stupendous egos without which they would not have become stars, inhibit the development of their gentler potentialities. Even so, Steve Allen gave many fine performers their first network exposure on Tonight and made the Hudson Theater on 45th Street a national shrine of nightly television entertainment and laughter.

A decade later, when the first participating program had blazed the way and its original players, behind and in front of the cameras, had moved on, some up, some down, some out, the long arm of Today touched me one more time. As president of InterTel, an Amsterdam based international television company, I got a call for assistance from an American TV production unit on assignment in the Netherlands, and when Hugh Downs accompanied by Barbara Walters walked into my office, relaxed, charming, thoroughly American, I felt a genuine rush of nostalgia for my NBC days. We talked about remotes, and suddenly I remembered a program, hosted by Dave Garroway, which consisted of nothing but consecutively hooking up with the four time zones, a breathtaking first: the New York skyline in bright sunshine, a rolling farm in the midwest, the Rockies in a soft early morning haze and finally, miraculously, Pacific surf breaking darkly on a California beach at dawn. The last picture was weak, as it should be so far away, like the end of our world. We all had tears in our eyes, even crusty old Garroway.

* * *

In the summer of 1953, more or less inevitably, I became an American citizen. It was not an act of renewal or rejection, and of the ceremony itself I remember only that there were a lot of people with whom I did not feel the slightest kinship. My days of strident nationalism were over, thank God, but as the Russians say, "On the day of his divorce the peasant remembers his wedding night", and I cannot deny that I immediately began to idealize Holland. However, I was also genuinely fond of the USA, and not being of an exclusive nature I allowed both loves to grow in harmony, making allowances intellectually and emotionally in both directions, keeping the ménage à trois in balance. As I foresaw little chance of serious trouble between its members, my administrative nationality mattered little to me.

I did not bother to inform NBC, where my colleagues never quite knew what to make of me, anyway. While working harmoniously side by side, we generally remained strangers to one another, but some of my background had leaked out and set me apart. This put me on the spot when Lawrence Olivier's epic film, Richard the Third, had to be shortened twenty minutes for American television. In view of the British star's giant - and tough - reputation, nobody wanted to touch it. Finally Pinkham, who habitually overrated my capacities, assigned the job to me as being "European and erudite."

Shakespeare is not part of Dutch education, and I had to look and listen five times to the movie before I knew what everybody was talking about. Whomever I approached for advice, shied away as if I had leprosy. After weeks of work, consulting dusty tomes of involuted commentary, I managed to eliminate twenty minutes from the film without making the story even more obscure. Blessing the fact that an ocean lay between England and me, I went on vacation.

On the day I returned, I was told to report at one of the executive screening rooms. The tiny, luxurious mini-theater was deserted, except for one viewer all alone in the front row. It was Lawrence Olivier. Without a word he waved me to a seat behind him, the lights dimmed and off we went: Richard the Third, American TV version, by yours truly.

Every screening room I've ever been in is air-conditioned to about minus 5, but this one beat them all. Even so, watching the endless movie in the otherwise silent little theater, I could feel the sweat drip down my spine. Olivier never said a word, never turned his head, never indicated approval or irritation by the slightest gesture. Suddenly it was over. He was on his feet before the lights came on, and strode out. In passing he tapped me lightly on the shoulder and said, "Good lad." It was a high point of my television career and inspired me to promptly write a half hour comedy, set in Mathes of Hollywood, composed entirely in Shakespearean verse and titled Shakespeare O'Haggerty. NBC shied away from it, and it's still available at a vast discount.

As the creative programmers began to skid and salesmen grew in stature, I saw more and more of Joe Culligan. He was a dashing New York Irishman who wore a black patch in place of the eye he had lost in the Battle of the Bulge. It had not slowed him down.

His other eye blazing with the color and intensity of a welder's torch, he sold his way to the top of the broadcasting industry, including the all important first sale of Today - to Washington State Apples - that saved the show from extinction.

In a new industry where every fresh idea was taken seriously, I caught Joe's attention by experimenting with printed ads and making them come to life on TV by means of match dissolves, thereby luring conventional advertisers into television. It led to the use of kinescopes, the forerunner of video tape, for sales purposes. As a result, Joe picked me out of Participating Programs and presented with me with my own "Telesales" department.

The first product I promoted was a TV remote control, one of the industry's new inventions. General Sarnoff, head of NBC's mother company RCA, showed personal interest and requested to view my 'kine'. Knowing that his mortal enemy was Colonel McCormick, the president of Zenith Television in Chicago, I included a picture of him in the demonstration. When it appeared it created the expected outrage, but then the general was encouraged to shoot the colonel off the screen with the new TV remote. This he did with great gusto, everybody present applauded and the future of the Telesales department was assured.

Here I wrote, produced and directed capsules of programs, performers and presentations to assist the sales department, as well as closed circuits for national corporate meetings and the like. Perhaps not as glamorous as network TV, it had a lot of advantages, such as independence, normal hours and a chance to direct, however shortly, almost all of NBC's stars who helped to promote their shows.

This was not always a joy. One afternoon I had to face a powerhouse of wit, Milton Berle and Martha Raye together, two of the funniest but not necessarily most considerate comics of those days. From the control room I tried to direct them through a kinescope for an upcoming event, but being relatively new at it I committed some blunders and became their victim, not undeservedly.

While they had the crew in stitches, including me, the situation rapidly got out of hand. Just as I was about to throw in the towel, a voice from the floor said calmly, "Why don't you just tell them what you want. They're very experienced, they'll be happy to give it to you."

I did, and they were, and the kinescope came out fine.

The man who saved me from failure while waiting for his turn to get on camera, was Mike Wallace. I don't remember what we produced together, but it obviously did not harm his rousing career. Somewhere in the line of duty I returned to Hollywood to direct the first TV color transmission from NBC's new West Coast studios, located in Burbank a stone's throw from the motel, now defunct, where Midge and I and baby Erik had lived for six long, tough but not unhappy months. The production was a commercial for Lux soap, involving lots of pretty girls. NBC was years ahead of its competitors in the development of compatible color, and while I wrestled with the impossible task of lighting the shiny soap wrapper, I was flattered to receive frequent visits from Humphrey Bogart who kept popping in from a studio next door. It soon turned out, however, that he was not so much interested in the effect of light on aluminum foil as on girls dressed in fluffy gauze and little else.

Staying in one of the fabulous cabins at the Beverly Hills Hotel, I took time out to visit the places where I had been poorer than ever before, or since. The gas stations where I had vainly tried to get a job, the cafeteria where a quarter had to do for lunch, the point of our nadir in Pacoima, now a stretch of new highway - they still turned my stomach into knots. Mathes of Hollywood was still there, but Whitey had gone. A quarter of a century later I stepped into a carpet emporium just off Kapiolani Boulevard, Honolulu, Hawaii, and there he stood, barely changed, but his own boss. We shook hands endlessly, and then he sold me a rug.

The transition of power to the financiers meant the end of the television road for the early pioneers, among them my allies Pat Weaver and Dick Pinkham. Both returned to to advertising world on Madison Avenue. Joe Culligan, next to leave, became president of Curtis Publishing, taking great pleasure in flying a helicopter from his home in Rye to his office in Philadelphia, every weekday morning zipping dangerously close past the glass enclosed NBC head office on the top floor of the RCA building. Out of his depth in the financial jungle of the publishing world, he almost paid for it with his life.

He developed a bleeding ulcer which felled him in the foyer of La Fonda del Sol, a Mexican restaurant on 6th. Avenue. It was a close call and a lengthy recovery, after which he fixed his fierce gaze on Ireland and set out to unravel his tumultuous origins.

With so much handwriting on the wall I conducted a holding operation under the guise of Director, Television Network Sales, a hazy position which somehow required my presence at both political conventions of 1956. It would be hard to devise a quicker way of thoroughly confusing a brand-new American. The arenas being the Cow Palace in San Francisco and the Stockyards at Chicago, I half expected to see people in cowboy hats a-whooping and a-hollering. In this respect I was not disappointed, and my overall impression was one of a huge, modern country trying to get by on a system designed for an archaic rural community. In the end Eisenhower and Nixon were elected, a foregone conclusion since they ran against Stevenson with a hole in his shoe and Kefauver wearing a raccoon on his head. Meanwhile Dinah Shore kept reminding us all to see the USA in our Chevrolet, at tens of thousands of dollars a clip for NBC, which was the sole reason for my being there.

It turned out to be my swan song. A new upheaval, closer to my heart than advertising rates and Nielsen ratings, was about to claim my attention and once again turn our lives upside down.

This time it was Hungary, and I could clearly hear the bell toll - it tolled, among many others, for me.

CHAPTER 21

Director, Radio Free Europe

Between August 6, 1945, when an atom bomb exploded on Hiroshima, and September 23, 1949, the date on which President Truman announced that the Soviet Union had developed nuclear capabilities, the United States of America pulled off a historic first of truly stupendous proportions. At the end of World War II it found itself in sole possession of a tool for world domination, and did not use it. From Hannibal with his elephants all the way to Adolph Hitler and his V2, this had never occurred before.

Even more remarkable, the USA did not even resort to saber rattling, except for one tiny clatter by presidential candidate Eisenhower during the Korean War, mostly for election purposes. It could, and perhaps should, have disarmed its one mortal enemy, the USSR, by the mere threat of nuclear annihilation, thereby saving half a billion people - Poles, Czechs, Hungarians, Rumanians, Bulgarians and even some Soviet nations - from four decades of slavery, and the world from half a century of division. Just imagine where we would be today, had the choice been Stalin's instead of Truman's.

America's break with the brutal past was a bellwether victory for humanity, but also a sign of self-confidence, not to say arrogance. They - now I speak as a Hollander, keeping my ménage à trois in balance - were quite confident of ultimately reaching their goals without the one-sided advantage of nuclear technology. The steps they took - Marshall Plan, Soviet containment, rehabilitation of former enemies, World Bank - were to their own advantage, but not exclusively. Whether Europeans like it or not, the world they live in today is largely built on Yankee dollars.

World War I spawned a popular and prophetic little tune, complaining, "How you gonna keep 'em down on the farm, after They've seen Paree?" Well, you don't. After coming home from WW2 young men and women from Maine to California turned right around and, leaving innocence behind, poured across the borders carrying American influence to the corners of the globe. They had little competition, one third of the world being in ruins, one terminally underdeveloped and one locked away in the suffocating grip of a utopian dictatorship. Like modern centurions, they represented a New World power surge, and somehow, after 36 years as a Hollander and three as an American, I became part of it.

At the core of this lurch in my career lay the Hungarian revolution, a heartbreaker if ever there was one. In the final months of World War II, Hungary had been overrun by the advancing Red Armies and subsequently disappeared behind the Iron Curtain. On October 23, 1956, the nation rose up against the communist regime and its supporting Soviet occupation forces, who after a week of fierce battles agreed to leave the country. On November 1 a new government proclaimed Hungary independent and retired from the Warsaw Pact. Now everything depended on prompt recognition from the West.

In one of history's most cruel quirks, England and France chose this moment to invade Egypt, where premier Nasser had nationalized the Suez Canal. The United Nations was in an uproar and NATO fell apart in recrimination and chaos, leaving the American government to face these crises single-handed. President Eisenhower and his administration, categorically opposed to foreign intervention anywhere on earth, suddenly found themselves confronted by two such problems simultaneously. They chose to block their former allies, a riskless venture, but shied away from possible involvement with Russia. Several days passed without the crucial recognition, the Soviets took heart, tricked the revolutionary leaders into captivity and attacked Budapest with tanks and artillery. On November 4, after three glorious days of freedom, the new Hungary ceased to exist.

It came as a personal blow to me. Not that I'm a rigid anti-communist; as a matter of fact, theories like "to each according to his needs" appeal more to me than the principles of capitalism where, as one high financier put it, "a little greed is a good thing". The vital difference is, the one does not work and the other does. Furthermore, I distrusted communism for a more pointed reason: As previously mentioned, a Dutchman's motto is "Liberty yes! Discipline no!", and I was well aware of the fact that the USSR offered none of the first and plenty of the second.

In any case, it shook me awake. The memory of living under enemy occupation came back to me like a call to arms, and the obvious flash points hovered over Hungary and the other captive countries behind the Iron Curtain. At the same time rumors started circulating in Toots Shor's restaurant and other broadcasting hot spots in New York that Radio Free Europe, a somewhat mysterious American organization based in Munich, Germany, was scouting around for replacements in top management. A little research disclosed that RFE blasted 376 hours and 45 minutes of anti-communist programming per week, three times as much as the BBC and VOA combined, into the five Russian-occupied states of Eastern Europe over 32 transmitters with a total rated power of about 1,450,000 watts. Who could ask for more?

Via a discreet intermediary I let it be known that, on the proper conditions, I could be available. The New York office of RFE became interested, because I had written a couple of studies about European broadcasting developments for Pat Weaver. After a considerable delay for security clearance they signed me up to head the news department in Munich. By the time we arrived there, I had been promoted to Assistant Director. A few months later the Director, Conny Egan, died of a heart attack and I took his place.

* * *

For a true Cold Warrior, whose memories of resistance under enemy occupation had been re-ignited by the Hungarian uprising, I found myself in the right place at the right time. The Iron Curtain, just a few miles to our east, marked the fault line along which the tectonic plates of hostile superpowers crunched against each other with primeval violence, subterranean, invisible, spawning every form of covert warfare along its edges. Opposing forces lay deployed on either side of it, with Munich as the American operational headquarters for the vital Central European sector. In the heart of the city a vast, low building crouched against the earth like a giant caterpillar: Radio Free Europe.

The more I learned about RFE - even as the director it took me six months to fathom all its aspects, such as the fact that it was essentially a CIA operation - the more I marveled at its size. Its basic components consisted of five giant radio stations, each broadcasting in its own language at a specific target: Poland, Czechoslovakia, Hungary, Rumania and Bulgaria. These were manned and operated by natives of those countries, now exiles, about 100 in each of the larger "Desks", as the stations were called, and 35 for Rumania and Bulgaria. The staff could draw on unique facilities, such as a formidable research department, which kept most of the Western governments including Washington and The Hague informed about conditions in Eastern Europe; the world's largest electronic monitoring capability, powerful enough to pick up a long distance telephone call in the Urals; and a translators section which functioned so smoothly that when Khrushchev was holding one of his interminable speeches in the Kremlin, the English translation on my desk never lagged more than twenty minutes behind.

To operate this gigantic enterprise, aimed at keeping the captive nations behind the Iron Curtain in contact with the Western world, almost 1400 people of 30 nationalities worked in the Munich headquarters, a former hospital of which the corridors alone covered more than three kilometers in length. When adding the personnel of the transmitter sites, located in Germany and Portugal, and of the ten news bureaus that covered Europe from Stockholm to Athens, the number of employees at one point in time rose to 2114. I was proud to be their director.

Also, I felt at home. Americans represented less than five percent of this Babylonic society, a thin crust of management over a dizzying group of Central Europeans, traditionally a crafty lot, many of whom were exiles with academic educations and formidable backgrounds. Forced out of top positions in their homelands, they now had to survive on minor jobs, taking orders from foreigners who were mostly younger, ranging from Harvard PhD's to some who had barely made it through high school. I knew their emigré mentality from battling the Dutch government in London, their schemes and intrigues, weak points and strong, their feeling of being cut off from home and loved ones, even the emotions of our audience listening to hidden radios. Their main problem was morale and the recovery of self-respect. I could not restore a former cabinet minister's sense of importance, but I did demonstrate the American concept by volunteering as a ball boy at the very first RFE tennis tournament, to the consternation of our rank-conscious German personnel.

Seriously concerned about our internal relations I hired two assistant directors - Charlie McNeill and David Penn - who, aside from being eminently qualified, were by nature guaranteed to deflate any occasional national arrogance. During an overblown dinner party given by the

American consul-general, a whole suckling pig with the traditional apple in its mouth was carried into the dining room, politely applauded by the awed guests. "That's a helluva way to serve an apple," commented Charlie, to the delight of some distinctly uncomfortable émigrés.

At another occasion in similar setting the owners of TIME and LIFE magazines, Henry and Claire Booth Luce, indelicately announced that they were going to stay with fascist Spanish dictator general Francisco Franco "to do some shooting."

"Shooting?" inquired a German count, not unsympathetically. "What's there to shoot in Spain this time of the year?"

"There's always Franco," suggested David wistfully. It didn't sit well with our bosses, the ultra conservative Free Europe Committee, but definitely endeared us to our polyglot employees.

In the end, it all came down to a matter of trust. We Americans bore the final responsibility for broadcasts in Polish, Czech, Slovak, Magyar, Romanian and Bulgarian, of which we did not understand a single word. All carefully designed control systems ultimately had to rely on a person who spoke the language and was ipso facto part of the exile community, at least emotionally. It did not take me long to realize that for us the Desks were sovereign, impenetrable entities, and our only guarantee the honor and loyalty of the five desk chiefs in charge. During my tenure, they never disappointed me.

They were tough, honest patriots, each strikingly representative of his nation. The Polish chief, Zdzislaw Jezioranski, had wisely changed this mouthful to his war name, Jan Novak, under which he later wrote the book "Courier from Warsaw", about his daring secret actions in WW II that it earned him America's Medal of Freedom, presented by President Clinton. He ran his Desk with iron discipline, and while he was a tough negotiator, with the Poles you always knew where you stood. His Hungarian counterpart, Istvan Bede, a cool former diplomat, matched his style but with a slightly lighter touch, as Budapest is lighter than Warsaw. Julius Firt, once a member of parliament, needed all his fatherly charm and political acumen to keep the fractious Czecho-Slovakian Desk together, a traditional problem of the country itself. Cheerful Ghiza Ionescu, romantic as he was, had no trouble keeping the Rumanians in line, and silent, melancholy Milev could be remarkably tough on his equally feisty Bulgarians.

The exiles created their own universes, based on language, but the Germans were different. Mostly competent in English, they fraternized easily with the Americans and vice versa. Yet underneath there was never a shadow of doubt about who had won the war. The Yanks were in charge, and took no crap. There was no stopping them; they were the conquerors of postwar Europe. In public their inborn friendliness hid most traces of arrogance, but over a couple of drinks in private, or when their authority was being challenged, they could lash out with uncommon fury. The Europeans, even those who had not lost the war, reacted with unctuous submissiveness, a cover for envy and even hatred of the self-assured bearers of America's wealth and power.

My own reunion with our former enemies, occupiers of my country proceeded more smoothly than I had expected. After twelve years I did not bear them animosity, which was not always the case in reverse once they knew I had been a pilot and bombed the hell out of their cities. Generally we got along, provided they did as they were told. The war rarely came up, except on television where - I must admit - the authorities did everything possible to disclose to German viewers, especially the young ones, what Hitler and his cronies had been up to, showing footage which no American household could ever have stomached.

Still, some never learn. At the Oktober Fest, a country fair, the villages surrounding Munich were represented by floats of flowers and beer barrels and such, carrying name signs, which included "Dachau". Commenting on my surprise at seeing the evil word proudly displayed, my companion, a stylish Bavarian matron, remarked, "Why not? It's a lovely old town."

Another time, at a dinner, the distinguished German guests expressed their horror at the RAF bombing of the Mohne Dam - immortalized by the movie "Dam Busters" - which wiped out a giant power station, several villages and hundreds of civilians. I frostily reminded them of Warsaw, Rotterdam, London and one or two other exploits of the Luftwaffe, to which they indignantly exclaimed, "Well yes, those were the Nazis. But the Allies were supposed to be the good guys!"

Even the president of our bank, whenever he found himself entangled in Germany's archaic procedures, always referred to a 1944 bombing raid - with an arch look in my direction - which had allegedly destroyed his files. I couldn't care less. Midge, Erik and I lived grandly in an elegant suburb in the house of ex-queen Soraya of Iran, next to our friend and neighbor Ed Page, consul-general of the USA, and got around in a chauffeur-driven Mercedes. I had not only joined the American tidal wave, I rode the crest of it.

Only once did the grim specter of the recent war arise forcefully. To maintain security at RFE we worked hand in hand with the German authorities, which occasionally took me to the only place in Munich where phobias of the past crept up on me, the offices of the Verfassung Schütz, the Bavarian counterespionage.

Its building faced the glockenspiel in the town hall tower with its little figurines cavorting around innocently on the hour, but inside, as I walked down the gray corridors listening to my own footsteps, an old terror would sometimes grab me by the throat and drag me back to the Occupation, to other corridors with closed doors, places of horror, and I had to restrain myself from turning around and running out the gate before someone locked it.

One such afternoon I knocked on the door of the Herr President, who as always received me with professional courtesy. While exchanging pleasantries we were joined by an inconspicuous man with clever eyes, an new employee who stepped into the light from a dim back room. While we shook hands he said, "At last we meet."

I could thank God that we had not met fifteen years earlier. As SS Sturmbannführer Joseph Schreieder, head of the counterespionage department in the Netherlands, he had done his utmost to catch me during our landings at Scheveningen, in the icy winter of 1941-1942. After a postwar trial in The Hague a Dutch court had cleared him of wrongdoing and he had returned to his native Bavaria. He was a fine intelligence officer, a pro, who had done his job correctly and cost many of my friends their lives. In our new positions our paths occasionally crossed. Harmoniously.

* * *

In World War II, when German officers wanted to learn the real state of affairs, they tuned their military radios to the BBC in London. It was a lesson on which I hammered away at Radio Free Europe, which due to Washington's confusing signals during the Hungarian Revolution had suffered in credibility. Every broadcast, every day, the news had to be true and accurate, without bias, however painful to the West. This grabbed the listeners, strengthened their confidence in us and made them receptive to our commentaries. It forced the communist sources of information to liberalize, which for a totalitarian regime is the kiss of death.

RFE fulfilled its mission. Proof came from the enemy himself, who kept over 2000 jammer stations grinding away in an effort to keep us out, at a cost larger than our entire technical budget. By placing the bulk of our transmitters in Portugal, our short wave signals bounced off the ionosphere into the target countries at an angle which sharply reduced the effectiveness of jammers. Frustrated, our opponents frequently attacked us directly, by sabotage or worse.

During one period a number of false memos were circulated within our building over my signature to create trouble between some of our ethnic personnel, such as Germans and Poles, which did not take much. I countered by organizing a multinational companywide sports club, everything from fishing to football to skiing, which became enormously popular and pulled the staff together. To celebrate its anniversary I brought over a soccer team from HVV, my old club in The Hague. Of course the Herr Director had to participate in the opening game, so the RFE backfield consisted of Stankoff, Ivanoff and Hazelhoff, promptly dubbed "the Balkan defense". To increase my chances of survival, I decided not to smoke for two days. The match was played in a foot of snow and we lost by three goals to nil, but I felt so good that I never smoked again.

Another time Spanish spikes were scattered around the parking lots, ripping our employees' tires to shreds. I replaced them from our stores, on the spot, free of charge, and although it put four new tires on some cars that weren't worth a single retread, it put an end to that gambit.

Sometimes it got serious. Shortly after my arrival one of our Czech editors was blown to bits at the post office, when a small parcel blew up in his hands. Another bomb exploded when the victim pulled the chain of a lavatory inside the RFE building. At our sister station Radio Liberty, the Ukrainian leader Bandera was ingeniously murdered by a Russian agent who later defected to the West. Under questioning this man disclosed that he had carried a glass vial of poison gas secreted in the crown of his hat, approached his prey by broad daylight in a hotel lobby, politely doffed his fedora and pushed it over Bandera's face, crushing the vial. The Ukrainian had died instantly, ostensibly from a heart attack.

One day they got to me. I had left my office for a moment and when I came back a cup of coffee stood on my desk, in the normal white china. Later nobody knew who had put it there. I drank it automatically, it didn't taste worse than usual, perhaps a little more bitter. Ten minutes later I left the building for a luncheon with Ed Page, the consul-general.

My chauffeur, Willi, drove me into town in the Mercedes, but on the Königsplatz I made him stop the car. I felt sick and told him to drive behind me, while I got some fresh air. Slowly we crossed the square.

Suddenly Munich started to whirl around me, first horizontally, then also vertically and all degrees in between. I waved my arms to keep upright, then crashed to the ground which seemed to hit me from above, and clutched the cobblestones not to be hurled off the earth into whizzing space. I started to vomit and had difficulty breathing. My head remained clear, I felt most embarrassed to be scratching around on that stately Platz, throwing up in broad daylight. All pedestrians hurried by in a big curve, except for one fat man in leather shorts and a plumed hat who watched with interest. He didn't lift a finger to help Willi get me into the car.

"Sozzled, is he?" I heard him ask with typical Bavarian logic and awe for someone who could achieve that condition so early in the morning. Ten minutes later I lay in a hospital where they kept me going with injections for two days, not without difficulty, until my own engine started ticking over again.

The poison in my coffee turned out to be atropine, a derivative of deadly nightshade, which indicates that their purpose was intimidation. For murder they had more effective stuff. We managed to keep the matter out of the newspapers, but for more than a year I had problems with my balance and perspective, which forced me to make my way along the endless corridors of our building with a finger stealthily tracing the wall, to avoid the impression that Herr Direktor had been hitting the bottle in the middle of the day.

The next attack made it into Time, Newsweek and all the major newspapers in Europe and America, and - in Time's snide words - as it happened just prior to the yearly funding drive, it did RFE no harm. Perhaps not, but only thanks to the alertness of our security unit and a tip from a double agent. Saboteurs, most likely of Czech origin, had placed atropine in the salt shakers of our cafeteria. As we all took our wives and children there, including babies, it could have led to disaster. I was incensed and felt the time had come to expose the bastards and their tactics. I should have known better: the "Spirit of Camp David" breathed détente and the subject lacked popular appeal. Facts are facts, but everyone believes what he wants to believe.

In the course of our activities we often kept contact with the real pros of the Central Intelligence Agency, and I must say, they were an engaging bunch. Considering my war record it is understandable that I am predisposed towards secret agents. The first spies I ever met in my young life were members of the Dutch Resistance, many of whom paid the price in concentration camps or before a firing squad. Their American counterparts at that time belonged to the Office of Strategic Services (OSS), a hastily concocted group of enthusiastic amateurs, as we were, just as patriotic, eager and reckless, and they fell like flies on secret missions from Norway to Greece. Those who survived formed the basis of the CIA after the war, a wonderful group of men, many of prominent families and highly educated, keen as samurais. They often turned up in Munich, where I had the opportunity of meeting some, such as Dick Helms, Cord Meyer, Frank Wisner and Richard Bissell. And on one occasion the big boss himself, Allen Dulles.

A car picked me up at the office and we drove to the outskirts of town, a beautiful villa surrounded by grass and greenery, and positively crawling with security people. I mean no disrespect, but when I saw the two chairs set out for us in the middle of a huge lawn to assure privacy, I suddenly thought of Karel Nikijuluw and our fishing expeditions on Long Island Sound.

The circumstances were different, but the technique still the primitive same.

Allen Welsh Dulles proved one of the most charming men I have ever met. The tasteless but popular quip "dull, duller, Dulles" - may have been applicable to his brother the Secretary of State, or his sister Eleanor, a severe lady whom I met behind the Iron Curtain on a secret, very unofficial visit to communist East Berlin, but Allen broke the mold. He reminded me of General van 't Sant, another perfect gentleman with a devilish streak in his character, but the American's aura struck me as lighter, with his little gray mustache and the twinkle in his eyes. He laughed more easily and spoke like a man who would take risks, even long shots, provided the payoff was commensurate. He looked like a tall, handsome professor, and his relaxed style instantly put me at ease.

We were served cups of tea in the middle of the lawn, while the conversation revolved around the new wonders of aerial reconnaissance and high definition photography, subjects which would soon lead to a CIA super spy-plane, the U2. Suddenly he asked, "What did you think of the South Moluccas?"

It should not have surprised me. Of course Al Charak had reported my activities to the intelligence community, from where they got into my security files, which reputedly were a foot high. Furthermore, it could have been a matter of some special interest to the Agency, because shortly afterwards an American pilot was forced down and captured over Indonesia. Still, I felt awed and pleased that knowledge of the Ambon trip had made it all the way up to the Director of the Central Intelligence Agency.

Allen S. Dulles

A decade later, when I had lunch with him at his home on Q Street, Washington, D.C., he remarked, "I have met all the big bullies of this era from Hitler on down, but the one whose personality I disliked most was Sukarno." I did not comment then and shall not do so now, but Nikki would agree.

* * *

While rising steadily on the social and economic ladder of American society, my emotional attachment to Europe experienced a rebirth during my years in Munich. This did not affect my performance at RFE, where we all struggled towards the same objectives. However, it was not an entirely new phenomenon. During my NBC days I frequently spent the lunch break by myself in deserted movie theaters, watching foreign films such as La Strada, Brief Encounter, Les Misérables, La Dolce Vita, even Carol Reed's movie The Third Man, set in Vienna, anything to be in contact with Europe for an hour or two. I also asked my mother, who loved soccer and could describe the action so well that at the word

"Goal!" I would jump up from my seat, to send me reports of the major Dutch matches, secretly in order not to upset Midge, to whom the Old World in general could go fly a kite. In Munich it was she who moped, bored and lonely, while young Erik, now a teenager, went to army school and I worked and traveled, soaking up the delights of a reviving continent.

It was not the Europe I had left. Thanks to the Marshall Plan and some very hard work, it had risen like a Phoenix from its ashes. Inspecting RFE's ten news bureaus, I sipped pastis in Paris on a bustling Champs Elysées, eyeing the girls; sniffed the aroma of roasting Easter lambs wafting up from Athens to the Acropolis above; discussed military tactics in London's Dorchester Grill, where Polish general Anders rated the Turks to be the best soldiers in the world; communed with the little mermaid in Copenhagen's harbor, so much smaller than I had pictured her; saw the sun rise over Rome from the Colosseum, and, closer to home, listened to Anton Karas' zither throbbing his Third Man theme in the bar at Sacher, then roamed the deserted, moon soaked Viennese streets in search of a cat that would lead me to Orson Welles.

The big treat, as always, was Holland. My parents, still firmly entrenched in Park the Kieviet and kept in the dark on the emotional subject of my nationality, were understandably mystified by my new position. I didn't tell them much. They had gotten old and seemed to have shrunk, especially my father who walked with a stick and wore the thick glasses of cataract operations. His mind rarely left the past, dwelling constantly on the fate of his beloved Dutch East Indies. He still beat me at chess, but preferred to spend his time watching ducklings frolic in the garden pond. Except Sundays, when he would sit in his own box at the soccer field of HVV, regular as clockwork, watching my venerable old club getting clobbered by some upstart newcomers.

A few streets away Ellen and Chris lived a happily married life with her three teenage children and a new baby, John, of their own. My old comrade, caustic as ever, still had trouble adjusting to peacetime. Liberty yes, discipline no, but not in postwar Holland which had reacted with admirable guts to the draconic measures required to revitalize the economy. But Chris had really never left "the Mews". My two other wartime buddies, one-time agent Tazelaar and the old Pathfinder Ben Hein, experienced similar problems that the old stone crock did not cure.

Meanwhile the country in general breathed optimism. The people, well fed and goal oriented, hurled themselves with relish and pride into the restoration of their prosperity. Boundless energy seemed to pump through every fiber of Dutch society, seething with confidence, as if the recent colonial crisis that threatened its existence had generated a countering force, a guarantee that in spite of the outcome of the Indonesian disaster the Netherlands would survive. I felt exhilarated, proud of my heritage, restored in the balance of my multinational ménage à trois, and returned to Munich invigorated.

All seemed to be going better than ever at RFE, but then the end came swiftly and for no good reason. Someone made an end run around me - an easy thing to do in an organization as multi- faceted as Radio Free Europe - at a time when my superiors in the USA were involved in political maneuvering and failed to back me up. Lust for power is a sign of immaturity, senseless and destructive as jealousy, and I refuse to accommodate it. I resigned overnight, regretfully, joined and supported to the end by my two loyal and brilliant deputies. As history has shown, Radio Free Europe got along quite well without us.

My little family and I returned to America by boat from Rotterdam. I usually stand in the bow on departure, tuning in on things to come. This time I wedged myself behind a derrick aft to watch the lights of Holland fade away in the stormy winter evening.

CHAPTER 22

Ups and Downs of a Businessman

If you don't believe that pride cometh before a fall, stick around, the next eight years of my life will convince you. I set the mood, immediately after leaving Radio Free Europe, by turning down the job of President, CBS News.

One of the pleasures - for me, not for Midge - of our years in Munich, was the constant stream of interesting guests from America, congressmen, senators, mayors, governors, generals, anybody sufficiently interested in politics to visit Radio Free Europe by choice and important enough for the government to pay the bill. Sometimes little things went wrong. The spokesman for a delegation of Midwestern mayors addressed our burgomaster and his welcoming committee, who had specially driven out to the airport to meet them, with a few words of thanks and the stirring conclusion: "It's great to be in Munich, Switzerland." And a two-star general in charge of the War Graves Commission who insisted on seeing our French news bureau, interrupted a lengthy but important briefing by complaining, "Ah come on, guys, I've been in Paris twenty hours, haven't seen a titty yet."

However, most of our visitors were hardworking servants of the people, who displayed sincere and intelligent interest. I showed them our operation, explained as much as it was safe to confide and invited them to dinner which, according to their personality, could vary from at home to a specialty restaurant called, with factual accuracy, "Suzanna im Bad."

Very rarely, a distinguished private person with the proper credentials would appear for an inspection, as was the case with Dr Frank Stanton, president of CBS. An elegant gentleman of international standing, high education and enormous prestige in broadcasting circles, he charmed both Midge and me with his cosmopolitan conversation and style. On parting he asked me to come and see him in New York, if the occasion arose.

As fate would have it, this presented itself sooner than either of us expected. Shortly after our return to New York I saw Dr Stanton in his old office on Madison Avenue, since CBS's new headquarters - the "Black Giant" - was still under construction on the Avenue of the Americas, previously a lowly neighborhood of delicatessens and Chinese hand laundries called Sixth Avenue. He introduced me to a young executive with the promising name of Frank Shakespeare, and after some general discussion about the future of television, the older Frank offered me a choice of three jobs, of which two were so insignificant that their nature escapes me. But the third was President, CBS News, Inc.

Life is a continuum of value judgments and decisions - as I wrote somewhere - most of them irrevocable and many crucial. Unless you opt for an unrewarding existence and a miserable old age, never ever second-guess a single one of them. Why did I turn down the leadership of such an exciting company? - Well, I wanted one of my own.

When I met Walter Cronkite many years later for the fiftieth anniversary of VE-day in Holland, where the roots of his family are as deep as mine, I recounted the above incident, adding, somewhat pompously, "So you see, you almost ended up working for me." He had every right to sneer me out of the room, but instead answered with his inimitable charm, "What a pity! We would have had a lot of fun together." It was as close as I ever came to second-guessing an old decision.

Don't blame me for wanting to be my own boss, it is part of the American dream. Only my scope was perhaps somewhat unusual.

Having learned a few things at NBC and RFE, I now intended to build the biggest television company in the world. What is more, for a while I came close. This was largely due to my new partner, Peik van Waveren, whose genius enabled him to translate my esoteric ideas into aggressive reality.

Peik, the son of a Dutch bulb grower - his father founded the Keukenhof, known to millions of tourists as Holland's most spectacular flower attraction - had brains, guts, charm, humor, and most of all, infectious and unstoppable enthusiasm. One word suffices to describe him: outrageous. No idea was too farfetched, no goal unattainable, and when trying to sell something however weighty to someone however exalted, his language became a torrent of superlatives which, from anyone else but Peik, would have made you laugh aloud or shrug your shoulders. Imagine convincing a Rothschild, a banker in the conservative mold of sophisticated European financiers, to invest his money in "the absolutely most super colossal television opportunity in the history of mankind."

Only Peik could get away with it, and did. And then delivered. He was a Leidener by nature, if not by education, fascinated by the outer limits of human imagination. Ten years my junior, he held his own in financial circles because he was used to money. He lived in Greenwich, Connecticut, with a beautiful wife, daughter of the owner/president of the largest privately owned company in the USA, manufacturers of compressors. Peik told me that when vodka was replacing gin in mixed drinks, a major event in his life, making the three-martini lunch undetectable on someone's breath, his father-in-law called the entire sales force together and forbade them to make the switch. "I'd rather my customers think that my men are drunk than stupid," was his reasoning.

My plans for an International Television Development Corporation - shortened to InterTel, our name of choice - were based on some studies I had made for NBC to determine the possibilities of a foreign connection. In a nutshell, it visualized a network of local companies that would support each other across national borders in all aspects of TV: production, recording, sales, talent representation and above all, financing. Its natural complexities were hugely augmented by the diversity in languages, currencies and technical aspects, such as voltages and number of picture lines per square inch, which differed between the USA, Britain, France and the rest of Europe. As a modest beginning- ha! ha! - we would pioneer the building of several 4-camera mobile units, at half a million dollars a shot, to produce and record programs for American television in Europe. No satellites existed yet, but the video tape which had just been invented would enable us to get foreign recordings onto U.S. networks in a matter of hours. After that we would march on, step by step, country by country, to integrate TV in Europe and, ultimately, the world.

* * *

For starters we needed money, lots of it. Peik, who knew his way around, came up with a list of the absolutely super crème de la crème of Wall Street, from which we picked 21 candidate investors that would give any entrepreneur goose pimples. These were all partners of the best banking houses, financiers fleshed out with chairmen and presidents of major American companies, with the managing editor of Time Magazine - Otto Fuerbringer - thrown in for luck. Then, after touching base with my old friend Prince Bernhard, who happened to be vacationing in Mexico and never let me down, we invited the selected group to a "Luncheon in the 'Recess Club', New York City, on Wednesday, April the Twenty- sixth, Nineteen Hundred and Sixty-One, in Honor of His Royal Highness Bernhard, Prince of the Netherlands." The hosts: International Television Development Corporation. All twenty-one came.

Very rich people and the institutions they represent do not invest only for money, but equally for the "romance" of a deal. In 1961, Europe was still pretty romantic for the American businessman, television even more so, and the aura of royalty in the background irresistible. Having been properly introduced, InterTel became fashionable, and Peik and I were catapulted into the heady heights of finance. Airy boardrooms with stunning views of skyscrapers and bridges and the Statue of Liberty; walnut- paneled suites in hushed houses along a 17th. century Dutch canal; a sunny, flower filled penthouse overlooking gray roofs against the Bois de Boulogne; the amazing warren of old banking offices in the City of London, with ceilings low enough to hit your head, short flights of stairs to nowhere, and curved corridors where at any moment you expect to bump into Charles Dickens or see Scrooge sitting on a high chair with a feather pen in his hand - the world of the big moneymakers is a special realm.

They themselves are men of rules and habit, who mask their towering ambitions behind modesty and charm. Money is never discussed except obliquely with an air of regret, and ostentation is the ultimate sin. Once, after a meeting in Munich, I was to fly to Paris the next morning with our two French board members, both of the Rothschild family. Being early, I emplaned and as president of InterTel picked myself a comfortable first class seat in the front section - in those days mass boarding was still rare - and waited for my two bosses. When the first one arrived I got up to invite him next to me, but he nodded frostily and continued on to economy class. The second followed suit a few minutes later, after which I hastily and sheepishly joined them.

Air France seats are very tight and we sat shoulder to shoulder three abreast. I was miserable all the way, but my companions showed no sign of discomfort and positively beamed with the bankers' pride of frugality.

The most illustrious occasion took place a few months later at Rothschild Frères in Paris. We were guests for lunch in the company penthouse, six board members and I, with Edouard de Rothschild our host. As his two cousins from London were present the small group contained four scions of the Rothschild clan, as well as our Dutch and Belgian bankers, surely the most exalted gathering of financiers ever attended by a former hobo from atop the roof of the 2412.

Did the conversation sparkle with intrigue, visions of gold and deals of the century? No, indeed! Only two subjects came under prolonged scrutiny. Firstly the recent visit of President Kennedy to Germany ("Ich bin ein Berliner!"), which InterTel had covered for CBS. It was unanimously agreed that the purpose of this trip had been to give him the opportunity for living it up a little with ladies other than his wife, a perfectly valid Parisian conclusion. The second revolved, endlessly and not without rancor, around the heinous fact that the Paris Rothschilds had succeeded in luring away the chef de cuisine from the London Rothschilds. I don't blame them, the luncheon was superbe.

✳ ✳ ✳

With the International Television Development Corporation the best financed TV venture in history, Peik and I had to prove the validity of our theories. The signs were promising. My vice president put his awesome genius to the test and I raised dust stirring op business all over Europe in a red Jaguar XKE, my pride and joy, one of the first on the Continent. Within a year ten InterTel companies were in operation from Amsterdam to Zürich, in New York and Buenos Aires. Our mobile units roamed from Prague to London to Madrid, recording programs, news events and sports for NBC, CBS, ABC, BBC, CBC, Australian TV, Associated Rediffusion, German and French television and countless advertising agencies, including ten hours from Holland for *Today*, remember? With Barbara Walters and Hugh Downs. Apart from news and sports we produced ballet, musicals and plays from rented studios, sometimes in five languages, starring Rita Moreno, Van Johnson, Bobby Van, Zizi Jeanmaire, Roland Petit, old Maurice Chevalier, and a host of other European talent. Already in 1962, InterTel productions were sold in sixteen countries, including Russia.

InterTel's Mobile Units

And then there was Roone Arledge, who at that time owned his own production company. From the beginning our operations filled each other's needs, and as he grew ever more prominent at ABC his programs, especially Wide World of Sports, became a mainstay of InterTel. In 1964 he produced the Winter Olympics from Innsbruck on our mobile units, with our crews, two unforgettable weeks of comradeship and hard work. He later became an giant of American television, but I remember him best at early morning production meetings in his chilly hotel room - with Stein Erikson, Jim McKay and InterTel's Bill Stone - his blue-white striped pajamas neatly buttoned all the way up.

In my memory that vision in Innsbruck, the morning sun shining from an azure sky through the window and somewhere out there our mobile units in the snow, has become InterTel's peak from which the road went rapidly downhill. On my return to our headquarters in Amsterdam, the chairman of the board informed me that in a special meeting the directors had voted for adding two financial experts to management, who in certain areas outranked me. It was NBC all over again. Of course, we had spent an awful lot of money, but our efforts at cross-borders integration, a crucial part of our concept, were also being sabotaged by national chauvinism at all levels. Anyway, the basic trouble with InterTel was that the board consisted exclusively of international bankers who knew nothing of TV, and management by television people lacking in financial experience. The two never met except in mutual bafflement. It's a miracle that we got as far as we did.

For me personally it meant the end of my dream. Others would run the company, succeed or fail; it was not my business anymore. I would return to the USA, perhaps work in the New York office for a while and then resign. I went home to the villa we had rented in Holland, on the edge of Wassenaar, to tell my wife.

I got the surprise of my life. The moment I saw a neat little envelope on the mantelpiece I knew that the unthinkable had happened: Midge had flown the coop. Of course she was right. For almost twenty years I had yanked her back and forth across the globe with little regard for her wishes, thinking only of myself. No peace, no security, no continuity, what kind of deal was that? She had been a great mother, but now young Erik, a 6'2" teenager, had left home for boarding school in Switzerland, and with me always on the road, what was there to stop her? Why was I so shocked?

I sat down on a couch and read her letter for the tenth time. She had gone off with a former school mate of mine from The Hague; frankly, a hell of a nice guy, the type that would put her on a pedestal and devote his life to her. Well, good for her. After reading the note one more time I tore it up, walked around the room and sat down again. I wanted some coffee, but didn't know where to find it. When two people have lived in a house together and one leaves, it gets an awful lot emptier. It turns into a jumble of ill-fitting squares of loneliness. My bag from Innsbruck was still packed. I threw it into the Jag and hit the highways of Europe. I wanted to see my son.

* * *

From the first time we met in Wassenaar, my son and I, about an hour after his birth, we got along. Even before he could speak he displayed a certain fearless directness that appealed to me, while showing approval of my efforts at communication. In Rye, where he rapidly turned into a human being, we used to sit together under a weeping beech to exchange viewpoints which, because of our difference in age, produced some mutual surprises. The subjects may seem a little weighty for a five, six year old, but through the years he has often referred to lessons learned under our "Thinking Tree," and so have I. For instance, I taught him that girls were great and deserved our early and sustained attention, with which he seemed to agree. I also urged him to sharpen his mind and remember that, to be successful in life, you have to be brilliant only once a week. He did not react to this at the time, yet it left a somewhat overly clear imprint on his later career.

Among his contributions to our dialogue, one surprise stands out. At six he announced that he was going to be a racing driver, nothing but. I paid polite attention, pointing out that it was a noble but risky occupation. However, I failed to oppose his plans there and then, because I did not worry. After all, there's a sea of time between six and sixteen, isn't there? Not so, parents beware! If your child has set its mind on a questionable future, it grows up twice as fast.

With the years whizzing by he turned the screws of fate a notch tighter at every opportunity. Only once could I argue him into a compromise: At the age of twelve he agreed that, prior to any irrevocable move, he should be tested by a recognized expert to determine whether he had the talent to carry him into the top ten racing drivers of the world - if not, why bother? We both thought we had won a decisive victory.

All this seemed like yesterday when I drove up in the Jag at his posh school in Switzerland - "Le Rosey", in Gstaad - and, by special permission from the headmaster, took him to lunch. He had grown another two inches and towered above me. About Midge I did not have to tell him anything, he was entirely aware of the situation and warmly approved of her beau, our new family member. As is usually the case, I had been the last to know.

"But I have news for you," he beamed at me, brushing off my troubles with sublime youthful egoism. "Just the other side of the Alps, in Italy, in Modena, Piero Taruffi runs a racing school. How about my test?"

Commendatore Taruffi had been world champion auto racing for several years in the thirties, even I knew his name. A deal is a deal, the time had come. We called Modena and registered for the five-day course, some time during the Easter recess. Once this was done, Erik seemed to lose interest in me. While I had a new urge to involve him deeper into my life, children do not want to be burdened by their parents' problems. Anyway, he was doing OK at school, in June he had to graduate and don't worry, Dad, everything will turn out fine. See you at Easter.

I got back into my car and with nowhere much else to go drove down to Munich. Conrad Adenauer's Bundesrepublik was in the middle of its Economic Miracle and the city looked rich and prosperous. The InterTel Building, headquarters of our German company, bustled with activity orchestrated by Peik van Waveren, my vice president and probable successor, who lived in the plush Hotel Continental. Our friendship had not suffered and I moved in with him until Easter, in order to get myself straightened out.

Meanwhile we hit the town, like old times. One day Prince Bernhard called from Italy. He was driving back to Holland and planned to spend the night in a old castle in Austria, a few hours drive away. Could we join him for dinner? Schloss Mittersill is a well preserved medieval pile of stones, artfully restored by a German nobleman and his American wife, who ran it as a dazzling boarding house, family style, very exclusive with a dozen rooms, fine cuisine and a stunning view, at prices high enough to satisfy any snob. Still, it had a hard time making ends meet. We set out on a misty afternoon, feeling no pain, and remembered halfway that we had failed to buy a present for the hostess, a mortal sin in a situation where every penny counted. "Never fear," my partner said, jauntily. "Peik is here."

At this moment a small hind, the size of a dog, jumped out of the forest and hit the Jag a slanting blow, slid alongside for a few hundred feet while I put on the brakes, and lay still.

Neither the car nor the deer had a scratch, but the latter was stone dead. We picked it up, decorated it with some pine branches and presented it on arrival to a grateful and delighted hostess for a future venison roast. InterTel or no InterTel, the gods were still with us.

Dinner was a joy, twelve of us around one table, with the Prince in great form, although clearly baffled by a couple from Philadelphia who, for no discernible reason, were dressed as Arabs with turbans and veils. At midnight he went to bed, after instructing his ADC, a promising young Dutch officer named Freek who had just been promoted to this high position, to have the Ferrari ready for departure on the dot of eight; as all royalty, he was a stickler for punctuality. The party went on, and somewhere along the line Freek, Peik and I left with a countess named Wipsy in her huge Daimler-Benz for a swim at her place, ten miles down the road. There we stayed the rest of the night, in the guest quarters.

At an ungodly hour Freek banged on my door, fully dressed, whispering, incoherent with concern about getting back to the Schloss in time for Prince Bernhard's deadline. "Should I wake Wipsy, you think?"

I looked on my watch. "Seven o'clock in the morning?!" I gasped. "At your own peril, the countess will have your head. - Why don't you just take one of her cars, they're all over the courtyard. We'll straighten things out later."

As Freek dashed out, Peik came in. He shook his head. "That boy takes everything too seriously," he said, while outside we saw a yellow VW "bug" tearing off the premises. Then he picked up the phone and asked for the Mittersill police, down in the valley. "The yellow Volkswagen of the Frau Gräfin has just been stolen," he reported. "It's heading east towards the Schloss. When he comes through the village, be sure he doesn't get away."

He didn't. It took Freek, who had problems with the local dialect anyway, more than an hour to convince the surly Polizist of his identity, a fancy tale involving princes and countesses, Jaguars and hinds and Arabs from Philadelphia. When he finally made it to the Schloss, Prince Bernhard, not amused, was on his third cup of coffee. However, both have forgiven us by now.

On the first day of the Easter recess, in brilliant spring weather, I picked up Erik for the drive to Modena. After Midge's departure and my disappointment in InterTel, his role in my life had grown commensurately. Whizzing together through the Alps in the red Jag, not a cloud in the sky, our mood was such that every incident turned into an adventure. Locked out of our car after breakfast one morning, we cut a hole in the canvas top of the Jag with a bread knife, to the groans of car-loving German bystanders; twice we outraced pursuing police in Porsches, and successfully hid in side roads; we sneaked through a railroad crossing on the wrong side of the road with the gates down, just beating the renowned Swiss railway system by an inch or two; in Modena, where we had blundered into a six-way traffic circle, blocking all exits, the fierce looking traffic officer on his pedestal motioned us close, looked down into the Jaguar and said, "Que bella machina!", before guiding us personally out of the jam. Commendatore Taruffi, trim, gray, handsome, fully aware of his standing in town, Italy and the world, waved us to a halt in front of his headquarters, like a pit stop, and welcomed us to his racing school.

For five days we cavorted around an abandoned airfield on the outskirts of Modena, in Ferrari's, Maserati's, a Bugatti and my topless Jaguar: Taruffi and his six pupils, including Erik and me, singly, in line, starting, sprinting, cornering, through S's and chicanes, curves and straights, slow and fast, and very fast. In the mornings we studied theory, forces and their resistance, centers of gravity, over- and under-steering, skidding, the perfect line through a curve, racing etiquette. The afternoons were for driving, putting into practice what we had learned, and enjoying ourselves. In the end, we were tested.

From the very first day, there had been no doubt: Erik was the best, by far, at everything. The commandatore awarded him a first prize medal and we all cheered. By now I was just as sold on racing as my son, and a vision of the "Thinking Tree" flashed through my mind. To the big question, put over a grappa around an outdoor table at sunset, Piero Taruffi answered, "He has the talent. The rest is application."

* * *

With Erik's future on track, I drove him back to school and continued home to organize a racing team. The Netherlands had never participated in big time international competition, which suddenly seemed preposterous to me. Gathering some friends we founded the Racing Team Holland, and as its first president I persuaded Prince Bernhard to become its Patron. In no time we collected around us a group of the most capable and dedicated enthusiasts, including driver Ben Pon whose father, sole importer of Volkswagen, provided us with Porsche racing cars - GT 904 and Carrera 6 - for a fraction of their cost.

The RTH was manned in all areas by Hollanders, including mechanics and drivers, most of them opinionated, brilliant prima donnas who never took no for an answer. It soon scored its first successes. I left to return to the USA, but others took over and their spirit and determination made Racing Team Holland a redoubtable factor in automobile circles. In the course of ten years Dutch drivers won many world class races, including ultimately the 24-hours of Le Mans by Gijs van Lennep, twice. But by that time I had long gone.

Racing is about money. If you are among the handful of top drivers in the world, you make a lot; if you're not, you pay plenty. Erik had a long way to go, and I did the paying. Before returning to the USA I bought a Mini-Cooper and a carrier van, tax-free at Schiphol Airport. The former is a small British car, like a match box on wheels, souped up by some genius to reach speeds in excess of 120 mph, a perfect starter for a racing career; the latter would serve as road transport, general headquarters and on occasion for camping. After graduation from "Le Rosey" my son was to pick them up, together with his mechanic, a young Danish aficionado called Nils. During the season, which more or less coincided with summer break at U.S. colleges, this little caravan would be seen speeding down the highways and byways of Europe, from one racetrack to another, Zandvoort, Francorchamps, Nürburg Ring, Snetterton, Monza,

Oulton Park, Monthléry, Le Mans, every place where a little prize money could be gained. After that Erik planned to go to college in America, then return to Europe the following summer to resume his racing career, perhaps on a Formula 3. I boarded the KLM plane, satisfied that an old promise had been kept.

When I hit New York the town was basking in bright spring sunshine, a perfect day to start a new life. Without wife and job I felt somewhat diminished, but I had enough money in the bank for one more serious roll of the dice. Television was out - after the glory days of InterTel, the turndown of CBS News, even the murky glamour of Radio Free Europe, the broadcasting chapter in my life was over. In the background of my consciousness hovered the magnum opus, as always, but not right now, thanks. First I had to make a lot of dough, for supporting my son's dash to the top of the racing world, and to guarantee the proper surroundings - a house on an island, perhaps, overlooking the blue Pacific? - without which writing would be a pain in the neck, really. As a start I rented an apartment in a brand new building on the southeast corner of 57th Street and Sixth Avenue, on the 24th floor with terraces all around, at the stiff price of $ 325 per month.

I had never heard of Joe Hirshhorn, the uranium billionaire who more recently stuck his museum slapdash right in the middle of the Washington Mall, until I met his son at a party in Greenwich, Connecticut, a few weeks after my return. If I consistently seem to run into the right people at the right time, it is not so much a matter of luck as of awareness, knowing what you are looking for. At that time I was honed for finding an area of endeavor new to me, with acceptable risks at bearable odds and at least the smell of money.

Gordon Hirshhorn, a young human dynamo with a prominent nose, turned out to be a terrific guy and president of Petrocana, a small company looking for oil in the Mediterranean continental shelf of Israel. To me this seemed just the thing, a totally irresistible combination of factors. We met again over lox and bagels the next morning, and when he offered me the opportunity I resigned from InterTel and joined his intrepid band, lock, stock, barrel and every cent I possessed.

It wasn't just the romance of the deal; Gordon, a very bright lad indeed, had an ace up his sleeve. The recently retired chief geologist of Standard Oil of New Jersey, Dr. Lewis Weeks, a man of towering stature in the oil world, firmly believed that Israel's continental shelf contained millions, maybe billions of barrels of crude. He had been right before.

Until he turned up in Australia, that continent had seemed barren of any and all petroleum reserves, but after his stint as a consultant it was - and is - swimming in them. The story goes that when the local entrepreneurs, Broken Hill Ltd., were huddled in front of a wall chart in their offices and asked the American geologist to indicate where oil might be found, Lewis turned his back to the chart and pointed out of the window at a spot some 800 yards out to sea. "That's where you should drill," he said. They did, and discovered Australia's first oil field. Dr. Weeks was now chief geologist for Petrocana, and as far as I was concerned he only had to be right one more time.

Through the hustle of the new job, which consisted largely of raising money and having stupendous Sunday breakfasts at Gordon's place in Stamford, everything from knishes to gefilte fish, I kept a distant eye on Erik Jr. He was doing well, racing once or twice a week all over Europe, often finishing amongst the first three. Then Holland's only Formula I driver, Carel de Beaufort, was killed in action. Not much later there was another crash. Then another. And another that killed the driver. Suddenly my eyes were opened to the fact that day after day my son was exposed to mortal danger. My pride in his career turned to fear. Entering the racing world was like returning to the front, to Finland, Scheveningen, the RAF, Ambon, realms where the dark prince had a presence by rights. Generally races took place on Sundays, and towards the end of the week I started to carry a lump of lead in my stomach. Saturday nights I never slept a wink. Allowing for the time difference, somewhere far away during those endless hours of darkness, in the daylight of Monza, Nürburg Ring or Zandvoort, cars stood in the starting grid, roaring and trembling. Accidents continue to occur, and only after Monday had passed without a message of doom, I began to breathe easier. For three days or so.

No news is good news, but not always. After a period of silence, in the middle of a week, the front page of a Swedish newspaper arrived, without comment. Spread over three columns was an extraordinary picture of a Mini-Cooper streaking along at full speed. However, it was traveling upside down, the driver's head less than a foot from the road surface. Of course it was Erik. On the back page a smaller photo showed him lying in the grass along the track, his car a heap of twisted metal behind him. He has a lucky streak, like me, and was unhurt, but too embarrassed to write. Two days later he turned up himself, none the worse for wear. I was so relieved that I refused to discuss the crash, not then, never. We set out on the town together, and the next morning I brought him breakfast in bed. He stayed with me for a week before entering Goddard College in Plainfield, Vermont.

As if my life weren't complicated enough, Prince Bernhard showed up in New York with his eldest daughter, the crown princess. We had dinner together in their suite at the Waldorf Astoria, then went to Lindy's on Time Square, lured by its renowned cheesecake. I had not seen Princess Beatrix since her return to the Netherlands in 1945, a child of seven whom I had lifted from the plane and planted back on Holland's soil. Now she was a young woman of twenty-six, chic and attractive, emanating an aura of strength that blew me away. I felt awkward and ill at ease, caught between my inborn respect for our future queen, somewhere way up there out of my league, and the powerful emotion I felt for this splendid girl. At a certain moment in Lindy's, relaxed after lots of cheesecake, she caught me admiring her hair, its thickness and color, a deep chestnut red-brown with golden tinges, very shiny... For a moment our eyes met full-on, but she did not allow any contact to develop and looked away over my shoulder.

* * *

My life in the oil business varied from arduous money raising for our exploration off the Israeli coast, to delightful sojourns in the country itself where, with Haifa as our main base, I shalom'ed my way through historical and geographical wonders from the Sea of Galilee to the Craters of the Moon. In order to maintain our mineral rights we had to progress according to a timetable, financed by our efforts in New York. The deadlines, many of which we missed for lack of funds, were fortunately not enforced, because the oil-poor Israelis needed us. After all, we were searching for what they desperately wanted and lacked, at least for the moment. Sometimes, watching our seismic tests blow spouts of white water from the Mediterranean shelf outside Ashdod, like orgasms of our money, I suddenly realized that the crude underneath represented my last hurrah.

In the spring of 1967 I was staying in London for Petrocana, on my way to Haifa, and read in a paper that Erik would be racing the next day, in the main event at Oulton Park, a track near Manchester. He was now driving a Brabham-Cosworth Formula 3, and while I cannot say the same for his college record, his racing career became impressive: he was the runner-up in the U.K. championships for F-3's. His problems, if any, were of a financial nature. The Mini-Cooper was written off as a total loss, and racing cars do not qualify for insurance. It was a hard blow for both of us, especially when added to the astronomical price of the Brabham. It could have been even worse, because the Dutch tax-authorities claimed import duties on the Mini, unless I could prove that it had permanently left the Netherlands. This I did by sending them the Swedish newspaper, with directions: "The number plate is clearly legible, provided you turn the paper upside down." And that was that.

I took the train, then a bus that dropped me somewhere in a meadow, and started walking towards the scream of engines. Just the sound was enough to give me a sick feeling. Soon I saw Erik standing in the dusty infield, behind the pits, the Brabham- Cosworth F3, barely reaching up to his knees, gleaming in the sun like a deadly projectile. He was wearing his sky blue, fireproof racing overalls and looked smashing. We embraced like Italians.

At the start he was positioned no. 4 on the grid, his tall body squeezed into the slender car as if this, too, he had outgrown. Apparently I looked so miserable, hunched up in the pits, that just before the 10 seconds signal he gave me a quick, encouraging wave. Immediately thereafter the shattering violence of the start stunned me, and when a few minutes later the machines stormed past at full speed for the first time, their pace struck me as totally unreasonable, out of control, catastrophic. Erik was in third place, and only after he had roared by five more times did I begin to feel a glimmer of hope that things might ultimately turn out all right.

"A crash! Ladies and gentlemen, we have a crash! A crash in the back stretch, at the curve! A total flip!" The announcer stammered with excitement. Ladies and gentlemen, that included me, very simply. The leading car whizzed by, tailed by number two. A short pause, there came number three - not Erik. Then the next... and the next...

When the last driver had gone by, there were no more straws to clutch. The silent emptiness trickled into my soul. Was parenthood really worth all this? I left the pits and wandered aimlessly in the direction of the back stretch. A Red Cross team hurried past me. Halfway through the infield my son almost ran into me, wheezing and puffing. In his left hand he still held the steering wheel, torn off in the crash. His face was smeared with blood.

"Pa!" he called, when he recognized me. "Don't worry, It's nothing. I'm sorry..." Then he collapsed.

Within an hour he was back on his feet, with here and there a Band-Aid. He had been thrown free, the Brabham landed a few feet away, ending up smashed, a total loss, ready for the scrap heap. We both knew that there was no money for a new one.

Tough, but right then I could hardly care less. For Erik it was the end of a dream.

We flew to Israel together, to get our breath back. In Tel Aviv I hired my usual driver, Ben Zvi and his car, and told him to head north. Just outside Haifa, in clear view of the road, Israeli army units were camped at the foot of Mount Carmel. Ben Zvi stopped his rickety Pontiac. When our dust had blown by we opened the windows; outside it smelled of orange blossom. The encampment was compact, full of life, a colorful rectangle against the drab hillside. Trees and shrubs hid the modern equipment, only tents were visible, brown and olive green, and everywhere the blue and white regimental pennants on tall, thin staves, fluttering in the breeze. It reminded me so much of the English bivouac of Henry V on theve of the Battle of Agincourt, that at any moment I expected to see my pal, Larry Olivier, strolling from tent to tent with some last minute words of encouragement for his longbow men.

"A friend of mine has a restaurant on Willoughby Street. That's where the parade goes by tomorrow," volunteered Ben Zvi.

"If you like, I'll fix it so you can sit on his roof. He's an Arab, you don't mind?" If Ben Zvi didn't, why should we? The annual national birthday parade of Israeli forces was just what we needed to get our minds off auto racing.

It was a tremendous show of military might, army and air force, which we enjoyed on a flat roof where our Arab host plied us with arak and various exotic delicacies. As the tanks rolled by and the jets roared overhead, I felt downright sorry for any hostile forces in the area. History proved me right. It was May, 1967. Three weeks later, in the Six Day War, the Israelis mercilessly clobbered their enemies and conquered half the Middle East in the process.

In that same process they also wrote finis to the gallant efforts of Gordon Hirshhorn and Erik Hazelhoff by capturing the Egyptian Sinaï, which gave them all the oil they needed. The next time we missed a deadline, not long thereafter, our rights in the Mediterranean offshore were revoked. A last minute appeal to Gordon's father, the billionaire, fell on deaf ears. Petrocana went down the drain, and with it every last penny I owned. I canceled my lease and moved into the Lambs Club, on West 44th Street, at $17 per week.

It was a bad year for dreams.

* * *

The next time you take a stroll in Central Park, or any other park in the world, take a good look at that bum sitting on a bench. Believe me, he could be you. It takes no more than one wrong decision, one stroke of bad luck, one moment of hubris to cross the line from benevolent observer to social outcast.

There I was, fifty years old, without a job, broke, no wife, no close family except a son who from now on would have his hands full with his own survival, and those far away in Holland whom pride prevented me from contacting. The roof over my head, the Lambs Club, was maintained by wealthy actors and inhabited by aging and unsuccessful male colleagues; my one room was smaller than half of Peik's bathroom in the Hotel Continental, and the only diversion I could afford was walking in Central Park. And when I got tired, I sat down on a bench, not quite sure anymore on which side of the line I should be classified.

I was still consoled by my philosophy, brought on by the war, of living life backwards, being grateful at fifty still to be alive, and able to afford... what? The clothes on my back? The little room with a ten-foot view on a blind wall? The Lambs Club had a nice restaurant, but most of the time I stuck to the deli across the street for chopped clams, the best food value nickel for nickel. What next?

Could I handle some dull job, nine to five with half an hour for lunch? I had to hurry - it is amazing how addictive idleness is, like a soft down in which to sink your weary spirit, and surrender your responsibility as a human being to the easy blandishments of the Salvation Army or a guru with a nose ring. Better to take a walk in the park and, well, sit on a bench.

Young Erik came to visit me in West 44th. Street, and was shocked. He had put the demise of his racing career behind him with surprising ease, even some signs of relief, as if he was ready for something new. He grew his hair longer now, and seemed content at Goddard College in Vermont, even if he had to support himself from various mysterious sources of income. His zest for life had not suffered.

We were sitting opposite each other in my tiny room, I on the bed, he on the only, straight-backed chair. On the floor between us stood a bottle of red wine, a welcome present from my guest. "Pa," he said. "I am worried about you, hanging around this miserable whore-infested shit neighborhood."

All fine and dandy, but if you can't afford anything else, you have to settle for a whore-infested shit neighborhood. It was not the kind of advice I craved. "I have an idea," I answered mildly, taking a swig from the bottle. "We're both big boys now. I don't worry about you, you don't worry about me. OK?"

Easier said than done, but he got the message. He stayed the night, in a sleeping bag alongside my bed on the floor, out like a light. In the morning he was in great spirits and had a huge breakfast in the restaurant on my account, which had not yet been blocked. Then he climbed into his newest acquisition which was parked outside, an antique, elongated funeral limousine called "Sebastian", from which he had removed the superstructure. He rose up out of the bare remnants like a chimney from a coal boat, tied on an old-fashioned pair of racing goggles with blue lenses, and shoved the monster into the street. Roaring, honking, waving, hair flapping in the breeze, he disappeared into the prosaic traffic of New York, a creature from a different world. By standing on my toes I could just see him turn right into Fifth Avenue, southwards, the only indication I had that my son was more likely to be on his way to Rio de Janeiro than to the North Pole. I really didn't have to worry about him. I bought a can of clams in the deli across the street and went for a walk in Central Park. When I got tired, I sat down on a bench.

That was the picture in 1967. Have I made myself clear? Not entirely, because I had a secret weapon which I shall now reveal. Karin.

CHAPTER 23

Soldier of Orange

Back to 1965, November 9, late afternoon. Gordon Hirshhorn and I are attending a Petrocana meeting on the 24th. floor of the Seagram building in New York. The Middle East is in turmoil, every day it becomes more difficult to scrape money together for our seismic exploration off Ashdod, Israel. Our accountant is reviewing our financial situation, dollars and cents, dollars and cents, dollars and cents, interminably. How can I pay attention to this mumbling old fart when beyond his bald head the view is unreal? The Big Apple is never so tempting as on an early autumn evening, when dusk creeps up into the workday and lights thousands of office windows that turn skyscrapers into glittering mirages, a feverish vision of glass and golden glow against the rising purple of night.

My southward view smacks squarely up against the new Pan-Am Building, which thrusts from Park Avenue like the infamous north face of the Eiger, now lit from inside all the way up to the 78th floor high above us, a gigantic, golden honeycomb. I sit there marveling at the spectacle, then it happens, right in front of my eyes: the top third of the honeycomb suddenly disappears. You don't just fall for that, one, two, three. I continue to stare at the building, stupidly, when all lights of the center section flick out, poof! like that, and then the rest. There it stands, a huge, dark, silent block, like a immense gravestone against the translucent sky.

No one else in the room has noticed it, they have their noses in annual reports and old Baldy mumbles steadily on. Have I gone nuts? But then, left and right of the Pan-Am Building, I see other towers of light disappear abruptly, as if someone throws a switch. Whole blocks are wiped out. I open my mouth, half rising from the chair, when floop! we ourselves are sitting in the semidarkness.

We look at each other, flabbergasted. Then to the windows - in the distance a few clusters of light still twinkle.. poof! out ...poof! out ...poof! out. That's it. New York, once a city in the eastern United States, has ceased to exist. The time: 5:27 p.m. It has taken less than thirty seconds, the last word of the accountant -"deficit"- still floats in the silent room. From the black chasms outside a crescendo of car horns begins to rise.

"Karin!" is my first thought. We have a date in the Brasserie of the Lexington Hotel, somewhere down the dark streets. How to find her? Old instincts take over: in moments of crisis I prefer to go it alone. God knows what's happening, perhaps the Russians have finally figured things out, but the 24th. floor of a building in the center of New York City is definitely not the place to await further developments. When my associates start deliberating on the next move, I slip out of the room into the pitch-dark corridor.

The Seagram Building is familiar terrain, I feel my way to the exit. As I come past the elevators I can hear the yelling and banging in the shafts - in all those dark towers people by the hundreds are hung up at various levels between floors, a grim thought. The door to the emergency stairs is unlocked, of course.

I start the long descent, blindly but counting carefully... 23... there... back... 22...there...back... 21... How many mezzanines?... Finally the ground floor, I hope. I push the door open, nothing but blackness and silence. "Hello!" I call out, and hear by the echo that I am surrounded by stone or concrete - am I too high or too low? Too low, I think, it smells of cellar. Step by step I climb back up, the next door is locked. Up one more, pretty anxious now, but the next one opens on candlelight flickering in the lobby. Some vague figures are hanging around, aimlessly. Beyond the glass walls cars are crawling down Park Avenue like stray beasts.

Once outside, I breathe a lot easier. I turn east into 52nd Street, right on Lexington. It's pitch-dark now, the hundreds of blocked cars only make the rest seem darker. Traffic lights are out and no police in sight. Here and there some guy tries to help solve the confusion at a crossing, waving his arms, making no difference whatsoever; the mess is total. Suddenly I realize that, after the first moment of confusion, nobody honks anymore. The biggest traffic jam of all time takes place in ghostly silence.

Something else strikes me, it takes a while to figure out. In the shop windows, one next to the other all the way down the street, candles are burning - business is business - which pour a soft light onto the jam-packed sidewalks while the darkness hides all else, including the skyscrapers: Lexington Avenue, pulled down, looks like a New York street of a hundred years ago, and the pedestrians in old-fashioned candlelight could have stepped straight out of a Thackeray novel. Even the mood supports this illusion, there's much smiling and everybody is friendly and helpful. Nothing like a good flap to make people nice to each other.

Everywhere free enterprise, indomitable, sprouts up on the sidewalks. Stalls, mostly for candles, have burgeoned like mushrooms in the dark, competing vociferously in mini price wars.

I buy a couple, as well as a big fried turkey leg, from a teenage entrepreneur. And so, with the candles in my breast pocket sticking up to my ear and the leg, bare and muscled, in my left hand, ready for an uncertain future, I step into the Lexington Brasserie.

The place is dark and jumping, like an après-ski bar in the winter sports, hundreds of strangers packed together around a few candles, talking, laughing, drinking, here and there some lighthearted necking. Yet there's an undercurrent of unrest, like London in wartime. As the hours of blackness continue, rumors multiply: Boston's dark... all flights to Washington canceled... Philadelphia just got it... all the way to Canada... all the way to Florida... Personally, I still think it's the Ruskies in the opening phase of a Final Solution. One thing is certain, I'll never find Karin in this dark refugee camp.

"Hello darling." She is sitting ten feet away, looking unbelievably lovely in the candlelight. She's surrounded by men, of course, who throw up their hands in mock desperation and good-naturedly make room for me. I kiss her.

"Thank God, I never thought I'd find you. I want to ask you something."

"Ask away."

"In principle, will you marry me?"

* * *

A popular saying has it that whoever agrees in principle, disagrees in fact. That's not our problem. I have a pretty good head on my shoulders and use it regularly, but all major decisions in my life have come from the heart. Yet somehow tonight in that crazy Brasserie, surrounded by strangers and candlelight, the world outside in darkness, tottering on edge, my head demands confirmation of my heart's most momentous resolution ever: Karin and I are going to be together as long as we both shall live.

Almost fifteen years have gone by since that dull cocktail party in New York, where our eyes met and held inside a silent tunnel across a room full of guests. We shied away from Fate and each other, bowing to circumstances. When next we met, at the London Hilton in 1964, we did not make the same mistake twice. Perhaps it's better this way, the first time around we may not have been ripe for emotions of this caliber. As we'll be together for the rest of this tale, let me introduce her.

Karin Steensma is the only daughter of a Frisian father and a Swedish mother, both immigrants, who met and got married in New York, where she grew up. Frisians are Hollanders, but special ones. They live in the extreme north, and - as they will surely tell you - contrary to the Franks and Saxons in the old Low Countries, were never subjugated by the Romans. They speak a different language that no one understands, from which English actually evolved. They are to the Netherlands what the Scots are to Britain, a proud and difficult lot who carry much more weight in the nation than their numbers would indicate. The Frisians are also romantic and emotion-al, and on occasion –particularly the female gender–beautiful.

The Swedes... what can I tell you? They eat smørgasbord, drink aquavit, swim naked - particularly the female gender - and are all beautiful. Karin is gorgeous. In view of the above, how can she help it? I shall not bore you - much - with any de-scriptions, except that she is tall, slender and blond, and has blue-and-yellow eyes. She's also smart as hell. And, as all Frisians of all genders, stubborn. The rest you may find out for yourself.

The obstacles to our joint

Karin in 1951

future are manifold, complicated and commonplace. They involve hus-bands, wives, children, divorces, money, pride. Karin and I are both still married, and Midge's plans have hit a snag. She's moved into the flat with me, where we live as friends, platonically, awaiting her future husband's divorce as well as our own. Karin has had enough of her spouse, a decent but unappreciative and ultimately uncooperative Dutchman, but she needs time to prepare herself for an independent future - none of us believes in alimony - by finishing college and becoming an interior designer. And I first have to make a lot of money in Petrocana.

We must have been asleep in our little corner in the Brasserie, like hundreds of others. It is 4:00 a.m. The Great Blackout of 1965 continues. Moonlight pours in from outside, so we decide on a walk. The lobby is packed with sleepers, some snoring or moaning; we have to maneuver our way around and over bodies in bags, under coats or in each other's arms. We stroll up Lexington and cross over to Park.

The avenue lies deserted. A hellish full moon blasts down and reflects its eerie light a thousand fold in the black glass walls and windows of the office towers. The silence is total. Then, somewhere, a male voice shouts, full-throated, sober, repeating a short cry which reverberates in the empty side street. It's the sound of a cantor or a Baptist minister or a muezzin or a guru. We cannot understand him. Then he turns the corner into Park Avenue.

"Pray for us!" he calls, strong and clear. "Pray for us!"

The voice rises in the moon drenched silence, up against the glittering walls. "Pray for us!"

All things considered, the guy's got a point.

* * *

I am convinced that long before our paths crossed Karin and I lived in each other's consciousness, like a sharply drawn emptiness to be filled only by a unique presence. When the two match up, everything falls into place, zoof!, a perfect fit, destined to dismiss all that stands in its way.

It took three years to clear the decks. By autumn, 1968, various divorces were final. Midge had long since left the apartment and joined her partner, while Karin graduated and became a member of the American Association of Interior Designers. We worried about the effect on our kids, especially Karin's daughter Karna, a lovely little girl of eight, but it's a moot point whether a child suffers more from a divorce or a bad marriage. I myself, having shot my bolt with Petrocana, living at The Lambs and walking in Central Park, occasionally sitting down on a bench, remained the only dud.

Not for Karin. She believed in me, not just as a person but as a writer. With mutual hilarity she proposed a household in which I poured out the talent while she brought home the bacon. On condition that I wrote my book, period. We moved to Washington, D.C. where, at a friend's home, to the strains of Mendelssohn and the scent of tuberose, the Reverend De Witt Dickey pronounced us man and wife. Then we both went to work.

It had not been since Rye, almost two decades ago, that I had quietly sat behind a typewriter. Those had been exciting years, Ambon, NBC, RFE, InterTel, Petrocana, but they had lacked something. Settling down does not mean slowing down, but integrating one's energies to provide the flow and rhythm of a mature life, of which writing a book is a microcosm.

Whatever your goal in this world, it's wise to think big and start small. A book will force it on you, hundreds of pages in concept, one word for starters. Then a sentence, a paragraph, a page, a chapter, over and over again. In an interview on Public Radio I heard a great writer, John Cheever, say, "Writing a book is like walking from Vladivostok to Madrid. On your knees." Change Madrid to Compostela and I'll go along with that.

On this seemingly endless journey you don't know what to expect and will find yourself in situations beyond your wildest dreams. All you can do is go on, just like life, go with the flow of the story and the rhythm of its days. It takes courage to start, determination to continue and perseverance to finish. When it's all over, look back without pride or disappointment - it's the best you could do.

Karin made it possible, not just as a meal ticket but as the missing link in my personality. We rented an apartment in Reston, a brand new town just outside the Beltway, and while she took Washington by design I wrestled with a curious question: Should I write the book in Dutch or in English? Commercially, the arguments were simple - 15 million versus 350 million potential readers. But emotionally I hesitated - after all, it was Holland's story.

The answer to the problem arrived by cable, and I was quick to take the hint. At this precise moment a telegram arrived from the Geillustreerde Pers of Amsterdam, stating that they were interested in publishing my war experiences as a series of articles, to be followed by a book. If I agreed, they would send a ghostwriter. I wired back, "Keep ghostwriter, send advance."

A happy marriage does not make for hot copy, nor do years behind a typewriter. However marvelous the experience, you'll just have to take my word for it. Together we were on our way, living by our talents, fulfilling our calling, on track at last. Of course, Washington has its own unique charms, too. As Karin moved up the ladder as interior designer, she was in due time hired to decorate one of the first apartments in the new Watergate complex. In the evenings I often helped her place or rewire some lighting or minor appliances, and as I entered the dark building with my pliers, screwdrivers, wire and electrical knickknacks I could easily have been arrested, to appear on television a few months later with Gordon Liddy, Haldeman, and ultimately Tricky Dicky himself. And when I rented a house near Bluemont in the Blue Ridge Mountains for writing purposes, I was shadowed for two solid days by a CIA helicopter team wondering who had set up shop in the middle of the winter right on top of Mount Weather, which - as I later learned - housed the secret underground command post of the U.S. Government in case of nuclear attack.

With our careers on a roll and the money coming in from both sides, I took out a weekend to visit young Erik. Plainfield, Vermont, the home of Goddard College, somewhere in the pine forest of New England, lay under a white blanket. He must have seen me come staggering through the snow, because he answered the front door himself.

"Holy Moses, what happened to you?" I couldn't believe my eyes. I remembered him as an ordinary, clean-shaven youngster, and now he stood before me like, well, the archangel Gabriel. Towering in the entrance he smiled at me through his golden beard, and flicked back his luscious mane like a beauty queen. "Hi Dad, great you're here!"

We went straight to dinner, all students together in a large hall, which reminded me of Fidel Castro's barbudos in the Oriente Mountains of Cuba. Afterwards we retired to Erik's room for a chat. There were no chairs so we sat side by side on a mattress on the floor, under an enormous abstract painting of his own creation, forerunner of things to come. The windows were closed and in the stuffy air I seemed to detect a whiff of incense. From two strategically placed loudspeakers music of some strange, exotic tonality trickled into the room. "Sitar," Erik explained. "Ravi Shankar."

I pulled one of his russet locks. "Is this hairdo strictly necessary?"

"Dad," he said patiently. "Don't be an ass. Does it really make any difference to you?"

Hell, no. Of course it didn't. I only worried what my friends would think. "Not really. You just look silly."

"Like our forefathers. You'll get used to it."

In the silence that followed I listened to the subtle melodies of the sitar, which along ever more roundabout ways kept turning back upon themselves. "What are you working on now?"

He avoided the question. "Pa, I never really thanked you for letting me work that racing stuff out of my system. It cost you lots of dough, I know, but it's very important to me. Life involves so much more than risking your neck for the glory of winning."

He caught me unawares. "Life involves lots of things. If it isn't one thing, it's another."

He shook his head. "Not quite. At least I've lost the urge of winning at the cost of someone else."

"Hey, wait a minute. Winning is always at the cost of someone else. It's what your whole future is based on, your whole career: that you have the ambition to get ahead of your fellow men. Whatever you do."

"Your career maybe, not mine. At least, not anymore."

Another long silence. Ravi Shankar kept picking away.

I felt shocked. What was going on? How about my son's future? "Well, what are you working on now?"

"Right now, I've gone into ceramics. It's fantastic what you can do with colors if you glaze and bake them. Want to see one of my tiles?"

I absolutely bloody well didn't know what to say. Tiles? He was supposed to be studying English Literature, which could lead to well-paying jobs like journalism or publishing. Tiles?!

"What in Gods name are you talking about? In a few years you'll have to graduate. And please shut up that whining Arab."

He turned off the music. It took a while before he answered. "Maybe I'll graduate, maybe not. Depends on what I feel like, it'll have to come from inside. Now this tile here..."

"Not graduate? Are you out of your ever-loving mind? I studied Law, four bloody years, it didn't interest me in the slightest, but I graduated. For my career, purely for my career. Four whole years!" I heard myself say it. The words rose like bats from a dank crevice and flapped disconsolately about the room. My son looked at me with a sad smile, full of sympathy.

"Well, hell!" I snarled. "You want to be a poor artist all your life?"

* * *

Starting on January 1st. 1969, I wrote one, long article a month for the Dutch publisher, many of them at a broken-down bungalow I had rented for this purpose in the Blue Ridge mountains. Initially I had to seclude myself in total solitude, sometimes for days on end, until I got my creative juices running again. Karin concurred, though somewhat miffed, and "Big Heavens" on Mount Weather filled the bill.

The one thing I had not counted on was the company of a raccoon, who, when I ignored him, retaliated in kind. For reasons of lighting I sat against a window on one side, he on the other on a bird feeding platform scratching around or chewing some complicated delicacy. The glass plate between us apparently gave him a sense of absolute security. If I came to the door he'd reluctantly depart, but seated behind the typewriter I did not seem to exist for him, even at night, when I lit a bright desk lamp. So we sat, head to head, separated by less than two feet, scratching for pay-dirt in unison. On the other hand, the little man who used to keep an eye on me had vanished, once and forever.

On December 31st. of the same year I wrote the last line of the series - and the book - and celebrated this milestone alone in a 17th. century castle near Arnhem, Holland, where Karin and I had spent the final months in order to be near Dutch sources of information. When I say "alone", I mean just that. My wife had returned to Washington to be with her daughter Karna for Christmas, and in Arnhem the blizzard was so intense that I stumbled into the restaurant of Castle Doorwerth as the only guest on that New Year's Eve. Fires roared, candles flickered, medieval splendor and all six lackeys in green and silver livery surrounded me during my solitary celebration meal. Missing Karin dreadfully I ordered two bottles of Veuve Cliquot brût champagne and invited the waiters to join me at midnight. The big, empty hall of the castle in the snow rang with male voices, song and the clinking of crystal, as seven lonely men greeted the year 1970.

During our stay in Holland I spent as much time as possible with my mother, who, after my father's death seven years before, had remained alone in their house in Wassenaar. Of my many visits one stands out, even now. To be truthful, I dropped in very late, merely looking for a place to sleep as close as possible to Leiden after a boozy reunion, and found the house in Park de Kieviet all lit up. She came to the front door while I was still fiddling with the key. "The moon," she said simply, with a glassy look in her eyes.

As it was pitch-dark outside and pouring with rain I thought for a moment that she was as sozzled as I myself, but then I saw the television in the living room and remembered that, my God yes, tonight was the night! She was so emotional that I put my arm around her shoulder while we walked to the couch and held her hand after we got there. And so we sat till dawn, with barely an interruption, my mother more or less in tears most of the time and myself rapidly sobering up as we watched Neil Armstrong and Buzz Aldrin land on the surface of the moon.

My reactions were mixed. While a strong supporter of the space program for romantic and scientific reasons, I saw no future for actual human penetration into the heavens. Contrary to popular myth, space strikes me as the most absolute, brutal and fearsome prison to mankind, and watching those two heroes and their pilot, Mike Collins, worming around in their tiny craft, locked up like sardines by an infinity of black, deadly space, or even cavorting outside within the pitiful restrictions of their clumsy suits in surroundings so patently hostile to every human grace, I could only admire their courage and mourn its waste.

The greatest moment in my opinion was therefore not Armstrong's famous first step on the moon, but the departure home when the little, square Mickey Mouse landing capsule suddenly took off and shot straight upwards like a disoriented cricket, on its way to the improbable rendezvous with Collins' orbiting spacecraft. When that came off without a hitch, miraculously, I joined my mother in her tears for the greatness of God and the brilliant folly of his children.

The principal reason for putting a man on the moon was furthermore the wrong one: not just any man would do, it had to be an American. The Kremlin was planning a similar stunt, and the entire multibillion dollar USA effort was motivated by the battle cry "Beat the Russians". Somehow Neil Armstrong and his crew had risen above this tawdry nationalism and turned these moments of history verily into a giant step for all mankind.

"We didn't even have electricity," my mother sighed. In the course of the long night she had said the same about cars, airplanes, radio, nylons, television, vacuum cleaners, telephones and all the other minor miracles of the 20th century. Outside the dawn glimmered coldly through dripping trees. "If only your father could have lived to see this."

It was a sentence she used constantly these days. On Christmas night of 1962, two weeks after Queen Wilhelmina, my father had died of a heart attack in my mother's arms, upstairs right above where we were sitting now. They had been married fifty years. The German Occupation had consumed him as a Hollander, the loss of the Dutch colonies as an Indies man. Meanwhile he had smoked and smoked, two packs every day of his adult life, even throughout the war. Now the cigarettes had come and claimed their victim.

Being in Europe for InterTel at the time, I had made it to Wassenaar by the next morning. Grief hung so heavily in the house that I tore myself loose from it by brute force, or the days would have disintegrated into chaos. "He was so proud of you," my mother reminisced tearfully, "and of his country. Always wanted Holland to do what's right and honorable. Way back already in the First World War. But he missed out on everything, and everything he stood for fell apart in his lifetime..."

I said goodbye to him by myself, in the same bedroom where he had slept for so many years. He lay peacefully on his bed, in his pajamas, neatly combed and shaven. What finally got to me in that silent room in Park de Kieviet, was one gray strand of hair which defied the neatness of it all and hung helplessly across his forehead.

At first my mother declined to move out of the house, where, according to her, she lived in close spiritual contact with her deceased husband. However, when due to her age the kitchen caught fire twice, my sister Ellen put her foot down - it was time for a service flat. In Holland that's no great problem, the country is dotted with apartment buildings, light, cheerful, on carefully tended grounds, where every old couple or person is guaranteed a flat, at whatever price they can afford, even for free. Does this make for high taxes? Indeed it does, but when once an American newspaperman asked Queen Beatrix, within my earshot, why there were no homeless persons in the Netherlands, she answered truthfully: "Because my people would not stand for it."

My mother held out in Wassenaar until a suitable apartment became available in The Hague, on the top floor for optimum communication with my father. When my book was finished she saw us off at the airport when we flew home, then met us again when Karin and I returned to Holland in April, 1970, for the publishing ceremony – a small, smiling figure waving a first copy exuberantly above her head. The moment I saw it, I knew we were in trouble.

The articles had been well received, twelve long installments about subjects of which the Dutch, who had spent WW II cut off from the free world under German occupation, knew nothing, such as escapes from Holland, exiles in London, secret landings on the Dutch coast, RAF attacks on Berlin, illustrated with unique photographs. I had expected the book to reflect this success, but what my mother was waving about so happily, looked like a miserable little paperback. Closer inspection only made it worse. It was a thin, cheap soft cover in which the articles were bundled without illustrations or the tight continuity required for a book. Had I worked so long and hard for this? Impossible! There and then I decided to get it republished the way I had visualized it, a nice, fat hardcover with a stylish jacket, a terse title and smoothly flowing transitions between the chapters.

We drove straight from the airport to the Geillustreerde Pers in Amsterdam, my mother at the wheel. Our average speed on Holland's matchless highways hovered between 75 and 80 mph., and as we whizzed by huge trucks and center railings with inches to spare, she explained that both the speed and the proximity were needed to counterbalance her failing vision, enabling her to identify hazy obstacles quickly and up-close. A monstrous green sign directing us to Amsterdam shot by overhead, unheeded, and my mother said, sweetly, "Erik, please let me know when we get to the sign for Amsterdam." When we got to our destination in spite of everything, I convinced her that it was going to be a long meeting and we'd make it home by train and taxi. The publishers were a friendly, helpful lot, obviously more interested in their magazines than the book division. To my surprise I learned that my paperback would not be available in stores, but was being peddled from house to house like a toilet brush, an experimental procedure of which they were proud. It was doing well, they assured me, and predicted total sales of about 23,000 copies. I asked them how I could get my rights back.

Copyright wasn't the main problem, it would revert to me in due time anyway, but I wanted to move fast and offered them a deal. In exchange for the immediate return of unrestricted rights to all material, I would supply the G.P. with a series of articles about a thus far totally unknown subject: my trip to Ambon. Not expecting me to succeed with my other project anyway, they accepted.

Now came the real hurdle - where to find someone crazy enough to publish a book for the second time, when the first version had just come out, and was not doing too well to boot? I asked my mother for advice.

"How about the fat fellow, next door?" she suggested.

We had never met in person, but our neighbor in Park de Kieviet, Ad Stok, had a certain reputation in our town, not just for his girth and dressing up like St. Nicholas in December but also as a gutsy and imaginative publisher. It being four o'clock on a perfect Sunday afternoon, I hopped over the back fence, crossed his immaculate lawn and found him at tea on the verandah. We discussed the weather, of course, and the state of the tulips, and the yearly invasion of German tourists, and then I put my proposition on the table: If he republished my book I would rewrite the text to create a fluid continuum and provide pertinent pictures. He smiled and shook his head sympathetically. I threw in a fine new title. He offered me another cup of tea. I mentioned that maybe I could get Prince Bernhard to write a foreword.

Ad Stok froze with the teapot in his hand. At this moment I suddenly remembered another of his reputations - a Dutch flag with an orange pennant always flew from his house at every royal birthday, and each time he went by it he doffed his hat.

"You get our Prince to write a foreword," he said instantly, pointing a stubby finger at me, "I'll publish your book."

I jumped on my 350 cc. FN motorbike, always at readiness during my visits in Wassenaar, and raced to Palace Soestdijk in Baarn, an hour's ride. Security in those days was rudimentary; I roared straight to the front entrance and ran up the stairs. Fortunately the Prince was home. As it was cocktail time he offered me a glass of champagne, but I wanted to get back before my publisher had time to sleep on his promise. When I returned he was still sitting on his verandah, only the tea had changed to a bottle of wine.

"The Prince will write a foreword," I gave him the good tidings. "You'll have the new manuscript before the end of the year." The fate of the 'orange soldier' was sealed with a superb glass of Chateau Lafite.

The rewrite took three months, as did the Ambon articles that bought back my copyright. The publishing date of the new version, an exciting-looking hardcover titled Soldier of Orange, was one year to the day after the paperback, 1 April 1971. The night before publication I appeared on television with Willem Duys, Holland's equivalent of Johnny Carson. At nine o'clock the next morning delivery trucks started lining up at Ad Stok's warehouse in The Hague and the books started rolling out of the stockroom at a rate of 3000 copies an hour, the first of forty-six printings. On March 25, 1994, the then publisher, Joost Bloemsma of Spectrum, presented me with the millionth copy, a figure Prince Bernhard lightly referred to as "encouraging".

CHAPTER 24

Echoes of Java

Life is a never-ending game of cards. Fate is the dealer, you play the hands. There's little you can do about the cards you get, but they're only half the story. We all know people who, with the deck stacked against them, made a success of their lives, and others who held all the trumps but botched the game. It isn't what happens to you that matters most, it's how you react to it.

The late sixties and early seventies were baffling times. With or without LSD, pot or peyote strange things happened. Men grew their hair long, women wore rags, families disintegrated, children ran away, strangers lived in groups together, heroes were despised. Long neglected forces pressed to the fore - love, altruism, honesty, compassion, gentleness - sometimes true, often phony, always controversial. Intuition challenged thought, vibes replaced reason, mystical powers claimed their ancient rights, and as people reacted, so they became. I, for one, did not feel out of place.

This may throw light on a bizarre shift in my story, often questioned but never before explained. Between 1968 and 1971, Age of Aquarius, two momentous developments occurred to me: 1) Karin and I joined forces for the rest of our lives; 2) "Soldier of Orange" fulfilled my writer's commitment. It also bombarded me to a media hero in the Netherlands. And now my reaction. Did I return to Holland to reap the rewards and take it easy? No - we bought a few acres of land and moved to Hawaii. Surprised? So was I.

Some foreplay preceded this powerful thrust. The winds of change touched even my former war buddies, all in their fifties now, and pushed them prematurely over some psychological threshold. One day I stepped into the Netherlands and noticed to my dismay that World War II once again loomed centrally in their consciousness. Reunions, which in our prime we had sworn never to attend, appeared to be daily occurrences. Ribbons and decorations that had been lying in a drawer for years, were worn again. A man's tie would tell you not only his wartime unit, but even whether he had stood eye to eye with the enemy. Everyone suddenly wanted it to be known that he had been a parachutist, or a pilot, a prisoner of war, an Englandfarer, even a secret agent. They had reverted to the past, and I did not like it.

"Oh hell," I was told. "It's just an excuse to get together over a beer now and then."

I don't buy that. The basic point is, are veterans driven together by memories of the war, or do they meet for the specific purpose of recalling the war? The latter is the case, it seems to me.

All those who had played a conscious role in the tragedy of 1940-1945, were approaching old age. Retirement was imminent, some of us already received pensions. They had reached that Great Divide where memories of the past begin to crowd out dreams of the future. Looking back from it we see the totality of our productive lives, and almost always it's below our childhood expectations. What have we really accomplished by all our efforts, sweat and tears - perhaps loved truly once or twice, raised our kids, occasionally stuck out our necks for a good cause, mostly in vain, helped a few people, remained human. They are all so unspectacular, those hard-fought, endless, exhausting achievements of our daily lives, they so easily pale in comparison with that one, dramatic episode which towers up from our common past: War! Occupation! Air raid! Gestapo! Dachau! Japs! Iwo Jima! Normandy! Victory! Were you there? Do you remember?

At commemorations and reunions the acceptable memories whirl around the flags and the beer bottles, above board, but somewhere deep down in our subconscious stirs the indigestible horror of violence, terror and mass murder. Could I possibly live in Holland forever, a country with a memory like an elephant and more monuments per square meter than anywhere I know, a place where they won't let you forget?

On the other hand, "ubi bene," as the Romans used to say, "ibi patria," which is a high sounding way of expressing a down-to-earth concept: "Follow the buck." I cannot possibly deny that I found the Netherlands a more desirable fatherland with a bestseller in the bookstores than with an unfinished manuscript in the attic. Except for one fact.

With almost a thousand inhabitants per square mile, Holland is also the most densely populated country in Europe. Sixteen million Dutchmen in an area the size of Rhode Island, largely overqualified for the jobs available, have created a "wheat field syndrome", which dictates that no one stalk shall outgrow the rest. It gets cut off, clawed down, crushed until the field is level again. But if it keeps growing nonetheless until finally out of reach, then it is applauded as a typical Dutch phenomenon. And a rare one.

Not standing in line for such heroics, I still had to endure its symptoms. They weren't new to me. After Queen Wilhelmina had awarded me the Military Williams Order for reasons which had to remain secret at the time, many whom I had counted among my friends in London scoffed and sniggered. Now the explosive success of "Soldier of Orange" produced similar reactions. The effect on me was chilling, I suddenly recalled all the reasons why I had left my country in the first place. Besides, writing should not be considered a serious profession, remember? -

After Soldier of Orange's publication and the concomitant hoopla in the press, on television and radio, we returned to Washington, where Karin could no longer afford long absences. Apart from our home life with Karna, she had developed a thriving business and sparkling social routine that spanned the political spectrum from crusty old Republican Senator Everett Dirksen to Democratic presidential candidate Gene McCarthy, an absolute charmer, especially towards women like Karin.

I found myself with little to do and, always eager to tighten the bonds with my son, went off to visit him. Erik had quit college some time ago, and for a while I seriously expected him to end up with crossed legs and bare belly on a mountain top in the Himalayas. However, he had opted for San Francisco, where he was staying in Haight-Ashbury - where else? As far as I'm concerned it could just as well have been Outer Mongolia. However, on my arrival in this hippy heaven the natives proved friendly and we exchanged ideas as if they were beads. They seemed to know exactly what they did not like, which left them little to go for in life.

In spite of my great age his ten house mates received me with surprising enthusiasm, which coincided with the arrival of a bag of brown rice that I paid for, of course. They offered me a bed underneath the staircase, perhaps in anticipation of more deliveries. I accepted, and in no time we were all sitting together on pillows and mattresses in a dusky room chanting Hare Krishnas- Hare Krishna, Krishna, Krishna, Hare Rama, Rama, Rama - an endless, monotonous drone that drove me nuts, but seemed to inspire the locals. Incense filled the air with exotic scent, which did not improve my cold, but I could not bring myself to ruin the mood by leaving.

Finally the chanting died down, the light came on, and Erik and I went to his room for a chat over a glass of unfiltered organic apple juice. Fat tomes lay scattered everywhere, among which I detected the Bible, the Koran, the Apocrypha and the Upanishads.

"I see that your attitude towards religion is.. ah.. tolerant," I remarked pleasantly.

He shrugged his shoulders. "Why not? They're all the same, God is God. Everyone looks for him in his own way. In India there are people who are meditating nonstop to find him. Thirty years already, some of them."

"Really? With their legs crossed?" In order not to lose touch with the times I had been practicing the lotus position, secretly in the bathroom, until an old soccer injury started acting up. Thirty years, my, my!

Erik nodded confidently. "But these guys are so spiritual that they can meditate themselves clear off the floor and float, just by the power of their minds."

"Do you really believe that?" I had a problem with it. When I had to get off the ground, I bought me a ticket at KLM.

"Why not? There are lots of things our civilization knows nothing about. Can you state positively that it's not so?"

Of course I couldn't. What did I know about floating and getting off the ground? Or about God, for that matter? I would have loved to follow my son on his spiritual adventures, but it is important that you remain true to yourself, no matter how much you love someone. Assuming that I could last half an hour in the lotus position and meditated myself silly, if after that time I still hadn't found God, I would probably turn on the television.

But then, is it really necessary to seek him so directly, with books and meditation, and hunt him down like a trophy in the jungle? Can't you just do your best in life and hope that from time to time you surprise him - and yourself - with something worthy of his grace?

* * *

To get back to Hawaii, the trouble was that my serious doubts about returning to Holland were almost evenly matched by the negative vibes we experienced in Washington. The country was in an uproar about the Viet Nam War, riots took place everywhere, students at Kent State University were shot dead by American soldiers, civilized society collapsed under lies and insults, everybody hated every one else. Karin and I joined anti-war protests all over town and finally marched on the Pentagon, watching my old CIA buddies take furtive pictures of the demonstrators, myself included. After all, there is a big difference between a war to throw the rascals out, like the Germans from Holland or the Russians from Hungary, and a military onslaught into somebody else's country for one's own purposes, however misguided. Nor could we stomach the president, Richard Nixon, and as the likelihood of his reelection grew stronger, so did our inclination to leave the country and await better times elsewhere. But where?

Then, one night in Reston, in the middle of these emotional upheavals, the telephone rang. It was young Erik. "Pa! I'm on Maui."

"On what?" I hoped it wasn't LSD.

"Maui. It's a little island in the Pacific."

"Good heavens, old chap. Can I do something for you?"

After Goddard, after Haight-Ashbury, I often labored under the erroneous illusion that my son needed help from me. If you're stuck on some godforsaken island, somewhere far from civilization, surely, you're in the soup? But he sounded excited, as if he were on to something, and urged me to come and take a look. Why not? A few hours on a plane... I told him maybe.

Karin and Karna were busy at work and school, and being frankly curious about Erik's discovery, I bought a ticket to Hawaii. To my astonishment I learned that the trip would take two hours longer than flying to Holland. I dug up a map and detected a few small specks in the middle of a vast, blue area, 3000 miles to the nearest land: Hawaii, half Erik's age as a state in the Union. Honolulu and Pearl Harbor on the island of Oahu, Kauai in the north, in the south the Big Island of Hawaii, rugged and empty, Molokai, Lanai.. bless my soul, there it was, Maui. After ten hours nonstop on a 747 and forty minutes in a Cessna, I deplaned in front of a little white structure alongside a single landing strip surrounded by sugar cane: Kahului, Maui. The scent of molasses, last smelled half a century

ago at one of my father's refineries just outside Surabaya, left me stunned
with recognition.

I had sent Erik a telegram to the post office, but there was no trace
of him. No problem - how many 6'4" youngsters with hair down to their
shoulders and a reddish beard could there possibly be on a funny little
island like this? I rented a car, and that first afternoon I saw at least ten
of them. Also, Maui turned out to be bigger and infinitely more beautiful
than I had expected. A massive mountain ridge, at least 10,000 feet high,
curved in the east, its slopes flowing down to the ocean in all directions
except westwards, where it was connected by a narrow plain to a second
group of peaks. The views were breathtaking.

I drove around till dusk, then stopped at a roadside stand under a
sign in Nipponese. I can tell a Japanese person when I see one, so I asked
the young man standing near me what it meant. "How the hell should I
know," he replied indignantly in unmistakable American. After this valuable lesson in local ethnology I ate a lonely cup of saimin soup, checked
into a motel and went to sleep.

Two days I cruised through Maui. I saw Asians in new Datsuns and
Hawaiians in old Chevys, Filipino's in pineapple fields and Portuguese
on horses, Caucasians with long hair and Caucasians with short hair, but
no Erik. Finally I called the police, the hospital, the nut house and the
graves registration, and then, in the last light of a golden sunset, I saw
him standing under a palm tree by the side of the road, waiting for a ride.
Kidding around with a blond wahine, laughing, tanned, leaning on his
guitar, he did not notice me at first - why did I ever worry about him? He
grinned when he recognized me, whispered something to his girl who
waved wildly in my direction, shoved his guitar on the back seat of my car
and opened the door. "Move over, Dad, I'll take you home."

Every breeze that touches Maui, from whatever point of the compass, has traveled across thousands of miles of ocean. Where the slopes
of the mountain - Haleakala, House of the Sun - force it upward, white
masses of cloud rise against the azure sky and deposit the moisture of
their long journey on the island below. The sun always shines on Maui
somewhere, and somewhere it rains; where the two meet rainbows glow.
From pine stands just below the crater, through impenetrable rain forests,
to the bamboo and palm trees along the coasts, hundreds of little streams
tumble unseen from waterfall to waterfall, splashing down into round,
crystal clear pools, five, ten below each other, until they lose themselves
on the black, polished pebble beaches of Koali and Kipahulu. Beside one

of those streams, in a shanty barely visible through mango and papaya trees and snow-white plumeria blossom, lived my son.

"It isn't much, but it's home," he said cheerfully as he guided me through the dusk to the wooden structure. The warm glow of an oil lamp shone from a window.

"No electricity, eh?"

He shook his head. "No electricity, no piped water, no telephone. And no racket, no stench, no heating, no pollution and no trouble with the neighbors." He stopped and put his hand on my arm. "Smell around you, Pa."

We stood sniffing together. A light, delicious fragrance floated on the evening air, I recognized it instantly from Sumber Agung, my father's coffee plantation on Java. Wild ginger... how many years had it been?

"But what do you do for water?"

"I'll show you tomorrow. Just listen..."

In the silence I could hear the purling of a stream, and behind it a soft, steady rush.

"The waterfall is a few hundred feet away, with one of the prettiest pools below it you've ever seen. There'll be water in your room from a hollow bamboo."

"Ok, great! - But no telephone..."

"Dad, sometimes you're a tiresome old fart." He took me by the elbow up the dark steps to the porch. I turned around and faced the night. The smell of ginger held me spellbound. I filled my lungs to bursting with the sweet scent of my youth. Between the treetops stars glittered fiercely around a sliver of moon, instinctively my ears tensed to catch the throbbing of tong-tongs. All I heard was the rippling and rush of water, and around it silence so pure that I had forgotten its existence. To my surprise tears stung my eyes. I felt the closeness not just of nature, but of all the mysterious forces that had formed me as a boy and sustained me through thick and thin ever since. The aftermath of World War II had wiped out my childhood along with my motherland, but all these years it had lain here safely stored away, awaiting my return.

* * *

On one point my son and I agree totally: It's fun to have money, but more fun to spend it. As the latter a priori rules out the former, our concept of wealth is not based on property but on income. "You are rich if you earn more than you need," is my definition. "You are rich if you need less than you earn," Erik turns it around. This difference seems negligible, but as my needs appear to grow as I make more money and his shrink as he makes less, I, according to my own definition, am poor and he's rich according to his. To make things worse I work like a demon for a living, while he couldn't care less.

We stepped inside the little shanty and I promptly almost broke my neck over a baby. "Oh Lord, what else is new," I groaned silently, patting it gingerly on the head. But when I straightened up the beaming proud parent was not Erik, thank God, but a boy with long, black curls. "Hallo," he smiled. "I'm Richard and this is my son, Sylvan."

Later that evening I found out that Richard's father was a deceased millionaire from Baltimore, who had left him a fortune. "He doesn't want to have anything to do with it." Erik turned down the oil lamp in the shabby room, were a wispy blonde called Susie had served us a dinner of fish and avocado with soybean sprouts, after which she and the others had gone to bed, tactfully leaving the two of us alone. We settled down for a beer and a chat, side by side on the rickety couch, feet on the coffee table. Outside the Hawaiian night was unbelievably silent. "The inheritance is being administered somewhere, but he ignores the whole thing."

"But why, in heaven's name?"

"He says money poisons the soul. He takes his yoga pretty seriously." Erik shrugged his shoulders. "Hell, you've got to respect it, everybody here lives his own life. Richard just wants to be a good person, no more no less. While I, for instance, believe you can be good and rich at the same time."

"Well, bully for you."

He laughed and poked me in the ribs. "Money just makes it more difficult, Old Man. You've got to work at it and keep a beady eye on yourself."

"And what does Richard do?"

"He surfs. Like me."

"I mean, what do you guys do for a living?"

"Oh. Of course we have our fruit here, and the vegetable garden, everything organic, only chickenshit and humus and stuff, and when we need money we work. Odd jobs, construction, fencing. But never something we can't get out off as soon as the surf's up in Maalaea, or if the weather is too great, or we just don't feel like it. And Deirdre, Sylvan's mother, has a job with retarded kids."

"Are they married, those two?"

Erik glanced at me. "Does it matter? You give a damn?"

"No - eh - no. Just a question."

"No idea, never asked them. Totally unimportant." In the silence outside a dog barked, nearby, then another in the distance. Was that rain I heard on the tin roof?

"Except, of course, for that little chap, Sylvan."

"Pa," There was a tremor of impatience in my son's voice. "All that matters is whether they love each other. And will go on loving each other. Don't you understand!?"

"Sure I understand. But why must you always make it so difficult for yourselves? Why can't you play the game according to the rules? As simple as that?"

"We didn't make the rules," he snarled at me. "Its YOUR rules. And YOUR game. And we're sick and tired of it."

Just as our talk was catching fire a bearded figure with a dripping wet blanket over his head stepped into the shack. "It's pissing with rain," he announced. "My groundsheet is wet. I'll sleep inside, if you don't mind." He spread a blanket underneath the dining table and, once comfortably installed, waved at me cheerfully through the chair legs. "My name is Rainbow. I live in a tent."

It broke the tension, we kidded around a bit and then went to bed. I spent a restless night in a sleeping bag on the porch. When I woke up, the sun sparkled in a spotless sky. The house was silent. I got up and walked along the jungle path towards the sound of the waterfall. There they all were, Erik and Susie, Richard and Deirdre with Sylvan, another young couple and a fellow called Michael, all of them stark naked in and around a perfectly round little lake. Only Rainbow was missing. They all cheered when I took my clothes off and modestly covered my ding-dong with my hands on the way to the pond. But one quickly gets used to nudity, and after a refreshing dip in the cool water we sat all mixed together on the rocks, soaking up the early sun rays in our bare bones. Michael turned out to be a major in the Special Forces, just back from Viet Nam and already with a pigtail where his green beret used to be.

I stayed a full week. Every day the magic of Maui grew.

Experiences gained in intensity by their sheer simplicity. In the early morning, floating bare-assed on my back in the round, clear pool below the hissing waterfall, staring up at blue sky between the trees, the exotic smell of guava in my nostrils, nothing in the world could be so vitally important as the breakfast being prepared that very moment by the women in the little house. Then, after basking a few minutes in the sunshine, listening to my stomach rumble, I would slip into my shorts, saunter home and feast on papaya with a touch of lemon from the garden, eggs straight from the chicken coop, a slice of Portuguese sausage created by Ah Fook in his store down the hill, home baked bread and half a dozen cups of ginseng tea. As the kids went surfing, I pushed off in the car to further inspect the island, lingering inevitably in spots where it would be great to build a house.

My son and I with the catch of the day

On the third morning I drove all the way from Makena Beach to the top of Haleakala, 10,000 feet high against a transparent sky. Behind the strips of golden sand, sugarcane filled the valleys and foamed up against the mountain slopes. The road wound its way past bungalows hiding behind bougainvillae and fire-red poinsettias to the pineapple plantations, the grooves as if drawn by compass in the terra cotta soil, a pert little fruit crowning each plant. Then through the grasslands between scented eucalyptus trees, endlessly upward to the barren crater wall. The horizon rose with me, and from the top it looked as if at any moment the deep blue ocean would gush down into the island. Up there, in the House of the Sun, where the icy wind howled over lava rocks, I made my decision, if it wasn't being made for me by forces far beyond my control. The next day I bought a piece of land.

Now I had to convince Karin of the inevitability of my action. With any other woman I wouldn't even have tried. We lived together contentedly in a house on a street in Washington D.C., with well-paid careers and a school-age daughter - how to make it acceptable that the necessity existed of uprooting this entire situation by moving five thousand miles to a little island lost in the Pacific Ocean? Love was just the beginning, but only Karin would trust my intuition that here our lives could grow into fulfillment, a home base free from the rubble of the past, with gentle people close to nature in a simple, mellow world. I called her on the phone and asked her to join me. Two days later she arrived.

From Kahului Airport we drove over Paia up the mountain, Karin at the wheel. She was bubbling with good news about her work. Ben Rome, president of Washington's largest construction company, delighted with the job she had done on his Watergate apartment, requested her availability for a number of major projects; the sky was the limit. She was so happy, I couldn't stand it any longer and dropped my bombshell without any mitigating preliminaries. After that we proceeded in silence.

I pushed my chair far back to keep my eye on her, this sophisticated woman in a summer blouse by Saks Fifth Avenue, to whom I had just suggested turning her back on the nation's capital and the entire spoiled world of America's East Coast, in return for living with me on this Mickey Mouse island. She drove with confidence, as she did everything, calmly, capably. Once, when she had to brake hard for a piglet, she put her hand on my knee, leaned forward and smiled at me in the mirror. Her eyes, light above strong cheekbones, hinted of a superior mind and culture; what in Gods name would she think of Maui?

At 2000 feet we came to Makawao, a little cattle town straight out of Bonanza, except for the tree ferns around the post office and oleanders along the gutter. Karin relaxed. She waved to a group of Portuguese cowboys with hat bands of plumeria blossom. They returned her greetings with dignity and smiles. At the Church of St. Joseph, where an enormous jacaranda tree wrapped the graveyard in purple shadow, I guided her into a right turn, up Piiholo. We were almost there.

A short shower had darkened the volcanic earth to the color of raw steak; against the clear sky glowed a rainbow. Tradewinds rustled the eucalyptus trees above sloping meadows; around a turn a stallion stood like a misplaced statue against a background of blue sea. A few more steep miles - now the powerful presence of Haleakala matches his rival, the Pacific Ocean; sea and mountain air are one.

We've arrived. I raise my hand and Karin stops the car.

We get out and silently cross the meadow up to the tree line, turn around and there, beyond the emerald island, lies the ocean.

"Is this land ours?"

"This is it."

She smiles at me, slowly. "I think I'm falling in love with it."

I kiss her. "How about your career? And Ben Rome?"

Karin shrugs her shoulders. "It's only money."

* * *

The ghosts arrive after sunset, but it's impolite to keep them waiting, so we left our house early for the graveyard. During a few hours each year they return to earth, especially those that have departed in the past twelve months. They come to see how the loved ones left behind are making out, and of course expect to be properly received after such a long journey. Everyone looks forward to this cheerful occasion, the Bon Dance, at which the local Buddhists remember their dead, and friends are welcome to help make the evening a success.

Our home, designed and furnished by Karin, had been solemnly blessed by a Hawaiian kahuna on completion, a small ceremony in which our new neighbors participated. It was time to return the complement, so we were off to the big temple near Paia, with the gold pillars and the red lacquered roof and the enormous bronze bell in the garden. In the late sun the flamboyants along the road blazed as if on fire, side by side with purple jacaranda and rainbow trees dripping with multi- colored flowers. My father we had buried on a bleak afternoon in icy rain, the elm trees bare against the Dutch winter sky.

All the way from Paia the cars were parked along the berms, we had to walk the last mile. We could hear the music ahead, shrill and gay, with the most unexpected variations of rhythm on the drum. The sun slid into the ocean and we reached the temple grounds in dusk. Before us lay the cemetery, all lights and colors and flowers and people. On almost every grave, around a bright paper lantern swinging gently on the evening breeze, a family huddled together enjoying a picnic in cozy reunion with the shades of their dear departed. They drank beer and wine, served the onetime favorite dishes of their ethereal guests and discussed intimate memories, soft voices around dim lights everywhere. The abundance of delicacies was meant to reassure the visitors, so that they would return to their vague domain free from worry about their progeny. The leftovers were stacked around a bunch of flowers, lit by the lantern, as provisions for the return journey. These would surely be gone in the morning - could it be the dogs of Paia, who were whining softly in the darkness beyond?

In the temple garden the Bon Dance gradually came to life. On a podium decorated in red and gold, fifteen feet off the ground, the musicians performed, not quite sober anymore but with tireless energy. The open area around the tower bathed in light, and here, in a circle three, four deep, the Buddhists of Maui and their friends danced the ceremonial welcome, forward, back, side step, courtly bow, moving slowly around the music, all together, every step a prescribed ritual. The ladies danced best, in their colorful kimonos with the little back pads which conferred unexpected dignity on the butcher's wife, the hairdresser, the woman of the post office. The men were less capable, but everybody could borrow a hapi coat on the spot and enter the fray, and while I let the colorful procession roll by me, forward, back, side step, courtly bow, I noticed a very tall, bearded reveler, forward, back, side step, courtly bow, who waved at me cheerfully as he danced by.

"Come on, Dad, join the party!"

I hesitated, of course. What the hell, me hopping about in a funny jacket to this weird music, but Karin and Karna had already floated past, a good head taller than the doll-like little ladies who smilingly made room for them. Not to join would be sheer cowardice, nothing less, so when Erik came by for the second time I launched myself with a graceful leap among my fellow Mauians and shortly afterwards tripped, turned and genuflected with the best, forward, back, side step, courtly bow, in a red silk hapi coat side by side with my son around the temple garden.

And suddenly I came to think of my grandfather with the wooden leg, who careened through Amsterdam in his Spijker, the first automobile in the Netherlands. And my other grandfather, the famous Leidener with his glittering heap of rowing medals and his spooky house on the edge of the jungle in Java. And of my own father, battered by the German Occupation and the loss of the Indies, peaceful at last on his bed in Wassenaar.

"Well, fellows," went through my head, and perhaps I spoke it aloud, "I have not the slightest notion where you are, but God knows, you too may be around tonight... funny business,of course..." - forward, back, side step, courtly bow - "...futsing around like this, but we mean well... So if by any chance you are here... - forward, back, sidestep, courtly bow - "I and my son, ...the tall one next to me, with the beard... wish you welcome from the bottom of our hearts."

"Pa, I have news for you!" Erik interrupted. He turned towards me, but after a somewhat extravagant pirouette a Chinese lady of exceptional proportions, as wide as she was tall, landed between the two of us. Only after she had spun along, chuckling with embarrassment, could he make himself heard above the ever increasing din of drums, flutes and an unexpected trumpet. "Susie and I, well, can't you guess?" He poked me in the ribs, threw back his head and laughed. "Grandpa! You're going to be a grandfather pretty soon!"

Someone pulled back the heavy wooden clapper and let it ram into the ten foot high temple bell. The bronze voice boomed over the sugar fields of Paia, rolled across the surf towards the ocean and shivered my molars while I - forward, back, side step, courtly bow - continued my dance around the drunken music men.

* * *

Even in Hawaii, the flow of life is marked by arrivals and departures. Shortly after the birth of our granddaughter - Meadow Melelani (Heavenly Song) Hazelhoff Roelfzema - we were invited for lunch at Sam Pryor's, in Kipahulu, alongside the Seven Sacred Pools near Hana on the far side of Maui. It was a tricky drive, three hours along a narrow, winding road full of blind curves, with Haleakala on one side and steep drops to the Pacific Ocean on the other.

Sam, one of the founders of Pan-American Airways, had retired to a double-sized A-frame beside a spectacular waterfall, where he lived with his wife and half a dozen gibbons. The monkeys, well loved and respected by their owner, wore diapers around the house for reasons of aesthetics and decorum. By the time I found the place, the other guests, including Mrs. Mellon from Philadelphia, had arrived. As had Charles Lindbergh.

Unless forced by protocol, I do not say "sir" easily, whomever I address, but this time it rolled off my tongue automatically, without the slightest hesitation. As if it were yesterday, I remembered that glorious time in 1927 when the entire world spoke about nothing and nobody else, by word of mouth, radio and newspaper headlines:

LINDBERGH ACROSS THE ATLANTIC!
LONE EAGLE IN HISTORIC FLIGHT!
NEW YORK - PARIS IN 33 HOURS!
LUCKY LINDY FIRST MAN ACROSS!

I was ten years old in Surabaya, a dump in a remote corner of the Far East, but not one boy in town didn't know about Lindbergh.

He stood as tall and straight today as then, only his gray-blond hair seemed curlier than I remembered from that strong, young face on the front pages half a century ago. I am not a hero worshiper, but Charles Lindbergh's presence thrilled me. He introduced us to his wife, Anne Morrow, a delicate beauty half his size, and asked after the health of our mutual friend, Prince Bernhard, with whom he had worked on the World Wildlife Fund. After this he concentrated on Karin, discussing their common Swedish heritage. At luncheon they sat side by side, with Anne Morrow as my meal companion.

The scene was no less than spectacular. We were seated around a circular table, ten persons, in a gazebo adjoining the house at about half the height of a 200 feet waterfall next to us, with a view of the tumbling torrent in one direction and the ocean in the other. To my relief Sam had resisted the temptation of inviting one or two gibbons to join us for lunch, as was often the case. Charles had just returned from Indonesia on some nature project, where he was appalled by the deforestation of my old island, Java. We also talked about an extension of Haleakala National Park, one of Pryor's pet projects, and life on distant planets, in which Lindbergh firmly believed.

Anne Morrow, a marvelous author, was fascinated by the phenomenon of longhaired youth, such as young Erik, about which I could tell her quite a bit. To my surprise she had never heard of the Whole Earth Catalog, the hippy's Bible, indispensable for life on Maui. She was astonished to learn that it regularly quoted writings and insights of her husband's, so I promised to send her a copy, and did. During our conversation I was startled to see Charles, across the table, leaning backwards and opening his mouth wide, and Karin peering down into it like a dentist.

She had apparently castigated him for putting four lumps of sugar in his tea, after which he now proved to her that, at the age of seventy, he still had perfect teeth without a single filling.

Yet he was a doomed man and must have been informed at just about this time that he suffered from cancer. Two years later when the end neared, he insisted on leaving the hospital in New York to die at home. The doctors assumed that he meant his family estate in Connecticut, but no, Lindbergh wanted to die on Maui. As Fate would have it, the Pan-Am pilot who flew him there on his final journey had also flown the Spirit of St. Louis in the movie of his historic flight.

The Lone Eagle prepared himself methodically for his last takeoff. His grave was dug in the remote church yard he had chosen, fifteen by fifteen feet, many meters deep. It was to be covered with pebbles from the beach right alongside the cemetery, Hawaiian style, one foot high surrounded by lava rocks, just enough to identify it, no more. After that, he selected the eucalyptus tree from which Kipahulu cowboys fashioned the coffin.

Then he said goodbye to his friends, calm and controlled, and died in the presence of his wife.

Karin and I went to pay our respects the day after the funeral. The road had been rough, squeezed between the mountain and the sea. I knew the place, still I could hardly find it. In the end we had to hike across a meadow, through a cattle gate which had been closed with wire, then slide along a rained-out mud path where a bull blocked our way, and finally climb a crumbling wall of sharp lava rock - Lindbergh was still hiding from the crowd that had pursued him all of his life.

I had expected a bunch of tourists around the grave, and heaps of faded flowers, but there we stood on the edge of the ocean, all alone, before a deserted heap of polished, fist-sized pebbles spread straight from the beach onto the bare ground. A single strand of plumerias, wine red and ivory, draped across the smooth, gray rocks. No gravestone, no name plate, nothing but our chance knowledge of Lucky Lindy's presence somewhere down there.

The earth lay scraped and scarred, behind a scruffy hibiscus hedge still stood the yellow bulldozer that had shoved the big hole shut. A little church behind us dozed peacefully in the embrace of a huge banyan tree. No sign of life, now or ever, except Anne's flower lei fragrant on the warm stone, as if he had wanted to wipe out any trace of his sojourn on earth. Already the ants were crawling over the plumerias.

Lindbergh's lonely grave; Maui, August 26th, 1974

Charles Lindbergh was the symbol of a generation - mine. He had picked his resting place facing east, as he preferred its soft, reflected sunsets to the mayhem in the west. The clouds, gently pink at first, gradually turned dull and gray; dusk gathered in the banyan tree. A shiver ran down my spine as I observed the pitiless approach of night.

* * *

Every so often, but especially when we have something on our minds, Erik and I get into the jeep and set out for the summit of Haleakala, the giant extinct volcano which is really the island of Maui. A few miles from the beach the road begins to rise. When we reach five-thousand feet, about halfway, we out-climb the woods, Eucalyptus first, then Hawaii's own red-flowered Ohia trees. The road strains upward in endless hairpin curves - reddish earth, measly tufts of grass, giant boulders, the occasional glint of a Silversword, not a tree to block the view.

We don't talk. Below us the broad flanks of Haleakala plunge steeply to the valley, ridges and dales that lose themselves in bays and beaches, sun-drenched, and the sea beyond in colors almost unacceptable to stoic Dutchmen. The horizon rises with us, the Pacific Ocean curves around Maui like a blue wall. Wisps of cloud whip around the Eastern mountainside and swallow us; we blindly creep along. When we reappear, high up in the rare atmosphere, the earth has turned to black lava-dust with an occasional tenacious shrub. You can drive to the top, 11.000 feet high, but we park the jeep on the side of the road and walk along a footpath that squeezes around a giant rock and boom! like a sudden blow, there it lies before us, the crater. "Godallbloodymighty," Erik mumbles into the silence.

Three thousand feet below us it stretches silently into the distance, Haleakala, House of the Sun, a black-purple bowl up to ten miles wide in every direction, sand and rock formations with here and there some nondescript vegetation, surrounded by almost vertical walls, the largest crater in the world. A number of volcanic cones with their own sub-craters rise from the bottom in strange colors of rust and magenta, several hundred feet high. Eruptions long ago have breached the crater wall at two locations, from which lava flowed which now stretches into the sea like a broad, frozen river. Through the breeches the trade winds blow, rise skywards against the far walls and suddenly manifest themselves in absolute silence as shreds of cloud that hurl over the edge.

Silence – it is the silence, total and majestic, that dominates the scene and overwhelms us. Against such a display of power our own demons cannot hold their own, and after a few steps down the path I feel a unique sense of peace enter my soul. After clambering down some way into the abyss, we install ourselves on a spot of grass in the shadow of a huge rock with our backs against the lava. Erik digs into his backpack for two cans of beer.

"Do you feel them?" With his eyes closed he pours the cool drink into his gullet. Then he takes a deep breath. "You feel 'em? The ur-powers?"

The effect of his words is somewhat deflected by a long, slow belch. He opens one eye. A pheasant tiptoes blithely out of a bush, gives us a startled look and dashes back where he came from. I sniff the mountain air, feeling light and cheerful and unbelievably alive, a tiny bit drunk perhaps after three swallows of beer.

"You've got to lean in to them," Erik says. "Ur-power charges your batteries, so you can sputter along a while longer."

"Never mind. For what reason did you bring me here?"

He acts innocent. "No reason. Except perhaps here we can talk a little."

I grin. I was cured long ago of giving unsolicited advice, especially to my son. But he has just become a father and that seems to worry him somehow. Perhaps he hopes that the ur-powers will inspire me. "About what?"

"My daughter, Meadow Melelani."

"Well?"

"Well... Suddenly I have a generation below me, I don't know whether I go much for that... Suddenly to be grown up. Brrr!"

"About bloody well time, you know. But being grown up has nothing to do with having children. Or with age or so. You're grown up when you draw a line under all the influences that have formed you, your parents, your heritage, your education, your family, every kind of trauma, the works. Draw the line, take the vow: 'From here on in I take total responsibility for myself.' Once you live up to that vow, you're grown up. Millions of people never make it."

"And then?"

"And then? And then? You want to talk?"

"Why not? It's nice here. Plenty of beer in the ice-bag."

We open two more cans and settle down cozily. "Well, then you start trying to live. It's strictly your business, a matter of reacting right to what happens to you."

He takes a long swig and scratches his head. "But surely, what happens to you does have something to do with it?"

"Of course. Some things that happen to you are pleasant, others unpleasant. The pleasant ones you accept gratefully and you think of them in bad times. The unpleasant ones are challenges. All of them. No more, no less."

"So?"

"Some challenges you win, some you lose. When you win, it makes you feel good and strong so that you're also likely to win the next one. The more you win, the easier it gets. Make a habit of it."

"And if something really terrible happens? I mean, gross?"

"Sometimes all you can do is wait. Give time a chance, it heals quicker than you think. It begins healing as soon as you accept the challenge, accept the reality. So accept it, immediately. By avoiding reality, you waste healing-time. Grab every challenge by the balls, as soon as it whacks you."

"God's truth, I don't know if I even want to be grown up." He hands me another beer and puts the empty one neatly in the backpack. "All those challenges. It gives me the willies."

For a while we don't say anything, drink our beer, perhaps snooze a little. I'm slightly irritated. "Why don't you start by getting a job?" I suggest morosely. "Babies cost money, you know."

This wakes Erik up, but good. "Yeah, yeah, yeah, there we go again. Get a job. Build a career. Make money. Screw your neighbor to get ahead. Pa, I just don't buy your world."

We're on familiar terrain. "OK. But do you really know of something better?"

"Everything is better. I believe in the abundance of life. In humanity, in the basic goodness of every human being."

"Oh boy, are you ever in for some surprises!"

"Dad, if I didn't believe that, I wouldn't even want to live."

So what next? "Well, if you don't dig our world, why don't you DO something about it?" Shades of my grandfather, God rest his soul: If you believe in something, fight for it. Always.

"Dad. I do everything about it. You've just got to begin with yourself. that's all. Be an example of what you believe in, the rest happens automatically. Why? Because the whole world is full of people, not presidents, not generals, not millionaires, but little people, ordinary people, and because ordinary people are basically good."

"Yes, but it's the presidents and the millionaires who have the power."

"For now, but not forever. Ultimately Good defeats Bad, sooner or later. If there's anything I believe, that's it. Because humans are basically good."

Silence. We drink our beer. The sun shines vertically down into the crater, it's getting warm. I like my son. He'll never get rich, but if he cheerfully accepts the consequences of his ideas his chances for happiness are reasonable. But he has also grown up and away from the incense-burning mystic who I once expected to end up with crossed legs on a Himalayan mountaintop. When I asked him the other day if he still practiced yoga, he answered: "Only exercise 9 in that book you once gave me."

I looked it up and read the instruction: "Lie down on your back. Close your eyes. Relax." - How could I not love him?

"So what are you going to do now, since you've become a father?" The air in the crater is starting to rise, quivering with heat. We collect the empty cans, it's time to leave. "I'm serious, you'll have to get a job. Believe me, babies cost money."

He takes a last swallow, chucks the can into the backpack and looks me in the eye, dead serious. "Your problem, Dad, is that you are a dirty capitalist with a Western linear consciousness who lives exclusively in the future and in the past and has absolutely no faith in Providence. Furthermore you're getting bald."

This I don't take. I look for something to throw, but by the time I'm on my feet with a dried horse-turd in my hand I see him in the distance bounding up the trail like an elongated mountain-goat.

$$* * *$$

Next day. The sun, as usual, sparkles over Maui. In the lazy swell off Makena the surfers gleam like otters on their boards, stark naked, as are the fair girls with their white bottoms and the kiddies building sand castles on the beach. Underneath the kiawe trees groups of Caucasian longhairs camp with their naturalfamilies, some for years already, who to the chagrin of the Japanese businessmen in Kahului have pronounced Makena Beach their paradise.

Karin and I are sitting on a blanket in the sand, slightly further down the bend. The picnic is over, we have eaten the chicken and the ribs and the lau-lau, drunk the beer and the chardonnay, and carefully cleared away the residue. Karna frolics somewhere in the sea, as usual, with her first real boyfriend, Chrysanto, a formidable Polynesian with an 'afro'. He plays a mean guitar. Some of his friends are standing at the water-line, studying the surf. Erik and Susie are strolling under the kiawes; Erik is wearing a little harness and when he turns around out pops, some-what forlorn against that endless back, the newest member of our clan, Meadow Melelani.

Gradually the rays of the sun reach diagonally across the bay. The islands Lanai and Kaho'olawe, sketched lightly on the horizon, suddenly gain in color and substance. A cool breeze rises, Karin and I cuddle clos-er together. Chrysanto and Karna, out on the dry, follow our example. He has grabbed his guitar, the chords glide smoothly around his husky voice. Karna smiles, proudly. The other boys, boards under their arms, walk out to catch a last wave or two. When Erik walks by he kneels next to me, his back with baby turned my way.

"Here Dad, can you hang on to her for a while?"

I take her over. "Hallo, Heavenly Song."

With my granddaughter on my lap I gaze around me, conscious of the fact that these are among the first impressions of her life, the earliest unconscious memories - the quiet beach, sea breezes and the scent of plumeria, Chrysanto's guitar, his voice against the whisper of the surf, blue ocean, white spume.

For a few moments I follow Erik standing on the backlit, sapphire crest of a wave, like a charcoal scrawl against the fiery sun disk, until he plunges down the slope, closely pursued by the hissing foam.

Then I become conscious of the fact that Meadow is staring at me with the brazen, steely look of babies. I read her mind without effort, flawlessly: "Well, it's you again. I've seen you before. How do you fit into my world, I wonder?"

Damned if I know, Heavenly Song, but somehow I'm a part of it.

CHAPTER 25

Hawaii No Ka Oi

MGB 320 slowly advanced on the Dutch coast near Scheveningen. An offshore breeze had flattened the sea, surf would be no problem.

Chris Krediet and Peter Tazelaar huddled on the foredeck, Bob Goodfellow and I watched from the little bridge. Even Colonel Rabagliatti had come along for this trip. Everything seemed normal, a confident repeat of many previous crossings, except that it was daylight, the sun was shining bright and we were all thirty years older.

AVRO, the largest Dutch television station, had embarked on a documentary mini-series of Soldier of Orange, and contrary to past experience we roared across the North Sea in perfect summer weather in the 320, which Her Majesty's Royal Navy had put at our disposal, in a fine new coat of paint. The beach, cold and hostile in our memories, stretched along the boulevard as a riot of color, flags, umbrellas and people. Only the old promenade pier that used to run from the Kurhaus far out to sea, was missing; on one of our escapades we had scraped past it and the Germans had blown it up.

Downstairs in the little cabin Colonel Rabagliatti, celebrating his first actual crossing in an MGB, hosted a small party - Plymouth gin, of course - for some other members of our group including Midshipman Dogger, who had been arrested with Peter on the boulevard one icy night in 1942, my old navigator Ben Vlielander Hein, who had just played his part in the RAF segment of the documentary, and our special guest, Karin. They were shortly joined by Tazelaar, who requested his straight gin in a water glass to make up for lost time.

None of this illustrious complement of World War II veterans had done well in peacetime. Chris had worked for KLM, but one day the president of the airline asked him for suggestions to improve the company. "Sir," my former sidekick answered true to form. "First of all you should resign." This cost him his job and now he was looking for a new one. Peter, who had gone through a number of short-lived positions, including - at my recommendation - a stint with U.S. Air Force Intelligence under Captain Al Charak, now found himself in the same predicament. Ben Hein's shipyard had hit the rocks, so he too was stranded. The same could be said of 390Gerard Dogger, who had taken up landscape painting. Rabagliatti, after heading the British Dollar Council in San Francisco, had resigned in frustration and retired to the South of France. And I, well, you know the story. Could it be coincidence that my onetime housemate, Paul Erdman, who stuck to his studies and ignored the war, had recently been elevated to Justice of the Court of Appeals in The Hague, as was his goal from the beginning?

Still, thanks to Queen Wilhelmina we didn't need to worry. In the middle of the war she had decreed that Resistance Fighters who were not covered by military provisions, would be eligible for special pensions from a new foundation for which the funds were allocated there and then, and have been growing ever since. Everybody in Holland, male and female, who fought the Germans in any capacity during World War II, is generously taken care of. Patriotism in the Netherlands is a two-way street.

The mini-series became a smashing success and the AVRO treated us to a sumptuous dinner, from Hors d'Oeuvre Contact Holland to Parfait St. Cergue. As usual I had a great time. Every trip to my old fatherland was an event these days, with interviews, parties, TV appearances and celebrations, anything we could want for action and entertainment. Then why was I always eager to get away?

Once again it has to do with pigeonholes, bane of my youth, and in Holland the one for age is iron clad. As a bona fide relic of World War II with Soldier of Orange as my certificate of authenticity, there is no escape. I feel automatically relegated to the past, a crumb of history to be doled out to ignorant school children, rattling towards my old age along a single, predestined small-gauge track.

In Hawaii we cannot categorize each other. Our backgrounds are like a closed book, our histories hide inscrutably in the furthest corners of the world. No artificial hurdles block our relations with our fellow men, no social grid, no pigeonholes. We move in all directions, no rails irrespective of age, the sky's the limit. You are free to play the game, any game, until you drop dead.

When early in the morning I drive our pickup to the harbor to collect a chair for Karin, interior designer, I get a friendly hello from Tatsuo, the freight clerk, who thinks to himself, "That truck driver is at it early this morning."

An hour later I give a lecture at Community College. The students address me as 'professor', because I know a little more about international affairs than they. Lunch usually takes place in the French bistro, where I am known as the journalist who can tell a Bordeaux from a Burgundy (mostly).

In the afternoon Karin needs the truck, young Erik has swiped the Honda, so I hitchhike to the beach. The tourist who picks me up says to his wife, "Let's give this hippie a ride."

I dive into the ocean, and a worker up an electric pole ashore sees me floating majestically off the coast and thinks, "Wish I, too, were a millionaire, with nothing to do all day."

Stay healthy, and in Hawaii it pays to stay alive.

* * *

As far as Maui is concerned, we miscalculated in one respect. If you belong to the millions who recently spent a vacation there, you know what I am talking about. No spot as perfect can escape the hot breath of our Western civilization.

One day we awoke and from an innocent sliver of lava, Maui had become the Pearl of the Pacific. Land prices had quadrupled, tourism risen 300 percent.

The friendly little airport in the sugarcane had been rebuilt to accommodate direct flights from San Francisco, Los Angeles and Tokyo on its grid of runways. Four-lane highways had appeared, busses rolled all the way to the top of Haleakala, supermarkets and shopping malls had taken the place of Ah Fook's. Along lonely beaches apartment buildings arose, ten stories high, with swimming pools, mini-golf, the works; here and there it became difficult to see the ocean. Makena, the paradise of the longhairs, had been sold to a company in Japan, to be developed as a resort; the naked surfers and their girls with the white bottoms had long gone. Along the coast near Kihei still curled the world's fastest left-breaking surf, but over the dusty parallel road thundered trucks and bulldozers and asphalt spreaders. Maui, opulent, luxurious and still gorgeous, had lost its soul. - We had one more move to make.

Across the Alenuihaha channel, barely twenty miles away, the formidable island of Hawaii arose against the southeastern sky. Millions of centuries ago a geological hotspot on the bottom of the ocean started to ooze lava, which slowly built up to an underwater mountain. After 18,000 feet its summit finally broke the surface of the sea. It did not stop there and grew another 14,000 feet which made it the tallest - not highest - mountain in the world, 32,000 feet from base to top. From Maui in clear weather we could sometimes admire the snowy crest that the Hawaiians have christened Mauna Kea, the White Mountain, equally high as its French namesake, Mount Blanc. Together with its giant sister mountain, Mauna Loa, it has created the island of Hawaii, the "Big Island", twice as large as all the other islands of the state Hawaii combined, and still growing.

This is the downward connection. Upwards, it's great height, pure atmosphere and above all the absence of light- pollution in the middle of the ocean, have made the mountaintop the best place in the world from which to observe stars. Astronomers from near and far have assembled on the Big Island - from the American mainland, Canada, England, France, Japan, Holland and the University of Hawaii - and built a powerful group of observatories. Night after night they penetrate into the corners of the universe, and from here mankind has reached the most distant star ever observed, five billion light-years away. Its image, by penetrating the crown of Mauna Kea, is in touch with the hotspot at its base on the floor of the ocean. This magical connection from the core of the earth to the farthest star is the Big Island.

All this has little to do with science and astronomy, of course, but it is the most acceptable explanation for the indisputable enchantment of this mysterious speck of earth, an island in the most remote archipelago on the globe with a multi- racial population of barely a hundred thousand who would not want to live anywhere else. Even in the state of Hawaii it is being looked at askance, a vague domain of snowy mountains, impenetrable valleys, fiery craters, misty rain forests, black beaches, and lava fields so rugged that they were selected as training-grounds for the moon landings. All this inhabited - apart from a handful of clearly mortal farmers and cowboys, artists and astronomers - by the pantheon of Polynesian gods and goddesses, from the all-powerful Madam Pele, goddess of volcanoes, to the respected heroes and half-gods who are seen to walk into the sea as men and proceed from there as sharks, or can turn themselves into a white dog at will. As a native of Surabaya this does not unduly startle me.

Hawaiians treat the Big Island with respect, as if behind its obvious beauty lurks another dimension that has to be approached with caution. A two-hour drive leads from mild, tropical beaches to icy heights where the wind whistles across snowfields. Lehua and orchids bloom around craters whose fiery lava flows hissing and growling into the protesting ocean. The volcanoes have not claimed a human casualty for decades, but the island trembles with suppressed energy. The number of seismographically measurable tremors surpasses three hundred per day, and from time to time one hits with a force of 7 on the Richter scale, leaving us shaking with impotent fear. Raw creation takes place all around, but in the night sky above your head glitter worlds that ceased to exist eons ago.

A small strip of hotels along beaches on the west coast takes care of the tourists. For the rest, Hawaii is out of civilizations' way.

We moved from Maui to the Big Island and built another house, 3000 feet high among tree fern and ohia forests, with snowcapped Mauna Kea as a backdrop and distant peeks of ocean. We call it "Cloud Cuckooland", after old Aristophanes' mythical state, not quite serious, where birdbrains rule the roost and all problems are solved in simple, unexpected ways. Here Karin and I reside in the rugged splendor of nature, close to a trail where spirits of ancient Hawaiians, respectfully called the Night-walkers, silently shuffle by on moonless nights. But by then Karin and I are long since in bed, cozy and comfortable, and wish them well on their murky mission.

We abide by the three conditions for successful island life: 1) come with a mate who satisfies you in every respect, physically, spiritually and intellectually; 2) work creatively, both of you, like designing homes and banging the word processor; 3) be rich or inventive enough to get away once a year for at least a month. Add lots of love, and pretty soon who cares about the rest of the world?

If it weren't for Holland.

* * *

The word was out - Rob Houwer was going to produce the biggest movie in Dutch history, to be directed by Paul Verhoeven. Its title?

Soldier of Orange. After the first excitement I found many things to worry about.

Houwer invited me to work on the film as a writer and consultant. It was tempting, a way to keep a finger in the pie and assure maximum accuracy in the story presentation. However, my experience at NBC had taught me that this is a fallacy. Book and movie are two different creatures; a faithful transcript makes for a dull film. Plots have to be simplified, characters built up or eliminated, conflicts accentuated and honed for effect, all the necessary steps that drive the author into a frenzy and guarantees trouble on the set. The best policy is to give him a bonus and send him on a long trip to, let's say, Hawaii, until the movie is finished.

My case presented an additional problem. Soldier of Orange is a true story, as accurate as humanly possible, and I stand behind every fact in the book. Nobody, as far as I know, ever attacked its veracity. Knowing that making a film would require changes, how then could I ever involve myself? You can't stand behind two sets of different facts. I declined Houwer's offer and consequently take no credit whatever for the film's superior qualities.

With one exception. The director, Paul Verhoeven, who later became an outstanding success in Hollywood with films like Robocop and Basic Instinct, was a Leidener like myself - he holds a master's degree in mathematics - which eminently qualified him in all areas of the project, save one. His style was highly individualistic. He would come onto the set at the start of day, quickly read through the script, cross everything out, make a few notes and start creating out of his own brilliance. I was usually around and enjoyed myself hugely. One morning we were discussing Wilhelmina, and he said, "Ah yes, that's the scene where she makes a bow at you guys," and he went down like a waiter after a hundred dollar tip.

"Paul," I protested, laughing. "Wilhelmina does not bow like that, she bows like this," and I moved my upper body forward slightly, straight-backed from the hips.

"How would I know?" he countered. "I was about six when she left for England." Because of his youth, he had never seen her in reality, and the same was true of everyone else who worked on the movie, except me. Then and there the director appointed me coach for Andrea Domburg, the actress who played the Queen.

On the night of the première, when finally the lights came on again, I asked Queen Juliana about Andrea's performance. She shook her head, pensively. "Remarkable," she answered, "It was uncanny. Often I thought, heavens, that's just like Mother."

Another of my worries, not unnaturally, concerned the question of who was going to play me. After all, if the film was successful in a small country like the Netherlands, we would be lumped together forever in the public eye. I could see years of emotional involvement ahead, with pitfalls and land mines, probably leading to a distressing relationship that would haunt our lives. So when I first heard his name, I could hardly believe my ears.

Rutger Hauer, one of Holland's up and coming actors, had just scored a notable success in a film called Turkish Delight, which even in France raised eyebrows with its explicit sex scenes.

Backed by the same producer and director, he had created an international stir based not purely on art alone. Being fairly innocent in this respect, especially by Dutch standards, I feared the worst. Was I to be represented by a porno star? One whose stage name, by sheer coincidence, had been "Erik" in the first movie and now would be "Erik" again, even further entwining me in the mesh of sleaze? Karin and I, just in from Hawaii and battling the usual twelve hour time lag, were still asleep when the phone rang in our Scheveningen hotel room. Hauer was on the line. I knew exactly what he looked like, both with and without clothes.

"Oh.. eh.. this is Rutger," someone stammered. "Are you Erik?" Pretty fresh, I thought, as this was well before I had witnessed him meeting Princess Beatrix for the first time and treating her like his little sister.

"Let's have lunch," I countered. "That new little French place behind the boulevard. One o'clock. OK?"

I must admit, he was big, blond and beautiful, although nothing compared to later, when many years of worldwide success had strengthened his confidence and gravitas. Now he struck me as awkward and unpredictable, with a hungry aura - not just as an actor - and we spent the better part of the afternoon devouring lobsters, sweetbreads, cheeses and several bottles of wine. We circled each other carefully, getting along fine, but he

Rutger Hauer, always the Soldier of Orange

was cagey, as if protecting a vulnerable and very private nature from a generally distasteful universe. Even then he displayed the intense aversion to phoniness and bullshit that affected his entire life, both privately and in his choice of professional output. What stole my heart, predictably, was his eagerness for the title role in Soldier for which - as he later confided - he received a mere pittance. It served him well, though, opening the door to Hollywood and a splendid career with over sixty films.

The producer, Rob Houwer, undoubtedly underpaid him through sheer necessity. A super-intelligent man, with all the advantages and disadvantages thereof, he considered nothing out of his range and had the guts to plunge spectacularly into shaky projects, confident that he could guide them to a successful conclusion - and he usually did. As it was, the production budget of the most expensive film ever made in the Netherlands did not exceed two million dollars, less than Robert Redford's pay for his short role in A Bridge Too Far, which had just been shot around Arnhem at the time. Even this amount of money was hard to come by in Holland, where movies did not rate as proper ventures for serious investors. The tight budget led to acrimonious clashes between the producer and his ambitious director, Paul Verhoeven. Paul may have become a success in Hollywood, but he got there on the strength of an under-financed Dutch film, which Newsweek described as"a superb war epic." Several other actors, like Jeroen Krabbé and Derek de Lint, also jumped on the Orange bandwagon and successfully made the transition to American television.

Rob Houwer approached his new venture with typical bravura. He solved his financial problems by the unique stratagem of involving everyone in Holland, public and private, from the Queen on down, in "Netherlands' National Motion Picture" - at no cost. The army supplied soldiers, the navy ships, bombing raids were flown in AT6's by private aero-clubs, even the same streetcar that had scraped by me that spooky night in 1942 when I was looking for a telephone, line 9, rode again around the square in Scheveningen, compliments of local Public Transportation.

The American filmmakers, finished with A Bridge Too Far, pitched in by lending us authentic WW2 heavy equipment like tanks and troop carriers. The ultimate Pathfinder, Group Captain Hamish Mahaddie DSO. DFC. AFC. DFM., after raising the largest private air force in the world for the film Battle of Britain, supplied us with Mosquitos and an antique DC3 for Wilhelmina's return scenes, if not for free - after all, he was a Scot - at least at cost. Shrunk, in civvies, a bowler hat pressed firmly down on his white curls, oozing humor and charm, he looked like a sly leprechaun. And finally, thousands upon thousands of unpaid extras filled the streets to welcome the Queen home - in a Packard, with an unexplained RAF officer on the rear seat - many of them once again in tears as they waved flags and threw flowers at Andrea Domburg, with Rutger Hauer in the back.

A book about yourself may build you up, a film will blow you away. Rutger, surpassing all expectations, had entered into my personality to a remarkable degree. For eight weeks I followed him through scenes of my youth, all on authentic location, our house in Wassenaar, the beach at Scheveningen, my student digs in Leiden, places where Rutger - the personification of the prewar Leidener asif he had never heard of Turkish Delight - appeared to feel totally at ease. To make things even stranger for me, he was always addressed on the set by his film moniker, Erik, as is usual, and after a few days I didn't even react when someone called my name. Another Erik was in the process of capturing reality, the old one faded steadily further into the vague domains of myth.

On the last day Verhoeven shot the final scenes in my old room on the Rapenburg, opposite the same, never changing university building. The camera whirred, I stood in a dark corner looking on, like an incarnation of the past, a ghost. Rutger excelled that afternoon, other actors reminded me of long lost friends - Aad Robertson, blown up in Russia; Jean Mesritz, perished in Germany; Paul, and Chris, others, gone out of my life, rarely recalled, oh! shades of Leiden - and suddenly in that crooked little room, so familiar, so full of memories, it wasn't Rutger Hauer anymore who stood there talking, gaily waving the sherry bottle... it was I, myself. And when the spotlights flicked out and I came forward to compliment Hauer on his fine performance, I saw in his eyes, too, a moment of doubt, ever so fleeting: Who are you? What are you doing here? - As if in that house, in Holland, in the world, there was no room for two Soldiers of Orange.

Suddenly it's a year later, the day of the première. Rutger and I, grown together by our joint experience like son and father, are standing alone on the brightly lit stage of the opulent Tuschinski theater in Amsterdam. The film has been publicly viewed for the first time, not always easy for me, being portrayed naked here and there making love to my first wife, in front of my present one, my mother, my daughter, the Queen, Princess Beatrix and her sisters, the Cabinet, the Chiefs-of-Staff and everyone else in that monstrous movie house.

All in all I'm satisfied. The first time I saw the film in preview, I frankly despaired. Verhoeven had created a masterpiece of action and mood, but to a secret service agent and Pathfinder pilot, the inaccuracies, the twisted details, the changed pace of events - it took Contact Holland seven failures before reaching the Dutch coast, in the movie off we go and bingo! - made me sweat with apprehension. But the film is being well received by an audience apparently low on secret agents and Mosquito pilots, and even I myself have become less critical. I face the audience with aplomb.

December 22nd, 1977, Film Premiere – Karin, Erik, 'Moesje,' Karna

Rows and rows of people, shoulder to shoulder, stretch away from us into the gloom. I can just see the royal box on the first balcony where Queen Juliana is sitting with Prince Bernhard and Princess Beatrix, who, like her mother, shielded her eyes during the torture scenes. For the rest the area is a sea of faces,anonymous in the dusk, my past and my present, and I know that even Waimea, our hometown on the Big Island, is represented here tonight. The stalls are getting up, then the orchestra, a standing ovation - not for us two, but for those who have been portrayed, a handful of ordinary Hollanders, symbols of the thousands who have done their best in World War II for their little country on the North Sea.

Rutger and I look at each other. He puts an arm around my shoulder. It is a touching, protective gesture, and I, perhaps better than he himself, know what it means: He tries to keep me in the focal point, while the reality of the leading character is slipping away from me to him. Impossible; for anyone who has seen the movie, Rutger Hauer will forever be the real Soldier of Orange. That's fine with me. My tale is meant to be the torch that illuminates a sliver of Dutch history. Rutger has taken hold of it and carries it high.

It would be great if I could report that the Dutch production in its American version surprised Hollywood and won an Oscar. It didn't, but only missed by a hair. It was nominated in the Foreign Film category and insiders reported that the final vote went between Soldaat van Oranje and Cage aux Folles, an amusing French comedy about gays. The Telegraaf of Amsterdam described this contest as "the battle between the heroes and the homos". The homos won, but Soldier of Orange captured the Los Angeles Film Critics Award for Best Foreign film of 1977.

* * *

Beware of memories, know them for what they are. Facts you recall with your mind, emotions with your heart. The former will recreate the face of the girl next door thirty years ago, a recollection; the latter how she made you feel, a memory. As you get old and start basing your life on the past, the distinction becomes ever more crucial. Mix them up, and you're in the soup.

What you believe to be memories of your youth, make you homesick, luring you back to your town or land of origin. When you arrive, all physical elements, the recollections, are still in place; what made them memories, your youth, is gone forever. If you are wise, you return to the present, wherever that may be. It's the only true home you have left.

In our early years on Hawaii, almost the antipode of the Netherlands, eleven time zones away, my life of contentment was often marred by homesickness. Recognizing its danger, I also suspected its fallacy. Testing it out in many trips to the old country, I found that our fun and satisfaction was based not on the past, on visits to former haunts, on reunions with one-time buddies, but on new ventures, new experiences, even new and invariably younger friends. Holland also has a present, full of marvelous opportunities and surprises and people, of which Karin and I took full advantage as often as we could afford two plane tickets. It seemed just the right relationship with the Dutch in my ménage à trois of nationalities. But even after the movie, the première, the media hoopla and the fact that Soldier of Orange was shown by Netherlands TV on

Liberation Day, May 5th, every year since - each time the wheels of our United Airlines DC-10 touched down on the compressed lava runway at Kona Airport, the squeal said "welcome home!"

On the American side, relationships also improved. At last the Vietnam War had run its disastrous course and the USA could lick its wounds and mend its fissures. The Watergate circus had made the most of its tawdry felonies and got rid of President Nixon, whose popularity promptly began rising to previously unattainable levels. Mostly, the mood changed, to an extent that Karin and I spent some delightful weeks touring the mainland. Yet again, when we settled back into our nest on the slopes of Mauna Kea, the world outside faded into insignificance. My life had achieved a delicate balance, with Hawaii as its base.

The Dutch have a proverb that states, "Blood crawls where it cannot go". The next event, which pulled me back even further into Holland's sphere, enveloped us three years later like a fairytale. Juliana announced her imminent abdication - which is the considerate custom of aging rulers in the Netherlands -, Princess Beatrix would shortly take over as Queen, and now she invited me to be her King of Arms for the Inauguration. I just wondered whether that evening at Lindy's on Times Square had anything to do with it.

Frankly, I had never heard of a King of Arms. It carried echoes of King for a Day, but Kramer's dictionary flatly called it a "herald". However, the Winkler Prins Encyclopedia was somewhat more encouraging. Its romantic explanation, which of course I promptly adopted, describes his medieval role as the protector of the designated but not yet anointed new king who, once crowned, will be King by the Grace of God and relatively safe by contemporary standards. Prior to this, however, in the interim period, he is fair game for all the other pretenders who feel they should be in his place and have till coronation day to get rid of him, one way or another. This the King of Arms has to prevent, at the peril of his own neck. That in my case the king was a queen, the queen was Beatrix, and most emphatically that times and mores had mellowed, all fanned my enthusiasm for the assignment.

We flew to Holland, where Karin volunteered to keep my 87-year old mother company and view the event on television at her apartment. As things turned out, they saw a very different inauguration from the one I attended. Amsterdam, always a rowdy town, was in a sour mood because of housing problems and some lingering resentment against Beatrix' husband, Prins Claus, who had the misfortune of being German by birth. As both previous queens, Wilhelmina and Juliana, had married Germans, one of which was the universally popular Prince Bernhard, it all seemed rather farfetched. Compared to other cities, the riots in Amsterdam were a social outing, but they produced lots of smoke and one injured policeman, and mesmerized the unspoiled Dutch TV crews.

In the Royal Palace on the Dam, however, where on April 30, 1980, the functionaries of the occasion gathered around the future queen and her entourage, everything was pomp, circumstance and Old Home Week. A batch of friends greeted me when I stepped in from faraway Hawaii, all of them looking splendid in dress uniforms with ribbons and gongs and decorations, colorful sashes, ceremonial swords and big smiles on their faces. Many I recognized from long ago - Robert van Zinnicq Bergmann, the Typhoon pilot who had taken over from me as ADC to Queen Wilhelmina, still in function as Aide to Queen Juliana; Freek Bischoff van Heemskerck, whom Peik and I got arrested in the Gräfin's yellow Volkswagen; the Commanding General of the Netherlands Air Force, who trained under me as a sergeant in Canada; army and navy officers, and even marines with whom I got along fine these days.

Meanwhile outside, the royalty of the world, preceding 2000 invited guests, strolled down the Mozes-and-Aäron Street to the main entrance of the New Church - in fact, of course, a very old church - where the ceremony was to take place. When all were seated, including the departing Queen Juliana who held hands with Prince Bernhard throughout the proceedings, our little group from the palace, escorting the designated new Queen and her husband, entered the church behind the Kings of Arms; there were two, in typical Dutch fashion. Beatrix, warm in a full length ermine trimmed cloak that had been worn by her ancestors at inaugurations for almost two centuries, glowed with health and anticipation. She mounted a throne on the podium with her court behind her, the Kings of Arms took up their position in front, to shield her from possible mayhem. I wore a rented morning coat loaded with full-size decorations and carried a red and gold staff, presumably to fend off the disgruntled pretenders. Before me stood the velvet-covered table bearing the Sword and Apple of State, the Scepter and the Crown. Straight from the Big Island I had plunged back into the heart of my ancient nation.

As I was three months older than the other King of Arms, an Underground Fighter named Liepke Scheepstra, mine became the honor of announcing to the world, in the church and via Eurovision to an estimated 200-million viewers, that a young queen had assumed the reign of

Holland. First the members of both Chambers of Parliament, assembled in the front rows, had to swear allegiance to their new sovereign. This took so long that my thoughts wandered to little Beatrix, seven years old, whom I had accompanied back to Holland from exile in 1945, and her warning to her sister Irene, even smaller, not to throw a candy wrapper out of a window of the old Dakota. "We're over Holland now. Stop making a mess." She would make one hell of a queen.

I smiled remembering, and suddenly noticed that you could have heard a pin drop in the huge hall. They were waiting for something - for me! Calling out loud and clear in the middle of a smile is not easy, but somehow I managed: "The Queen is inaugurated! Long live the Queen!"

$$* * *$$

As time went by, my involvement with the Netherlands grew with our advancing years. Hawaii continued to be our home, but my actual and emotional point of gravity shifted from the USA farther and farther back across the Atlantic. In this I wasn't alone - Karin's love of nature and its elements brought her into close contact with Princess Irene, one of Holland's most spiritual naturalists. They became friends, and together with my longtime ties to her father and the above coronation of her sister, our bonds with the Dutch Royal Family grew steadily closer.

Whenever a phone call wakes us up around six in the morning - cocktail time in Holland, when he likes to drink a glass of pink champagne - we know what's coming: "This is Palace Soestdijk. I'll connect you with Prince Bernhard." One day, snuggled up closely to Karin in the chilly dawn, I had hardly said hello when he unfolded a plan to come over and stay with us for a week. Would that be convenient?

One of the dangers of living in Hawaii is house guests.

Everybody wants to visit paradise. However, it's a long way from Holland, and distance works like a strainer: the greater the distance, the finer the mesh. But could we handle royalty? A whole week?

After sincerely assuring the prince of his welcome, we jumped out of our enormous bed and slipped into robes. Karin disappeared into the kitchen, and when she got back with some ripe papayas and a pot of herb tea, I had a crackling wood fire going in the bedroom fireplace. The occasion called for a pre- dawn meeting of the minds.

The problem, of course, was that hosting royalty takes money, lots of it, because you want everything to be the best, to which they are accustomed without any notion of expense. Prince Bernhard generally stayed in regal mansions, while Cloud Cuckooland can only be described as a modest home in the forest of a backward island with nothing but ocean all around. The lines were drawn almost immediately when a few days later his aide-de-camp sent us a list of all the foods and wines that our imminent guest enjoyed most. I faxed back that half the items on the roster were unavailable in Hawaii and the other half we could not afford, so His Royal Highness just had to take potluck with us.

This turned out to be exactly what he had in mind. As a typical Dutchman, he came over to see where and how his friends lived. When as his very first dinner Karin served Indonesian nasi goreng - his favorite dish, not on the list - he finished it to the last grain and then, having solemnly asked his hostess' permission, licked his plate clean. The following morning he helped me take out the garbage to the dump.

The prince arrived with his usual guard, a quiet secret service man who started out covering all bases. The Netherlands Ambassador in Washington had instructed me to make the necessary security arrangements, but I informed the Chief of Police that we needed nothing. He insisted on alerting at least the office in charge of our local station, a brawny Portuguese, who called me a few minutes later. "Erik!" he bellowed excitedly. "This new friends of yours, Bernhard Prince, he's a pretty big fish, eh?" The Dutch guard we put up with a Hawaiian widow down the road, and that's about the last we saw of him.

Cloud Cuckooland – Erik, Karin, Prince Bernhard

To give Bernhard the best of times, worthy of our island, we mobilized the entire community. The Benz agency lent us a big Mercedes for a week, free of charge. A total stranger took us on a morning's sightseeing flight in his private plane, an open three-seater, on condition that we have lunch at his home. HPA, the local prep school, invited us for an afternoon's sail, during which a large whale surfaced slowly close to starboard, coal-black against the last, fiery speck of the setting sun. Very much appreciated, specially by our guest, was a case of the prince's favorite pink champagne, Pommery & Cremo. For the farewell party, presented by ourselves and Big Island Mayor Herb Matayoshi, we borrowed the beach residence of people we hardly knew. All meals in hotels and restaurants were on the house - a royal prince has substantial PR value - except for one super snooty place. When Bernhard saw me inspect the astronomical bill he asked, "What's he matter? You've got to pay?"

I nodded, sour-faced."Well," he grinned, shrugging his shoulders, "you win a few, you lose few."

Even the Gods cooperated. Of the hundreds of measurable earthquakes each day, most are not noticeable, but a few are, very much. Sometimes you hear them come rattling down the road, others hit the house like Mohammed Ali's right hook, followed by severe shuddering and shaking for ten, fifteen seconds or more. To withstand this ordeal structures are built of wood and stand loose on concrete blocks, four feet off the ground, all but eliminating the danger of collapse. Even so, it is a frightening experience of complete helplessness in the clutch of dizzying primeval forces. It often precedes volcanic outbursts, and in the night before the airplane ride we got a whopper.

The next morning Prince Bernhard, our pilot and I were purring over the eastern slopes of Mauna Loa, the Long Mountain, Mauna Kea's lively sister mountain, basking in brilliant weather, when I smelled smoke in the air.

"Probably pot," the prince volunteered, knowledgeably.

At that moment we saw two columns of molten lava, light orange even in the bright sunshine, spouting right out of the grassy terrain below to an altitude of about 500 feet. As they were well separated we flew between them, and when the pilot throttled back we could hear the roar of the flaming fountains. It proved to be the first stage of an eruption that built a new mountain, Pu'u O'o, whose glare, now a good twenty years later, is still visible at night from time to time, as the rivers of red hot lava flow towards their tumultuous meeting with the ocean.

I trust it convinced Bernhard of my exceptional connection with Madame Pele, Goddess of Volcanoes, with whom - I assured him - I had specially arranged the fireworks in his honor.

Another occasion occurred on which we impressed the prince with our occult acumen. No slouch himself on the subject of mythical powers, he kept a tiny jeweled elephant by his bedside, given him by some foreign potentate, probably female, on condition that every Thursday it be presented with a white rose. One afternoon on returning from Volcano National Park, Karin realized what day it was and telephoned a friend, Betty Nakashima, who owns a flower nursery near Honokaa on the way to Cloud Cuckooland. Driving along the highway through the cane fields, we reduced speed at a certain milestone and stopped. Bernhard, thoroughly puzzled, turned down the window as he saw a fairy appear from the sugar cane, a delicate little figure exquisitely dressed in a pink mu'umu'u, with a flower in her hand.

"Here," said Betty, offering the prince the white rose.

"For your elephant. It's Thursday."

The end came all too soon. At the farewell party close to a hundred guests of every shade, shape, race and age congregated in the garden of the residence we had borrowed, right along the beach with a sunset view. From there we would drive directly to Kona airport. When the time came to part, a local kahuna blessed Prince Bernhard and wished him a safe journey, a speedy return and aloha. We made a large circle around the music and the hula girls, all held hands and sang "Aloha Oe". At just the right moment the sun sank below the horizon, and not an eye was dry. The prince, up to his chin in a lei of ilima flowers - orange, which also happens to be the Hawaiian royal color - turned to Karin and said glumly, "I don't really want to leave, but I know 'aloha' means Goodbye."

"More than that, Bernhard. It means Love," Karin answered, and kissed him on his nose.

* * *

Shortly after these events I returned to the fold and re-emigrated in the other direction. By Royal Decree No. 90.004795, dated 26 February 1990, Queen Beatrix granted my request for Netherlands citizenship. Accompanied by the Dutch consul in Hawaii I promptly reported to the Head of the United States Immigration and Naturalization Service in Honolulu, Mr. Douglas Radcliffe, and inquired about the political consequences of my move as far as the American authorities were concerned. He informed me that there were none. "If you show us your Dutch passport, we'll treat it as a travel document," he said, smiling, and slapped me on the back.

And then added, with more charm than I'm used to from immigration officials, "We don't let go of a good man that easily."

I am enchanted. The two countries that I love have both accepted me - in America I am an American, in Holland I am a Hollander. The ménage à trois can continue on a perfectly balanced basis.

Another problem, solved in a simple, unexpected way. Aristophanes clearly knew what he was writing about.

CHAPTER 26

Grande Finale

Relax everybody, the razzmatazz is over. With the stage set and the players in place my life is heading for its inevitable grande finale. The signs point to a happy ending, but the playwright is notoriously unpredictable. Let me tell you about the last act, and confidently leave the dénouement to the director.

We look back on the story of the 20th century, and my own. For both of us it mirrors the tail end of the Big Bang theory, an explosive beginning followed by lots of confusion and a long period of putting things together again. History still has a way to go - we hope - but my final days boil down to a simple love story in the implausible setting of a tropical paradise.

I have long since discovered that under Karin's lovely looks flourish the warm heart and generous spirit of a regular girl from Manhattan, with her share of human frailties, while in me she has awakened a social conscience, love of nature and, not always my strongest point, humility. Hawaii? Well, geologically it may be the most isolated archipelago on Earth, one glance at the globe will convince you that it's clearly the center of the world. Paradise, but the telephones work.

The key to our bliss is a discovery we jointly made over martinis in the Georgetown Hotel, Washington, D.C., on our honeymoon. "You know," Karin said, with tears in her eyes. "I have decided to dedicate my life to making you happy."

I was totally overwhelmed. Nobody had ever exposed herself to me like that, absolutely serious, completely reckless.

My reaction was instantaneous and reciprocal, and for thirty-nine years it has been our guiding principle. When you love somebody - or something - more than yourself, your entire life straightens out. It's like discovering magnetic north, after which every point of the compass falls into its place, showing you the way. For this, you don't even have to live in paradise.

Paradise? Of course Hawaii knows many of the same problems as other human communities, but generally they are solved peacefully, friendly and with a sense of humor. The leading concept is 'aloha', the slightly overworked expression for all degrees of emotional warmth, from love to comradeship, from hallo to goodbye. It is supported by a unique society.

As the ultimate melting pot of the world we only use first names, because we can neither pronounce nor remember each other's last (except the dentist's, Dr Au). This creates a family feeling of intimacy and informality. Racially all but perfectly integrated, we are the only state in the Union sufficiently relaxed to tell ethnic jokes about each other on television, unless you're a malahini (newcomer). Since our backgrounds are untraceable, mutual trust has survived as an essential element of society. And last but not least, money can not buy social acceptance. Envy - that national blemish on the Dutch character - does not mix with aloha. Nobody keeps up with the Jones's, thus forcing wealthy newcomers into gated ghettos until they learn to respect the aloha spirit. Some never do and spend the rest of their days impressing each other.

Our house, Cloud Cuckooland, stands in the fringe of a rain forest. The lanai overlooks a shady gully, which attracts all kind of exotic birds. Red Cardinals and a rare Hawaiian I'iwi flash through the foliage like winged flowers, blue-necked Himalayan pheasants cackle in the underbrush and flocks of wild turkeys, tame as pets, take to the air like prehistoric monsters when our miniature Chihuahua, Lulu, feels the need to throw her 1 pound weight around. If you believe in Nature as an intrinsic part of Heaven, it's a good place to age, because sometimes you imagine yourself already halfway there.

Meanwhile our children have left home, but our very existence continues to fulfill an obligation towards them and their contemporaries. They don't know it, but we give them a sense of security. We die, and suddenly they find themselves in the front-line, vulnerable and shaken: We are gone, so they are next.

Young people have not the slightest idea of age. They consider life a lost cause after forty, and anybody over sixty a threat to the nation.

Frankly, I like my eighties just as well as my thirties and forties, different kinds of fun but no less enjoyable: a house full of flowers, a swim in the ocean, breakfast on the lanai, a dozen roses for or from Karin, a John le Carré book, Eurocup soccer on television, a beer with a neighbor, candlelight dinners for two, an occasional siesta with a wood fire in the bedroom and a noggin of Glenfiddich and a touch of Calèche in all the right places... Our friends, mostly around forty, approach the half century mark as if it were the guillotine. Until they see Karin and me, not just coping, but loving life and each other. Yes, Virginia, there is life after eighty.

This is as close as I'll come to lifting the veil. Love and happiness between two people are based on endless intimacies of the spirit, the mind and the body, which cease to be intimate once disclosed. While I fully meant to write more about my life with Karin, the all-embracing joy and enchantment, fun and comradeship of our days and nights together, I have shied away from it. I cannot do it. Forgive me, but what we have is private and ours alone.

Erik and Karin – Home at last!

* * *

"Honorable Old Fart," a letter from Herman van Brero, would-be dualist, one time Englandfarer, sardonic critic of both America and the Netherlands, always enchants me. I freely translate from the Dutch:

"Bad enough that I am here in Rye wasting my time in unutterable bore-dom instead of spending my life drinking costly wines surrounded by hundreds of stunning women, as behooves a man of my standing and age, and now I hear that they have promoted that A-1 asshole of a soap manufacturer (read: President of Unilever. EHR) to become a cabinet minister. High time I hurry back to Holland to salvage what is worth sav-ing, which isn't much considering that all they do out there is play soccer and pay taxes, neither of which is high on my list of priorities. As soon as I am appointed Prime Minister I shall put the death penalty on both, but so far Her Majesty has failed to invite me to form a government, an oversight for which I shall never, never forgive her..." etc.

Count B, what a character! He was still living in Rye, had never ap-plied for U.S. citizenship or returned to the old country, and still bitched in both directions with equal gusto.

He had always followed my career with interest, and I remember the tail end of our last conversation: "Are you never worried about the future?"

"The future, Herman, is a matter of faith."

"Faith? Or confidence?"

"Both."

"And when you kick the bucket?"

"Same thing. And you?"

"In Gods' name, Erik, it scares me shitless!"

His last letter picked up on this subject, and I decided to answer him. It took another two months before I got around to it. My lighthearted note remained unanswered. Herman van Brero, alias Count B, was gone. He had died on his post as the last of Holland's half-assed immigrants. I recognized the warning: the dark prince was back in the picture.

If you want to grow old comfortably - pay attention, young whip-persnappers, it's later than you think - go to the Netherlands. The pro-visions for "the advanced in years", as they accurately call themselves, are excellent and you'll have lots of company. If you don't want to grow old at all, come to Hawaii. The provisions for "senior citizens", what-ever that means, are all but nonexistent and you can't afford to get old. Consequently life expectancy in these islands is the highest in the USA.

Statistics show the Netherlands with even better average figures than Hawaii, but my friends are not contributing much to these. One by one my contemporaries are signing off. It must be their lifestyle, but late-ly it looks as if funerals have replaced cocktail parties as the main social diversion in our circles, averaging one a week.

My old buddy and brother-in-law, Chris Krediet, led the way shortly after my father. They were the smokers, they go first.

My sister, Ellen, continued to preside over the marriages of her noble breed to scions of the finest families in Holland, which gradually promoted me to one of the best connected uncles in the country. Meanwhile she looked tirelessly after my mother, who died at the age of eighty-eight, after twenty lonely years without her husband. All the way from Hawaii, I barely made it to the funeral. As with my father's lock of hair, it was a detail that got me: the smallness of her coffin, buried in flowers, as if it contained the body of a child. Such a long life, so little left.

Some ten years later Ellen contracted Lou Gehrig's disease and, in her usual uncomplaining way, quietly faded away. In some mysterious way I did not get the news of her death until several days later, too late for the cremation. It was par for the course - we always got along fine, but were rarely on the same wavelength.

When Peter Tazelaar, secret agent par excellence, finally lucked out, he had been so ravaged by decades of booze that one of his friends wrote, "Peter's life was like a James Bond novel. We buried its sodden cover with proper respect."

Ben Hein we saw one more time, before - as they say in the RAF - he "went for a Burton." He lived in France and took us to the best restaurant in the Bordeaux countryside, situated on a hillside like a painting by Monet, ringed by a whitewashed wall with roses around the gate. After a copious lunch Karin and I staggered to our car, Ben waving us off. I looked in the mirror for what I knew to be one final view of my intrepid navigator. Unruly as ever, disdainful of all authority, he was standing in the roses facing the wall, taking a leak.

* * *

When you die, the sun rises just the same the next morning, and nature doesn't seem to care. I have often wondered whether I should feel insulted about this, or comforted. Nature itself was good enough to give me the answer.

One early morning in 1991 we expected a total eclipse of the sun. Karin prepared the scene on the porch with a bottle of champagne and pâté for breakfast. It was only seven o'clock, but as the days grow fewer anything unusual becomes an excuse for a party. Our next-door neighbor Richard Waller, now pushing fifty with a gray-flecked beard, had joined us after staying the night because a family of wild pigs had moved in under his house, and the suckling of the piglets kept him awake. The din of morning was everywhere, birds singing, cocks crowing, dogs and cows and the indignant quacks of Richard's unfed geese. Then, at 7:23, it started.

As the golden day turned gray, one by one the sounds stopped. The roosters went first, next the silver voice of the Hawaiian thrush, then the racket of the mynah birds, finally Richard's geese gave up as if embarrassed. The usual early chorus of dogs diminished, with one hysterical basso profundo the last to shut up. The light weakened to dusk without a compensating glow of sunset somewhere, a deadly, darkening gloom turning to black that seemed irreversible, final. At the moment of truth, blind as midnight, a bull bellowed insanely.

It was the end of the world. The tong-tongs of Java's moon eclipse had at least provided a ray of hope, a sign of resistance against the forces of destruction, but Hawaii with its spraying and chopping and building and hundreds of endangered species seemed to have resigned itself to extinction. In the eerie darkness I glimpsed the epitaph of civilization: anything for a buck. We sat silently, the delicacies untouched.

At 7:32 the first dagger of light, flashing from behind the black moon-disc, fierce and brilliant, dispelled the nightmare. At 7:35 the champagne popped open and we drank a toast to the reassurance of the rising sun - may it rise, now, every day, forever, in sickness and in health, and on the day after death, mine included.

Prince Bernhard has his own ideas about such matters and made a historic contribution to the annals of age. At eighty- four he developed Multiple Organ Failure, a condition fatal at almost any age, and went into a coma for two months. Towards Christmas, 1995, his aides were told to get their dress uniforms ready for the funeral. The managing director of AVRO informed me that they were flying a TV crew to Hawaii in order to record an interview about our old friendship, but I stopped him.

"Hold everything," I advised. "I know the Prince. If he doesn't feel like going, he won't go."

Two days later he started his remarkable recovery, which left him entirely undamaged in body, mind and spirit, and landed him in the Guinness Book of Records as the oldest person ever to recover from M.O.F.

And what on earth ever happened to Midge? One day Karin picked up the phone, talked, laughed and invited someone for cocktails at Cloud Cuckooland. "That was Midge," she said, lightly. "She and Blinkie have bought a house in Waikoloa, the other side of Waimea. She wants to see a little more of young Erik. They're coming for drinks on Thursday."

I swallowed a couple of times. Midge's marriage to Blinkie van der Flier, an old schoolmate of mine from The Hague, had proven an unqualified success. I would be delighted to see them again, but a home on this very same island?

"She's having trouble with the curtains for their bedroom," Karin went on. "The windows are triangular or something. I promised we'd give them a hand."

For an interior designer the problem was a minor one. For the husband of that designer, who often helped her with the actual hanging of such curtains, even in people's bedrooms, the situation had bizarre overtones. All the same, Karin and I did hang the curtains in Midge and Blinkie's bedroom. It certainly broke the ice, as the two ladies undoubtedly intended, and since then we have frequent luncheons together, in peace and harmony. Even triangular windows have their use.

* * *

More and more, with the Old Country emptying out, Hawaii is becoming the focus of our lives. We stay away from the U.S. mainland as much as possible. I've loved America throughout the dramatic 20th. century - my century - and now it's just too painful to see it come apart in the 21st. I recognize the symptoms, the slanted news, the veiled threats, the arrogance, I've lived through this before, and as there's nothing I can do about it we let the simplicity and peace of the Big Island quietly envelop us.

Slowly but surely no place on earth welcomes me more warmly than the spacious lanai of Cloud Cuckooland, where I feed the birds, chat with friends, and have lunch à deux and a glass of Chardonnay with Karin. Sometimes I just sit there, by myself, thinking and communing with nature. Then, I must admit, the black primordial turkeys flying against a yellow sunset occasionally turn into peacocks across the lawn of Sumber Agung, with my father drinking a stenga on the porch. I look behind me for the number two boy lighting the lamps, like a ghost.

These are the evenings that young people come and visit me. Age is a respected condition on the Big Island. I am by now known far and wide as "Big Pa", and people listen when I speak.

The young ones actually come to me for advice. My own father never explained anything. He taught me by example, I suppose, but his generation did not communicate with its children about their problems. Kids still ask questions of anyone rather than their parents. From me they expect wisdom.

They will be disappointed. Like the difference between memories and recollections, wisdom tends to be confused with experience and common sense. On that basis I, too, can give advice, but wisdom cannot be taught. It is inspirational, the result of a creative process like a work of art. Scriptures, seminars, books, lectures, tracts, sermons, nothing can convey it except silence, through meditation, contemplation of nature, introspection and similar profound practices. Wise men don't speak, and if they do it's usually in obscure terms merely hinting at an area to be explored. If you are searching for wisdom, only listen to people who keep their mouths shut.

Sometimes young persons want to know about war, and there I can be helpful. Among others, here follow some questions and answers:

"I wouldn't have the guts to do what you did. What do you think?" - I think you're wrong. Courage is a reserve on which one draws as needed. You'll never know how much you've got, until forced to use it. War forces you, the response may surprise you. Besides, we were lucky. Fate confronted us with Adolph Hitler, a monster we could liquidate in eminent good conscience, assured of being on the side of Good against Evil. Find your own dragon and vanquish him. There are plenty around.

"How can you sleep at night, after bombing all those innocent women and children?" - Always judge by the standards of the times. War isn't worth one wounded child, but as soon as violence breaks out it transforms humanity. I witnessed Rotterdam in 1940, London and Coventry in 1941, and in return bombed Bremen and Berlin and a few dozen other German cities with chilling satisfaction. I sleep fine, thank you.

"Would you do it all over again?" Give me a break!

* * *

The party is in full swing. Holland's best restaurant, Auberge de Hoefslag, has spared money nor effort. The dining space, a large version of an elegant hunting lodge, its classic white-decked tables splashed with masses of orange tulips, manages to look both cozy and exuberant. Familiar faces, old and not so old, some very young, eat and drink and talk and laugh, and beam and smile in our direction, a century and a world compressed into an evening and a room. Karin and I sit at the head table between Princess Juliana and Prince Bernhard. The former Queen looks around the multitude, perplexed, turns towards me and says, "Who in God's name are all these people?"

They are my life, from Surabaya to Hawaii, from London to San Francisco, from Prague to Portugal, and above all, from all of the Netherlands. It's the ultimate party, gastronomically superb, geographically diverse, racially mixed, intellectually challenging, socially chaotic, a perfect cross section of my long existence. It is my birthday, but as far as I am concerned, it's a farewell party. The 20th century lies behind us, my century, and I don't expect to venture far into the next. Old soldiers never die, etc. etc.

We specially flew over for it, Karin and I; also to attend the opening in Amsterdam, in one of the leading galleries of a show by an artist called Erik Hazelhoff Roelfzema. My son. Young Erik has pulled the switch of a lifetime on me.

I know from experience that achieving happiness through idleness requires talent and determination, and had begun to suspect that in my son I had produced a master of the art. Our daughter, Karna, after switching from horses to boys to computers, was already making a living in software somewhere around San Francisco. Even Meadow edited books while having a crack at education, and just as I'm beginning to think that Erik is an island boy good for little else but surfing and drinking beer, suddenly there he is in the Netherlands, publishing poetry, writing lyrics for songs that stay for months on the bestseller list, opening expositions showing - and selling - his creations called "Modern Fossils and Power Objects" and God knows what else, appearing on television, endangering my position in town as the Erik Hazelhoff Roelfzema. He'll never cease to surprise me.

A few years previously Karin and I, as usual, were spending May in Holland together, celebrating Spring. The country had changed profoundly since my first, hesitant arrival almost three-quarters of a century ago. World War II and the mighty national effort at reconstruction afterwards had pulled people together, softened social strata and eliminated the blight of "pillarization". The economically disastrous loss of the Dutch East Indies had been overcome by international expansion of trade and industry, and the resulting prosperity was changing attitudes towards arts and culture. In the modern Netherlands writing for money lost its social stigma and became an honored profession, though rarely a profitable one. Artists in general were "in."

Leiden, still clinging to its centuries-old traditions, had nevertheless changed dramatically. The Student Corps, after much harumphing, finally welcomed the ladies into their ranks. It did the town a lot of good, bringing colorful flower boxes into dull gray streets, girls waving out of windows, cozy little bistros everywhere, a general lightening of mood we could well have used fifty years ago.

One evening, at a party in my old digs on the Rapenburg, Karin and I met a student who lived a few doors down the street and turned out to be Queen Beatrix' eldest son, Crown Prince Willem-Alexander, the Prince of Orange. The Prince of Orange! I must admit, the realization went through me with a shock of emotion, as if I were suddenly wired into five-hundred years of Netherlands history. That famous title, which got its origin from a small medieval princedom in France, reverberates through our national consciousness all the way back to our country's very inception. It was William the Silent, the Prince of Orange, who led a handful of rebellious Dutchmen through the endless horrors of the Eighty Years War against Spain (1568 - 1648), until his assassination. His sons, both Princes of Orange, pursued the lopsided struggle to victory from which the Netherlands emerged, free and proud, blossoming into Holland's Golden Age. Thirty years later his great grandson, William the Third - "and Mary" - became King of England, but first and foremost he also was and remained the Prince of Orange, ancestor of my own Queen Wilhelmina, her daughter Queen Juliana and granddaughter the present Queen Beatrix. And now this blond, strapping youngster here in my old student-room in Leiden was the first Prince of Orange I had met, who, when his mother considers the time ripe to abdicate in his favor, will become Holland's first King in more than a century.

But he's also a Leidener, like me, and my favorite picture of our future king shows him standing on the roof of his submerged car in the middle of a Dutch canal, after missing a curve.

More importantly, we have become friends, and since that first evening in 1987 we dine together once every year, alternately picking up the tab, accompanied only by Karin and the Prince's lady of the hour. This, in due time, became Máxima Zorreguieta, a beautiful, sparklingly intelligent and altogether lovable daughter of the Argentine pampas. In the course of several intimate little dinners Karin and I, as bellwethers of the Dutch nation, fell for her lock, stock and barrel. In February 2002 (2-2-2002!) the two year old love affair culminated in Europe's biggest royal bash of the century.

For us it started on the slopes of Mauna Kea, where the modest little post-office was lit up one morning by the arrival of a letter clearly from an other world - outsize, opulent, embellished with an eight-point royal crown on the back flap: the invitation to the wedding of Willem-Alexander of Orange and Máxima Zorreguieta.

It was accompanied by an organizational questionnaire of which two inquiries caught my attention: 1) How many servants will accompany you? and 2) Will you arrive by private aircraft? - Oh boy! Just our type of party!

Believe it or not, but that was actually what it turned out to be. From the moment we set foot in Amsterdam airport we were swept up in the joy of a nation mesmerized by the glamour and romance of a fairy tale and its two principal characters - the Prince of Orange and the girl from Argentina, both young, both beautiful, both in love. Nothing could possibly go wrong, and nothing did. One of the joys of communing with royalty is the aura of self-confidence they radiate. Once amongst peers - or just in the majority, which is rare enough - they can eminently afford to be themselves, and their social advantages come into their own: broad education, impeccable manners, unique perspective, concern for others, and a surprising amount of humor without which their lives would be unlivable. And they were there, at one time more than seventy 'royals' together in the entertainment halls of the Amstel Hotel, mostly princes and princesses, but also kings and queens and world figures like Nelson Mandela and Kofi Annan, all joyful and exuberant. Prince Charles of England, a charmer if there ever was one, apologized for stepping on Karin's toes while - in his own words - "sidling towards the door;" when a director of protocol tried to hustle me out of the way of the arriving bridal pair, Willem-Alexander broke rank to give me a public hug. Unforgettable moments, for a couple of old Hawaiians!

The festivities lasted three days and, of course, also provided the perfect setting for a classical blunder. At the Wedding Reception in the Palace on the Dam dozens of lackeys in uniform, many wearing service medals, silently moved among the guests with drinks and refreshments. One of them, an older fellow standing by himself and looking tired, caught my attention. Meaning to cheer him up, I chatted with him for a moment, Hawaiian style, asked what he thought of the party, and told him, "it wouldn't be long now, so hang in there." He thanked me for my concern, in Dutch, and after a friendly clap on his shoulder I moved along.

"Nice old chap," I remarked to my companion of the moment, Queen Beatrix' sister Princess Margriet.

"Yes," she answered, somewhat to my surprise. "He's a very nice man."

"You mean, you know that fellow personally?"

"Certainly. - That's Albert, King of the Belgians."

The indispensable tear was also shed, and not by Karin and me alone. Sitting in church, watching the wedding ceremony, I became conscious

Crown Prince William-Alexander
and his bride Máxima Zorreguieta

of Máxima's inevitable loneliness, the solitary figure in white, surrounded by thousands of foreigners far from her people and country, in the middle of a Dutch winter while the summer sun bathed the wide fields of her faraway home. At this moment the sounds of a bandoneon, the classical hand-organ of Argentine music, trickled through the church, played by a local artist, a poetic, moving gesture to the bride's sentiments. The mellow notes of a tango named "Farewell, little father" hung forlornly within the gray church walls, and our future Queen was the first to dab away a tear. But not the only one; not an eye in that church - or in Holland for that matter - stayed dry.

And then they were gone, on their honeymoon to Bora Bora. We packed our bags and went home, one fairy tale richer. Four months later we had our first little dinner again, my turn to pay. Would you believe it, they hadn't changed a bit.

* * *

To return to Erik, apart from the joys of tulip time Spring 1994 found us in the town of Hilversum for a special occasion: Soldier of Orange, still going strong, had passed the million copies mark, a Dutch record. Then, on our last day there, the telephone in our hotel room rang and triggered a sequence of events neatly orchestrated towards an unlikely result, reminding me of old times. A publisher wanted to send a photographer to take some pictures for a magazine. I had to turn him down for lack of time.

"It's Patricia Steur," he insisted, naming one of Holland's most renowned photographers. I expressed regrets, but no, and the following day we returned to Hawaii.

Not easily discouraged, Miss Steur surprised us by flying to the Big Island just for a photo session; I had no objections. She turned out to be a beguiling young lady in her thirties, with black hair and green eyes not uncommon in persons of Indies background. Her vibes were strong and positive, as if plugged in to ancient, familiar power sources. We worked well together for two days, after which she was eager to see the island. "My son can show you around," I offered. "He isn't exactly busy right now, anyway."

Well, they met, drove off in his car, and disappeared.

Weeks later they were spotted in Indonesia, then popped up in the Netherlands where Patricia divested herself of previous entanglements - Erik and Susie had split up years ago - after which they officially tied the knot. From that moment Erik, sustained by a happy marriage with the right woman, took off like a multiple rocket in several directions. He, too, had entered the realm of unselfish love. And if the feeling is mutual, as is theirs, then you've really got it made.

Meanwhile Karna, a leggy adolescent version of her mother, chose a different route. Hawaii is not for young people whose ambition goes beyond the laid-back lifestyle; jobs and money are hard to find. Our daughter, growing up into a beautiful strawberry blonde, wanted both. She left for the mainland and a computer career, during which she met and married an engineer named Maurice, a spitting image and possibly reincarnation of the Duke of Alva, a Spanish grandee who four centuries ago gave the rebellious Dutch a very rough time.

To wrap things up, my granddaughter Meadow Melelani, now some thirty years old, with fine features and imperious blue eyes, is a young, blonde edition of my grandmother, the wife of the one-legged lawyer with the first car in the Netherlands. She moved from Hawaii to Amsterdam to California to Seattle to Arkansas and then to Oklahoma, living a life which to me is a complete mystery. After myself and my son she is -so far- the last of our line, which reaches back into the annals of the year 1572. Does she remember that day on the beach in Maui? No - but I do. We are still trying to figure out how we fit into each other's world.

Back to the party. When I had reassured Juliana that in spite of their ebullience the guests did not pose an immediate threat, she remarked, "I hear that your book is almost finished. And then what?"

I answered by quoting - if I may be allowed to drop yet another name - Alfred, Lord Tennyson: "..something ere the end, some work of noble note, may yet be done..."

She looked at me suspiciously and said, "Please, I like straight answers."

"My dear Princess," I explained, "like every writer, I still dream of producing a Magnum Opus."

She nodded, somewhat impatiently. "I know, I know. But what are you going to do after this book is finished?"

"That's when I'm going to write my Magnum Opus."

"Speak up!" Prince Bernhard intervened. "She's a little deaf."

"So are you," Juliana bounced back, laughing.

"As a matter of fact, all three of us are," I concluded, not really sure whether I got through. And so the Magnum Opus, still unwritten, remains in its usual place on the back burner.

Then the main course arrived.

* * *

If by now you are wondering where this idle chitchat will lead us, you probably suspect its purpose. I am trying to avoid the one subject you really want to hear my opinion about: Death. However, the moment is appropriate, because a few years after this party Prince Bernhard died.

It started with one of his usual early morning phone calls. "Greetings! Do I wake you up?"

"Not at all," I lied, passed the phone to Karin and went back to sleep. After a few minutes I woke up again - Karin was in tears. I took her in my arms, shocked. "What's the matter? What's wrong?"

"Bernhard asks us to come to his funeral. He says that he's reserved two fine seats for us in the church."

She was sobbing disconsolately, but I didn't know whether to cry or laugh. If he was serious, he certainly had matters well in hand. Prince Bernhard and I had never paid Death too much respect in our lives, but for this I took off my hat. And he meant it: five days later he died, clearly well prepared.

Assisted by the Court, Karin and I somehow made it to the Old Church in Delft in time for the funeral. Being shown to our places I had to smile: once again "PB" had not let me down, the seats were the best. And when his youngest daughter, Princess Christina, sang her father's favorite song - "La Golondrina" - in a crystal clear soprano that ripped the somber silence in the church to shreds, I knew Prince Bernhard would have approved.

Outside a "missing man formation" of three modern fighter-jets and one WW II Spitfire roared overhead, until the stout little "Spit" peeled off, higher... higher... higher... away into the clouds... gone. The people below waved their Prince farewell.

Death awaits you as surely as me, and you are dying - excuse the expression - to know a very old man's view about it. Having in these final pages tied up all loose ends of my life, I shall now endeavor to connect my origin and my demise.

Polynesians believe that the souls of their dead leap into the ocean and return to the original land whence their ancestors came. As a courtesy to the Hawaiians, who are my hosts and brothers, and in absence of any specific preference, I have no objections to joining their faith in this respect. After all, even our wind chimes, five lengths of bamboo cut and fashioned on Java, babble their homesick secrets whenever westbound breezes stir the air. To serve these homebound souls all our islands have "leaping places", prominent rock formations sticking out into the ocean facing westwards, the direction of our mythical destination. The name of this hallowed spiritual haven? Are you ready for this? It's Java. The name Hawai'i, derived from the original Hawa-iki, means Child of Java. Well, what else am I? So you see, I am already halfway home.

But this is not what you mean. You want to hear it first hand from an old man on the threshold, one who should know, and whom you have followed through all his life: What do you think of Death?

The answer is simple. I don't. I don't want to, because the thought of leaving everything I love, including you, I find unbearable. I don't have to, because at a very early age I became convinced of two things: a) whether by the grace of God, nature, religion, a central intellect, dark powers, electromagnetism or the simple urge for survival, the system functions; b) as it is quite clear that I do not know, nor ever can find out, how and by whose grace it functions, I am not going to worry about it. I accept it with unquestioning gratitude. As I wrote before, you don't have to know your benefactor to acknowledge your debt.

How do I know the system functions? Because if one part of it does, no matter how insignificant, a white ginger flower, a Hawaiian honey bee, a little Chihuahua, any of the billion small miracles you encounter every second of your life, then they all do. Why is it clear that I'll never find out how? Stop kidding me, and appreciate all the time and frustration I have saved myself. Better men than I have tried, and ruined their lives in the process; yet even so we are all sparrows.

The one remarkable fact, perhaps, is that I came to these conclusions at the age of six. It happened when I passed by the Black Cave and the pebble in my mouth worked. The wave of gratitude which overwhelmed me at that moment, never let go. Of course, I have to credit whatever spiritual forces influenced me at that time. This leaves me no choice - those were the days of old skin-and-bones, the shark and the crocodile, my friend the Banyan tree, the Dutch gentleman in the white suit floating in the lake, sun rays shivering through the water like dancing spider webs. As I grew up and older, these concepts remained the same, only their values kept pace with me and expanded. Did I learn nothing, then, in the lifetime that followed? - I learned that there was nothing more to learn.

So I accept Death as I accept Life, because there is no choice. Having acknowledged one, you can't reject the other. Life did not scare me once I knew that, whatever its purpose, it functioned. Nor do I fear the dark prince, on similar grounds. I respect his grim assignment and, let's face it, he has been generous to me.

One of these days, soon, while the world will be worrying about other weighty matters, I'll run in to him, on a black lava flow curving down Mauna Loa, or a wind swept dike along a Frisian lake, or a sweltering New York street. I'll recognize him instantly. After all, we've stood eye to eye often enough in the past. Our conversation will go something like this.

"I have been looking for you."

"Try Samarra."

"It's time you came with me."

"You've said that before."

"This time I mean it."

"Are you sure?"

"Yes."

"Quite sure?"

"Quite sure. Your time has come."

No use arguing.

Hora est. - Goodbye...Vaarwel...Aloha.

BIOGRAPHY

Erik Hazelhoff Roelfzema

Erik Hazelhoff was born on the island of Java and wrote his first two books as a student in Holland, one a bestseller about America. He held a law degree from the University of Leiden, where his career was interrupted by World War II. He joined the Resistance, spent some time in an SS-jail but later escaped to England.

After four years of warfare he returned to liberated Holland as ADC to Queen Wilhelmina after having been knighted by her and awarded the equivalent to the Medal of Honor for his actions in the Secret Service, and decorated with Dutch and British DFC's for his many missions as an RAF Pathfinder pilot.

At the end of the war he emigrated to the USA, where after a stint as actor in Hollywood he joined NBC in New York. In due time he became head of the *"Today"* and *"Tonight"* shows (Manager, Participating Programs) and ultimately a vice-president. In 1956 he rejoined the (Cold) War as Director of Radio Free Europe in Munich.

When at age fifty he decided to go back to writing, he settled on the Big Island in Hawaii, where he wrote the international bestseller, *"Soldier of Orange"* which was turned into a movie directed by Paul Verhoeven and awarded the LA Film Critics award for best foreign film of 1979.

His final book, *"In Pursuit of Life"*, published in 2005, is his autobiography that encompasses the book *"Soldier of Orange"*, which he rewote in Dutch with several updates. In 2006 he returned to his original title, *"Win a Few,"* for this English version.

Erik Hazelhoff passed away gently on September 26th 2007, age 90, at home in his beloved Hawaii. Early in 2006, he had been approached by producer Fred Boot, wishing to make a Dutch musical of *Soldier of Orange*. It premiered October 30th 2010 with Queen Beatrix, Princess

Irene and Prince Pieter Christiaan in attendance. In 2013 it became the longest running musical ever made in the Netherlands.

On April 30th, 2013, Queen Beatrix abdicated after 33 years on the throne. Erik was King of Arms at her inauguration, and would have been delighted to see his very favorite student-Prince follow his mother, as King Willem-Alexander of the Netherlands, with Queen Máxima at his side, to the cheers of an entire 'Orange' nation.

Made in United States
Troutdale, OR
07/02/2023

10936415R10235